THE COVENANTS
WITH EARTH AND RAIN

The Civilization of the American Indian Series

BY JOHN MONAGHAN

(with Robert Hill) *Continuities in Highland Maya Social Organization: Ethnohistory in Sacapulas, Guatemala* (Philadelphia, 1987)

The Covenants with Earth and Rain: Exchange, Sacrifice, and Revelation in Mixtec Sociality (Norman, 1995)

This book is published with the generous assistance of The Kerr Foundation, Inc.

Monaghan, John.
    The covenants with earth and rain : exchange, sacrifice, and revelation in Mixtec sociality / by John Monaghan.
        p. cm.—(The civilization of the American Indian series ; 219)
    Includes bibliographical references (p.) and index.
    ISBN 978-0-8061-3192-4 (paper)
    1. Mixtec Indians—Social life and customs. I. Title. II. Series: Civilization of the American Indian series ; v. 219.
F1221.M7M66   1995   95-2527
306'.089976—dc20   CIP

The Covenants with Earth and Rain: Exchange, Sacrifice, and Revelation in Mixtec Sociality is Volume 219 in The Civilization of the American Indian Series.

THE COVENANTS WITH EARTH AND RAIN

EXCHANGE, SACRIFICE, AND REVELATION IN MIXTEC SOCIALITY

BY JOHN MONAGHAN

UNIVERSITY OF OKLAHOMA PRESS : NORMAN

CONTENTS

List of Illustrations   vii
List of Tables   ix
Preface   xi
Acknowledgments   xiii
Notes on Orthography   xv
Abbreviations Used in the Text   2
Introduction: Community in Mesoamerican Ethnology   3
Part One. Nuyoo as an Association of Households   17
    Chapter   1.   Love and Care in Domestic Life   19
    Chapter   2.   Marriage and Renewal   51
    Chapter   3.   Gifting   78
Part Two. Fertility, Renewal, and the Sacred in Nuyooteco
  Sociality   95
    Chapter   4.   Earth and Rain   97
    Chapter   5.   Jesus, the Sun   118
    Chapter   6.   Tachi, the Wind   131
    Chapter   7.   The Mountain of Tiñu   167
Part Three. The Community as a Great House   191
    Chapter   8.   Blood, Milk, and Semen   193
    Chapter   9.   Sacrifice and Kinship   213
    Chapter 10.   Commensality and Community   233
    Chapter 11.   Cargo and the Human Condition   247
Part Four. Revelation and History   257
    Chapter 12.   Corporate Holdings and Liberal
               Reforms   259
    Chapter 13.   Gift Exchange and Privatization   285
    Chapter 14.   A New Saint, a New Beginning   307
    Chapter 15.   The Indio de Nuyoo   335
Summary and Conclusion   356
Bibliography   367
Index   379

ILLUSTRATIONS

MAPS

1. Oaxaca, Mexico   20
2. The Mixteca   21
3. The Nuyoo region of the Mixteca Alta   24–25
4. Santiago Nuyoo and surrounding municipalities   271
5. Nuyooteco territory in dispute with Ocotlán and Nopalera   276

CHARTS

1. Average number of deputies, 1860–1884   292
2. Average number of deputies, 1910–1935   295
3. Average number of deputies, 1936–1945   296

FIGURES

1. The landscape of the Mixteca Alta   23
2. A man on his way to the Sunday market at Nuyoo Center   29
3. People praying before a household altar   35
4. Compadres dancing at a wedding   73
5. *Lista Kɨ'ɨ* of the *mayordomo* de Nuestro Señor de la Santa Cruz, May 1984   82
6. The *koo savi*   107
7. The *koo savi*   108
8. A man clearing a field with his machete   110
9. Corn plants   113
10. Sowing corn with a digging stick   116
11. A man encounters a *tachi* outside its house   142
12. Dancing *velu*, including a *ñatuun*   150
13. A *velu* troupe with its accompanying musicians   151
14. The return of the dead on All Saints'   160

vii

15. Dying "outside the house" 162
16. Transferring the saint's chest to the house of the
    new *mayordomo* 183
17. Nuyooteco ancestors inside the earth 203
18. Nuyooteco ancestors emerging from the earth at
    Soko Usha 210
19. A curer offering pulque to a *nu ñu'un* on behalf of a
    patient who lost his *ánima* 214
20. Corn 219
21. Three Nuyootecos, a priest, and Misericordia 274
22. A *tachi kuka* 320
23. A *cacique* addressing the assembled citizens 322
24. A *tenuvi* smoking seven cigars to bring rain 350
25. Remigio Sarabia creeping through the Royalist
    lines during the siege at Huajuapan de León 352

TABLES

1. Objects that expectant mothers and fathers may dream
   of that indicate the sex of their unborn child   58
2. Ratio of tortilla countergifts to tortilla initial gifts 84
3. Average value of *mayordomía* principal, 1925–1944   279
4. Number of deputies in the Rosario, Santa Ana, Santa
   Cecilia, and Santiago *cofradías*, 1860–1945   292

PREFACE

WHEN I first arrived in Santiago Nuyoo—a small Mixtec-speaking town in the southern Mexican state of Oaxaca—my intention was to study how people who had grown up in distinct historical periods developed age-specific relationships to social and cultural change. I began by focusing on processes such as bilingualism, the commercialization of agriculture, labor migration, and religious conversion. My eventual aim was to see if the dynamics and sequence of change in an indigenous community could be related to generational cleavages within the population. Accordingly, I spent time researching local and regional archives, collecting life histories, and listening to older people talk about what Nuyoo was like when they were young.

I arrived in Nuyoo in May 1983, and I was to live there almost continuously until January 1986. By the beginning of the second year I had begun to modify my research, in response to things Nuyootecos were saying about themselves. A particularly good example occurred during a rancorous town meeting, when the two sides to a land dispute argued their claims before the assembled citizens. The problem had been brewing for years, and the people involved had managed to convince so many relatives and friends to take sides that the members of at least a dozen households were caught up in it. When I arrived, the debate had degenerated to the point where people were doing nothing but shouting at one another ("Liar!" "Egotist!" "You're pig-headed!" "You're envious!"). Then an old man stood up, staring straight ahead, and people began to quiet down. He was a *tañuu*, or father of the community, a respected elder who had served in all the major posts of the civil-religious hierarchy. Obviously pained by the bitterness of the dispute, he asked, "Are we just a bunch of drunks from Yucuyaa murdering one another in a fiesta? Don't we all eat from the same tortilla?" These words had an immediate effect, and the venom seemed to drain out of the discussion. One official later told me that the old man's words had embarrassed the people who called each other names.

After hearing statements like "we eat from the same tortilla," I realized that Nuyootecos have their own vision of what their community is and what it is that makes them a people distinct from other peoples. This meant that before I could analyze how Nuyootecos responded to new situations, or before I could presume to make statements about how the community changed, I needed to develop an understanding of just what community, for Nuyootecos, means.

ACKNOWLEDGMENTS

THE fieldwork for this book was carried out over 33 months between 1983 and 1986, 3 months in the summer of 1989, 2 months in the summer of 1991, and 3 months in the summer of 1993. Of that time I spent 30 months living in Nuyoo. Most of the rest of the time was spent in archival research in Tlaxiaco, Teposcolula, Oaxaca City, and Mexico City and living in another Mixtec-speaking community in the coastal region of Oaxaca.

Funding was provided by the Boyer Fund of the University Museum, the Department of Anthropology of the University of Pennsylvania, the Mellon Foundation, the University Research Council of Vanderbilt University, and the Wenner-Gren Foundation. Logistical support was provided by the Instituto Nacional de Antropología e Historia, the Instituto Nacional Indigenista, and the Centro de Investigaciones y Estudios Superiores en Antropología Social. I especially want to thank Barbro Dahlgren, Manuel Esparza, Nancy Farriss, Joyce Marcus, Ruth Paradise, Kenneth Pike, Eunice Pike, Father John Reuter, Angeles Romero Frizzi, Anita Sanchez de Downs, Ronald Spores, María de la Luz Topete, Enrique Valencia, and Mark Winter for their kind introductions and words of advice. Arjun Appadurai, John Chance, Catherine Good, Thomas Gregor, Stephen Houston, Laura Junker, Mark King, Joyce Marcus, Ruben Reina, Anita Sanchez de Downs, and Anthony Wallace have all read drafts of this book, and I want to acknowledge their helpful comments.

My greatest debt is, of course, to people living in Nuyoo. I have used pseudonyms for many of those whose statements I cite in the text, and have tried to obscure the time and place of some of the incidents I describe (Nuyoo is a real place and can be found on most maps of the Mixteca). However, I do want to mention that Juan López Nuñez drew most of the illustrations that accompany the text, with some contributed by Indelecio Vasquez García. I thought it was important to include these because they help us to understand what people in Nuyoo highlight in their social and religious practices, and many of the conventions used by Tata Juan López Nuñez can be found in the works produced by the ancient Mixtec scribes, even though he had never seen a codex. Also, most of the myths, legends, and oral histories I cite in the text were told to me by the storytellers Tata Fausto Modesto Velasco, Tata Guadalupe Rojas, the late *tee ka'a shini nu ñu'un* Lorenzo Rojas, the late Ñanuu María Sarabia, and the late Tañuu Carmen López Feria.

NOTES ON ORTHOGRAPHY

THE orthography I use for Nuyoo Mixtec is based on the practical orthography developed by Alexander (1980) and Ortíz López (1982) for the Mixtec dialects spoken in the Nuyoo-Yucuhiti and Atatlahuca regions, with the exception of geographical names, for which I use conventional spellings. Other sources on Mixtec linguistics are included in the bibliography.

CONSONANTS

	Bilabial	*Labiodental*	*Dental*	*Alveolar*	*Palatal*	*Velar*	*Glottal*
Occlusive							
unvoiced	p		t			k	'
voiced		v	d				
Nasal	m			n	ñ		
Fricative							
unvoiced		f		s	sh	j	
voiced					y		
Africative					ch		
Lateral				l			
Vibrant				r			

VOWELS

	Front Unrounded	*Central Rounded*	*Back Rounded*
High	i	ɨ	u
Mid	e		o
Low		a	

All vowels may be nasalized. This is indicated by the addition of an *n* to the vowel.

Mixtec is a tonal language, in which contrasts in tone mark lexical and syntactic distinctions. Tone is transcribed by the use of ´ for a high tone, – for a low tone, and no mark for a midtone. I have minimized the use of diacritical marks as much as possible, indicating tone only when the contrast it marks is important in the context of the book.

THE COVENANTS
WITH EARTH AND RAIN

ABBREVIATIONS
USED IN THE TEXT

AGN   Archvio General de la Nación
ARM   Archivo Regional de la Mixteca, Tlaxiaco, Oaxaca
AEO   Archivo del Estado de Oaxaca
APT   Archivo de la Parroquia de la Virgen de la Asunción, Tlax-
       iaco
AMN   Archivo Municipal de Santiago Nuyoo
AMY   Archivo Municipal de Santa María Yucuhiti

INTRODUCTION

COMMUNITY IN
MESOAMERICAN ETHNOLOGY

"INDIAN peasant community" (like that other famous triad, corn, beans, and squash) has long epitomized Mesoamerica for anthropologists. Despite our current uneasiness with the categories of Indian and peasant, the idea that Mesoamerican people live in communities continues to inform ethnographic accounts of the region. Part of the reason for the concept's durability is, no doubt, its useful ambiguity, referring as it does to a people, a place, a state of mind, an administrative unit, and so on. But "community" is also a term the people of Mesoamerica themselves invoke in discourse and action, and many of us, when using the word, are simply following the lead of those whom we study.

This is not to say that our understanding of community has remained static over the years. In fact, for some of the earliest modern ethnographers, Mesoamerica was divided not into communities but into tribes. Like indigenous peoples of the western United States or the European colonies of Africa, each "nation" spoke the same language, occupied a well-defined territory, and maintained a unifying social and political organization. Of course, calling Mesoamerica "tribal" implied that it had a low ranking relative to the "civilized" West, so that the distinctive features of groups in the region could ultimately be accounted for by the rung they occupied on the ladder of human evolution. But even as early as the 1920s it was clear to some that Mesoamerican tribes were not like those in other places. Blom and La Farge (1926–27) noted in their account of the 1925 Tulane University expedition through southern Mexico and Guatemala that

> The Tribes are very different from those of North America . . . it appears there was none of that deep feeling of loyalty towards the group, of essential, almost mystic unity with all the members that characterizes our own Indians. Similar customs, common interest, and geographical proximity hold each Tzeltal group together; bonds that are easily broken. (1927:354)

3

In the same report Blom and La Farge called the Tzeltal town of Bachajon a "village-tribe" and contrasted it with other Tzeltal-speaking "village-tribes" of the region. What they tried to capture by using the term "village-tribe" was similar to what Tax systematically formulated in his 1937 article, "The Municipios of the Midwestern Highlands of Guatemala." Tax observed that Indian municipalities in Highland Guatemala differ radically from one another in such things as dress and craft specialization. He also noted that each municipality is highly endogamous and maintains a distinct civil-religious hier-archy that structures the political life of inhabitants and consumes much of their time and wealth. Although earlier ethnographers spoke of the "Quiché tribe," referring to the thousands of people who speak related Quiché dialects and inhabit dozens of municipalities across the central highlands, Tax argued that they should not be seen as a group except for linguistic reasons. In most instances, Tax pointed out, the relevant social unit is the municipality (or more generally, the community), with its separate dialect, its distinct dress, and its bounded political, ritual, and connubial systems.

The focus on community in Mesoamerica did not, at first, have major methodological or theoretical implications for anthropology. It is true that Tax argued for a redefinition of units of analysis and that the survey approach (in which ethnographers traveled from one place to another on expeditions, stopping only briefly to collect information) began to die out at this time. However, this practice was being replaced by "intensive work" in anthropology more generally. No innovations ensued because anthropologists continued to conceive of communities in much the same way that they conceived of tribes. The community-studies approach, which aimed to produce a holistic description of the institutions, values, and culture of individual communities, was in essence the same kind of study anthropologists carried out in "tribal" societies in North America and Africa. In Mesoamerica the only difference was that one worked in "village-tribes."

For the most part, the terminological switch from "tribe" to "com-munity" did not reflect major revisions in the way anthropologists conceived of their object of study. However, Robert Redfield's at-tempt to place the Mesoamerican community within a comparative typology of human groups was a significant theoretical contribution that would eventually move Mesoamericanists to the forefront of the developing area of peasant studies. To account for the variety of groups he found in the Yucatán, Redfield suggested that we should think of the region as containing a continuum of settlement types. At one extreme was the small, homogeneous, and traditional folk society with its strong, kin-like bonds of moral solidarity and isolation from modern industrialized life. At the other extreme was the large, heterogeneous, and secular urban society with its complex divisions of labor and multiple connections with other social and urban centers. A particular group could be placed along the continuum, Redfield explained, depending on the degree to which it approximated one pole or the other (Redfield 1941).

Two points about the folk-urban continuum have had continuing implications for our understanding of community in Mesoamerica. First, Redfield defined community as a universal ideal-type. He considered his "folk society" and later his "little community" as concepts that reflected life not only in the societies of Mesoamerica, or in rural agricultural settlements throughout the world, but also in urban neighborhoods and even groups as distinct from one another as the Siriono of Bolivia and the Nuer of Africa (Redfield 1960:5–6). Although societies could be classified according to the degree to which they conformed to this ideal, community functioned within this scheme as a major premise rather than something to be demonstrated. On the one hand, this meant that theorists would not have to worry overmuch about defining community in, as they put it, "particular ethnographic terms," because community was a condition of human life, like politics or the family. On the other hand, it meant that those working on the "particular ethnographic" level would not have to deal with the problem of defining what they meant by community. Thus in the community-study ethnographies produced through the 1970s in Mesoamerica, one can find detailed descriptions of kinship terminologies, local rituals, political institutions, and settlement patterns of particular communities; however, they contain no statement about what community is. Because ethnographers saw community in foundational terms—almost as a natural social unit—it was not something to be critiqued or investigated. It was important to describe its institutions, and all agreed that communities might vary, but the existence of community was not in question.

The second element of Redfield's scheme that has had continuing implications is his use of the term community itself. When Redfield writes that the "folk society" or "little community" is a small, bounded moral universe, homogeneous and self-sufficient, one can see in this echoes of Aristotle, Rousseau, the nineteenth-century anarchists, and many others who imagined the ideal social setting to

be a rural agricultural village where inequality, hierarchy, and exploitation would be effaced by communal bonds of neighborliness and
mutual respect (Lewis 1970:435–36). Although much has been made
of this aspect of Redfield's thinking (to the point where some feel it
has been overexaggerated), it is worth pointing out that it is still
something of a revelation that Mesoamerican communities, despite
an ethos of shared poverty, may be stratified into different economic
classes with competing interests (Schryer 1990:38–42), and we have
yet to deal adequately with the view latent in much ethnographic
research that community is something that empowers people, that
coercion and alienation happen only when people lose community or
wander outside it. Among all the terms used by anthropologists to
describe social life, community stands out as being the most value-
laden, and many of our advances in understanding rural Mesoamerica
have required us to overcome our own deep feelings about what a
community should be.

In the 1950s anthropologists began to focus on what made rural
communities in Latin America different from the "primitive" societies their colleagues were describing in other parts of the world:
namely, that these groups were parts of larger societies, and that they
had been for hundreds, if not thousands, of years. They were "peasants" who occupied a rural hinterland linked economically, politically,
and culturally to urban centers, colonial empires, and nation-states
(e.g., Aguirre Beltrán 1967; Cámara 1952; Kroeber 1948; Redfield 1960;
Wagley and Harris 1955). This research set in place the enduring—and
sometimes stifling—areal concern with ethnicity, development, rural
links to urban areas, and peasant dependence and subordination.

By far the most influential of these analyses, in terms of Mesoamerican studies, have been Eric Wolf's (1955, 1957, 1962). Like
Redfield, Wolf placed the Mesoamerican community within a comparative typology of human groups; however, unlike Redfield, he
classified communities in terms of their articulations with the "wider
social field" of which they were a part (Wolf 1955, 1957). Wolf saw the
community as the unit of Indian adaptation in an environment of
economic crisis and colonial exploitation. In response to severe economic depression and attempts by outsiders to gain control of local
resources, the community closed itself off, drawing sharp boundaries
between insiders and outsiders. As evidence for this "closed" and
"corporate" community, Wolf pointed out that communities in Mesoamerica place restrictions on membership, prevent the sale of land to
outsiders, and encourage village endogamy. Also, the onerous bur-

dens of service in the civil-religious hierarchy channel the accumulated surpluses of community members into collective celebrations and prevent the formation of potentially disruptive class differences, promoting a democracy of the poor (Wolf 1962:214–16). These and other mechanisms block members of the community from forging alliances with dangerous outsiders and prevent outsiders from playing a role in the life of the community. Wolf (1957) then identified examples of the closed corporate community in Java as well as Mesoamerica.

Although Julian Steward's cultural ecology has often been cited as an inspiration for Wolf's model (e.g., Hewitt de Alcántara 1984:73–78), Fortes's work on the unilineal descent group was of equal importance, as Wolf himself pointed out (Wolf 1955, 1986). He noted that survival is a collective activity for Mesoamerican peoples as it is for the members of a unilineal descent group. Also, Wolf saw that both the Mesoamerican community and the descent group are defined in terms of ownership of the most valued productive property in the society and by the place it occupies in what Fortes called the "total social system" (Fortes 1953:29, 35; Wolf 1986). Most importantly, Wolf believed that the closed corporate community, like the unilineal descent group, should be analyzed in structural terms. As he put it, "a typology of peasantries would be set up on the basis of regularities in the occurrence of structural relationships, rather than on the basis of regularities in the occurrence of similar cultural elements" (Wolf 1955:454). The purpose of this exercise was, as was true for Redfield, cross-cultural generalization: "since structure rather than culture content is our main concern here, we shall emphasize the features of organization which make this type of community like corporate communities elsewhere, rather than try to characterize it in purely ethnographic terms" (Wolf 1955:456).

In defining the community in this way, Wolf gave structure a causal primacy: "the persistence of Indian culture content seems to have depended primarily on maintenance of this structure. When the structure collapsed, traditional cultural forms quickly gave way to new alternatives of outside derivation" (Wolf 1955:456). If "culture content" was at all relevant, it was to express, regulate, and reinforce structure (see Fortes 1953:21). Thus the characteristic institutions, values, and customs of Mesoamerican people operate in the closed corporate community model to level differences in wealth and to maintain boundaries.

The perspective suggested by Wolf proved to be crucial: it turned

Mesoamerican studies away from a view of indigenous society as existing in a timeless, functionalist vacuum, and it anticipated many theoretical and methodological developments that were to take place in anthropology over subsequent decades, such as world systems theory, the use of historical materials in anthropological analysis, and a regional rather than a village focus of research (see also Aguirre Beltrán 1967; Cámara 1952). Its timeliness and the broad truths it articulated created some serious problems, however: it was so widely applied that many groups described as closed corporate communities turned out to be strikingly different from one another, making comparison meaningless (Greenberg 1981:10).[1]

Several criticisms of the closed corporate community model have emerged that are relevant to the present discussion. For one, we have come to realize that the relation between "culture" and "structure" is much more complex and contingent than was proposed in the model. After all, if any social group had their traditional system of land tenure radically changed, it was probably under assault in other ways as well, so one cannot say that "structure" disappears first, and "culture content" follows. Also, we now know that some "culture content"— even aspects, such as marriage, that are defined as particularly important in regulating and reinforcing the structure of the closed corporate community—can vary independently of the closed corporate structure (e.g., Farriss 1984; for general statements on the distinction between closure in an economic sense and closure in a sociocultural sense, see Dow 1973a; Greenberg 1981; Sheridan 1988). We have also begun to realize that the whole focus of the closed corporate community model, while teaching us to see communities in terms of historical processes and changes in the wider economic and political field, has also caused us to misperceive Mesoamerican societies in important ways. Its structural bias has restricted the meaningful aspects of social life to one or two core functions (Wolf 1986:327; Schryer 1990:43) and has made indigenous ideas about the

1. Watanabe takes Mesoamericanists to task for "canonizing" the closed corporate community, making it an index of "Indianness" instead of seeing it as a Weberian ideal-type and situating actual communities along a continuum of "open" and "closed" configurations (Watanabe 1992:227). Wolf makes a similar point when he criticizes those who accuse him of pigeonholing Latin American peasantries into a limited number of types. Like Julian Steward, he tells us, he may have used the word "type," but not as a classificatory device. Instead, he used it to refer to causally enchained elements in interaction (Wolf 1986:325). In all fairness, however, the language of Wolf's 1955 and 1957 articles is not consistent, and it can be read to intend type in a "classificatory" sense (e.g., 1955:468; see also Roseberry 1989a:148). Moreover, he made no note of the specialized way he was using the term "type" or of Julian Steward's clarifying article, which he did, however, cite in 1986.

processes of group formation incidental to discussions of rural social organization. As Wolf wrote in his 1986 review of the closed corporate community concept it even caused us to overlook village-specific structural features of great relevance to social life: "The top-down perspective led to a disregard of territorial entities and kinship structures intermediate between household and community, as well as to a disregard of connective networks among people in communities, networks other than the market" (Wolf 1986:327).

In any event, it has now become clear that a variety of things not immediately reducible to interactions with macro-level economic and political forces are important for understanding the particular form corporate communities take.[2] Sheridan, for example, has shown that ecological relationships are crucial to the persistence of corporate control over property in northern Mexico (Sheridan 1988), whereas Chamoux (1987) and Schryer (1990) argued that corporate institutions in central Mexico must be seen in terms of systems of stratification internal to the community. One also wonders if the success of the corporation analogy, with its focus on landholding, did not overly limit us in the way we have imagined community in Mesoamerica. It would not, for example, be a distortion to view Mesoamerican social units as congregations.[3] In other words, instead of seeing the group defined by its corporate holdings, it would be defined by its special relationship to a god, with its members functioning as the god's servants. As in other sacred communities, the leaders could be seen as a corps of adepts most advanced in certain spiritual exercises (i.e., service) with the performance of this exercise constituting the formal rite of admission to the group.

I raise this possibility because we now understand that the categories we use in our ethnographic descriptions are not objectively neutral, but are based on particular relationships with the subjects of our analysis and circulate within broader discourses of which we are not always aware. For example, the highly valued practice of ethnological generalization has meant that most of the theories of community we work with function within comparative typologies. The

2. Wolf explicitly stated that the economic and political forces that determine the structural regularities of the closed corporate community lie "within the larger society to which the community belongs, rather than within the community itself" (Wolf 1955:454, 455, 469; 1957:7; 1986:326).

3. Dow suggested something like this when he examined territorial divisions among the Otomi as the products of the organization of religious corporations, rather than seeing religion as fulfilling functions with respect to community control over territory (Dow 1973b:138).

problem is that economic, political, social, and cultural variables have produced a rural complexity that is simply not captured by these typologies. As the ethnohistorian John Chance tells us,

> One of the most important things we have learned from current research on the history of Indian Mesoamerica is a healthy respect for diversity—in culture, social structure, and economy, among other spheres. Even within regions that were once treated as culturally homogeneous— such as the Valley of Mexico—it is becoming increasingly clear that patterns or structures characteristic of one community may not apply to others located just a short distance away (Chance 1989:xiii; see also Chambers and Young 1979; Schwartz 1983).

From the time of Redfield, it has been practice among theorists in Mesoamerica to deemphasize—one might even say suppress—the diversity of Mesoamerican communities in the interests of generalization. This is also characteristic of the epochal analysis that became popular in the 1970s. "Indian community," when used in this discourse, is either a subsystem of capitalism, which the analyst proceeds to locate in a worldwide division of labor and unequal exchange, or it is a noncapitalist mode of production that the analyst usually goes on to show exists to fulfill the needs of capitalism. Such perspectives tend to make local social arrangements and practices residual, things that are in themselves of little interest. And if there is any doubt about the existence of strategic links between ways of knowing and political agendas, then we have the example of those theorists working within this general paradigm who concluded—in a way that was perfectly consistent with their use of the term "community"—that the "Indian community" is no more than a deformed product caused by external domination. If the legitimacy of the "Indian community" could be questioned in this way, then it could be argued—as some went on to do—that it should be abolished (see Hewitt de Alcántara 1984:115–16 for a review).[4]

It would be useful to examine more fully how community functions

---

4. An alternative to this latter perspective emerged in Latin America's own brand of "subaltern studies," or *culturas populares*. Its leading proponent in Mexico, the late Guillermo Bonfil Batalla, rejected the assumption that native cultures retarded social progress, and defined them as valuable and interesting in their own right. Bonfil Batalla and others also worked to preserve local languages, nurture folkloric traditions, and stimulate expressions of cultural creativity (Arzipe 1988:150–52). However, because the *culturas populares* approach has tended to focus on groups sharing a similar structural position within the broader context of Latin American society, it has tended to deemphasize the differences between Native Mesoamerican and non–Native Mesoamerican groups, and links between cultural expressions and rural social organization have not been a central concern.

within social science paradigms. My interest here however, lies in sustaining a tradition of ethnographic inquiry that treats the culture of indigenous people in a way that does not immediately reduce it to class, economic position, structure or some sort of marker in an ethnic field. I began with community because it seemed to me the closest thing to what I—as an anthropologist, working in the 1980s—saw as being significant to people in Nuyoo. But at the same time, what had been said about community in Mesoamerica was more of an obstacle to understanding than an aid. One problem is that there is little appreciation that Mesoamerican people themselves might have definitions of community. Even when this possibility is acknowledged (e.g., Oettenger 1980:19; Schryer 1990:60–61), the theoretical traditions the ethnographers work in do not allow that this might be significant, and so it is not explored in any depth. In order to really listen to what Mesoamerican people say community is, what is needed is an approach that views the processes of group formation in the region in communicative (symbolical) terms. Fortunately Kay Warren in the late 1970s, and John Watanabe more recently, have undertaken projects in Maya-speaking towns of Highland Guatemala with this aim in mind.

At the time she worked, Warren (1978) was uniquely aware of the problems overhanging ethnographic work on community in Mesoamerica, and she set out to describe what she called the "local model of social reality." She made the valuable point that in order to discover what this model is, our focus should be on conceptual idioms, in the same way Schneider focused on conceptual idioms to delineate American models of kinship (Schneider 1968, 1972, 1984). Warren concentrated on mythological and ritual idioms, as well as everyday statements by people about "why we are the way we are." The focus on creation myths allowed her to determine what are, for the Maya of San Andrés Semetebaj, elementary social categories. In the context of ritual, she was able to witness people building definitions of the social order. Finally, by listening to what people said about themselves, she was able to learn how persons were locally defined. The result is a portrait of the community as a series of social classifications and their related moral codes, in terms of which the Maya make sense of not only themselves, but also their relationships to the non-Maya, or ladinos, who live in the town.

Warren's primary interest in her ethnography was in "how Indians have created a social philosophy to make sense of subordination to non-Indians" (Warren 1978:6). Since for Warren subordination is a

structural position (1978:6–7), the question became "how subordination and powerlessness are reflected in Indian ideas about themselves" (Warren 1978:3)—that is, "the symbolism of subordination."
Her aim was to complement studies such as Stavenhagen's (1975) on
the interactions of ethnicity and class by exploring the "extent to
which self-perception and belief are marked by changing colonial and
class relations" (Warren 1978:17), a topic ignored in the materialist
analyses of the 1970s. This perspective narrowed her focus, and
despite her concern with Maya social idioms, we do not come away
with a comprehensive understanding of what is distinctive about the
San Andrés community (Gossen 1982). Warren's approach does clearly
show, however, that it is in terms of their own idioms that people
comment on, question, and seek to influence the ongoing process of
social life, and that close attention to these idioms is necessary in
order to understand the nature and direction of local change.

The Mixtec speakers of Santiago Nuyoo, like the Maya of San
Andrés Semetebaj, have a richly inflected conceptual and moral
vocabulary for describing social relations, and within this vocabulary
the *ñuu*, or community, plays a prominent role. For example, one of my
neighbors would often tell me that he served as *mayordomo*, *comisariado*, president, and other *cargos* "because it was the will of the
ñuu"; another officeholder used to say that he worked hard in his
gardens and cornfield not for himself or his family "but to feed the
ñuu." Yet when I tried to get them to be more specific about what they
meant by "ñuu," I was continuously frustrated—there did not seem to
be a "model" that everyone could agree upon, or even articulate,
despite their frequent use of the word. This brings me to another
obstacle that the broad use of community in Mesoamerican ethnology
has brought with it: that we assume it exists. Helpful at this point is
Watanabe's recent work, based on the research he carried out in the
Mam-speaking town of Santiago Chimaltenango (Chimbal), in which
he rejects the "totalizing" of social conventions "into such monolithic
analytical abstractions as culture, ethnicity, or class" (Watanabe
1992:16). We might add community to his list.

Watanabe's interest is in how the people of Chimbal define their
ethnic distinctiveness. Because Highland Maya ethnicity is, as Tax
observed long ago, inseparable from life in a community, Watanabe
asks what community is for the people of Chimbal. Life in community, according to Watanabe, involves "participation in local contexts
of conventional discourse . . . and commitment to an investment in
the concerns of that discourse" (Watanabe 1992:15). Watanabe de-

fines conventions as regular acts of symbolic communication that require "interlocutors" to particularize symbols in reference to ongoing events, and that conventionalize the events to make them recognizable (Watanabe 1992:13–15). He then shows us how the Mam of Santiago Chimaltenango "identify and engage" one another through a "formal language of community" made up of "saint and *witz*, souls and soul-loss, and public recognition and community service" (Watanabe 1992:129). At the same time, his perspective allows him to emphasize the open-ended, emergent, and creative dimensions of communication, as opposed to the constraints it places on actors. Thus we can see that although the institutional forms traditionally associated with the Maya have disappeared from Chimaltenango (in an earlier period we probably would have called them "acculturated"), the people of Chimbal remain Maya and continue to be a community, even though they are not the Maya of the past, and even though the community is not the same today as it was when Charles Wagley worked there in the 1930s (see also Foster 1991:19–23, 167–71).

This view follows a more general rethinking of the nature of symbolic activity, which critiques the idea that we can understand symbols only as a representation of people's understandings (in anthropology, see Bloch 1980; Bourdieu 1977; Ortner 1984; Sperber 1975; Strathern 1988; Wagner 1975; Weiner 1988). Thus, when the people of Santiago Nuyoo define themselves, they usually do so in terms of customary practices, as when they say "we eat from the same tortilla." As we will see, it is out of such usages as these that the institutions we find typical of Mesoamerica emerge, such as the feasting complex. But like having a soul in Chimbal, these practices are not contingent upon the continuity of specific institutional forms (see Simmel 1964:22–23). More broadly, when we look at Nuyootecos performing rituals, making exchanges, or telling myths, they are not only representing social life but also intent on creating effects; Nuyootecos explicitly speak of these activities as being instrumental and efficacious. Nuyooteco ritual, exchange, and myth, then, are less symbolic representations than they are theories of social action (Strathern 1988:171–190).

The question, What is the Nuyooteco definition of community? should thus be shifted from a search for models of finished social groups to a focus on local articulations of how collectivities form and accomplish goals. After all, the key elements of our own general sociological vocabulary—culture, society, institution, education—were originally nouns of action or process. Before attaining more familiar levels of abstraction, "culture" meant to honor by worship, to cultivate, or to tend; "society" meant active unity or fellowship; and "institution" meant an act of origination (Williams 1976:76–72, 139–40, 243–47). It should not be surprising that the ethnosociology of other people starts from a similar active, experiential, and transactional basis.

This suggests that the view latent is most of the work on community in Mesoamerica—that it exists as some kind of established entity out of which action flows (a view reinforced by the people themselves when they speak of community as something that has a "will" and causes them to act in certain ways)—should be shifted to one that views community as decidedly secondary, something that emerges out of particular relations and interactions. In the early part of this century Simmel similarly invited us to see social life through "forms of sociation," or "forms of being with and for one another . . . in which individuals grow together into a unity and within which their interests are realized" (Simmel 1971:24; see also Simmel 1964 and 1990:174–75). Simmel's term has several advantages. First, it turns our attention to how people create and maintain relationships. This is something potentialy obscured by perspectives that view the social unit as operating upon individuals, a heritage of the legal discourse used to build classical theories of society (Giddens 1984). Second, like Chimalteco conventions, it forces us to see "community" as enactment, without the high level of coherence and systematization that is implied in so many other elements of our general sociological vocabulary.[5] Finally, it focuses our attention on agency and interests, on "knowledge about the way in which people impinge upon one another" (Fardon 1985:134; Simmel 1964), which is of particular importance for situating small communities like Nuyoo in history.

Forms of sociation that seem particularly important—in Nuyooteco mutual engagements, in defining Nuyoo as a place distinct from other places, and in transforming Nuyoo from one kind of place to another— include marriage and gift exchange, cargo service and communal labor, pooling and distribution, sacrifice and revelation, and, alas, *yatuni* or "envious" acts. As individuals seek to reproduce, negotiate, and transform their relationships with one another through these usages, they are rarely concerned with community as a complex or comprehensive whole—hence my frustrated search for a Nuyooteco "model" of community. But at the same time, these forms of sociation

5. Although I use Simmel's terminology, I so so without the universal and ahistoric status he gave to such things as "exchange" or "competition" (Simmel 1964).

culminate in what I will argue are two "summating images" (Weiner 1988) of Nuyooteco sociality: Nuyoo as an association of households, and Nuyoo as a "great house." I see these, however, not so much as defining social types but as embodying a sense of purpose; they are less underlying structures than they are enduring truths. And even though they are my abstractions — as an outsider and an as anthropologist — they are grounded in Nuyooteco idioms, and individual Nuyootecos have found them to be acceptable generalizations.

Nuyoo, of course, does not exist in a vacuum, but I think a good place to begin the ethnography, as I do in Part One, is with a synchronic analysis of commensality, marriage, gifting, and ritual practices. I do so, however, with the proviso that Nuyoo is not something that is foreclosed or finalized. It unfolds through time, and the different forms of Nuyooteco sociality are part of history, so that they combine and recombine in particular political and economic circumstances. As I noted, when Nuyootecos themselves describe village life they do not do so in terms of fossilized institutions, but with verbs and nouns of action that suggest an ongoing process (e.g., "gifting," instead of "the gift exchange complex"; "service," instead of "the civil-religious hierarchy"). If we think of Nuyooteco forms of sociation in this active sense, we can better understand that practices such as gifting and service might have alternative uses and considerable flexibility, and that far from being things that resist change, they can be resources people draw upon to change, as they seek to mobilize others, solve problems and accomplish goals. This brings me to the subject of revelation.

In speaking with Nuyootecos about what we might call "society" — institutions, roles, traditions, norms, and social categories — it is clear that, for them, these things are the byproduct of human interaction with the gods. When Nuyootecos talk about the past, their accounts are structured by such things as holy covenants with the Earth and Rain and the sudden appearance of sacred beings, who bring new knowledge, such as agriculture, or who institute new moral regimes. The example I focus on is a saint, called Misericordia, who appeared on the steps of the old church in Nuyoo on the morning of December 8, 1873. The saint's appearance, and the ritual and mythology associated with it, were connected to the creation of new mechanisms for financing collective activities, to the redefinition of households as property-holding units, and to the emergence of new relationships mediating households. In other words, the sudden appearance of Misericordia gave Nuyootecos the opportunity to interact with the sacred in a new way and, by that, to change the way they interact with one another. This is significant because if we are to see community as both historical cause and consequence, as many sensibly argue we should (e.g., Good 1988; Handy 1991; Smith 1990; Watanabe 1990), then, because Nuyooteco social forms are instituted through revelatory experiences, the dynamics of these revelations become important to understanding the way things in Nuyoo change.

Nearly every Nuyooteco has been in the presence of a god at some time in his or her life: for instance, a man once was in the town jail for drunkenness, and the patron Santiago came before him to indicate a weak spot in the adobe wall, which the man was able to kick through and thereby escape). But there are revelations that have significance for all Nuyootecos, not just isolated individuals, and that not only speak to individual dilemmas but authorize collective action. The question we have to ask is, How do certain appearances become significant for an entire group of people? For Misericordia, this will involve exploring the historical context of the revelation. What we will see is that a small group of individuals were active in promoting worship of the saint, and their interests, which were in part shaped by developments in the region's economic and political life, were served by the changes that followed the saint's appearance. Their actions, moreover, had important consequences for the distribution of power in Nuyoo today. As Simmel teaches, "sociation is the form around which the interests of human beings crystallize" (Simmel, cited in Frisby 1990:46). In other words, Nuyooteco forms of sociality are relevant for our understanding of historical process because it is through them that people seek to influence others (and in turn find themselves conditioned by others), something that links history (change) in Nuyoo to particular individuals and gives it its own communal and cultural logic, even as individuals and groups respond to broader economic and political developments.

I end the book by tracing the history of Nuyoo up to the present, examining the migration of young Nuyootecos to Mexico City in search of work. My focus is on how the revelations brought by another sacred personage have allowed Nuyootecos to expand the boundaries of Nuyoo, and to reconfigure their identities in ways that not only make them part of a broader nation but also highlight their distinctiveness. In addition, by identifying the principal players in this revelation, we will obtain a nuanced view of the kinds of interests, efforts, and purposes that coalesce around images such as that of Misericordia, and how these images become dynamic sites of innovation.

PART ONE

NUYOO AS AN ASSOCIATION OF HOUSEHOLDS

When the cacique was to marry the daughter of a cacique from another pueblo . . . he broke off a piece of tortilla with a piece of meat, and he gave it to the cacica to eat, and the cacica did the same, and thus they were married.
— Relación Geográfica de Juxtlahuaca, Pueblo de Putla, 1580

All the heathen customs (of the natives) were based on on eating and drinking—worse than the Epicureans.
— Diego Durán, *Book of the Gods and Rites and Rites of the Ancient Calendar*, ca. 1576

CHAPTER 1

LOVE AND CARE
IN DOMESTIC LIFE

THE Mixteca region of the Mexican states of western Oaxaca (map 1), eastern Guerrero, and southern Puebla contains hundreds of small, indigenous settlements clustered around central market towns and district capitals, where mestizos predominate. Most indigenous people in the Mixteca speak a dialect of Mixtec, though the area also contains Amuzgo-, Chatino-, Cuicatec-, Chocho-, Trique-, and of course Spanish-speaking settlements.

The Mixteca is usually divided into three large geographical regions. At the center is the mountainous Mixteca Alta. A humid coastal strip lies to the southeast of the Alta, called the Mixteca de la Costa. Finally, to the northeast of the Alta lies a high, dry region known (to the confusion of many) as the Mixteca Baja. Although useful, one should not allow this partition to obscure the climactic and ecological diversity that exists within each region. (The ancient Mixtec appear to have divided the area into more than three subregions (e.g., de los Reyes 1976:2–3).) My focus in this book, the Mixtec-speaking town of Santiago Nuyoo, is located along the border of the Alta and the Costa (see map 2).

Nuyoo lies about 10 km due west of Oaxaca City. It covers 48.5 square km and is centered on two canyons, at the base of which lie the Río Golondrina and its tributary, the Río Corral. After these two rivers join, they empty into the larger Río Verde, which in turn drains into the Pacific Ocean. The town center of Nuyoo is located at the high end of the largest canyon, surrounded on the north, east, and west by sharp mountain walls. These walls form a pocket in which the town center of Santa María Yucuhiti lies just above that of Nuyoo, which is almost at the base of the cliffs. Looking out from Nuyoo Center to the south, one can see the Golondrina draining through the canyon. The base of the canyon is filled with coffee plants and lush groves of banana, zapote, mamey, orange, and other fruit trees. Farther up, running in a band across the canyon sides, are the cleared lands where

19

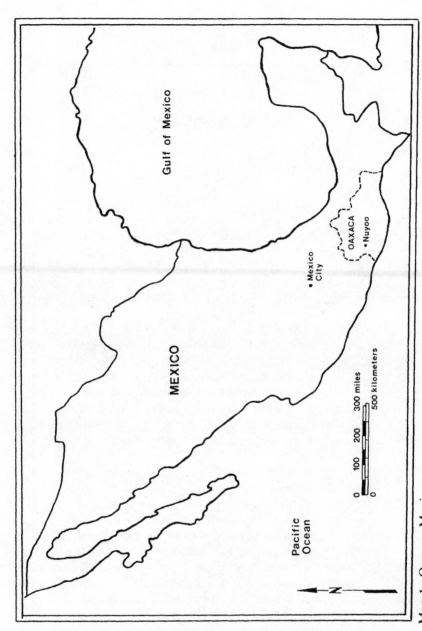

Map 1. Oaxaca, Mexico

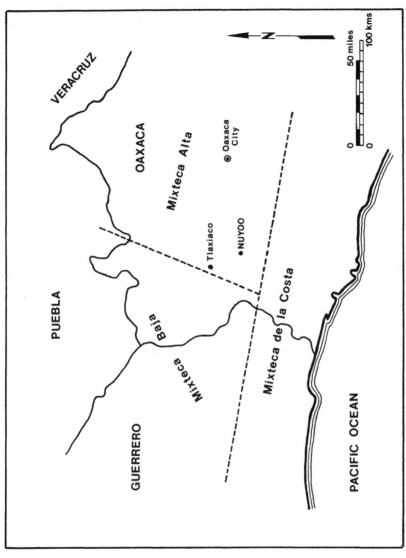

Map 2. The Mixteca

Nuyootecos sow their corn; above them are the pine forests where they cut firewood and hunt for deer. Along the canyon side to the north, one can detect the narrow switchback road cut into the hillside in 1977 that connects Nuyoo to its district capital, Tlaxiaco. On the wall to the south the same road, which loops around Yucuhiti, climbs up to San Pedro Yosotato and then descends into the Cañada of Yosotichi (see map 3).

The terrain gives the people of Nuyoo an advantage over many other settlements in the Tlaxiaco region. Although level land is at a premium (one travels either uphill or downhill, as there is almost nothing in between), the varied altitude of agricultural plots allows people to grow cold-weather crops like maguey and potatoes at the higher elevations and warm-weather crops at the lower elevations (figure 1). This is because Nuyoo (using the traditional three-part division of the Mixteca) occupies a transitional zone between the high mountains of the Mixteca Alta and the hot, tropical lowlands of the Mixteca de la Costa. The center of Nuyoo, for example, is at 1000 m above sea level, while Yucunino, one of its hamlets, is at about 2500 m. As one travels south down the canyon from the center the land descends to below 600 m, and when traveling northwest from Yucunino it rises to over 3000 m. This gives the area an Andean atmosphere since diverse plants are cultivated in the various altitudinal zones, all of which are integrated into a complex agricultural schedule (Katz 1990; Monaghan 1994). Because farmers can produce tropical fruits and colorful flowers not found in other areas of the Mixteca Alta, the Nuyoo region is sometimes called "the garden of the Mixteca."

At the outset I think it is useful to highlight some of the things that make this part of the Mixteca distinct from the better-known areas of Highland Mesoamerica. Unlike many municipalities of Chiapas or Highland Guatemala, where populations may exceed 50,000, most municipalities in the Mixteca Alta are small; in the Tlaxiaco area, they are also ethnically homogeneous. Thus almost all 2,500 inhabitants of Santiago Nuyoo speak the Nuyoo variety of Mixtec, and about a third of them are monolingual. From colonial times to the present, there has never been more than one or two non-natives living in the town at any time, and those, for the most part, have been women married to Nuyooteco men. Although Nuyoo is by no means an autonomous political entity, its ethnic homogeneity has meant that local government and decision making have largely been left in indigenous hands. To my knowledge there are no communities in the Mixteca Alta that have the kind of parallel indigenous and mestizo municipal administrations one finds in Guatemala and other parts of

Figure 1. The landscape of the Mixteca Alta. This is a line of mountains to the southeast of Nuyoo Center. Yuku Kasa, the highest, has a lake near its summit, which the artist represents as a rectangle on the mountain's side.

Mexico. In Nuyoo the absence of a Mestizo ethnic group—whose position in so many other places is often based on the subordination of indigenous people—has allowed strong, local Mixtec-speaking leaders to emerge who, while by no means unselfish, are nevertheless still Indian. This, I think, has contributed to the strong sense of confidence and security in their own purpose one finds among Nuyootecos, something that is often lacking in indigenous peoples living in towns characterized by hierarchical ethnic divisions.

Nuyoo is also located in an area I call the "swidden belt" of the Mixteca, where there is little or no irrigated land and the steep gradient makes plow agriculture impossible. (The abrupt and rocky terrain creates such a challenge for walking that people often say good-bye to visitors with the words, "don't fall!"[1]) This difficult

---

1. "Don't fall" is more than a simple warning about difficult paths. On the one hand, it is a warning about soul loss, where the emotional shock of a slip or fall causes the soul to fall out of the body, where it is seized by a *nu ñu'un* or some other creature. If it is not recovered by a curer, the patient will gradually waste away and die. On the other hand, "don't fall" is a warning of the moral dangers we face. Thus a man who squanders an inheritance, or a woman who becomes pregnant out of wedlock, is a person whose "feet have slipped" (cf. Burkhart 1989:61).

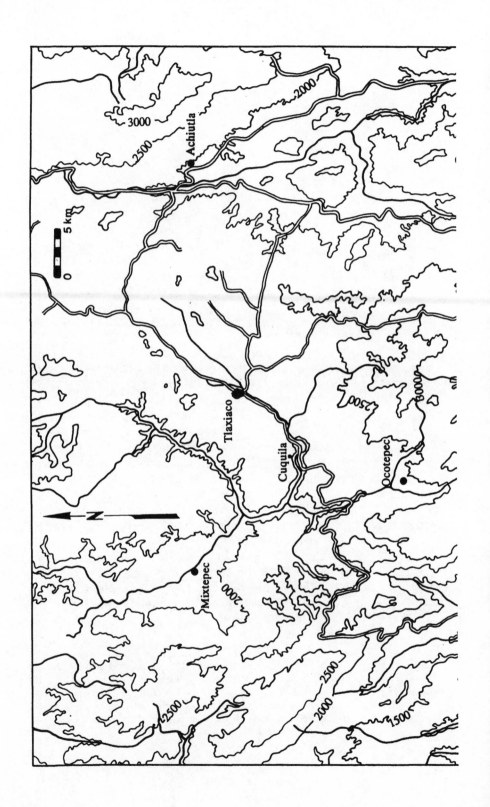

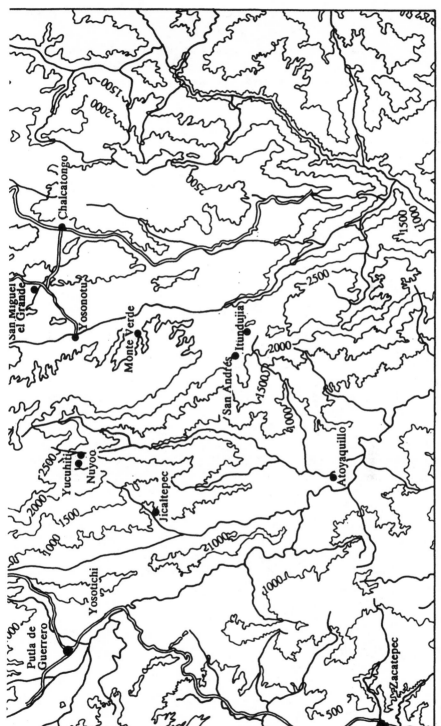

Map 3. Topographic map of the Nuyoo region of the Mixteca Alta. Drawing by Inez Verhagen and Laura Junker.

landscape made the area unsuited for intensive commercial agriculture until the coffee boom began in the 1940s. Also, religious conversion has not been a major dynamic in the region. In Nuyoo the
catequistas, who are nominally the representatives of the Catholic
church, function primarily as prayer leaders in traditional ceremonies
and do little proselytizing. The high rate of monolingualism and the
lack of sustained contact with a Catholic priest makes communication
about doctrinal matters difficult, even though Nuyootecos see the
priest as an authority on religious matters. (The priest assigned to
Nuyoo oversees a parish of over two dozen communities, many of
which are accessible only on foot or horseback, so the time he spends
in any of them is limited.) By 1991, about a half-dozen people had
converted to evangelical sects; however, their small numbers and
their continuing participation in communal and religious institutions
have kept conversion from becoming a divisive issue, and Nuyootecos
maintain a degree of uniformity in belief and ritual practice that has
not existed in other areas of Mesoamerica for generations.

Finally, the Mixteca region, like most of Oaxaca (Dennis 1987), is
distinguished from better-known indigenous areas by a high level of
intercommunity conflict. Before the Mexican state began a period of
expansion in 1950s and 1960s, communities were usually in competition over land. Now disputes also involve the locations of schools and
rural clinics, where roads will pass, and where government-subsidized dry-goods stores (CONASUPO) should be established. These
conflicts often erupt into shooting wars, and in the 1980s more than 40
men were killed in a single battle between two municipalities in a
district adjacent to Nuyoo. Intercommunity warfare not only has been
an important factor in political and economic developments in the
region but also has a lot to do with how people define themselves.
Nuyootecos, for example, use images drawn from indigenous people
of neighboring communities as stereotypes of negative behavior,
along with images of Spanish and Mestizo people, and they are just as
likely to be concerned with boundaries between themselves and other
Mixtec speakers as they are with the kinds of people anthropologists
traditionally evoke when speaking about "outside exploiters" of
Native Mesoamericans.

LOCAL SETTLEMENTS

Nuyoo is divided into six hamlets (Yucunino, Yucubey, Loma Bonita,
Unión y Progreso, Tierra Azul, and Zaragoza) and the town center.
Each hamlet contains a school, an agent's office, perhaps a govern-

ment-subsidized cooperative store or CONASUPO (in Yucunino and Unión y Progreso), a church or chapel (in Zaragoza), a few storage sheds, and, in most hamlets, one or two poorly stocked stores.[2]

In political terms, each hamlet is represented by several officials, the most important of whom is the hamlet agent. The agent administers hamlet funds, reports to the municipal government, and directs hamlet public works projects. All married men and men over 18 years of age who belong to the hamlet are eligible to serve as agent or in the other hamlet offices. Hamlet members owe *tequio*, or corvée labor, on hamlet projects and must also make monetary contributions to meet hamlet expenses. Nuyoo Center, which functions in many ways like a hamlet, was represented by the municipal *síndico* until 1993, when the post of "representative of the center" was created by municipal authorities (see below and chapter 7).

Yucunino and Yucubey are the oldest hamlets in Nuyoo and are situated near Soko Usha, where the founders of Nuyoo emerged from the earth. Zaragoza, the youngest hamlet, was established as a stronghold early in this century to guard against encroachment by the

2. The statement that Nuyoo contains six hamlets is only partially correct; one other hamlet, Yosotato, lies to the southwest of Nuyoo Center and is officially part of the municipality of Nuyoo. I did not include it among the others because Yosotato is a unique case. It has its own well-defined territorial boundaries, and no one from the other Nuyoo hamlets has access to its lands (nor does anyone from Yosotato have access to lands in the rest of the municipality). People from Yosotato seldom marry people from the other hamlets, never join in the communal work parties, and almost never attend meetings held in Nuyoo Center, preferring to arrange most administrative matters among themselves, led by their agent. Yosotato also has its own church and, in the 1970s and early 1980s, even served as the parish seat for the entire region.

Yosotato is unlike the other hamlets because it was once an outpost of a Mixtec kingdom whose people, according to oral history, came from outside the immediate region. In contrast to this, the other Nuyoo hamlets are either very ancient, as is true of Yucunino and Yucubey, or were founded by the descendants of the original inhabitants of Yucunino and Yucubey. Since the sixteenth century, Yosotato has changed hands several times in political disputes, and it finally ended up as part of Nuyoo after it seceded from Yucuhiti. It is true that many settlements in the region have split off from larger polities, either joining some other polity or becoming independent. But in Yosotato's case this occurred much more frequently, and over a longer period, which served to reinforce the identity of the people of Yosotato as a unique group. Also, during each secession, Yosotato's boundaries became an issue and were precisely defined, something that not only made Yosotato into a landholding unit but, no doubt, contributed to its people's strong sense of identification with a particular territory.

When people in the region talk about the differences between Yosotato and the other hamlets, however, they do not mention Yosotato's complicated history. Instead they simply explain it by saying that Yosotato is one ñuu and that the rest of the municipality forms another ñuu, and Ñuu Nuyoo. This highlights the importance of local definitions of the social order for understanding social patterns in the Mixteca.

people of nearby Ocotlán and Nopalera. No hamlet is more than an hour's walk away from its nearest neighbor; however, it can take three to four hours to go from Yucunino to Zaragoza, since Nuyoo territory forms a long, narrow rectangle running northeast to southwest and Yucunino and Zaragoza lie in opposite corners.

About one-fifth of the population of Nuyoo lives in Nuyoo Center. The center is unique because it functions like a hamlet (the men of the center, like the men of the hamlets, are eligible to serve in local offices and must join communal work parties) but is, as its name implies, the municipal seat. Concentrated within the center are the municipal buildings, such as the *presidencia* or town hall, the office of the *comisario* (see chapter 7), the school district office, and the main church. This makes Nuyoo Center the hub of public life. Anyone who wants a child enrolled in school, a tax matter arranged, a marriage registered, or any other official transaction completed must report to the center. This traffic makes a relatively high level of commercial activity possible, and it is in the center that one finds a weekly market and the best-stocked stores in the region (Figure 2). The center also has the densest population, since many people have chosen to live there to take advantage of municipal services. Houses in the center stand close together, and vacant house sites are scarce, in contrast to areas outside the center, where people usually live dispersed across the landscape.

Hamlets and Intercommunity Conflict

When the men of Nuyoo gather on the veranda and lawn in front of the municipal hall for communal meetings, they cluster together in loose groups based on hamlet affiliation. They also vote together, raising their voices in unison when the authorities call their hamlet's name. As this suggests, hamlets form important subgroups within Nuyoo, and the significance of hamlet-based identities appears to be much greater today than ever before. Hamlets have grown tremendously over the past 50 years, becoming the locus of many activities that had been restricted to the town center. Also, patrilineal inheritance and virilocal residence tend to concentrate kin within specific hamlets, further isolating the people of one hamlet from those of another. This can be clearly seen in the distribution of patrilineally inherited surnames, which are identified with particular hamlets. A Velasco is invariably from Yucubey, while a Rojas is most frequently associated with Tierra Azul.

In spite of the forces that isolate the people of one hamlet from

Figure 2. A man on his way to the Sunday market in Nuyoo Center. Ancient Mixtec scribes also represented markets as circles, but enclosed footprints within them rather than trucks and roads.

another, one cannot say that Nuyoo is strongly divided by its hamlets. Such divisions do, however, exist among hamlets in surrounding towns, whose inhabitants battle one another over resources and where some have attempted to secede from their municipal seats. Nothing like this has occurred in Nuyoo.

There are three reasons why Nuyoo's hamlets are different from those of neighboring Mixtec-speaking municipalities. The first has to do with the loose link between hamlet and territory in Nuyoo. Even though each hamlet owns the land where its school and other public buildings sit, there are no boundaries between hamlets or between a hamlet and Nuyoo Center. Coupled with this, the average Nuyooteco owns several plots of land scattered throughout the community territory. It is not unusual to find a man from one hamlet (say, Yucunino) working a plot of land near the agent's office of another hamlet (such as Tierra Azul).

The negative consequences of drawing boundaries between hamlets and making hamlet membership the criterion for owning land within the hamlet (as in nearby Monteverde and many other places in the Mixteca) are not lost on Nuyootecos. We can see this in remarks made by the town president, a man from Yucunino, during a town meeting when people criticized him for his handling of community affairs. In the heat of the moment he blurted out, "All right, if that is the way you feel, no one from Yucunino need ever come down to the center and serve in municipal positions. From now on we will just name our own authorities up there." A man then shouted back, "If you do that, then you need not come down to work your land, either." Nuyoo Center, Tierra Azul, Unión y Progreso, and Zaragoza sit in the semitropical zone of Nuyoo territory, where most cash crops are produced. The people from Yucunino, who live in the cold uplands, have extensive holdings in the tropical zone, where they grow coffee, corn, and bananas and other fruits. After hearing the president's statement and the replies it provoked, his fellow hamlet members (who would normally be his first line of support) remained silent and later even criticized him for saying what he did. Nuyootecos recognize that there are economic and subsistence-related reasons to keep hamlets from becoming socially, politically, or territorially isolated.

The second factor that counterbalances the tendency for hamlets to nucleate and fission has to do with the way hamlets recruit members. In Nuyoo, hamlet membership, or membership in the center, is not ascribed; a person is free to join any hamlet he or she may choose. Although hamlet membership is usually based on how close one lives to a hamlet center, people sometimes quit one and join another, particularly if they are feuding with fellow hamlet members. The process is simple: all one has to do is attend a meeting of the new hamlet and announce that one wishes to join. For example, two households located quite close to the hamlet office of Loma Bonita belong to the center, which is several kilometers distant. Likewise, one man lives only a few steps from the market in Nuyoo Center but belongs to Zaragoza, a 2½-hour walk from his house. In the first case the households were originally part of Loma Bonita, but they broke away and joined the center because they were mad about the way officials from Loma Bonita expended hamlet resources. In the second, the man moved from Zaragoza to his house near the market some years ago but continues to consider himself a part of Zaragoza. My survey data suggest that at least one man manipulates this situation to obscure which hamlet he belongs to. I suspect he does not belong to any hamlet and thus avoids communal labor requirements and financial contributions altogether.

The final factor limiting the growth of serious divisions among hamlets in Nuyoo has to do with population transfers within the community. The movement of women to their husband's household in marriage counterbalances the concentration of kin ties within a locality, in that it creates lines of communication and alliance between households of different hamlets. In one bitter political dispute, two hamlets united to impeach a municipal office holder, and the office holder's brother-in-law, who was from one of the hamlets, secretly informed him about what his neighbors planned. He did this even though hamlet officials warned him not to tell his affines what was going on.

Over the past 70 years, there have also been large-scale residence shifts in Nuyoo, which have, like marriage, crosscut hamlet boundaries. About 40 years ago, people began to move into Nuyoo Center in order to take advantage of the services provided there by the Mexican government. Prior to this, beginning in the 1920s, there was a movement of population toward the hamlet of Zaragoza, when the "wars" with the neighboring communities of Nopalera and Ocotlán turned in Nuyoo's favor and a large area of land became safe for farming. Both movements resulted in the redistribution of households within Nuyoo boundaries, so that people in Yucunino, Yucubey, Loma Bonita, Tierra Azul, and Unión y Progreso have many relatives in Zaragoza and the center.

In all this, Nuyoo Center plays a crucial role in mediating local divisions. Besides being populated by people who have moved there from all the different hamlets, the center is the focus of ritual and political life, and people from throughout Nuyoo frequently visit it for one reason or another. This allows those who live far from one another to regularly interact, since almost everyone spends some time in the center during the week, and many with duties in the civil-religious hierarchy move there for their period of service. Moreover, all Nuyootecos have a place to spend the night in the center because they either own a house there or have relatives and ritual kin who do. This again is in contrast to other municipalities in the region, such as Monteverde, where people in many of its hamlets have never traveled to its center (though they do make equally arduous trips to other towns in the Mixteca). As we will see in chapter 15, a key factor in the growth of a strong center in Nuyoo has been the cacique (a kind of political boss), who has worked to concentrate municipal services in one place.

The forces that cause hamlets to separate and compete in the Mixteca are thus counterbalanced in Nuyoo because hamlets are not landholding units, membership in them is not ascribed, and most individuals participate in networks of social relationships that crosscut hamlet divisions. This is not to say that the people of different hamlets are always in agreement or that divisions between them will not become significant in the future. It is only to make the point that groups lying between household and community are not overly significant in Nuyooteco social life.

THE HOUSEHOLD

Late one evening in January 1984, I was in the home of a religious official, waiting for him to return from an errand. I arrived in the company of two prayer leaders who wanted to discuss the details of an upcoming fiesta with him. It was cold, and the men sat huddled together, leafing through a school science textbook belonging to the official's son. Eventually they came to a chapter on human evolution, illustrated with the inevitable picture of a hairy, stoop-shouldered Neanderthal standing in front of a cave. The prayer leaders looked to me for an explanation, and I told them that the Neanderthals were a primitive people who lived long ago. "Ah," one of them said, "the *tiumi.*" At that point, the official arrived home, the book was put away, and the discussion turned to the fiesta.

After asking around, I discovered that all Nuyootecos—men and women, young and old—can talk at length about the tiumi, whom they also call "the primitives," "the unbaptized ones," or "the people of the wilds" *(ñivi yuku).* The tiumi lived before the sun was born, when tall forests (yuku) covered the world. They were hunters, and they ate the animals they took raw, since they had no fire. The tiumi did not know how to grow corn, they lived in caves rather than houses, they mated freely (as one woman put it, "the tiumi did not know who was a son, or who was a daughter"), and they did not sacrifice to the gods. Some speculate that the tiumi did not even know how to speak. Their world came to an end with the cataclysmic birth of the sun, whose searing heat burned them. To escape the sun, some tiumi retreated into caves where, according to people who have ventured in, their abnormally large bones may be found today. No one knows if all the tiumi died after the sun was born, and some say the survivors became the ancestors of modern humans (cf. Jansen 1982:200–201).[3]

---

3. *Tiumi* is related to the Mixtec word for owl. The term probably came from sixteenth-century Dominican sources, who, in their efforts to translate Christian concepts for indigenous populations, hit upon the Nahua *talcatecolotl,* or "owl man," a fearful, nocturnal shapeshifter, as an equivalent for

When Nuyootecos talk about the tiumi, it is clear they do so to establish contrasts with people today. Thus, the tiumi hunted, but modern humans practice agriculture; the tiumi ate their food raw, but people today cook their food and season it with chile and salt; the tiumi did not worship the gods, but those who have come after them make sacrifice and sponsor fiestas for the saints. I will discuss the tiumi from time to time over the course of the book; here I want to start with the household, something that is—along with agriculture, cooked food, incest taboos, and sacrifice—one of the things Nuyootecos identify as making them different from these primitive beings.

THE HOUSE

When Nuyootecos build their dwellings, they usually begin by digging into a hillside to create a level plot. People say these sites are "cooked" (chi'yo; see Smith 1973). Cooking is, of course, a widespread metaphor for transformation, and in Nuyoo, once a place has been "cooked," it is no longer part of the wilds (yuku). If the tiumi were "people of the wilds" (ñivi yuku), Nuyootecos are civilized people of households (ñivi ve'i).

Most Nuyooteco households consist of at least two structures: the house, where people sleep and store most of their belongings, and a smaller kitchen hut. The house may be made from a variety of materials. In the town center and other places where the road passes, people sometimes build their houses out of concrete and steel reinforcing rods, which involve considerable expense; such materials signal high status. Most houses, however, are made of adobe bricks and have tin or wood roofs. People living above 1800 m elevation frequently build their houses out of pine logs or boards because wood is readily available from nearby forests and can be chinked and used as insulation from the cold. At the warmer, lower elevations, people sometimes construct houses with the cane that grows along the rivers and thatch the roofs with straw or the waterproof husks of the trunk of the banana tree. In the past almost all Nuyootecos at lower elevations lived in houses made of cane. Many Nuyootecos also cooked inside these structures because separate kitchen huts were not always built.

Nuyooteco houses are typically dark inside, since people build

---

the Demon (Burkhart 1989:40–41). Although the tiumi represent a more generalized Mixtec view of a presocial existence and cannot be reduced to European ideas about evil, they are identified as "unbaptized" and are linked to the velu, troupes of masked dancers who circulate among the households of Nuyoo in the weeks before Lent, and who are spoken of as demons.

them without windows, and the floors are of packed earth. (The exceptions are houses with walls of cane, since ample light filters through.) Sleeping platforms made out of cane, or wooden beds purchased in the Sunday market, are placed along the walls, interspersed with wooden chests, baskets, pots, tools, glass jars, and plastic containers. Baskets, sacks, and clothes hang from the rafters to keep them from mice and dogs. The family altar (figure 3) is usually set to the left of the doorway. It consists of a table holding several small images of saints and, perhaps, an unusually shaped rock, such as those that contain the outline of a human face; Nuyootecos identify these as a kind of *ndiosi*, or "god," called the *nu ñu'un* (see chapter 4). The table may also contain candleholders, an incense dish, and several tin cans to hold flowers. The space underneath the altar is used for storage. The walls of many houses are covered with calendars, which are given out annually to customers by stores in Tlaxiaco and Putla. People hang these up not because they have a great interest in keeping track of time but because they enjoy looking at the colorful photos on their covers. (I have seen some that are as many as 30 years old.) Most people have a radio tuned to the Instituto Nacional Indigenista station in Tlaxiaco, the only station that can be picked up in Nuyoo during daylight hours.

Nuyootecos spend very little time in their houses, entering only to sleep or to retrieve items stored inside. Most activity occurs around the patio between the kitchen and the house and in the kitchen hut. The kitchen hut usually faces the main house across a patio. It is made of less substantial materials than the house and is intentionally drafty, so that smoke can escape from the cooking fires. The kitchen hut contains a hearth; at least one griding stone; numerous pots, bowls, and plastic buckets stacked around the walls; a clay griddle for baking tortillas; several stools; and, perhaps, a metal corn grinder. Bunches of bananas, sacks of dried tortillas *(totopos),* and seed corn may be strung from the roof, again so that dogs and mice cannot get to them. In many respects the kitchen is what defines the household for Nuyootecos. It is where people collect in the morning to warm themselves before heading out to their individual chores, it is where people consume meals together, and it is where they gather at night to chat after everyone returns from work.

The Household and Nakara

At the outset of his ethnography on the Maya of Panajachel, Tax remarked,

Figure 3. People praying before a household altar. A framework of cane, called an arch, is set up over the altar. Household members affix palm leaves, flowers, and other colorful decorations to it during religious events.

> In making this study, it was striking to find how many of the data had to be gathered by households rather than individuals on the one hand, or family or neighborhood groups on the other. Thus, in discussing marketing, it was useless to try to deduce which individuals went to certain towns regularly, but it was easy to find out which households were regularly represented by one or another individual in a given town. Likewise in land ownership, it was not difficult to discover which plots were owned and worked by a certain household . . . . (Tax 1953:11)

As in Panajachel, the people of a Nuyooteco household have a strong collective identity and easily substitute for one another. A five-year-old, for example, may refer to a rifle his father uses, or to a cornfield worked by his grandfather, as "his" rifle or "his" field, since the members of a household hold property in common. Household members are also accountable for one another's behavior. In 1985, for instance, a fire set to burn the stubble in a cornfield got out of control, destroying many fruit and coffee trees and killing the man who set it; the man's brother, who lived with him in the same household, was forced to pay damages to neighboring property owners. Although household members have different perspectives and act independently of one another (as Wilk 1984:239–40 cautions), Nuyootecos usually speak and act as though the household were a single person; even a thing as personal as a dream, which Nuyootecos say represents the wanderings of the soul, is considered a foretoken not only of the health and future of the dreamer but also that of all the members of the dreamer's household.

Ideally, a household consists of a man and a woman, their unmarried children, and their married sons, since residence is virilocal and males receive the bulk of the inheritance (Romney 1967:207). I lived for a time in one such household. The couple who headed it had three children: one married son with two children, a daughter with two children who returned to live with her parents after her husband died, and another daughter who, at 15, was just reaching marriageable age. The adults worked together, dividing the day's tasks among themselves early in the morning. The males would go to different plots of land, or to the same plot, depending on the job at hand. At least one of the adult women stayed at home to prepare food and care for the children who were too young to accompany their parents to the fields. The people of the household lived in a compound with several different structures, but there was only one kitchen hut. They cooked their food together, they apportioned it equally, and they stored the harvest in one place. The eldest male held the money the household received from the sale of cash crops; he distributed it to household members as needs arose, such as when a grandchild needed a new pair of pants or when his son needed a new machete. Although there were conflicts (especially between the widowed daughter and her sister-in-law), it was an arrangement where people were said to "live well," forming a single landholding unit, a single unit of production, and a single unit of consumption.

Nuyootecos say that the people I lived with form a distinct, cohesive, and functioning domestic group because they have *nakara* for one another. Nakara might be translated as "love," since it is an intense, emotional relationship that people say exists not only between parents and their children but also between men and women who are romantically involved with each other. Yet nakara does not connote desire as much as a willingness to take responsibility for another by providing what is needed for a healthy life. Thus Nuyootecos frequently define nakara as the act of one person's feeding another *(nsikaji ma,* or "he feeds him") or clothing another *(nsikuniji ma*, or "she dresses her"). The most common, everyday expression of nakara occurs in the kitchen hut. In a scene I saw repeated hundreds of times, children would go to their father, who was seated near the hearth, and he would break off a piece of the tortilla he was eating and hand it to them so that they could dip into the bowl of beans or squash he was holding. His wife, who had served him the food, might then come over and eat from the same bowl. Among household members, there is no need to apportion food separately. They share in the most intimate way possible, eating out of the same bowl and drinking from the same cup. This stands in contrast to visitors, who, when invited to eat, are served separate portions of food, in the house or out on the patio, but never in the kitchen. Outsiders always seem a little uncomfortable in someone else's kitchen hut, as if, by coming inside, they have suddenly entered a place where they have no right to be.

Food, Clothing, and Nakara

Nuyootecos do not speak of the giving of food and clothing by one person to another as an expression or symbol of nakara. Instead, those items give form to the relationship; they put it into force, so that nakara exists only as long as the nurturing flow of food and clothing continues. An older woman once observed that "It is better if your parents are poor and have nothing. That way you will not feel it so much when they die." From her point of view, poor parents who do not have many things to give will have a correspondingly less-intense relationship with their children. This also holds true for godparents. When a godchild goes to the home of his godfather, the godfather should rejoice and offer whatever food is in the house. I once heard a young man complain about how little affection his godfather showed him and how he didn't even think of the man as his godfather anymore. When I asked if he was going to visit his godfather, he replied, "I'm not going to go any more because he starves me."

Because nakara is contingent on the flow of food and other items between persons, these items have a significance for Nuyootecos that at first seems excessive. On a superficial level, it makes them appear to be overly concerned with material things, since they are constantly talking about how much particular items cost and where they can be obtained. For example, a young boy named Pedro was showing off a new pair of sandals to other children in front of the house where I stayed. His older "brother" Luis (FBS) told him that he saw Pedro's parents Sunday and that they didn't buy the sandals but found them on the side of the road. This made Pedro sad, and he began to cry. Later I asked Pedro's mother about this. She said "Oh, that's why he asked me if we really did buy them. I asked him, 'Who would leave a new pair of sandals by the roadside?'"

I have seen Luis and Pedro grow to be young men, and they still do not get along with each other. But what is interesting about the incident is that of all the nasty things Luis could have said to Pedro, Luis chose to tell him that his parents came by the sandals easily, and that this hurt Pedro deeply. Parents rarely demonstrate physical affection for their children. There is little caressing or hugging once they are no longer infants. Yet the children proudly display the clothing and other items their parents give them as a demonstration of their parents' affection. What Luis was telling Pedro was that because the sandals were obtained so easily, this showed that Pedro's parents didn't care for him as much as Pedro believed.

The notion that the goods one person gives to another constitute their relationship in substantive and emotional terms is something that is true not just in nakara but in a variety of other relationships as well. For example, if a man borrows a piece of land from another, and the crops he plants do poorly while those on other plots in the vicinity flourish, the man who borrowed the land can be sure that the man who lent it to him did so unwillingly. Likewise, when someone eats a meal and later becomes ill, this is a sign that the person who prepared the food, despite appearances, did so with great reluctance. People are accordingly very concerned if someone becomes sick after eating, since it bodes ill for their relationship. But it is not just that the items that pass between people objectify their relationships in such a way that the state of the relationship becomes characterized by the physical properties of the items—it is also through these items that people experience one another: in the food in their bellies, through the clothes on their backs, and through the illnesses they suffer.

Nakara—the idea that deep affection is inseparable from the intimate sharing of food and clothing between people—should also be placed in the context of a society where scarcity and hunger have been regularly experienced by nearly everyone. Although outsiders consider Nuyoo a "garden," life is not easy for the people who live there. Because little land is suitable for irrigation, and because outside supplies of corn are often difficult to obtain in late summer, people rely for subsistence on the rainy-season corn harvested in October to December, which inevitably runs short by the next July. This produces what Nuyootecos call the "months of starvation" in the late summer and early fall, when the supply of corn dwindles and people anxiously await the harvest.[4] It is not coincidental that nakara is constituted in the giving of food and clothing; with hunger and privation all around, anyone willing to feed and clothe another must truly be bound to them by loving ties.

Nakara and the Household

The close connection between intimate sharing and domestic life can perhaps best be seen in the way Nuyootecos speak of the process of household fissioning. Although the ideal domestic arrangement is an extended family household, sons often live apart from their fathers, and brothers move away from one another and establish separate households. What is interesting about this is that Nuyootecos talk about the breakup of a household as something caused by the interruption in the free circulation of food and clothing among household members (cf. Wilk 1984:225, 226). One example of this occurred between 1983 and 1985 in Nuyoo Center.

Prior to 1983, this household was considered a place where people "lived well." It consisted of a couple, their two recently married sons, and their sons' wives. However, not long after the boys married, a rift began to develop, and within two years the household had split.

According to several household members, problems began when the wife of the eldest son took a dislike to the wife of the youngest son, and the two began to bicker. This became more serious when the wife of the eldest son accused her mother-in-law of showing favoritism to the other son, by giving the young man and his wife more than their proper share of the money from the cash crops the household produced. One day, she and her mother-in-law had a bitter fight in which the two screamed insults at each other across the house patio. When the men returned from the fields and discovered what had taken place, the father ordered the daughter-in-law to return to her father's household. Over the next few days, tempers cooled, and the eldest son went to his in-laws' house to ask for the return of his wife. They granted his request, and the couple was reunited.

Even though the husband and wife were together again, bad feelings persisted. While in her father's household, the wife had told her relatives, neighbors, and just about anyone who would listen how badly her in-laws treated her. She went into explicit and embarrassing detail about how they denied her food, how they forced her to work so

---

4. This period is called *yoo yuu* in Mixtec.

hard she lost weight, and how often they insulted her. Her in-laws, she said, did not care for her (nakara) in the way they should care for a daughter-in-law. Her complaints were so effective that during the celebrations at Christmas her father shocked the community by taking the plate of food presented to him by his daughter's father-in-law and throwing it on the ground. This was both a great insult and a dangerous thing to do, since wasting food is sinful to Nuyootecos and may be punished by the gods with the loss of a harvest.

The conflict continued, and within a month the wife was back at her father's house. This time it was almost two weeks before her husband came to ask for her return. Yet from this point on, the relationship between the woman and her husband improved. She bore a son, and the proud father received his first cargo in the municipal government, which requires close cooperation between husband and wife (see chapter 8). She continued to be on bad terms with her in-laws, however. Gradually, according to her account, she brought her husband around to her point of view—that is, that there was no nakara between them and her in-laws. She argued that the father was not giving them enough food to eat and that they were not receiving the money necessary for the well-being of their little son. Once the husband was convinced, he informed the other members of the household that he would stop going into the fields with them. This was a bitter time for both sides, and the husband and wife went to live with the wife's parents for about a week. When they returned to the compound, the husband no longer went to work with his father but, instead, worked as a wage laborer. He, his wife, and his son lived in his parent's house as before, but they no longer ate the corn and other foods prepared by his mother and sister-in-law. Instead, they purchased corn in the market, and although they used the same hearth, they cooked and ate their food separately. From their point of view, they were no longer a single household, even though they continued to live in the same structures.

When it was time to plant in May of 1985, the husband borrowed a plot of land from another man and sowed his own field of corn. He continued working as a day laborer and, just before the harvest, completed the construction of a house and kitchen hut alongside his father's house. Although the separation from her father-in-law's household made the wife very happy, her husband seemed a bit doubtful about the new arrangements. My impression, after seeing them again in 1989 and 1991, is that the tension between the two sides gradually diminished over the years and that both have become accustomed to the new situation. (For another example of the breakup of a household, see Ravicz 1965:140.)

There is a tension between the notion that in nakara people freely share what is necessary for a good life, and the obvious asymmetries that exist between parents, who hold the purse strings, and their children, who receive from them. But Nuyootecos point out that the persons who administer household wealth will change with the succession of generations, so that those who were initially subordinate and on the receiving end of a nakara relationship become the administrators, incurring the responsibility of giving to those who maintained them when the latter are no longer able to support themselves. This symmetry is expressed in several aphorisms: for example, *nteeo je kajira chi teera je nkajio* ("we sow so that they may eat because they sowed so that we could eat"), when a son is speaking about an aged parent, and *saa saa nuvi siio* ("well, then, the son [or daughter] has become the provider"), when an aged parent is speaking about a child. Also, the items that flow from children to parents have the same significance as the items parents give to children. Just as children brag about a new piece of clothing bought them by their parents, old men brag about a coat bought for them by a daughter or money sent to them by a son working in Mexico City. There are, of course, many reasons why children might not provide for their parents. Nevertheless, in a society where a domestic unit's productivity is often a function of where it stands in the household developmental cycle, a son's household, at the height of its productive power (Pastor 1987), will often take in and support parents, or his grandparents, uncles, aunts, and even godparents.

Earlier I pointed out that Nuyootecos say living in households makes them different from the tiumi. Beyond the contrast between living in caves and living in structures with rooms and hearths, what they are saying is that their willingness to assume responsibility for others by providing the things needed for a healthy and prosperous life—even at the expense of their own well-being—is what makes them "people of households" and therefore civilized. In this context, it is significant that Nuyootecos do not define the household in terms of the genealogical connections of its members. Although the household is ideally an extended family built up around a core of agnatically related males, the household's developmental cycle, fissioning, selective mortality, and divorce make for a great deal of variation. There is a household in Nuyoo Center, for example, made up of widowed sisters and their children; another has a widower and his deceased daughter's husband and children, and yet another has a widow, her adult, unmarried son, and her deceased daughter's two children. Nor do Nuyootecos define the household in terms a list of specific functions. These are actually quite flexible and change over time (see Wilk and Netting 1984). Rather, Nuyootecos speak of the household as emerging out of acts of nakara, which can occur between a variety of people and which is instantiated in things as diverse as a mother nursing her child or a son in Mexico City sending his father a new coat.

JESUS AND THE MORAL COMMUNITY

When I would ask Nuyootecos about local social conventions, they would often refer me to the time when Jesus walked the earth. I heard the complete story from Guadalupe Rojas, a man from the hamlet of Tierra Azul. Before I met Tata Guadalupe, others told me of different incidents of Jesus' travels, but it was Tata Guadalupe who strung them together in an epic narrative that took him almost two hours to tell. When I recorded his version in the mid-1980s, he was in his late sixties, and he told me he had learned about the incidents as a young man from storytellers who are now deceased.

Several older men and women in Nuyoo, like Tata Guadalupe, are known as good storytellers, and I worked with most of them over the course of my time in Nuyoo. However, I found that a detailed knowledge of myths, legends, and other examples of Mixtec oral literature is not restricted to this circle of virtuosos but is widely diffused among Nuyootecos. I also found that when Nuyootecos tell stories, they, like other Mesoamerican peoples, usually do not do so in discrete storytelling sessions (although the texts I am going to present were narrated in formal interviews). Instead, the stories are told in the context of ongoing activities and are often evoked by some chance remark or event, so that they are a part of the way people interact with one another.[5] When Nuyootecos tell stories while working in the

5. For example, I was working *tequio* (communal labor) with about 25 men from Nuyoo Center one day, when a pretty woman passed by near where we were working, carrying a load of wash and dragging a small pig behind her. Tequio is a strongly gendered activity for Nuyootecos, and it did not surprise me when one of the men commented on the woman's presence. He called to her in a suggestive way, and introduced himself as "Pedro Ordemala." Pedro Ordemala is a trickster figure in Latin American folklore, and it was obvious to those present that the man was referring to a ribald story that involved Pedro, a pretty woman, and some pigs. Fausto Modesto Velasco, who was also working tequio that day, then launched into the story, in which Pedro told a rich man that his pigs were buried up to their tails in mud (Pedro had cut the tails off the pigs, and stuck them in the mud), and while the man was busy trying to get the "pigs" out, Pedro went and had sex with the man's

fields, or walking together on a path, or sitting on the veranda of the municipal building waiting for a general assembly to begin, they are, of course, doing so for entertainment purposes but they are also, in a very explicit way, talking about what they share, their relationships to one another, the dilemmas they face, and, most importantly, how these identities, ties, and problems relate—at that moment—to the things they are seeing and experiencing together.

Tata Guadalupe's stories occurred at a time when the world as we know it was just coming into existence. Thus in one part of the narrative he tells us that Jesus went around naming everything in the world; this device is found in many oral traditions to mark creative events, since naming brings things into the scope of human significa-tion (see chapter 4). The main action in the stories of Jesus' travels— which Tata Guadalupe relates to his flight from demons, called variously *tachi* (demons), *velu* (the ancestors), *reyes* (kings), and *jurrios* (Jews)—occurs when he comes upon several households, whose in-habitants either aid him or turn him away. These stories become important because they provide a moral context for certain key social practices, as we will see below. Here, I will cite only the beginning of Tata Guadalupe's narrative, when Jesus came upon the first house during his flight. (Other portions will be cited in subsequent chap-ters.) I have organized the text to give the reader a sense of Tata Guadalupe's poetic style:

> He was a man who traveled through the country, so the story goes;
> He traveled in a humble and frugal manner, he who was Jesus;
> Well then, he arrived [at a house].
> The owner of the house was not a good man.
> Because Jesus arrived and asked:
>> "Will you give me a piece of tortilla so that I may eat and live?"
>> And Jesus asked, "Will you give me a drop of water, so that I may drink and live?"
> He spoke humbly.
> "Well then," said the owner of the house:
>> "Make your own tortilla and eat it, because I make my own to eat.
>> "Make a tortilla and you shall eat, go and fetch water from the river and you shall drink, just as I go to carry my own water to drink," he said.

---

wife. After the story ended, Fausto continued with other Pedro Ordemala stories while everyone else continued working (and laughing), until the men tired of this and the conversation shifted to other topics.

"Build a house and then you shall live in it, just like I built the one I
live in," he said.

"Well then, all right [Jesus replied], you can rest in your house, and
don't ever leave your house, because it is the house you made;

"Then cook what you will eat;

"Go and bring the water you will drink;

"And so I am leaving, I am going to pass by," he said, because the
man did not give him a place to rest.

Well then, the wife of the man carried [on her back] an infant, who had
just been born.

As the gray light of dawn appeared, [the baby] spoke, and said:

"Father," the baby said.

"Father," the baby said.

"What predicament are you in?

"You did it to yourself:

"What should not have been said, you said.

"What should not have been done, you did.

"What distress your soul is in.

"You did it!

"You did it!

"Now!

"Now!

"Right now!

"Go, leave!"

Because this tiny infant spoke.

"Right now, right this instant, leave, go . . . leave!

"You cannot stay here because if you stay, you will suffer, and then I
will see.

"Perhaps I will cry, I will be very sad—go now, leave!

"You know what you should do,
when you go,
if you leave."

"Go!" he said.

"Go!" he said.

This tiny infant, he who commanded.

And he left.

The man went.

But he did not stay on the road, as he plunged
into the brush (ku'u),
into the forest (yuku).

He fell on the rocks;

He fell into the canyon;

He fell onto a bed of thorns which clawed and cut him;

He ran like a madman, falling, stumbling, rising up and falling again,

cutting himself, bruising himself, bumping into trees;
And then it became hot, because *Sakramentu* [the sun] appeared;
And under a tree there was some shade;
And he thought, "It is very hot; if I go under the tree then I may rest
    in the shade."
And so he ran, and went under the tree.
But he found that the shadow had moved to the other side.
So he went there, but the shadow had moved again.
And so he did not get any relief from the hot rays of the Sun *[nkanii];*
And so, well, his entire body was inflamed.
And so he was burned, inflamed:
    the man who ran through the brush,
    the man who ran along the rocks,
    the man who ran through the forest.
He suffered tremendously, the man who is called Señor Monte [the
    Man of the Wilds].
So says the story.

In another incident, Jesus turns the people who refuse him hospitality into pigs. As we will see in chapter 7, Nuyootecos associate the pig with the demon and with velu dancers, both symbols of evil.

Two episodes in Tata Guadalupe's story deserve special comment. In the first, the man refuses to give food and drink to Jesus and is forced to go into the forest (yuku). As I noted earlier, a significant distinction exists around house sites between wild areas and settled areas. Things belonging to one or the other domain are marked in everyday speech by suffixing to them either yuku (forest, brush) or ve'i (household). Thus, *kiti yuku,* "animal of the forest" refers to wild animals, while *kiti ve'i* refers to domestic animals, such as dogs, cats, and pigs. The passage in the story where the man is driven from his household and into the forest can therefore be taken to mean that he has become like a wild animal and has lost his place in human society.

The second important episode in Guadalupe's story occurs when the man is burned by the sun because he can find no shade to protect himself out in the wilds. It is significant that in Postclassic and early Colonial times, Mixtecs called the sun "flaming heart" (King 1982). Although no one in Nuyoo whom I spoke with would translate nkanii as anything other than sun, they did agree that the sun is an *ánima,* or heart. As several explained, the sun is an ánima because just as the ánima is the "center" of the person (being the principal source of vitality for the body), the sun is the "center" of vital life on earth. In the absence of the sun, there would be no light and no way to sow and reap. The sun animates the world, just as the ánima gives life to our bodies, and just as the ánima is the source of the vitality that heats our bodies, so too the sun heats the world.

When Nuyootecos speak of the sun, they often make no distinction between it and Jesus. (When referring to the Mixtec Sun, I will therefore capitalize it as a proper name; I will do the same for Earth, Rain, and Wind, each of which is both a celestial force and a sacred being.) For example, people sometimes call the Sun Sakramentu ("Sacrament"), referring to the miracle of holy communion, where the priest transforms bread and wine into the body and blood of Jesus during the Mass. In church ritual and doctrine, the communion wafer is associated with the sacred heart of Jesus, which Nuyootecos in turn link to the Sun, "the ánima of God." Thus people call the celebration of Corpus Christi *Viko Nkanii*, "the fiesta of the Sun," and Nuyootecos say the monstrance—the "saint" of this fiesta—represents a sunburst. Also, Nuyootecos locate the place where Jesus was born as "where the Sun rises, Bethlehem" and say that he died "where the Sun sets, Jerusalem." This connection between the life of Jesus and the movement of the Sun recalls the ancient Mesoamerican belief that the Sun must overcome death when it sets so that it can be reborn each day at dawn. (A common word for death in Nuyoo is *na'vare*, "he is extinguished," the same verb used for the act of shutting off a light or dousing a fire.) Another ancient belief recalled in Nuyooteco stories is the idea that when the Sun first rose into the sky, it did not move at all. It was Jesus who, through his death, caused the sun to move, just as the ancient gods caused it to move through acts of self-sacrifice (Sahagún 1977:259–62, vol. 2; see also Burkhart 1989 for a discussion of the colonial Nahua association of Jesus with the Sun).

But while Nuyootecos see both Jesus and the Sun as "sacred hearts," they also associate them on another level, which involves the role Jesus plays as the embodiment of truth, goodness, and purity for Christians. When people in Nuyoo speak about the Sun, they often speak of it as Christians do of Jesus, as a moral force. They say the Sun penetrates all things, that it sees and hears everything. In the words of several people, the Sun is "the eye of God" (cf. Jansen 1982:297)

The purity and goodness of Jesus Christ/the Sun are in turn closely associated with the light and heat the Sun emits, and the resulting contrast drawn between nighttime, when the Sun is absent, and daytime, when it is present. On the one side, darkness brings with it a variety of evils. It is the time when the demons prowl, when witches cast their spells, and when illicit activities take place. In contrast to this, *niji*, ("brightness," "clarity") is used as a metaphor for truthfulness, sincerity, and respectability. We will see an example of this in chapter 3, where, in marriage negotiations, the groom's party emphasizes its sincerity by arriving at the bride's house at first light and speaking "the dawning words."

In the passage from Guadalupe's story where the man is driven into the wilds, then, his being burned by the Sun is the equivalent of a punishment administered by Jesus.[6] The reason Jesus punishes him by driving him into the brush is that in refusing to share his food and offer hospitality, the man repudiated social life.

Food sharing is central to Nuyooteco thinking about moral action. A popular phrase for injustice is derived from those very instances where people do not share food. I first realized this when I gave a group of Nuyootecos an example of two people who committed the same crime, but only one of whom was punished for it. I then asked them if there was a way of describing this in Mixtec. They all agreed that in this example the person punished "was looking at the mouth." The meaning of this was unclear to me, and I asked them if they had any thoughts about why they would use such an expression. One man volunteered that it probably comes from a situation where there are seven tortillas and four people. If they divide the tortillas, three get two tortillas, and one person gets only one. "When the person with only one tortilla finishes," he explained, "the others are still eating. This person is then 'looking at their mouths.' This is injustice."

If going hungry because others do not share is the height of injustice for Nuyootecos, then the hoarding of food is the most reprehensible of sins. Parents teach their children from the time they are young to share food with others, and they punish them when they fail to do so. I once saw a father give a quantity of sweets to his young son and tell him to distribute them among all the people present. "And if there are any left over, you may have one, too," the father perversely told him, forcing his son to overcome the urge to dip into the bag immediately. Likewise, anyone who "eats in the dark" *(kaji neeo ma)*, or eats surreptitiously *(kaji yu'uo ma)*, so that others will not know they have food, is committing a sin *(kuachi)*. The person who sins in this way risks being accused of committing crimes, even though they are not at fault. The reason for this, people explain, is that by "eating in the dark" it is as if the person had stolen the food. The

6. The child who ordered the man to leave is also associated with the Christ Child, or Santo Niño, whom Nuyootecos say was able to speak only a few days after being born.

selfish act of hoarding food is morally wrong and, like other kinds of sins, will not go unpunished.

The willingness to share food is a primary characteristic of the *tee va'a*, the "good man" and the *ña va'a*, the "good woman." When I asked people to define *tee va'a* and *ña va'a*, they would invariably say something like "a man who always shares his food, even if it is only half a tortilla" or "a woman who serves the men her household has hired as day laborers the same food as she serves her husband." In each case, the *tee va'a* and *ña va'a* are not stingy with food and are always willing to give part of what they have to others.

Although custom demands that food be shared in a number of different contexts, it most commonly occurs when visitors come to call. When a visitor arrives, or even if someone only passes near the house, they should be invited to rest and served something to eat. If you arrive at a house and its members do not invite you to eat, or if they give you something to eat but do not invite you to sit, then one can be sure that you are not welcome and that the owner is hostile.[7] Indeed, hospitality is the most basic expression of being social in Nuyoo (see Kearney 1972:70–80 for another example from Oaxaca).[8]

The kind of food sharing associated with hospitality should not be confused with nakara, however. As I noted, when outsiders receive an invitation to eat, they will usually be served away from the kitchen hut, either in the patio or inside the house. Similarly, each outsider receives a separate portion of food.[9] Nuyootecos may share food with outsiders, but they do not do so in the intimate way that household members do, who scoop food out of the *same* bowl, and eat from the *same* tortilla.

7. In the sixteenth century Diego Durán wrote that when Nahua peoples "go to visit someone—whether ill or in good health—if they are not fed and given drink, they will not return, even though he is their own brother or close kinsmen" (Durán 1971:151).

8. The etiquette of hospitality is also the model for the serving of food in fiestas. I was always surprised at the differences between people's descriptions of a fiesta and what I could see going on when I attended one. If I relied solely on what people had to say about the fiesta, I would have never known that much of the activity involves people making prestations and counterprestations to one another, which are often governed by calculation and mistrust. When gift exchanges are mentioned, they are not described in terms of a sequence of tit-for-tat reciprocities but as a case where the gift-exchange partners arrive to "visit" the sponsors, who fix some food to share with them. In other words, the most significant collective rituals in Nuyoo are discussed as instances where hosts offer food and hospitality to guests. (See Ortner 1978 for a parallel case.)

9. If it is a man and woman who visit, the men of the household will serve two portions of food to the male visitor, who in turn gives a portion to the female with him. Only men and women who are kin, affines, or ritual kin should serve each other food, and even in these cases it is sometimes seen to be improper.

What is most significant about hospitality and the sharing of food for Nuyootecos is that they take these acts as an index of the host's ability to put themselves in the place of others. As they often say, a man who shares "knows what it is to suffer"; that is, he knows what it means to go without. Thus when Jesus arrived at the house, hungry and thirsty, he confronted the owner with an important test: whether to be sociable and offer hospitality or to turn Jesus away. By refusing to share his tortillas and water, the man not only denied Jesus but showed he was unable to act morally; consequently, he could not be part of society.

It is for this reason that the man in Tata Guadalupe's story is linked to the tiumi, the race of beings who lived before the coming of the Sun. Earlier I noted that Nuyootecos call the tiumi *ñɨvɨ yuku*, "people of the wilds" in contrast to ñɨvɨ ve'i, "civilized people." The tiumi lived at a time before the Sun was born. "The moon was their Sun" (the moon is called *ña'nu*, "the eldest one"), and they hunted in its dim, cold light, since they were able to see at night, like animals. As one man put it, the tiumi had a kind of mind *(anduni)* that was suitable for the world of the moon, unlike today's people, who have a mind that is suitable to the world of the Sun. And in the world of the moon, which was a time of "dim light," people led an amoral existence. Indeed, one man explicitly compared the tiumi to dogs, since the tiumi "did not recognize their mothers or fathers." As we will see, Nuyootecos associate dogs with promiscuity and incest. When the Sun appeared, it was the end of the world for the tiumi *(ficio,* from the Spanish for Last Judgment). Many died of fright, and the Sun burned the others. In a vain attempt to escape, some tiumi hid themselves in caves. By retreating before the Sun, whose light and regular movement Nuyootecos consider the epitome of truth, integrity, and rational order, the tiumi signaled their close attachment to the dark, presocial world of the moon and their ineligibility for life in the Christian era.

Returning to Tata Guadalupe's story, we can see a close connection between the man who did not offer hospitality to Jesus and the tiumi. Because he refused to share food and offer Jesus a place to rest, the man was driven out of his household to live in the wilds, like the tiumi, who are people of the bush. Also like the tiumi, the man is pursued by the Sun. There is no place he can go to hide from its rays, just as the tiumi, who retreated into caves, were eventually destroyed by the Sun. If the tiumi represent the idea of an amoral and uncivilized life, then the man who refuses to share and be hospitable sets himself apart from society. And his acts not only cause him to lose his place in a household but, by associating him with the tiumi, bring him to the point where he has reverted to the primitive, presocial state of those people who existed before our world came into existence.

Lying behind the explicit moral lessons contained in the stories Nuyootecos tell about the time when Jesus walked the earth is a social landscape composed of households. Although household members are often in conflict with one another, and decisions are sometimes made without any attempt at achieving consensus, it is still within the household that crucial decisions are made: about whether to purchase or sell land, when and how much to plant, what tools and other items will be purchased, and whether money will be spent to send children to school. And the people of the different households that Jesus visits do not act corporately but independently of one another. Some turn Jesus away, while others aid him.

Within this setting, collective activities are contingent upon the relationships that exist between households, and much of Nuyooteco discourse about "community" is about households and their interrelationships. Indeed, incidents in the myths about Jesus' travels—and these are creative events, occurring at the very origin of the world—are concerned with how the people of different households are able to establish and maintain relationships with one another through ritual kinship, marriage, and gift exchange—the topics of the next two chapters.

CHAPTER 2

MARRIAGE AND RENEWAL

THERE is a group of men in Nuyoo known as *tee ka'a sha*, "men who speak respectfully." Typically these are older individuals who have reputations as skilled orators. Other, less-gifted Nuyootecos will seek out *tee ka'a sha* to speak for them when large numbers of people must be addressed, such as in marriage negotiations and fiestas.

One thing that distinguishes a man as a *tee ka'a sha* is his skillful use of metaphor. The famous *iya* vocabulary used by the ancient Mixtec elite and published by Reyes in 1593 is probably a list of such oratorical metaphors.[1] In any event, it was while listening to a *tee ka'a sha* that I first heard households called "seed beds" and "nurseries" *(yava)*. Initially I thought he was referring to the household as a place for raising children. But it became apparent that my interpretation was only partially correct, and the notion that households are nurseries has to be put in the context of the Nuyooteco view that they are not born into their "true households" but must move to them later in their lives, so that people are like the tender shoots a gardener nurtures in a force bed until he can transplant them to a permanent location. This process of transplantation is most obvious in marriage, where a bride (and sometimes a groom) is "let go" so that she can move into "her true house," that of her affines. This also occurs, in Nuyooteco reckoning, in baptism, and in death, when the deceased is said to move to his or her "true house," in the cemetery. For Nuyootecos, the community is a place where people are in constant movement among households.

In this chapter, I am not so much concerned with how the circulation of persons among households forms a "total" system of exchange, which is a subject I will deal with in chapter 10. Instead, what I focus on here is the way Nuyootecos bring outsiders into their households

1. The sixteenth-century Mixtec nobility were believed to speak the language of the first Lords of Apoala. Although there is no evidence for a distinct, elite dialect, nobles do appear to have used a set of conventional Mixtec terms that, when morphosyntactically marked with a -*ya* suffix, took on deep metaphorical meanings (King 1988:290–303).

51

and make them insiders, and how the relationship between different households is transformed by the transfer of members from one to the other. I begin with an examination of the way a child is "given" by one household to another in baptism and follow this by analyzing the process by which a household "lets go" of a girl, and sometimes a boy, so that they can take their place in the household of their affines.

THE GIVING OF CHILDREN IN BAPTISM

In baptism, two things occur that are of great significance in children's lives. The first is the blessing they receive from the Catholic church. Although people in Nuyoo do not feel that original sin stains their souls, they do feel that baptism is what makes them *cristianos*, or civilized beings. Thus people call the stillborn and others who die without baptism tiumi, the same term they use for the wild people who lived before the birth of the sun. It is the rite of baptism that distinguishes Mixtec children from the wild tiumi and brings them into the realm of truth and light. In this respect, baptism is linked to two other significant "blessings" *(bendiciónes)* received over the course of one's life: marriage and the nine days of prayers said after death. Each of these rituals is crucial to one's spiritual well-being. A person who dies unmarried, unbaptized, or without the full nine days of prayers after death risks being taken by a tachi, or demon, to live with it in the wilds.[2]

The second important event that occurs at baptism is the acquisition by the child and his or her parents of ritual kin through the institution of *compadrazgo*. Compadrazgo creates a tie of godparenthood between a man, a woman (usually the two are husband and wife), and a child of another household. At the same time, ties of coparenthood are created between the child's parents and its godparents. Each tie is marked by mutual rights and responsibilities. A godchild should show deference, obedience, and respect for his or her godparents, and coparents should demonstrate high and equal regard for one another (Ravicz 1967:238). There is wide agreement that people in Latin America use ritual kinship to extend ties of solidarity, in both a vertical and a horizontal sense (Gudeman 1972; Mintz and

---

2. Although the Church distinguishes between the blessings received by the pouring of water on the child's head at baptism and other occasions when holy water may be used to bless, most Nuyootecos do not (usually referring to both as *jia nute*). Thus people frequently say that they "baptize" their children to protect them from illness, that they "baptize" their animals, and that they even "baptize" the trucks owned by the different hamlets.

Wolf 1950). One advantage is that it allows people in small villages like Nuyoo to give some measure of stability to relationships they have developed with persons not linked to them by kinship, or even by community membership. Compadres, along with one's close kin, form one's core of important allies. Compadres should speak up for one another in political matters, and they can rely on one another for emergency loans and other forms of economic support.[3]

Compadrazgo and the Household

My purpose here is not to provide a comprehensive description of Nuyooteco ritual kinship (for more details see Monaghan 1987), but only to call attention to the Nuyooteco view that the contracting of compadrazgo ties is not something that occurs between individuals, or between sets of nuclear families, but between households. One can see this in the extension of Nuyooteco compadre terms (npaa for males, kumadri for females) to all the members of the households involved, not just the couples linked in ritual kinship. Also, the process of selection of compadres is often part of a household strategy for building alliances. There are several young men in Nuyoo Center, for example, who have as compadres for their children someone who is a generation older. In each case, it was the young man's father or grandfather who arranged the tie, since the compadre maintained a close relationship with senior members of the household. These senior members saw in the birth of their grandchild or great grandchild an opportunity to cement and upgrade this link. That compadrazgo links households as well as individuals can also be seen in situations where, for some reason or other, a compadre is unable to fulfill his or her ritual duties. In these cases, senior or junior household

3. The Nuyoo system of compadrazgo contains the possibility of making almost everyone in Nuyoo the compadre of everyone else. In fact, there are many other occasions besides baptism when one may acquire godchildren. There are godchildren of evangelio (se'ya stola or se'ya ii), which requires only that one be present when he or she is blessed, godchildren of confirmation (se'ya ii), godchildren of graduation from school, and godchildren of marriage. Ties of compadrazgo are also created to improve the health of a child, as the sponsor is felt to have a beneficial influence on the godchild. There are, in fact, people who have a large number of godchildren and compadres. However, there is a custom in Nuyoo that works against the unlimited extension of compadrazgo ties. Most people, once a set of compadres is selected, will continue to be godparents for all a couple's subsequent offspring and will also serve as the godchild's sponsors in all the life-crisis rituals that will subsequently be celebrated. This rule has the effect of reinforcing the ties between pairs of particular households, at the expense of expanding the system to include ever greater numbers of households.

members may substitute for the absent compadre without any embarrassment to either the godparent or the sponsors of the ritual.

When Nuyootecos speak about baptism, they often say that one household "gives" a child to the people of another household. This is not just a rhetorical convention, since there are many cases where godchildren reside in the households of their godparents. A godchild whose parents die prematurely may be taken in by his or her godparents, and there are several cases where parents have sent a child to replace the deceased child of a compadre or to provide childless compadres with children. The children in these situations will inherit from their godparents. Although they may be forced to divide the estate with their godparents' other relatives, a godchild raised in the godparent's house has a legitimate claim to a share in the estate he or she leaves behind, even if the godparent has living children.

Most godchildren do not take up residence in their godparents' household, but they do acquire a status similar to a child. In the first chapter I cited the example of a young man who no longer goes to his godfather's house because, as he said, his godfather "starves him." Godchildren who visit their godparents should be brought into the kitchen and fed, as a member of the household. Members of the household will also address the godchild as a kinsman or kinswoman. It often confused me when someone would call a particular individual their "brother" or "sister," and then someone else would say that the two were not consanguines. Later I realized that Nuyootecos extend the brother and sister terms, along with the incest taboo, from the ego who is baptized to the sons and daughters of ego's godparents. Although the terms can be qualified with *nute*, "water," which refers to the holy water used in baptism *(ñani nute* for a male's godparent's son, *ku'va nute* for a cross-sex child, and *ku'vi nute* for a female's godparent's daughter), in practice people simply refer to the child of their godparents as "brother" or "sister." The reason for this, they explain, is that the children of compadres should treat each other as brothers and sisters, playing together and supporting one another, and if one is older than the other, the elder should serve as the younger's guide and protector.

The pattern established by the "giving" of a child in baptism can also be seen in marriage, where a member of one household, usually a woman, is "let go" and takes up residence in another household. But before marriage can be usefully compared with baptism, something must be said about the roles of males and females in the household.

Males and Females in the Household

In Nuyoo, males and females are economically interdependent. As one man explained: "You cannot get ahead without a woman to aid you, no matter how hard you work on your own. Your wife must help you; working by yourself you cannot sustain [nakara] a household no matter how hard you try. A wife must have a business on the side, or any kind of work that brings the corn in, because a man by himself cannot." This interdependence is, in turn, the basis of the household. Another man put it this way: "The two of us, who are people, are in our house. I believe there could be no household if there were only one of us males, and there could be no household if there were only a woman. It is when we are two that there can be a household."

As those remarks suggest, any household that lacks the proper complement of male and female labor is in danger of failing. For example, it is quite common to hear widowers *(tee na'vi,* "poor men") complain that being alone in the house makes it difficult for them to obtain tortillas. Almost every male in Nuyoo is a farmer, and dispersed landholdings mean that fields and gardens are often an hour or two from home. The work involved and the distance traveled require periods of absence, and men frequently spend the night in their fields rather than travel back and forth on a daily basis. Consequently, males describe their work as requiring them "to leave" *(keenio),* and "male work" translates as "going to work" *(ki satiñu).*

In contrast to male work, Nuyootecos call female work *(saa sii,* "what women do)* yi'i tiñu ve'i,* or "work inside the house." One of the most important tasks for a woman is the processing of corn to make tortillas. She must first remove the corn from the cob and then boil it in water with lime added to it, so that the hard outer husk of the kernel falls off. She then rinses the corn and grinds it into dough. Only then can she begin to pat the dough into flat cakes to be baked on the fire. Women usually rise at 3:00 or 4:00 a.m. to complete this task, so that they can have tortillas ready when the men of the household leave for their fields. Given the labor required by these tasks, it is impossible for one person to work in the fields and prepare the daily meals. For this reason widowers say they "suffer for tortillas."

Beyond bemoaning how they "suffer for tortillas," widowers also complain that when they are at work, their empty house is an invitation to theft. Without a woman present, they cannot keep turkeys, chickens, goats, or sheep, since tending domestic animals is time consuming and is usually a female task, especially if there are no older children in the household. Chickens and goats are an important means of accumulating and storing surpluses, and they provide an occasional meal with meat. In this, women's work in the household is invaluable; as one man put it, "the woman *is* the household."

For their part, widows *(ña la'vi,* "poor women") complain about cutting wood, about having to haul heavy loads, and about the physical labor demanded of them in agricultural tasks. If widows do not regularly use the land their husbands worked, they will have a hard time maintaining control over it, since men from outside the household may begin to use it and then claim it as their own. Widows also find it difficult to raise money to buy corn and other food items to supply the household. While the labor of men is usually in demand, women have few opportunities to work as wage laborers. One widow once told me that "the man must work so that the woman may eat well . . . a widow sees green" (i.e., lives in poverty).

The terms *ña la'vi* and *tee la'vi* have an interesting range of meanings. While Nuyootecos use *ña la'vi* and *tee la'vi* for widows and widowers, they also use them for any woman or man who is not part of a complete household. Thus, an orphan can be referred to as a *tee la'vi* or a *ña la'vi.* People even call children who have only one deceased parent *tee la'vi* and *ña la'vi,* because they live in a household that lacks a male or female component. Similarly, a bachelor is a *tee la'vi,* because he too lives alone. This lumping together of widowers, widows, orphans and bachelors underscores the difficulties of living in an incomplete household, regardless of one's age or marital status.

"Standing up Together"

Nuyootecos often say that husbands and wives "stand up together." One of the things they mean by this is that the couple face the rest of the community hand in hand, as complements to one another. For example, in the sponsorship of civil-religious hierarchy fiestas and life crisis commemorations, the members of the sponsoring household organize activities in gender-specific ways. The males of the household greet the male guests, accept the gifts of cash, beer, and liquor they have brought, and make note of how much of each item the guests bring. They then invite the male guests to rest and eat. The women of the household greet the female guests, take the baskets containing the prestations of tortillas and beans the women carry, count the tortillas, estimate the weight of the beans, and serve the women food. In any such event, women congregate around the kitchen area, which is often a hut facing the main house, while men gather around and inside the main house, near the altar. The men of the household are in charge of organizing the public rituals associated with the fiesta, securing the assistance of ritual specialists, and ensuring that the paraphernalia needed for the rituals is in sufficient supply. The women of the household are in charge of preparing the food that will be served in the fiesta and of apportioning it so that there will be enough for all who come—a skill much admired in Nuyoo.

The social and economic interdependence of husband and wife also explains part of the stability that characterizes Nuyooteco marriages, even though philandering by men and women is quite common, and violent disputes often result. Marriage is stable because women and men are unprepared to live by themselves. Several times when I was in Nuyoo men drove their wives out of the house, only to repent once they were alone. Faced with the problem of fending for themselves, each went to his in-laws' house to ask for his wife's return. It is true that in extreme cases a man will begin searching for another woman to take her place, but continuing to live alone will not be an option for him. I have heard parents and brothers use the threat of removing their daughter or sister from a man's household to keep him from abusing her: "We will take her home with us, and then we will see if you are a potent man," suggesting that men can complete themselves only in relation to women. Likewise, women who leave their husbands usually decide to return because "that is their true household" and because the options open to a single woman are so restricted that remaining with her husband, even if he abuses her, appears more attractive than living alone.

Gender Symbolism

The classification of domestic and other activities into areas of "male work" and "female work" is paralleled by a symbolism that associates gender and sexuality with specific productive tasks. For example, the birth of male children is foretold to expectant mothers and fathers by dreams of new machetes, tumplines, large net bags used for hauling heavy loads, and by dreams of money. Machetes, tumplines, and large net bags are all agricultural implements used by males. People associate cash with males because male children "add wealth to the family" in their work as wage laborers and are the ones most closely involved with cash cropping. Dreams of round, open things—usually associated with cooking, such as small baskets, jars, and all sizes of pots—presage the birth of female infants (table 1). A type of large pot,

TABLE 1.
OBJECTS THAT EXPECTANT MOTHERS AND FATHERS MAY DREAM OF
THAT INDICATE THE SEX OF THEIR UNBORN CHILD

Female	Male
Cooking Pot	Machete
Tortilla Basket	Tumpline
Ring	Hat
Rebozo	Shoes
Huipil	Shirt
Skirt	Pants

the *ko'o*, is also a metaphor for "vagina." If women and men work for, and complete, each other, then Nuyooteco gender symbolism emphasizes what this work is.

One theme running through Nuyooteco discussions of gender is the idea that females negatively affect male productive activities. This is best illustrated in the way the sexes are partitioned by a left/right symbolism, which divides the world into negative and positive poles.

Nuyootecos explicitly associate females with the left *(satin)* and males with the right *(kua'a)*. For example, midwives say they can tell the sex of a fetus because a female has her head to the left in her mother's womb, while a male has his head to the right. In all social gatherings, husbands and wives sit separately, with women to the left, and men to the right. In the marriage ceremony, the bride's family sits along the left side of the house, while the groom's family sits along the right side. Like other places in Mesoamerica, the left connotes evil and danger (e.g., Gossen 1972; Hunt 1977; López Austin 1980). The left is associated with the west, the region of sunset, darkness, and death. The left hand is also the hand of *Tachi*, or Demon (see chapter 8). Eating with one's left hand makes food innutritious; presenting gifts with the left hand expresses ill will. "Putting something on the left" is a phrase commonly used for thievery and embezzlement.

In addition to corruption and evil, the left is associated with foreigners. *Ka'a satin*, "speaking leftly," is the speech of someone "who does not pronounce words clearly, a stranger." The people of the Mixteca Alta speak many different dialects and languages, and Mixtec speakers sometimes refer to the indigenous inhabitants of linguistically distinct communities as "people who do not speak clearly." These communities, moreover, are generally hostile to one another. One who does not speak clearly is thus a potential enemy, not someone to be trusted.

Women are associated with outsiders in several ways. Since residence at marriage is usually virilocal, women are in effect "strangers" in their in-laws' household. This, as we will see, places newly married women in a difficult position, since they are not, at first, trusted by their in-laws. Also, the vast majority of people who come into Nuyoo from other Mixtec-speaking communities are women who wed Nuyooteco men and move into the house of their affines. They are people who are not only new arrivals to the household but also who "do not speak clearly."

The association of females with the left and with untrustworthy outsiders is consistent with the idea that female sexuality is "polluting" *(te'en)*, something that male Nuyootecos link to promiscuity. Males value exclusive sexual access to females but feel that most women are incapable of being faithful. This is partly due to the belief that women have a stronger sexual appetite than males, which married women satisfy through illicit affairs. The more women have sexual intercourse, the more polluted they are.[4] Male sexuality, on the other hand, is not harmful in itself, and the right does not have sinister associations.

The pollution that comes from female sex organs makes women inimical to corn, beans, squash, coffee, and fruit trees. Both men and women say that if a woman steps over any kind of seed, such as corn, the household may lose its crop in the coming year. This is not true for males, who may step over seeds with impunity. Males cause no harm because, as one elder told me, "a man suffers to make the seed grow, while a woman does nothing." Similarly, if a woman climbs a fruit tree, she will cause he tree to wither and die or become sterile (particularly the mamey). Several people told me, however, that this is not true for prepubescent girls.

The idea that women may harm corn and other seeds causes Nuyootecos to place restrictions on women's participation in agricultural production. A woman should not sow or weed cornfields because she may get sick, the field may die, or a wind may come and knock down the plants.[5] Males also keep their implements away from

4. Women who are the most te'en are ones who are called *ña'a teni*, women who have a voracious sexual appetite.

5. Note that when a woman weeds a cornfield and the wind destroys it, the punishment is also directed at her husband, who, out of sloth, forced his wife to do his work. Indeed, Nuyootecos

women. A woman who steps over a machete will, because she is te'en, cause it to break.

As I noted earlier, even though females should avoid male productive activities, male performance of female tasks, such as grinding corn or cooking tortillas, is not taboo.[6] However, males become polluting after having sex. Thus men should not go into their fields after intercourse, since they may damage the plants growing there. Similarly, men who have had sex should not go near where other men are making lime, or where men are cooking in underground ovens, since they may affect the fire in such a way that it will undercook what is being produced.

Although Nuyootecos say females are polluting to males, and they often oppose male and female activities, the negative qualities associated with females do not get in the way of the close cooperation between husbands and wives. Even though males may assert that all women are polluting, they will, simultaneously, refer to their wives as "my right hand" *(kuenta ña'a kua'a kuvi)*. Several men likened their wives to their machete, the preeminent symbol of male dominance, virility, and productive capacity (see chapter 4). The basis for this trope is that as a machete allows a man to clear land and sow crops and thus have food to eat, a wife also provides a man with food, since she grinds his corn and prepares his tortillas. While generally "sinister" and "contaminating," wives lose these qualities for their husbands when they join together in a household. Within the household, males and females complete one another; they transcend the things that divide them. Thus, when I asked one couple why both of them were weeding their cornfield (after they both told me that women are prohibited from doing agricultural work), they replied that it was all right if the woman is of the household; it is the women who come from outside the household who are dangerous.

MARRIAGE

The complementary relationship of males and females in domestic and other arrangements is fundamental to understanding marriage in Nuyoo, since it forms the backdrop to people's decisions about who, when, and where to marry. Many older people say that their parents

---

consider it a woman's prerogative to refuse to perform male labor, and a woman whose husband forces her to work in the fields is justified if she leaves his household.

6. However, people do say that if a male places a *tenate* (a basket, a female implement) on his head, dogs will attack him.

forced them to marry at young ages (11–13 years old) because, by marrying, they "would be able to eat"—that is, to live in a household that is equipped to meet the needs of its members. One man even told me that his father had him marry because his mother could not process enough food for the six males in the household. They decided to obtain another woman—his wife—so that his mother would have someone to aid her.

This last example illustrates one of the more important factors in the decision to transfer persons from one household to another. Through marriage and, to some extent, adoption and resettlement, Nuyootecos try to balance the household's supply of male and female labor. An imbalance between male and female labor threatens the household's ability to function as a social and economic unit. A household with many daughters will therefore attempt to reduce their number by marrying them off as quickly as possible; if it controls sufficient land, however, it will try to persuade sons-in-law to settle uxorilocally. A household with many sons will similarly attempt to find wives for them as soon as possible, even before the boys are sexually mature.

"Marrying Well"

Nuyootecos distinguish two different ways domestic unions might be formed: one in which the couple "simply comes together" and one in which the couple "marries well." As these descriptions suggest, strong value judgments are made about each type of union. The first, in which people "simply come together," is something shamefully or badly made *(nke'e ni va'a)*. Nuyootecos call this "speaking in the market" or "speaking in darkness." It occurs when a young man convinces a woman to come to live in his household, without negotiating with her kin for her hand, and without the customary ritual that celebrates the transfer. There are many reasons people might choose to "simply come together." Chief among these are the high costs of the marriage ritual, which may place the young couple in debt for years after the wedding. Another reason may be that an affair the woman has had has become public knowledge or that one partner is divorced or widowed. The most desired mates are, of course, young, unmarried, and without children, and those who do not meet these criteria may feel the formal marriage ceremony is unnecessary or that it calls too much attention to the match. Other people say that the frequency of unions where people "simply come together" has increased over the last 20 or 30 years. I suspect that these kinds of arrangements may be less stable than those where people "marry well," but it should be kept in mind that they are not stamped for all time as immoral. Initially, people who "simply come together" may be ashamed to appear in public. However, the couple will eventually establish an identity as a cohabiting pair, and town officials will recruit them to serve in the civil-religious hierarchy. Also, their union can always be upgraded with the performance of the appropriate rituals, even if it has been several years since the couple began to live together.

Traditionally, heads of households were responsible for seeing that other household members "marry well." Most middle-aged and older people say that when they married, 20 or 30 years ago, they had little or no contact with their future spouses. Their paths may have crossed, but chances were they had never spoken or considered each other as potential spouses.[7] Parents sometimes forced their children into marriage. Tañuu Manuel Velasco told me that when he was 12 years old his father denied him food until Manuel agreed to marry. This experience was much harder on the girl, who suddenly found herself in the presence of a group of strangers intent on taking her away from her parents, brothers, and sisters. It was such a shock to Ñañuu María Sarabia when she found out she was betrothed that she was unable to say anything at first and cried herself to sleep for months afterward. Despite the gradual increase in average age at time of first marriage (from 11–15 years to 14–19 years) and the input the bride and groom now have in the choice of their partners, the experience of the woman in marriage has not changed significantly. She is still in a very stressful situation, since she faces so many unknowns. What will her husband be like, and how will he treat her? Will her in-laws be mean spirited and make her work very hard? Will they beat her and be stingy with food? Marriage today, as in the past, is not a happy time for the bride. Indeed, to dream that a young girl is dancing at her wedding portends her death.

---

7. Along with marriage at an early age went a very strict separation of the sexes. Except for spouses, parents, and siblings, people were sharply constrained in their interaction with members of the opposite sex. "Just speaking with a woman," Simón Sarabia used to tell me, "would land you in jail, even if she was on the other side of a canyon." Her father could claim damages and perhaps even force the boy to marry her.

The sanctions on interaction between the sexes holds today, in a more attenuated form. The verb *ka'a ra,* "they are speaking," is a metaphor for the sexual act, and *ku kuentan* (from the Spanish verb *contar,* "to talk, to chat") refers to a partner of the opposite sex with whom one has illicit sex. People are very interested in who is publicly speaking to whom, since "speaking together" suggests intimacy. This information makes a great difference in marriage arrangements. I know a boy who broke off marriage negotiations when he discovered that his prospective bride was speaking, literally, to someone else.

The Marriage Negotiations

The girl and her kin discover that someone is considering her as a marriage partner when a *tee ka'a sha* appears at her house early in the morning. As I noted, the *tee ka'a sha* is typically a well-spoken, respected older man, skilled in the arts of rhetorical persuasion. "An old man is like a bottle of liquor," Nuyootecos say, "because you take in (his words) and end up doing something you might wish you hadn't." When he arrives, he presents his request to the girl's father or, if her father is no longer living, to her brothers. The girl's mother may also be present, but she does not usually take an active role in the negotiations. People carry out these discussions with *tu'un sha'u*, "grave words," and those involved are standing, not sitting, since sitting is appropriate only in relaxed, informal situations. Each *tee ka'a sha* has his own stylized manner of presenting his request, governed by Mixtec canons of politeness: speech should be neither abrupt nor direct but circuitous, and it should be made with as much humility as possible. The way the man presents the request is important, since it will be taken seriously only if he makes it with decorum and respect.

Soon after the *tee ka'a sha* begins his speech, he, or a helper, will pass out cigarettes and a bottle of liquor to those who are present. After about 20 or 30 minutes of talking about human nature, about honor, and the hard life we all have, he comes to the point of his visit: that so-and-so has charged him to ask to "buy" *(ke'e)* a daughter of the household. Once he makes his proposal, the girl's father or brother will—in an equally long and self-deprecating manner—either inform the *tee ka'a sha* that he should return for their answer (usually in a week) or that the girl is "closed" *(nasi)* since they have accepted the request of someone else.[8] Occasionally, the father accepts the request outright, telling the man to return with the boy, his father, and the boy's godfather. Such an immediate response is, however, rare.

While debating whether to accept the petition, the girl's family will consider several factors. Chief among these is the reputation of the people who have made the request. The habits of the boy's father have a great deal to do with this, since he often determines how the other members of the household live. If the father is a drunkard, or if he is vicious or lazy, the girl's parents will think twice about sending their daughter there. The girl's parents may also request advice from distant relatives and seek out compadres who know the suitor's

8. The girls' being "closed" connotes, for Nuyootecos, that she is in her house and that the door is shut to other suitors.

household to see what they think of the match. If they decide that marrying into the boy's household is not in the best interests of the girl, they will look for some pretext to explain their refusal. The father may say to the *tee ka'a sha* something like "I think it would be a good match, but the girl's brothers do not want her to marry," or he may say that his daughter is unworthy, and would make a terrible wife. In the case of widows, or in the case of widows who have daughters with children out of wedlock, the woman herself may make the reply. Their suitors are usually widowers, or they may be unmarried men who are mentally or physically deficient in some way. Women's refusals are often ingenious in these cases. One woman who had a child out of wedlock told the *tee ka'a sha* of a dim-witted young man that she "did not want to marry someone who would probably be given many posts in the civil-religious hierarchy, and thus make his wife work hard." As everyone, including the man's family, suspected, his backwardness would preclude his being named to important posts. Yet the woman managed to turn down his request without insulting him or the other members of his household, and for that everyone was grateful.

If the *tee ka'a sha* returns, and he finds that the girl is "open" *(nunee)* and the father is willing to allow her to marry, he may place a string of rosary beads around her neck and negotiate a date for the final request to be made. The rosary beads show that the girl is now "closed" and "cannot answer to another." The father than tells the *tee ka'a sha*—and the boy's father, if he is present—to return with the boy, the boy's mother, and the boy's godfather so that he can ask the boy if "he really believes that his wife is going to come from my house." This usually takes place a week after the *tee ka'a sha* places the rosary beads around the girl's neck.

At the final request, *siin nu na'vi* (which can also indicate an agreement made outside the marriage context), the boy's wedding party sets out early in the morning in order to arrive at the girl's house just after first light. The timing is important and is sometimes referred to during the marriage negotiations, as when one *tee ka'a sha* said,

Tu'un ora vaji kaa nka nii
The dawning word

Ora nutuun nu'u
The time of first light

Vajira ni
We come

Nsaa tu'un nkuaa vi
Not on a dark mission

In su tu'un naa vi
But to deal clearly (with you)

As noted before, light and its source, the Sun, imply truthfulness, integrity, honor, and good faith. When the *tee ka'a sha* stated that the boy's party spoke "the dawning words," he was saying that they genuinely wished the boy to marry the girl, that they were there to make the request in the manner established by tradition, and that the boy had no intention of running off with the girl.

Just as the boy's party speaks "the dawning words," the girl's household is called "the place of light." Marriage, as I pointed out earlier, is one of three great blessings Nuyootecos receive during their lives. When a married person dies, he or she goes to a place where there is "light," where people are happy and where there is comradeship. Those who do not marry "walk in darkness" *(jika nee)*, like a criminal, or like the presocial tiumi. The church bell does not toll for these people at their death in the way it does for others, and they go to a place where they are "sad" and "alone."

When the members of the boy's party arrive to make the last request, they bring with them a large quantity of cigarettes, beer, pulque, and liquor. The girl's household will provide food and may slaughter a goat or sheep. In one petition I witnessed, the father of the girl questioned the boy. He asked, "Do you really want my daughter? Will you care for [nakara] her? Will you have only her, and no other?" After the boy replied in the affirmative, the bride moved to the center of the gathering, and the father of the boy asked her the same questions (cf. Flanet 1977:97). When she finished, her family huddled together for one final meeting. They then emerged, accepted the boy's petition, and began to make the wedding arrangements. I was told that if the *tee ka'a sha* had not already placed a set of rosary beads around the girl's neck, the father of the boy may do so at this time. The members of the boy's party then served the food and liquor, and a small celebration began. After it was over, the boy's party returned to their house.

MARRIAGE AS CONTRACT

Nuyootecos use the verb *ke'e* to describe a household's acquisition of a bride for one of its sons, the same verb they use for purchasing things in the market. Bilingual Nuyootecos will also translate the boy's father's activities in marriage as "going to buy a woman" *(va a comprar una mujer)*.

As is true of other places where a similar idiom is used for marriage, the idea that one side "buys" something from another suggests that marriage is a contract in which two households cede certain values to one another. We can best see what these values are through an examination of the transfers that occur at the time of marriage.

Transfers in Marriage

Nuyootecos say that the expenses of the wedding ceremony are the major transfer made by the groom's household. Wedding expenditures can be considerable; people say it is necessary to slaughter an animal for the feast and provide liquor for the guests. The rationale people give for this is straightforward: the groom's household is receiving another member, while the bride's household is losing one, so the feast is in exchange for the bride. Consequently, if a couple divorces soon after marriage, the groom's household will attempt to recoup the expenses of the wedding ceremony from the bride's household. Disputes such as these are civil matters, and in the two cases I am familiar with, officials awarded the groom's household a large part of the wedding costs. In addition, it seems that one factor affecting the size of the marriage expenditure is the status of the bride's household. In discussions with men about marriage, they often said that "we make a large expenditure to get a good wife." One man even told me that his poverty "closed" several marriageable women to him, since the members of the women's households, who are relatively well off, would expect a large marriage feast.

Besides the expenses of the wedding feast, the groom's household makes two cash transfers to that of the bride. The first occurs just after the bride-to-be has the rosaries placed around her neck in the final marriage negotiations. Here the boy's father presents the girl's father with a sum of cash, about twice the daily wage of an agricultural laborer (800 to 1,000 pesos in early 1986). The rosary beads show that the girl is "closed" to other suitors and that both sides are in agreement about the marriage. Before the beads are placed on the girl's neck, all those involved in the negotiations take turns blessing the beads to show their satisfaction with the proposed union. This means that at the moment the members of the two households agree to the marriage, there is a transfer of wealth from the boy's household to that of the girl. We can therefore call the cash handed over to the father of the girl a bridewealth payment. Although these are small sums, marriages in other Mixtec communities are often accompanied by larger and more-formalized payments at this time.

Almost immediately after the groom's party makes its payment, a second transfer of wealth occurs. Here the groom-to-be gives a sum of cash, again one or two times the daily wage, to his future mother-in-law. It is significant that it is the mother of the girl who receives this portion of the bridewealth, because it shows that all members of the household are involved in the transaction, not just the eldest males.

There are two things transferred from the girl's household to the boy's household in marriage. The first is labor. One *tee ka'a sha* told me that during the questioning of the boy in the marriage negotiations, either the boy or his parents may say to his future in-laws, "I believe that from your house will come the tortillas I will eat and the water I will drink" *(ve'i ra ña kua ña niñi kenee ista kaji nute ko'o kachin ya)*. This is a very rich metaphoric statement, since it equates women and affines with tortillas and with eating and drinking. I will expand on the association between women and corn plants both below and in chapter 4, where we will examine the circulation of tortillas in exchange and why Nuyootecos say corn is "the daughter of Rain."

The second thing transferred at marriage are rights to a woman's sexuality and reproductive functions. Because the entrance of the bride allows the groom's household to replace its aged members (see below), and because she will be the mother of a new generation of children, the transfer of persons in marriage becomes the key to household continuity. People consider this one of the primary values transacted in marriage; thus Nuyootecos sometimes speak of marriage as *tu'un teeyii ra*, which can be translated as "an infusion of life" from one household to the another. I even heard people joke during a wedding, *retu sa'a-re fuerza je saa nakuni-re nuu shu'un je koo litu*, "If the groom makes an effort, he will get a reinvestment right away on the money he put out, with a baby." For good reason people consider it a woman's moral duty to bear children, and infertility is sometimes cited as a reason for divorce.

THE MARRIAGE CEREMONY

When Nuyootecos "marry well," they have three ceremonial options open to them. First, almost all celebrate what I will call the "Mixtec wedding" *(viko tana'a)*. Second, a civil service is performed by the municipal president. Many people choose to have a civil service performed because federal law requires this before a marriage can be considered legitimate. This is what usually happens on the morning that the Mixtec wedding is celebrated: The groom's family send messengers to ask the bride's family to join them in the municipal building. There the president marries the couple in the civil ceremony, and the party then moves to a house where the Mixtec ceremony is performed. Alternatively, people may go through the civil service a few days before or after the Mixtec ceremony.

The final ceremonial option is to be married by a priest in the church. Many people hold the church wedding on the same day as the Mixtec wedding, early in the morning before festivities begin. Most often, though, a church wedding is held some months or years after the couple go through the other ceremonies, when their first children are born. Couples often wish to have a church ceremony at this time because if they wish to baptize their child (and acquire ritual kin), they must be married by a priest.

The civil, church, and Mixtec ceremonies are thus three discrete activities. Moreover, the civil and church ceremonies are secondary to the Mixtec ceremony, which is morally and affectively the most important rite for Nuyootecos. For this reason, I make the Mixtec ceremony the focus of discussion.

The Viko Tana'a (Mixtec Wedding)

The groom's household usually hosts the Mixtec wedding ceremony. Those invited to the celebration include kin, ritual kin, and neighbors. Others may also join in the festivities if they happen by and someone they know invites them in.

Just after dawn on the day of the wedding, the groom's baptismal godfather goes to the bride's household to see about her journey to the household of the groom. Sometimes he brings porters with him to help carry the bride's baggage. The godfather may stay and accompany the bride and her party, or he may return and inform the groom's household about what time they can expect the guests to arrive.

When the members of the bride's party reaches the groom's house, usually in the afternoon, the men of the house usher them inside. The girl's people gather to the left of the household altar, and the boy's gather to the right. The *tee ka'a sha* serving as spokesman for the groom's father may welcome them. Other participants may also have a *tee ka'a sha* speak for them. In one wedding I attended, the bride and groom sat together on a reed mat, between the two groups. The *tee ka'a sha* announced the solemn reason they had for coming together and stressed the respect each group had for the other. He then introduced the key participants by name (the bride and groom, their parents, their baptismal godparents, and other notables). After the *tee ka'a sha* finished, the godfather of the boy welcomed the girl's party and asked their forgiveness for any inconveniences he may have caused. Following this, the girl's father spoke. He introduced his party as humble people who came to see the couple married in an appropriate way. The girl's godfather followed, saying much the same. When he finished, the groom's and bride's mothers took turns addressing the group. These women were so embarrassed at having to speak publicly, however, that I could not understand what they said. Later one of them told me that they both had also stated the solemn reason for the gathering and asked pardon for any discomfort they may have caused the guests.

After the parents and godparents finished their speeches, there was a break in the activities, and people chatted among themselves. The next stage of the ceremony began when the couple knelt on the mat, facing the altar. The parents, godparents, and grandparents of the couple then approached and took turns making a sign of the cross over the bowed heads of the young couple while whispering words of advice. Once they finished, other kin also gave their blessings, which began with the child they were related to.

In most weddings, what follows the blessing is perhaps the most significant part of the ceremony for the participants. In the weddings I attended, the father and mother of the groom embraced both the bride and groom, they moved off and embraced each of the bride's kin. As they embraced, they called each other "compadre." When they finished, the bride's parents repeated the process, embracing the kin of the groom, followed by the godparents of the boy and girl, who did the same thing. In one marriage, emotions ran so high at this point that the groom sobbed openly, bringing tears to everyone's eyes. From this moment on, each of these people addressed one another as "compadre," with the decorum and respect this relationship entails.

In Nuyoo, as in most other places, marriage creates strong ties between people of different social groups. One way this alliance is marked in Nuyoo is when the godparents of the bride and groom exchange roles; the girl's godparents provide the wedding clothes for her groom, and the boy's godparents provide the wedding clothes for his bride. This transfer of clothing is highly significant because it demonstrates the new status the bride and groom have with respect to the households of their in-laws. When presenting the clothes, the godparents tell them, in a casual way, *ku'u sa'ma*, "dress in these clothes." Like the clothes the godparents give in baptism, these items are not gifts, and the godparents do not expect to be formally acknowledged. They are instead part of a relationship in which the people of a household assume the same responsibility toward an outsider as they do "a child of the household."[9]

After the transformation of affines into ritual kin, people relax, and the father of the groom serves alcohol to his guests. In one elaborate wedding I attended, the father brought out several cases of beer, giving one each to the father of the bride, to her godfather, and to the groom's godfather. These men then opened the boxes and began to distribute the bottles to the groom's family, on the opposite side of the house. The father of the groom also distributed a case of beer, with the aid of his son. As the alcohol flowed, the new compadres came together to chat, crossing the invisible line between the bride's and the groom's sides of the house.

The groom's family should serve the guests food along with the alcohol. The meal should include a meat dish and plenty of tortillas. While helpers serve the food to the guests, one of them will set a large plate of tortillas in front of the bride and groom. The godfather of the groom then approaches and tells the couple that they should "eat and grow together." He takes the top tortilla, tears it in half, and then sets the two halves back on the plate on top of each other "in the form of a cross." The bride and groom each take a half—the bride the top half, and the groom the bottom half—and carefully eat them.

It is rare to see Nuyootecos consume tortillas without something on them, even if it is only salt or chile; in other fiestas, where beans, meat, and condiments are plentiful, eating tortillas by themselves is unheard of. The absence of other dishes when the bride and groom consume the tortilla highlight the special nature of this meal, and I want to take time to examine it in detail.

Eating from the same tortilla. People say that by eating the tortilla together, the bride and groom will "speak together" *(ka'a nuu ji)*. This means that they will treat each other as persons worthy of respect. "As the tortilla is our sustenance, and we must respect it, so too the man

9. The godparents' relationship to the household of their godchild is analogous to the relationship an in-marrying spouse has with his or her in-laws. As the godparents are the child's "parents" but not of his or her household, the spouse is a "child" of the household but was not born in the household. This special relationship makes godparents and spouses both insiders and outsiders to their ritual kin and affines. This also gives the godparents—who are the first to have a *nakara* relationship with an individual without being a part of his or her natal household—a unique mediating role in all other transfers of personnel between households.

must respect the woman, and the woman must respect the man," an old woman once explained to me. Along with this respect, the consumption of the tortilla means that the new couple will "grow old together" (the verb *kue'nura* is used). This means they will remain together throughout their lives, they will always sustain (nakara) each other, they will grow familiar with each other *(kaa yo'ma, sikaa ta'a)*, and they will have true affection for each other, so that "if one is away, the other will feel sad" *(kukuekani)*. Eating together will also diminish conflict between them. As one woman said, "we will be of one heart, one mind" *(in ni nasa'o animao, andunio)*, and she went on to add that the couple who eat together will work for the good of the household, rather than for their individual interests. One man explained that a major cause of conflict between husband and wife arises when one does not share food with the other. The wife may receive a gift of food while her husband is away from the house and, rather than wait to share it with him, eat it herself. Similarly, the husband may find himself with extra money and, instead of buying something for the household, spend it on drink. It is then that the accusations start. This same man proudly noted that he and his wife "had always eaten together" and have had no serious problems in their marriage.

The efficacy of the ritual parting and consumption of the tortilla lies not just in its being a sign of the beginning of a relationship between husband and wife. Rather, it is an act that *creates* the relationship. People are quite clear about this. By eating the tortilla, the bride and groom are "standing up together" *(kuini kuta'a)*, and they "accompany one another" *(kuji'i ji; nuu nuu ta'a ji)*, so that they complete themselves and become a functioning domestic unit. The married couple even serves as a single legal person, since the only instance in which a woman may attend a town meeting is when she goes as proxy for an absent husband. Moreover, the sharing of the tortilla is not an isolated, ritual act, confined to the wedding ceremony, but something that is part of a couple's life together; a husband and a wife should share the same food at each meal. Once again, we see here how Nuyootecos define relationships in terms of their enactment, and that relationships continue to exist only if the act that created them is performed regularly. By the same token, it is a sign of undue intimacy and familiarity if a man and a woman who are not married eat from the same tortilla.

The parting and consumption of the tortilla in the marriage ceremony also reveals something significant about the household. In the first chapter, we saw that Nuyootecos define the household in terms of its members sharing with one another all that is necessary for a healthy life—what they call nakara. But people also *become* members of a household through acts of nakara. In baptism, this occurs when the godparents provide the clothing in which the godchild is to be baptized. In the past, the godmother wove this clothing, but most people now purchase what they need in the Sunday market. The godparents then come to the house of their godchild, dress the child in the clothes they have brought with them, and then take the child to the church for the ceremony. In marriage, the bride and groom are similarly provided with clothing, this time by each other's godparents. This giving of clothing in baptism and marriage, like a husband and wife's sharing of a tortilla, is not confined to isolated "ritual" contexts. Often godparents will buy their godchildren clothing when they purchase clothing for their own children or, if the godchild is married, stop by with food or give the couple parcels of land for them to farm.[10]

The Loaned Daughter and Replacement

Musicians are invited to many weddings, and after everyone eats the meal served by the groom's family, people begin to dance (figure 4). When there is a dance, chances are that the celebration will last until the next morning and that participants will drink heavily. Two additional meals will then be served to the guests: one around midnight and another just before dawn. If no dance is organized, the members

10. The act of clothing the godchild is repeated in all compadrazgo rituals, even when an animal, a saint, or some inanimate object is the "godchild." Thus, in the case of a bull, it is the godfather's task to adorn it with ribbons and colored streamers. In the case of a saint, it is the godfather's task to paint it, and have the niche where it will be set built by a carpenter, before he takes it to the priest to have it "baptized." A dilemma presented itself to one man I knew, who was named godfather of the new cement basketball court constructed by the Instituto Nacional Indigenista in Loma Bonita. How could he "dress" a basketball court? His solution was to travel to Oaxaca City and buy a Mexican flag, which was hung over the court. Everyone agreed afterward that this was, indeed, an appropriate way for him to adorn the court.

Besides providing the baptismal clothes, it is the godparents who must make at least two further transfers of clothing to the godchild during life-crisis rituals. The first is at marriage, and the second is at the death of the godchild, when they provide the clothes in which the child is to be buried. (If the godparents are no longer alive, another member of their household should provide the clothing.) In marriage, it is the baptismal godparents' duty to provide their godchild's betrothed with wedding clothes, a ring (if the child is to be married in the church), and, if the child is the bride, a pair of earrings. In the past, this meant the weaving of a huipil and skirt for the spouse of a male godchild and the weaving of a blanket, shirt, and pants for the spouse of a female godchild. Today, the parents and godparents usually purchase these items and split the costs, rather than produce the clothing themselves. Also, if the girl is old enough to have learned how to weave, she may make a tortilla bag and a blanket for her husband.

Figure 4. Compadres dancing at a wedding. When a groom's household organizes a dance, the first people to take the floor are often the godparents. The godfather of the boy begins by asking the godmother of the girl to dance, and the godfather of the girl asks the godmother of the boy. Other couples may then take the floor, as people in one party ask people in the other to dance. Dancing with another's spouse is unheard of in this area of the Mixteca, but in a wedding it shows the high regard ritual kin have for one another.

of the bride's party will be invited to spend the night in the house of the groom. The bride and groom do not sleep together—each lies down with his or her relatives on opposite sides of the house.

Early in the morning, after everyone is awake, the groom's family serves breakfast and the final rite in the marriage ceremony begins. Here the mother of the bride brings her daughter into the kitchen of the groom's house—an area where females preside—and introduces her to the groom's mother, saying, "here is your daughter-in-law." The word daughter-in-law, *sia nuu*, comes from *se'ya nuu*, which means, according to Nuyootecos, "loaned daughter." The mother-in-law then becomes *shi sia nuu*, "the caretaker of the loaned daughter."

As I noted earlier, corn preparation and the drawing of water are primarily female tasks, whereas sowing and weeding are male tasks. Without someone to perform each of these activities, a household cannot be a viable unit, since no single person can successfully perform both male and female tasks. In marriage, the groom's household receives someone to aid its females in doing the work of preparing tortillas and drawing water. This means, however, that the women who remain in the bride's household lose a helpmate. The boy recognizes the women's loss when he presents his future mother-in-law with a portion of the bridewealth "in payment" for her daughter. Among themselves, the senior women of the two households also acknowledge this transfer, when the girl's mother brings her daughter into the groom's mother's kitchen and presents her to the other woman as a "loaned daughter."

Nuyootecos explain that the term "loaned daughter" means that even though the girl may come to reside in another household, her natal household retains rights over and responsibilities toward her. Her parents and other relatives can warn her in-laws not to mistreat her, and they can even remove her from her in-law's household if things are bad. It should be recalled that the bride, traditionally of a very tender age, is usually ignorant of all the tasks expected of a woman. It is up to her mother-in-law, as the "caretaker of the loaned daughter," to teach her and, in a sense, socialize her into the work habits of the household (see also Gwaltney 1970:86). This continues to be a point of conflict between daughters- and mothers-in-law, since mothers-in-law are often overbearing and daughters-in-law frequently resist older women's authority. In any event, the first several months of the daughter-in-law's stay in her new household are crucial to the development of her relationship with her mother-in-law. The mother-in-law will scrutinize her performance to see if she is a good worker, even-tempered, and trustworthy. The last is particularly important, since the daughter-in-law is a stranger to her in-laws. Sometimes a new wife steals things and then returns to her own household. This is a risk people say widowed or physically deficient men take, since, by marrying women of dubious moral standards and bringing them into their household without other women to watch over them, they will lose money and goods if the wife decides to leave (this occurred twice between 1983 and 1986).

Another risk is that a new daughter-in-law will turn out to be a gossip. In a small, face-to-face society such as Nuyoo, it is difficult, at best, to keep anything secret. Since a daughter-in-law acquires detailed knowledge about the private life of her affines, she may make closely guarded secrets known to outsiders. If she does, it will not be long before the entire community will know and gleefully comment on the most intimate details of life inside the household. This is why one man, when discussing the merits of different women as wives, said he had an excellent wife because she never complained to outsiders that she was not being fed well or that she worked too hard. "Even if she does feel this is true," he said, "she keeps it to herself."

After the daughter-in-law has been in the household for several months and the mother-in-law sees that she is a diligent, trustworthy worker, the older woman is able to state (as one woman told me), "The day that I die my daughter-in-law will be in my place. It will be as if I do not die, because my daughter-in-law is going to continue doing exactly as I am doing." As another woman explained about her daughter-in-law,

Nanda nakunasi nuuni
The one who is going to be in my place has arrived

Re kue'i nke'enu
And if sickness overcomes me,

Re suvi nsu nee in kuvi kinoo nuun
It isn't as if there is no one to remain in my place

Chi ya'a va na ni'ini yaa kuvi se'yan
Because I found who is my child

Nakunasi nuun kinoo nu ve'ini
Who will cover my place and remain in my household.

Kua in neen kua nee va nakunee
As I was, as I am, she will be.

These remarks show that when the daughter-in-law is brought into her "true" household through acts of nakara, she becomes the replacement of her mother-in-law, and that marriage in Nuyoo is a process by which a substitution of identities occurs between mother-in-law and daughter-in-law. This process in turn allows the household to perpetuate itself, by replacing other members with younger members.

If we take "replacement" (Foster 1986; Weiner 1980) as a primary social value transacted in marriage, then the young age at which people traditionally wed is not surprising. A 10- or 11-year-old girl is more easily socialized into the ways of a household than is a 17- or 18-year-old woman, who has already been involved for a number of years in the domestic life of another household. Members of Nuyooteco households are fastidious about their particular styles of doing things, and this frequently results in conflict between a mother-in-law who has an established way of carrying out her duties and an older daughter-in-law who cooks, grinds, weaves, and performs domestic chores in a way she became accustomed to in her natal household. The bride's sexuality and fertility, although important, is thus not the sole (or even most important) issue at the time of the wedding; traditionally, when the couple married, neither the bride nor the groom were sexually mature. What is crucial at the time of marriage are the bride's role in the division of labor and the way her entrance into the groom's household allows for the eventual replacement of key household members, ensuring household continuity. The bringing of a bride into her husband's household is a first step in the transmission of identity between her and her mother-in-law.

The central role of senior women in the marriage transfer also shows that there are as many relationships created in marriage as there are kinds of persons in a household. Moreover, because the relationship between the mother-in-law and daughter-in-law is of key importance for the unity and future success of the household, it is a focus for Nuyootecos. Over the 2½-year period of my initial fieldwork, I saw the transfer of responsibilities (and identity) between mother-in-law and daughter-in-law take place in two households. One case was interesting because the daughter-in-law had been badly treated by her mother-in-law. After moving to her husband's house in 1983, the mother-in-law began to criticize her and to find fault with everything she did. On several occasions, the mother-in-law beat her. However, in 1985 the older woman became sick with a wasting illness that confined her to a mat laid out on the kitchen floor. The daughter-in-law then took over, preparing food for her husband, his younger brother, her children, her father-in-law, and her mother-in-law. When I returned in 1989, I found the older woman's power reduced, since everyone recognized that she was no longer the head of the household. She remained as prickly as ever, but she no longer criticized her daughter-in-law, and the younger woman's situation was much happier than it had been.[11]

11. The idea that marriage in Nuyoo is a contract in which people move from one household to another to replace senior household members can also be seen where the newly wedded couple lives uxorilocally, or as Nuyootecos describe it, where the bride "buys the groom." A household that has a good deal of land and no sons usually makes this kind of transaction with a poor household that has little land and many sons. At the time of the marriage negotiations, the father of the girl will communicate to the boy's family that he will accept the suit, but only if the boy comes to live with him. A very small wedding feast may be sponsored by either the groom's or bride's household, and the boy settles in his father-in-law's house. The groom will work with his father-in-law on his

To return to the scene in the kitchen, after the daughter-in-law is introduced to her mother-in-law, the bride's party prepares to depart for its own homestead. They may be given food to take with them and will be warmly sent on their way. When the guests leave, the marriage ceremony is over.

Although the two parties separate after the two or three days of the marriage ritual, the people of the households involved in the marriage will see much of one another in the future. Before the marriage negotiations, the people of the two households may never have spoken. After the marriage, each becomes part of the core group of the other's allies, and the members of the two households consider themselves ritual kin, addressing one another with respect and deference.

Marriage in Nuyoo is thus a transaction whereby women, and sometimes men, move from one house to another, replacing its senior members. In the process they, like children given in baptism, create especially close ties between the household that gives them up and the household that receives them. What I want to do now is place this discussion of baptism and marriage in the context of the exchange of gifts between people of different households. If the "giving" of a child in baptism or the "letting go" of daughters in marriage transforms the relationships between the households involved, then it is also true that social ties for Nuyootecos exist in their enactment. It is through gifting that affines and ritual kin most frequently experience their relationships with one another.

---

father-in-law's land, and the groom's children will inherit the father-in-law's property. (This is one of the few cases where land passes through female links.) Just as the girl who marries and lives virilocally replaces her mother-in-law, a boy's entrance into his affines' household also involves a gradual transmission of identity, in which he comes to "cover" the place of his father-in-law.

Although uxorilocal postmarital residence does occur with some frequency, it is a distasteful situation for males. Men who live with their wives' families are criticized for being "like women" and for "eating the money of women." Indeed, the three men I know who live uxorilocally in Nuyoo Center keep a low profile and have not assumed leading roles in the town government. One man who had lived uxorilocally after marriage and eventually moved away from his father-in-law told me he moved to avoid the taunts of other men in the community, who never missed an opportunity to remind him that he was "bought by a woman."

CHAPTER 3

GIFTING

I FIRST arrived in Nuyoo Center in a jeep driven by an economist from the Tlaxiaco center of the Institutio Nacional Indigenista. He was on his way to a meeting of the district's beekeepers in San Pedro Yosotato and had promised to drop me off on the way. The road to Nuyoo was only a few years old, and we spent the whole day navigating deep ruts and digging through mud slides. When we finally arrived in Nuyoo Center, I unloaded my bag, and the economist drove away. I can remember standing in front of the municipal hall, which faces the church, and looking around to see all the public buildings closed and padlocked. The only sign of life was a small child who stared at me from the door of a distant house. It surprised me that my arrival attracted so little interest. In the Maya towns of Highland Guatemala where I had previously worked, there always seemed to be people around the main plaza, and it is not every day that someone like myself alights in the center of a town like Nuyoo. Later, as I sat on the veranda of the municipal hall (where I slept for several nights), people began to trickle in, first women carrying baskets of bananas and succulent shoots on their heads, then men carrying firewood. After living in Nuyoo for a while, I realized that the emptiness of the town center during the day is typical. Early in the morning, an hour or two before sunrise, the men — and later, women who carry the day's food — go off to their gardens and fields. Only small children and one or two of each household's women stay behind, to prepare the evening meal and to carry out household chores. Then, beginning about 3:00 o'clock in the afternoon, the town comes alive again as people return from their work. By late afternoon there are men and women lounging in front of each household, children running in the streets, and young men and boys playing basketball on the court next to the Nuyoo church.

In sharp contrast to Nuyoo Center's usual sleepy appearance are the

78

times when fiestas *(viko)* are celebrated. On these occasions people stream in from the hamlets, and they often stay several days, sleeping in the house of a relative if they don't own one in the center. During the most important fiestas — such as the one held to celebrate the feast of Nuyoo's patron saint, Santiago — agricultural work is prohibited, since these are holy days *(kivi ii)*, and many non-Nuyootecos also gather to take advantage of the market and to enjoy the festivities. At these times, the noise and hubbub are tremendous. Merchants from Tlaxiaco and other places arrive to hawk their wares, caling out to prospective clients with bullhorns. Religious officials set off a constant barrage of fireworks, interspersed with the ringing of the church bells. Women and men mill about, visiting with relatives and friends that they may not have seen for some time. By the afternoon, the religious processions on their way to the different mayordomo's houses criss-cross the center, and the alcoholic beverages dispensed by plaza vendors begin to take effect, filling the town with rowdy drunks.

The fiestas Nuyootecos sponsor can be divided into two types.[1] First, there are the fiestas held to commemorate life-crisis events. Of these, the largest are those that commemorate death. If the deceased is an older person who had a long record of service to the community and many kin and ritual kin, hundreds of people may attend the rituals, which last nine days. Next in size are marriage celebrations. Depending on the status of the bride and groom, these may attract anywhere from 20 to well over 200 participants. The smallest are those that mark baptism. Typically, attendance at the baptismal fiestas is restricted to a few relatives. Although it is difficult to say with precision how many large death rituals and major marriage celebrations there are each year, I estimate that from 1983 to 1985 there were, on average, 39 held annually.

The second kind of fiesta is celebrated by civil-religious hierarchy officials. The civil-religious hierarchy, or cargo system, is an organization in which adult men and women occupy a series of rotating offices dedicated to both civil and religious aspects of community life. Based on an ideal of service, in which officeholders dedicate themselves to community affairs, the offices are arranged in the form of a pyramid, so that there are many at the base and few at the top. If a husband and wife are astute, hard working, and lucky, they will, over the course of

1. While mayordomo fiestas, baptisms, marriages, and patriotic holidays are all called *viko* in Mixtec, death rituals are not. Nevertheless, the exchanges made in the death rituals link them to each of the other rituals in the ceremonial cycle.

their lives, serve in all the levels of the pyramid and become respected elders (Cancian 1967).

For the religious cargos, there are a total of 29 major fiestas held annually. This number includes the 23 saints' feast days celebrated by each of the 23 mayordomos, the four *viko luli* ("small fiestas") celebrated by select mayordomos (see chapter 7), and the two fiestas the church caretaker *(fiscal)* must sponsor; one during Holy Week and the other during the Posadas in December. Civil officials annually sponsor 14 fiestas. These commemorate patriotic holidays, although several civil officials also sponsor fiestas commemorating saints' days. If we add the number of civil-religious hierarchy fiestas to the number of major life-crisis commemorations, we arrive at a figure of 82 fiestas celebrated in an average year in Nuyoo. As one can see, the sponsorship of fiestas is something that dominates public life, and seldom does a week pass without at least one being celebrated.

At first, the different fiestas do not appear to have much in common. Not only do they commemorate different kinds of events, but they are, in ritual terms, quite diverse. In some, sponsors make complex sacrifices; in others, participants carry sacred images in processions; and in still others, the representatives of different groups make long speeches. Many life-crisis rituals are not held in Nuyoo Center, especially if the sponsors do not reside nearby. Yet every fiesta, no matter where, when, or how it is celebrated, involves the consumption of massive quantities of food and drink. Few of those who sponsor fiestas have the labor available to prepare all the necessary meals; nor do they have the resources necessary to accumulate all the corn, liquor, and ritual paraphernalia required to attend the many hundreds of guests who might arrive. As Nuyootecos say, "no one has the strength *(yɨɨ)* to do these things by themselves." What they do, then, is finance the celebration through gift exchange. The details of these exchanges will become clear over the course of this chapter, but what happens is that people give prestations of food and money to the sponsors, which the sponsors then expend in the celebration. Some of these people come to repay the sponsors for prestations the sponsors made to them in the past, and others come to make new prestations to the sponsors, which the sponsors will have to repay in the future. Nuyootecos call this practice *saa sa'a*.

The food items exchanged between *sa'a* partners in life-crisis celebrations and civil-religious hierarchy fiestas include tortillas, usually in multiples of 60 (60 tortillas equals "one basket," *ɨn tunoo*, which is a standard measure in the region); other items include beans, salt, chile, pasta, liquor, beer, soda, fermented sugar-cane juice *(aguardiente)*, and pulque. The rule in *saa sa'a* is strict reciprocity. Thus, Nuyootecos describe the flow of goods between gift exchange partners as *niko kani*, or *na niko maa*. The first is used for the motion of a log rolling over, while the second is used for the up and down movement of a yo-yo. Also, of a complete sequence of prestation and return prestation, people say *ii yu'u kua'a*, "once again to the (owner's) mouth it went." Each of these expressions evokes an image in which one's gift, even if it is out of one's control for a while, eventually returns.

Nuyootecos are careful to keep track of how much they owe their gift exchange partners. This is partly because they want to know what they must return and partly because they want to be sure their partners are not cheating them. When they receive tortillas in exchange, the women of the sponsoring household count each one to see if the number of tortillas given is the number the partner claims. Some women are able to judge if a basket contains the correct amount by lifting it up and feeling the weight. People worry about being deceived, and almost every woman in Nuyoo has a story about a time when someone fooled her by giving her a basket that was light a few tortillas. (By implication, almost every woman in Nuyoo has been accused of trying to cheat a partner.) A household that chronically cheats others will earn a bad reputation and find it difficult to attract gift exchange partners for future exchanges.

In the past, the women of a household kept track of the household's gift exchange credits and debts without the aid of written records; today, however, the men of the household record credits and debts in what Charles Leslie has called "account books" (Leslie 1960). In one book—Nuyootecos favor the small notebooks used in schools for taking notes—the men mark the names of all the people who make prestations to them and the kinds and quantities of goods they bring (gift debts). In the other book, they mark the names of people to whom they give prestations and the kinds and quantities of goods given (gift credits). As people arrive with the goods they owe, they cross off the names of these latter individuals, since the debt has been paid. Nuyootecos call the book in which the sponsors keep the names of those who make gifts to them the *lista ki'i* (figure 5) and the book where sponsors keep the names of those who owe them a gift the *lista ña'a*. *Ki'i* and *ña'a* are motion verbs that indicate that something or someone makes a round trip, by leaving with the intention of returning *(ña'a)*, or arriving with the intention of leaving *(ki'i;* Kuiper and

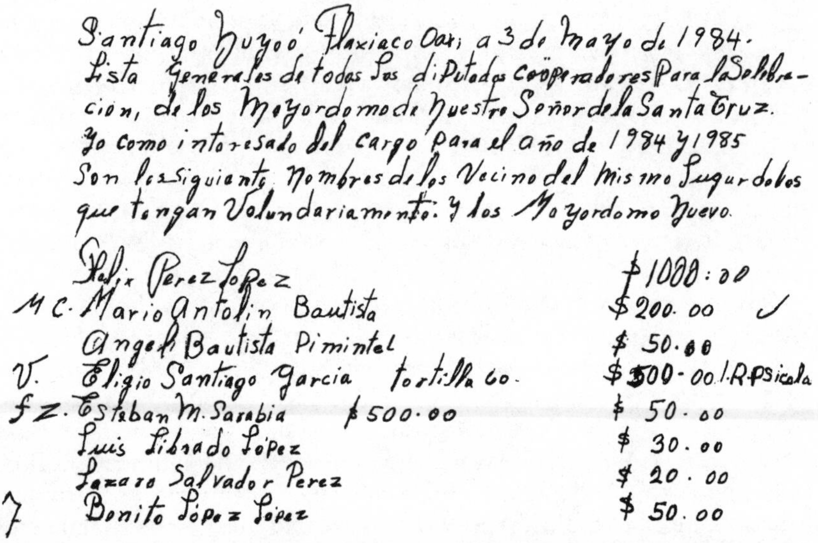
Santiago Nuyoó Tlaxiaco Oax; a 3 de mayo de 1984.
Lista Generales de todos los diputados coöperadores para la Solebración, de los Mayordomo de Nuestro Señor de la Santa Cruz.
Yo como interesado del cargo para el año de 1984 y 1985
Son los siguientes nombres de los Vecino del mismo lugar de los
que tengan Voluntariamente. y los Mayordomo Nuevo.

	Felix Perez Lopez		$1000:00
M.C.	Mario Antolin Bautista		$200.00 ✓
	Angel Bautista Pimintel		$ 50.00
V.	Eligio Santiago Garcia	tortilla co.	$500-00 1 R Psicola
f z.	Esteban M. Sarabia	$500.00	$ 50.00
	Luis Librado Lopez		$ 30.00
	Lazaro Salvador Perez		$ 20.00
7	Bonito Lopez Lopez		$ 50.00

Figure 5. *Lista ki'ɨ* of the *mayordomo* de Nuestro Señor de la Santa Cruz, May, 1984. This is the first page of the notebook in which the mayordomo of Santa Cruz recorded the gift debts he acquired during the saint's fiesta in 1984. The left column contains the names of the gift exchange partners, followed by the quantity of tortillas they gave (only one man on this page gave any), followed by the amount of cash, and any drink, such as Eligio Santiago García's gift of one case of Pepsi Cola (García is the mayordomo's godson). The man who kept the list is also one of the few who maintains the custom of calling those who aided him with prestations *diputados*, or "deputies" (see chapter 13).

Merrifield 1975). The items the sponsor receives in gift exchange are thus seen as arriving but eventually leaving, while those given in gift exchange are seen as having left but eventually returning.

The advantage of *saa sa'a* to those sponsoring a celebration is that it allows them to spread the costs of sponsorship over a long period of time—up to five or six years. When the members of a household first make plans to sponsor a fiesta, one or two years before they hold the event, they carefully calculate what they will need and come to a surprisingly precise number of tortillas, cases of beer, liters of liquor, and other items necessary to feed their guests. They then begin to make prestations in the fiestas sponsored by other households, depositing one-third to one-half the goods they will need by the time of their celebration. For example, if they calculate they need 10 cases of beer, they will make prestations of 4 cases before their celebration and expect to receive these 4 cases back when their own celebration occurs. This allows them to "bank" (Beals 1970) household surpluses by investing them with other households. When they celebrate their fiesta, they also can expect to receive 3 or 4 cases as gifts from people who are themselves preparing for a celebration. This latter transaction, in effect, permits the sponsors to borrow against future household surpluses, since debts are due only when a partner's celebration is held. These occasions are staggered; some take place within a few weeks, but many do not take place for months or even years. (This also has the effect of linking any particular celebration to a series of celebrations that took place in the past and to those that will take place in the future [Monaghan 1990c].)

The remaining cases of beer sponsors need, which are not circulated in *saa sa'a*, make up part of what I call the start-up costs of the celebration. I say "start up costs" because a sponsoring household cannot depend on the incoming prestations to meet their initial outlays. Prestations only trickle in at first, and they do not provide the sponsors with the supplies they need to serve the first of the meals to the people who arrive or to make proper countergifts for the gifts received (see below). For any large fiesta the sponsors will therefore ensure that they have on hand some 500 to 600 tortillas, 20 to 40 liters of beans, 2 or 3 cases of beer, 1 to 3 cases of soda, and some 20 liters of liquor before the celebration begins.

The countergift. When a husband and/or his wife leave their prestation at the house of a fiesta sponsor, the sponsors ask them to "wait a bit" while the women of the household count their gifts and the men write the quantities in the proper account book. The sponsors then serve the partners a meal consisting of three to five tortillas, a bowl of beans or meat, and something to drink. While the partners eat their meal, the sponsors present them with one or more countergifts. Sponsors make countergifts for each item they receive. For tortillas, the countergift is about 20% of the initial prestation (see table 2). For cash, the countergift is usually a bottle of beer or soda (something that must be purchased with cash), but it can also be a quantity of tortillas. Sponsors never return cash as a countergift. As the sponsors present each countergift, they state the purpose of each item: "These [six tortillas] are over the tortillas" or "this [beer] is over the cash."

TABLE 2.
RATIO OF TORTILLA COUNTERGIFTS TO TORTILLA INITIAL GIFTS

Size of Initial Gift	Size of Countergift	Ratio	Number of Cases
105	10	1 to 16.5	1
60	10	1 to 6	32
60	20	1 to 3	3
45	10	1 to 4.5	4
30	10	1 to 3	2
30	8	1 to 3.75	1
30	7	1 to 5	7
30	5	1 to 6	1
AVERAGE:		1 to 5.49	

Depending on the number of things the partners brought with them, they may soon find three or four piles of tortillas stacked before them. The partners take careful note of what they receive, since the countergifts are not subtracted from the initial gift. Rather, they are a separate prestation made from the sponsor to the partner, and the sponsor expects to receive a countergift of equal size when the partner sponsors a fiesta.

I could discover no word in Mixtec for the countergift, although people were quite willing to describe its purpose. The countergift, they say, is "for the meanwhile; to hold people over until the exchange can be completed." What I understand them to mean is that the countergift is a formal recognition of the loss incurred by the partner over the time goods are with the sponsor (Sahlins 1972). Put another way, the countergift acknowledges the labor that went into preparing the prestation. (Nuyootecos say the gift embodies the labor of those who made it). This may explain why the countergift increases in proportion to the size of the initial gift (see table 2). If the countergift is to be a proper recognition of the partner's labor, then it must increase in proportion to the value of the labor present in the gift.

Sponsors also use the countergift to communicate something special in the celebration. Amid the confusion of the milling guests, the sponsor singles the partner out and thanks him or her for the prestation. The sponsor then presents the partner with the countergift of tortillas and beer, which the partner can consume on the spot or take home and eat later. This shows those present that the partner aided the sponsor and that the partner's gift was well received.

Finally, the countergift has the function of redistributing any inordinate surplus a household may accumulate by sponsoring a celebration. If the women of the household realize that they have more tortillas then they will need for the meals, they may increase the proportion of tortillas they give as countergifts, thus creating new debt with the surplus. They may also expend this surplus in another day of celebration. Another way to dissipate a surplus is to make prestations to selected households immediately after the fiesta has ended or to distribute the surplus among the close kin who have come to lend a hand in preparations for the celebration.

The Gift in Its Social Context

Nuyootecos say that when they exchange gifts, they exchange labor. It is labor, they explain, that goes into the preparation of tortillas, and it is labor that produces the beans, chile, pulque, and other items served with the meal.

Labor is not, however, a homogeneous category for Nuyootecos. People say the labor that they transact in *saa sa'a* is *chineei ta'a*—literally, aid *(ta'a)*. This is not to be confused with muzu labor, labor sold in the market for a wage. For one, *chineei ta'a* always implies some kind of reciprocity, so that if one works a day in someone's fields, or if one produces 60 tortillas to give to someone else, the person who receives the labor or tortillas must return the same amount at a later date. This contrasts with wage labor, since the muzu who works in another's fields receives a salary, and his employer does not reciprocate in kind.

Another difference between *chineei ta'a* and wage labor is that *chineei ta'a* circulates among ta'a. *Ta'a* is a term that contrasts with *to'o*, or "outsiders," and people do not usually transact *chineei ta'a* labor with those who are not Nuyootecos. For example, in 1983, I joined the men of Nuyoo Center to clear brush from around the spring the center uses for its water supply. As we pushed a large log that had fallen over the spring, three men carrying loads of fruit from the hamlet of Zaragoza happened by on a nearby trail. They put down their burdens and joined in the work. People said the men did this to show their solidarity for the center and that the men from the center would have done the same for them, if they saw a work party from Zaragoza struggling to move a log. This show of support, people said, was *chineei ta'a*, because they aided ta'a (i.e., fellow Nuyootecos).

A similar incident occurred in 1989, when I walked with six Nuyootecos through the neighboring municipality of Ocotepec. We came upon a group of men struggling to move a log, this time one that blocked a road. Instead of stopping to help, the Nuyootecos hurried by and made no effort to join in, even though 5 or 10 minutes pushing the log would have been of great help. The Nuyootecos did not feel any obligation to aid the men trying to move the log because, as one of my companions explained, the men were not ta'a; they were from Ocotepec, and Nuyootecos do not "aid" them.

Given the restricted sphere in which *chineei ta'a* labor circulates, it should not be surprising that the gifts circulating in *saa sa'a*—which Nuyootecos explicitly say embody *chineei ta'a* labor—are similarly restricted to Nuyootecos. One might explain this by proposing that the exchange of gifts, like the exchange of labor, is embedded in a sectorial moral regime that is closely tied to Nuyooteco ideas about the identity of community members. Indeed, as one woman put it, gifting is an "act of honor," and it does not appear to exist among the people of different towns.[2] In fact, the municipal archives of both Yucuhiti and Nuyoo are full of letters demanding that the authorities take action against members of their municipalities for reneging on a debt to someone from another town. The chance of the authorities intervening on behalf of an outsider is slim, and such debts usually go

2. This should not be taken to mean that Nuyootecos exchange gifts among themselves in a disinterested or uncalculated way. A good illustration of the way self-interest enters into Nuyooteco gift exchange can be seen if we compare the Calenda mayordomo fiestas of 1984 and 1985. The Calenda mayordomo is a position associated with the sponsorship of a fiesta in November, prior to the feast of Santa Cecilia, the patron of musicians. The mayordomo whose household sponsored the fiesta in 1984 was a member of the town band and a diligent worker, and members of his household were often present at the celebrations of others. People considered him to be a good man, and his household to be made up of trustworthy people. The man who succeeded him in 1985, however, had an extremely bad reputation. This man has tricked many people into loaning him money or tools, which he never returned. He rarely showed up on time for communal work parties, and the town policemen were constantly in pursuit of him for various legal infractions.

Many of the variables that influence attendance and the quantity of goods received in prestations can be held constant in these two fiestas, since both men are from the same hamlet and both are musicians. Moreover, since their households are closely related, they share many of the same core gift exchange partners. Attendance at the fiesta sponsored in 1985 by the household with the poor reputation was less than a third of that for the 1984 fiesta. The amount of cash given in gift exchange was also correspondingly lower. Many people who made prestations in the 1985 fiesta were part of the sponsors' core of gift exchange partners. They thus had an obligation to attend and to aid the household in its sponsorship. However, the strategy these people followed, knowing the man's reputation for unreliability and deception, was to protect themselves by reducing the quantity of goods given, so that if they were not reciprocated the loss would not be a severe one. This is readily apparent in the lower number of tortillas per prestator in the 1985 fiesta. Whereas in 1984 the average was 51.2, in 1985 it was only 37.2.

uncollected. Notwithstanding this level of mistrust, there are cases where people of different towns do establish enduring gift exchange partnerships. Admittedly, these are few: out of 2,469 *sa'a* exchanges I was able to record only 13 that occurred between Nuyootecos and non-Nuyootecos. But these few cases do show that *saa sa'a* can sometimes extend beyond the boundaries of Nuyoo.

Saa Sa'a and the Household

In 1987, a man who served as mayordomo the year before passed away after a brief illness. He still owed many people for the gifts they had brought to his fiesta. But these gift debts, and the few gift credits he accumulated, did not die with him. They became the responsibility of other members of his household, even though these other household members did not formally hold the office, select the gift exchange partner, or make the prestation (cf. Diskin 1986). Gifts—like children "given" in baptism and young women and men "let go" in marriage—are transacted between households, not individuals. Even though the mayordomo passed away, his household continues, and so do the obligations created by the credits and debts he accumulated.

In circulating between households, gifts also mark the outer range of commensality, since household members do not engage in *saa sa'a* transactions with one another. In the nakara relationship all resources are pooled, and strict accounting would violate the spirit of the relationship (cf. Wilk 1984:225, 226). This does not mean that fathers and sons, or mothers and daughters, never become gift exchange partners. It means only that when this does occur, it is because these individuals are no longer the members of the same household. (When households fission, however, it is also true that the bad feelings created by the split often cause people to refuse to exchange gifts with one another).

Given the way that *saa sa'a* defines who is and who is not a member of a household, *saa sa'a* can function as one of the formal acts constituting a household. Recall from chapter 2 the case of the man and women who established a household separate from that of his parents. Once the couple began to eat separately from his parents, the parents turned over to the couple the list of gift debts they had accumulated from the couple's wedding feast. By beginning to repay these debts, and eating separately from the man's parents, the couple took on an identity as a household distinct from other households—well before the son had been able to construct a dwelling that was physically separate from his parent's dwelling.

Alliance and Saa Sa'a

We have now come to realize that gift exchange in many societies does not conform to the universal ideal first defined by Marcel Mauss (e.g., Parry 1986). What I will do here is examine some characteristics of Nuyooteco *saa sa'a* that make it different from better-known gift exchange systems. This will, in turn, allow us to see how the form of the Nuyooteco gift and the context in which it is given function as evaluative comments on the partners who make the exchange.

A feature common to many gift exchange systems around the world is what Andrew Strathern called "alternating disequilibrium" (Strathern 1971; see also Foster 1967:223–24). This can best be illustrated with a hypothetical example from Nuyoo, in which the people of household A attend the celebration sponsored by the people of household B. When the people of household A arrive, they make a prestation of 60 tortillas. Household B then owes household A 60 tortillas according to *saa sa'a* accounting. When A sponsors a celebration, B arrives with 90 tortillas: 60 to pay off the debt, and an additional 30 to create a new debt. Then, when B sponsors a second celebration, A arrives with 60 tortillas: 30 to pay off the debt, and an additional 30 as a new prestation. The exchange relation may continue in perpetuity, A and B making prestations of 60 tortillas and incurring debts of 30 tortillas. The two thereby alternate in the role of debtor and creditor, depending upon where they are in the exchange cycle.

Two reasons are commonly given in the literature for this oscillating indebtedness. The first is that if the return gift exceeds what is owed, then the exchange relationship between transactors is maintained, since they remain in debt to one another (Foster 1967:233–4). In Strathern's account of the Mount Hagen gift economy, it is this increment, or *"moka,"* that is the defining feature of the system (Strathern 1971). The second reason has to do with competition for social rank and prestige. In New Guinea a man's status rises or falls according to his ability to outgive a rival. The Native American societies of the northwest coast of North America carried this competition to an extreme when low-ranked individuals obtained access to trade goods and attempted to muscle their way into the traditional hierarchy by staging huge potlatches. Such competition is consistent with sequences of gift exchange that exhibit alternating disequilibrium, since each side tries to put its rival into unrepayable debt (Strathern 1971).

Nuyootecos, like the Melpa of Mount Hagen, also have a special word for the gift increment, *"yɨɨ,"* which can be translated as "strength," "heat," or "potency" (see chapter 5). Although they say that every prestation should be returned with an increment, in practice the number of people who increase their gifts is small. Of the 317 separate gift transactions I was able to trace through at least one complete sequence of prestation and counterprestation, only 70 (22%) actually involved an increment in the gift, and only 25 (8%) increased the number of tortillas (most of those who increased their gifts did so only with small amounts of cash). Do these figures mean that some in Nuyoo are interested in outgiving rivals and achieving high status in the community, while others are not? Should we see Nuyoo as a place where only some people are interested in maintaining their relationship with their partners, while the majority are not concerned if they lapse?

First, compared with the "big man" distributions of New Guinea or the potlatches among the Native Americans of the northwest coast, Nuyootecos do not compete with one another through their prestations and counterprestations. *Saa sa'a* is by no means warring with property, and indebtedness has little to do with political power in the community. This is not to say that people feel that it is better to owe than be owed. On the contrary, Nuyootecos speak of their debts as "stringing them up" *(nitoo).* Being strung up by the wrists, or under the arms, is a form of corporal punishment inflicted by civil authorities on those who have committed serious crimes. Instead, people participate in *saa sa'a* to "prepare themselves" *(tu'vara);* i.e., they invest surplus goods with other households so that the goods will be returned when needed.

As I suggested earlier, the key to understanding gift exchange in Nuyoo is to look at it as a way of dealing with the practical problems of financing a celebration. In being host to a celebration, sponsors depend on others. As one man put it, "suddenly, something happens" (such as a death in the household, requiring a ritual commemoration), and the sponsor "does not have things ready, and people say, 'the poor man, let's go to see him,' and they bring the things he needs so that he will be prepared." This makes the relationship between the giver of a gift and the one who receives it quite different from what one finds in New Guinea, with its antagonistic undercurrent, or from the open hostility with which partners sometimes confronted each other in the northwest coast. In Nuyoo, the sponsors of a fiesta feel a kind of warmheartedness (kukuekani) for the people who come to make a prestation to them. Sponsors take it as a great favor *(kumani inio)* that someone would make the sacrifice to lend them "a word of strength" *(tu'un teeyii)*, since "they know Nuyootecos are poor" and do not have such large surpluses that they can easily afford to give their supplies food to others. People say the sponsor of a celebration is in a serious predicament, in need of the help of others to "save himself." And in Nuyoo, sponsors are able to overcome the difficulties of sponsorship only through exchanging goods with people of other households.

The absence of competition in Nuyoo gift exchange can clearly be seen in the way people view the increment on a return gift. In New Guinea, this increment is the focus of the whole exchange. Its size has much to do with the standing of big men relative to one another, and it shows just what kind of resources each is able to mobilize (Strathern 1971). In Nuyoo, however, the increment does not play such a central role. People see it only as an extra help to an esteemed individual to aid him in "saving himself" from the current crisis. Thus, while it is true that *saa sa'a* establishes a relationship between givers and receivers, this relationship is not one of domination and subordination. It is instead one in which a household is able to invest surpluses in other households and simultaneously support a partner in a crisis.

Yet if Nuyootecos are interested in preserving the ties that bind them to other households, then we may question why they don't usually keep their accounts imbalanced, so that one side continues to owe the other, and the relationship continues, as in the Mexican community of Tzintzuntzan (Foster 1967:223–24). The reason is that the most important question for Nuyootecos is whether one does or does not arrive with a gift when an ally faces a crisis. Since the average household sponsors a celebration once every three years, and since a large number of fiestas are celebrated annually, there are plenty of opportunities for the members of different households to show their loyalty to one another, and nearly every household is involved in making prestations all the time (Monaghan 1990c). People do not look upon a failure to increase the gift as placing the relationship with their partners into question; sponsors appreciate any increment, but the key is appearing with a proper gift when it is needed.

Core Exchange Partners and Fiesta Attendance

Nuyootecos judge a fiesta to be a success or failure based on the number of people who attend. In a mayordomo fiesta with a particularly large turnout a man once observed, "they should feel proud because they have an understanding with all sorts of people." It is thought to be especially notable if people from all the hamlets attend the celebration, not simply those who live near the sponsor. A big crowd means the sponsoring household is well liked and respected. Also, the more guests who attend, the more food, money, and liquor they bring, and the more there is to distribute. Nuyootecos speak of the guests in the fiesta as making the sponsor "potent" *(nu teeyii* or *tunee i ini)*. In contrast, celebrations that are poorly attended are said to be sponsored by people who either "don't go to the celebrations of others" and "have no friends" or who "cannot be trusted."

Although sponsors say they would like to receive gifts from every Nuyooteco, they make the bulk of their exchanges with just a few categories of persons. First, the sponsors' household can expect to receive prestations from households that will sponsor celebrations in the near future. These latter use the civil-religious hierarchy fiestas and life-crisis commemorations preceding their own as a way of storing labor and food surpluses. Second, the sponsors' household can expect prestations from fellow hamlet members. The relationships between households of the same hamlet is, as noted in chapter 1, a strong one. Hamlet members share many responsibilities and participate in many collective activities. The ties generated by their close cooperation extend to the realm of gift exchange, so that even though the celebration may be held in the town center—a site that is quite distant from hamlets such as Yucubey or Zaragoza—the sponsors' fellow hamlet members will attend in a proportion exceeding those of other hamlets.

By far the most significant and permanent set of people who exchange gifts with the sponsors are those I call the "core" partners of the sponsors. The first component of this core is made up of the sponsors' affines—that is, a male sponsor's wife's siblings and parents, and his married sisters' and daughters' spouses' households. Also included here may be the affines of any of the sponsors' siblings, if these siblings are living in the same household as the sponsor. Ritual kin make up the second component. Within this category fall one's children's godparents, the parents of one's own godchild, and certain kinds of affines, since ego's offspring's spouse's parents and ego's brothers' and sisters' affines are transformed as a result of the marriage into ritual kin. The male sponsor's relatives by birth who are living outside his household make up the final component of the core. Included in this category are siblings and cousins, as well as the households of mother's brother and sister and father's brother and sister, again if these people are living apart from the sponsors. However, bad feelings often exist among those who were once part of a

single household and who separated, and it is not unusual that
consanguines (such as brothers) living in different households do not
exchange gifts. One can see from this that even though the "core" of
the sponsors' gift exchange partners is made up of the kindreds of the
different members of the sponsors' household, the most important and
permanent members of the core are those who are related to the
sponsors by marriage and ritual kinship. The 13 *sa'a* exchanges I
recorded between Nuyootecos and people of other Mixtec communities all involved households that were linked by ritual kinship
and/or marriage.

A chief responsibility of core partners is to arrive early to aid the
sponsors in preparations for the celebration. Prior to the fiesta, the
males may haul a load or two of firewood and the females may
cooperate in cooking the food. Core partners should also pay any gift
debts they owe the sponsors a day or two before the celebration to help
the sponsors to accumulate what they need. The gifts exchanged
between the core partners and the sponsors should, moreover, be
substantial ones. Throughout the celebration the core partners should
remain sober, and they should offer to help the sponsors in performing
rituals, in carrying water, and in the running of errands.

Even though the core partners expected at a fiesta may number over
50, the sponsors keep a precise—albeit informal—account of who is
and who is not present. A ritual kinsman who fails to make a prestation
gives the sponsors pause. They will question themselves: "What have
we done to make him upset with us? Have we wronged him in some
way?" Core members must have a very good excuse if they are not able
to attend the fiesta, and even then they should send someone to take
their place. On several occasions I was present when people took out
their account books to look over the names of those who made
prestations to them in past celebrations. They smiled and nodded
when the name of a person who brought an especially large gift was
read, and they fell silent when someone asked about the gift of some
compadres, and their names did not appear on the list.

The interest Nuyootecos show in their lists of gift exchange partners might be interpreted as providing them with an index of the
support they will have when they are faced with a "real" need for
allies, such as in political or economic disputes. However, Nuyootecos
identify fiesta sponsorship as a real crisis, and, along with cargo
obligations, fiesta sponsorship may be the most serious crisis most
Nuyooteco households face (see chapters 13 and 14). This makes gift
exchange more than just a sign of a willingness to support an ally—it *is*

that support. Furthermore, given the large number of fiestas held annually in Nuyoo, and the frequency with which people make prestations (I calculated that the average household makes prestations in 14 fiestas annually [Monaghan 1987]), the people in any circle of core partners continually exchange gifts — and, in particular, tortillas — with one another. *Saa sa'a*, then, is not only an act of support but also a consistent feature of their interaction. Like the husband and wife who "eat from the same tortilla" regularly, the exchange of tortillas among affines, ritual kin, and kin is the form through which they experience one another.[3]

This exchange of tortillas among core partners is significant in another way. Recall from chapter 2 that obtaining a wife is expressed in terms of being able to obtain tortillas, the main items circulated in *saa sa'a:* people call her household the place where the groom's "water will come from, where his tortilla will come from." The bride's sexuality is also associated with the tortilla. Female sex organs are referred to as a variety of nutritious foods, such as "meat," "a folded tortilla," and "a tamale." People also equate children given in baptism with ears of maize. This suggests the items circulated among core gift exchange partners are related to the persons who, when they moved from one house to the other, were made into affines and ritual kin. Just as the tortillas a husband and wife eat together each day are related to the first tortilla they shared (which made them into a married couple), the exchange of tortillas in *saa sa'a* among affines and ritual kin is both an integral facet of their continuing relationship and related to the acts that first created this relationship.

To understand the consistent parallels Nuyootecos draw between women and corn plants, or between children and ears of maize, we cannot end by simply noting the correspondences between the items that circulate in gift exchange and the persons who circulate in baptism and marriage. What is required for a deeper understanding is that we move beyond the normative account of interhousehold transactions I have presented thus far, and place marriage, baptism, and gift exchange in the context of wider processes of fertility and renewal, which Nuyootecos speak of as embodied in corn growth, rainfall, and the movement of the sun.

3. Although affines, ritual kin, and hamlet members constitute their relationships with one another through saa sa'a, this does not exclude an intense concern with the gift as a material item — people do want others to return the things they give to them (see note 3).

PART TWO

RENEWAL, FERTILITY, AND THE SACRED IN NUYOOTECO SOCIALITY

[A]ll the services that they performed for their gods served no other end, and no other purpose, than that they might be granted health and life and sustenance.
   —Diego de Landa, *Relación de las Cosas de Yucatán*, ca. 1566

Now I want to set down . . . the origin story that Indians of New Spain tell, such as those of the Zapotec kingdom, Guatemala, and many others. . . . Before the creation of the world, there was no earth, nor sky, not sun, nor moon nor stars . . . there was a divine husband and wife . . . who engendered three sons. The eldest was arrogant and envious of the other two, and wanted to make, by himself, living creatures . . . but the work of his hands was just some old cups, like pots and jars, to use in lowly matters, and other base things. The younger sons . . . made the heavens, plants, fire, air and earth.
   —Gregorio García, *Origen de los Indios del Nuevo Mundo*, 1607

CHAPTER 4

EARTH AND RAIN

In Preconquest times, the most important shrine in the Mixteca was on a mountaintop near Apoala. According to early Spanish accounts, the Mixtec believed this site to be special because it was there the two great halves of the cosmos, Earth and Sky, met. This partition of the cosmos into two halves *(sava)* continues to be relevant to Nuyootecos, and my discussion of Nuyooteco cosmology follows this ancient Mixtec scheme.

In the first part of this chapter, I describe Earth, or Ñu'un. Although I translate Ñu'un as Earth, Nuyootecos do not use Ñu'un for the planet on which we live, or for the sphere of mortal life, as we might use the English word "earth."[1] Instead, they use Ñu'un in contexts where they emphasize the physical presence of the earth—a rock, some soil, a mountain. Thus Ñu'un may refer to a specific plot of land or to the consistency of soil. For Ñu'un to be used, some feature of the earth must be the immediate referent.

The second part of my discussion of Nuyooteco cosmology examines the Sky (Sukun) and, in particular, Rain (Savi). As we will see, Rain is the counterpart of Earth, and the shrines and "gods" associated with the Sky complement those of Earth. If Earth shrines are located in fields and at the base of cliffs, then Sky shrines are in mountain caves or atop the mountains themselves; if the earth deities, or *nu ñu'un*, are seated in Earth, then the rain deities, or *ñu'un savi*, ride the rain clouds.

In the last part of this chapter, I examine Nuyooteco ideas about how Earth and Sky interact to create new life. This will be significant for our discussion of community because Nuyootecos draw clear parallels between the flow of things between humans and Earth and Sky, on the one hand, and the movement of the bride from her parents' house to that of her affines, on the other.

1. Nuyootecos employ the word *ñivi* for this concept, or metaphorical phrases such as "seven mountains, seven valleys, seven lakes, seven swamps," which encompasses all the geographical features of the world.

THE EARTH

When Nuyootecos speak of Earth, they speak of it as something that was here long before people appeared and that is destined to be here long after they are gone. In this sense, Earth is something that is constant and eternal, and Nuyootecos contrast it with that which is ephemeral and in flux.

Nuyootecos often use corporeal images when speaking about Earth. Soil, for example, is flesh *(kuñu)*, rocks are bones *(yikin)*, rivers are veins *(tuchi)*, water is blood *(niñi)*, and marshy places are hearts (ánima). Thus, when men first tried to plant, the place where they sowed "shouted in pain" and was "very angry" because they poked it with their digging sticks. This continues to be true today, since each time people sow, break a rock, or excavate a house site they cause pain and should ask the place where this occurred for forgiveness.

Consistent with their use of corporeal images for Earth is the idea that it is alive. *"A teku,"* they say; "it lives." In point of fact, most things are, for Nuyootecos, alive. As one man explained, "You may not think the rocks are alive and feel things, or have a mind as we do, but it is true. How else could trees or plants grow from rocks?" Another man I spoke with pointed out a place where, for some reason, all the vegetation had died out the year before. The area was now covered with new growth. "How could this be possible," he asked me, "if Earth were not alive?"

Rocks, cliffs and mountains not only are alive, they also grow, like a plant or animal grows. Thus people say boulders were once pebbles and mountains were small hills. They also say it is a bad thing to drop a stone in a deep hole, because after you die you will be sent to remove it, only to find that it has grown and become impossible to extract.

Although the examples I cite concern life as it is manifested in processes of growth, growth is not the defining characteristic of life. What does define things as living—and differentiates living things from one another—are the sounds they make. People make sounds, animals make other sounds, and rocks make still other sounds. Given this criterion, there is almost nothing in the world that is not alive.[2] If the division between spirit and matter is axiomatic in Judeo-Christian thought, Nuyootecos begin in a different place, assuming that every-

---

2. The only objects in the natural world I could find that Nuyootecos classify as truly dead were rocks that had been burned and cracked by fire. As a consequence, hearthstones and rocks used in ovens are extremely dangerous, and people avoid stepping over them or placing things on them for fear they will become ill.

thing is existence is endowed with a life principle (Mak 1977:110; Townsend 1979:28–37; for general discussions of Otomonguean religious concepts, see Marcus 1983, 1989, and Spores 1984).

The notion that a single sacred force animats all of existence is important for our understanding of Earth—as well as for the later discussions of Rain, Sun, and Wind—because these represent properties of the life principle. Rain, as we will see, is generative power and is likened to semen; Sun is vital heat and is related to the blood that courses through our veins; Wind is self-preservation and is manifest in images that suggest greed and self-containment, such as ravenous or hermaphroditic beings. As for Earth, its specific properties are most immediately revealed and experienced through the *nu ñu'un*, which translate as "the face of Earth" or "the place of Earth."

The Nu Ñu'un

To begin, I should make it clear that there is no one single form or "face" of Earth. Some say *nu ñu'un* appear in their dreams as old men with white hair and a beard. One woman told of a dream of a kind of *nu ñu'un*, called the *nu ñu'un yuku*, in which she saw it with the face of a puma and the body of a human being. A man described the *nu ñu'un yuku* as a small man, only one or two feet tall, with long ears "like a jackrabbit," and the *tachi ñu'un* as an ugly, filthy man or woman with a hairy face. A local curer once told me that there is a *nu ñu'un* that is like a giant snake with seven heads. It cares for "the wide world" (seven mountains, seven valleys, seven lakes, seven swamps), and can be found in the houses of all the *nu ñu'un*. Unusually shaped rocks, rocks that look like human faces, and the Precolumbian figurines that people occasionally find are all *nu ñu'un*. Some people bring these things home and place them on their family altar. More frequently, however, they leave the *nu ñu'un* where they find them because, in Nuyooteco thinking, *nu ñu'un* are closely tied to place.[3] Thus, when speaking Mixtec, people usually distinguish *nu ñu'un* by the locale they occupy:

Ñu'un ichi	"*Ñu'un* of the dry land"
Ñu'un mini	"*Ñu'un* of the pond or lake"
Ñu'un no'yo	"*Ñu'un* of the swamp"
Ñu'un ñi'i	"*Ñu'un* of the sweatbath"
Ñu'un yute	"*Ñu'un* of the river" (also *Ñu'un nute*)

3. Jansen (1982:298) recorded a Spanish translation of *nu ñu'un* by a Mixtec speaker as "Santo Lugar."

Ñu'un nu'un	"*Ñu'un* of the hearth"
Ñu'un itun	"*Ñu'un* of the oven"
Ñu'un yuu ñu'un	"*Ñu'un* of the hearth stone"
Ñu'un yuku	"*Ñu'un* of the forest"

This list of different *nu ñu'un* shows that the earth, for Nuyootecos, is a complex and varied cosmos. At first I had a little difficulty picturing how something as solid as the earth could be a place where so many different beings reside. I owe a debt of gratitude to Adolfo López López, who, when trying to enlighten me, hit upon the following metaphor. He compared the earth to the sea: "When we look out upon the sea, we see a solid surface. Yet there are many happening that we cannot see. The same is true for the earth. There are many things in the earth that we do not know about, and cannot see. There are many *nu ñu'un*, just as there are many fish and other things seated in the water." Thus the *nu ñu'un* are like the different fish of the sea, but instead of sitting in water, they sit in Earth *(nee nu ñu'un)*. The idea of "sitting" somewhere connotes, for Mixtec speakers, permanent residence and proper place. The *nu ñu'un* protects and administers the area under its control, called its "house," and does not leave it.

Although the *nu ñu'un* "sit" in Earth, they generally wander about in the morning, just as men and women do, and return to their houses in the late afternoon. Extending Tata Adolfo's metaphor, the *nu ñu'un*, as creatures of Earth, are able to move through soil and rock, just as fish and other creatures of the sea move through water.

Nuyootecos consider all *nu ñu'un* to be ndiosi (from the Spanish word for God) or, as they translate it, "saints," just as they call the images of Christian saints in the church ndiosi. Like the saints, the *nu ñu'un* have Christian names. So, San Marcos is the ñu'un of the swamps, San Cristóbal is the ñu'un of the dry land, and the Virgen de la Luz is the ñu'un of the sweatbath. There is considerable variation from one Nuyooteco to another over which *nu ñu'un* go with which saint's names (Jansen 1982:305–6). The three cited above, along with San Eustacio, the *ñu'un* of the forest, are the ones most consistently paired. As for the others, when I would ask people about inconsistencies in the "Christian" names given them, no one thought it all that important because any *nu ñu'un* has a number of different titles, and worshipers often invoke all the *nu ñu'un* they can think of, to ensure that they hit upon the one who is most able to help.[4]

4. Many people assert that there is a chief of all the *nu ñu'un*, and if you know its name and

There are male and female *nu ñu'un (nu ñu'un yɨɨ* and *nu ñu'un sɨ'ɨ;* Jansen 1982:298). Female *nu ñu'un* are, like Catholic saints, *yan si'i,* which Nuyootecos translate as "virgins." Being a *yan si'i,* however, has nothing to do with virginity as we might define it, but instead indicates sacredness and femininity. *Yan* is the prefix for sacredness, and John Pohl points out that *si'i* may be related to the word for grandmother (John Pohl, personal communication, 1989). While people see the *nu ñu'un* as differentiated by sex, most express a doubt that the *nu ñu'un* would engage in sexual relations. They feel that the *nu ñu'un* are eternal. They were always there, and will always be there. No new *nu ñu'un* are ever created, so people reason that there is no need for them to engage in procreative acts. Rather, the division of the *nu ñu'un* into males and females may be part of a division of the Nuyooteco sacred into paired halves, which occurs on each level of the cosmology.

There are many different types of *nu ñu'un,* and each type has many members. Thus, the *nu ñu'un* found in one bend of the river is not the same as the one found further upstream, even though they may carry the same name and be addressed in the same way.

All the *nu ñu'un,* no matter where they sit and what kind of *nu ñu'un* they are, are thought to come together to coordinate their activities (usually in general assemblies at noontime), just as Nuyootecos periodically do. For example, each spring all the *nu ñu'un* meet to decide how much corn they will produce in the coming year. The *nu ñu'un,* being the face of Earth, control and apportion Earth's transformative vitality. As one man put it, "they decide whether they want to work, and how hard." They can cause a bounteous corn crop to grow, or they may prevent crops from growing and cause famine. The decisions they arrive at in their general assemblies are thus of acute interest to people and may be influenced by sacrificial offerings.[5]

---

where its house is, then you can speak to it and get it to order the other *nu ñu'un* to do what you wish. One man referred to this chief as the "president" of the *nu ñu'un,* and that its name is San Barrancón. San Barrancón does figure prominently in all the prayers to the *nu ñu'un* I was able to record.

5. The role *(tiñu)* of the *nu ñu'un* in regulating the fertility of Earth makes people very interested in their activities. As mentioned, the *nu ñu'un* are the ones who "work" to produce corn and other domesticated plants, and they can be stimulated in their "work" through sacrificial offerings. To choose an example that does not concern agriculture, but that illustrates the same principle, the *nu ñu'un yuku* has, as part of its area of control, wild game. Some people say that the game animals go into the earth during the day and emerge at night, when the *nu ñu'un yuku* graze them as if they were flocks of sheep or goats. All agree that it is the *nu ñu'un yuku* that causes animals to be taken in the hunt, by exposing them to the hunger (or, if it doesn't want them taken, it hides them when the

The *nu ñu'un* will also come together when they wish to take revenge on a person who has slighted them in some way. They retaliate by taking his or her ánima[6] — one trips the person up, and another "grabs" the person as he or she falls. One man suggested that the *nu ñu'un* have a shared consciousness or, as he put it, "a single mind" (anduni). This allows them to come to decisions instantaneously and unanimously, unlike people, who may argue and disagree with one another.

Much of what the *nu ñu'un* do parallels human activities. They eat three meals a day — at dawn, noon, and sunset (people make offerings to the *nu ñu'un* in the morning and late afternoon and avoid bathing, washing clothes, or working in the fields at noon, since the *nu ñu'un* of the river or dry land may seize their souls as part of its meal) — they live in households, and they come together in general assemblies. When people talk about the *nu ñu'un*, they often refer to them as "the respected, older people" *(ñɨvɨ ña'nu)*. Moreover, in prayers to the *nu ñu'un* it can be seen that even though people view the *nu ñu'un* as superior beings, they do not view them as different from people in the kinds of things they need or in the desires that motivate them (see Monaghan 1987:683–86). Just as some humans are good humored or generous while others are reckless, impulsive, or mean spirited, so too the *nu ñu'un* have different personalities, which affect the way they interact with people.[7] The *nu ñu'un* may be the embodiment or "face"

---

hunter draws near). If the hunter wishes to ensure success, he should make sacrifices of pulque and incense to the *nu ñu'un*, which consumes them. One experienced hunter recited a story of a man who encountered a *nu ñu'un* while out in the forest. He gave it an offering of pulque, and, as the *nu ñu'un* drank it and became intoxicated, it promised the man a large animal from its herd. No sooner had it said this than a large animal sprang out of the forest, making itself an easy target.

6. The *ánima* is taken when a person experiences certain emotions, principally when he or she is "frightened" *(yu'u ni)*, "angry" *(kitini)*, or "remorseful" *(kukuekani)*. If one slips and falls, for example, one is often momentarily startled. Alternatively, one may become angry and curse at skinning a knee or elbow. Either way, the *nu ñu'un* find the ánima an easy target. Falling on the ground or slipping into a river or stream is by far the most common way of losing ánima. The *nu ñu'un* themselves try to trip people up, by "pulling one's feet" to make one angry or frightened. You can always tell when this happens, Ñanu María Sarabia once told me, because when you look to see what you stumbled on you find there is nothing there.

7. The different *nu ñu'un* also have different relationships with people. Some *nu ñu'un* are easily upset and will immediately retaliate against those who have disturbed them. Others are not so easily offended, and one is safe around them. People stress that the *nu ñu'un* are like people; just as there are people with different personalities, so there are *nu ñu'un* with different personalities. San Cristóbal, for example, who sits below the leaf of the *tineca* plant that grows along stream courses, enjoys taunting people *(saa kani ya kuvi ñu'un)*. Anyone drinking water near this plant should make a sign of the cross first to prevent San Cristóbal from causing the drinker to become ill. The fiercest *nu*

of a sacred force, but they nonetheless form an internally differentiated pantheon.

Any number of things will offend the *nu ñu'un*, all of which people
classify as kuachi, "sin, fault, transgression." Fouling the house of the
nu ñu'un is perhaps the most serious. One should not urinate or
defecate in rivers, streams, or swamps or on a path. Washing your
hands and allowing the dirty water to run back into the stream,
drinking from a stream with bad breath, or drinking with chile or salt
on your lips is similarly offensive to the *nu ñu'un*. For this reason
people usually carry cups with them. Bathing while one is ill is also a
transgression, since the coldness or heat of the illness dirties the water.
Similarly, only fresh water may be poured on fires, since dirty water
would offend the *nu ñu'un* of the hearth. Drunks have a particular
problem, as their bad breath often offends the *nu ñu'un* when they fall
asleep out in the open. Many people, while drinking, will make
periodic libations to the *nu ñu'un* so that nothing bad befalls them.
The *nu ñu'un* are also said to be offended by the odor of women, who,
because of sexual intercourse, become polluting *(ten'en)*.

Other serious transgressions against the *nu ñu'un* include the setting
of forest fires, the overkill of animals by hunters, the breaking and
burning of rocks, and unwarranted excavations. The *nu ñu'un* may also
become angry if they are not given a proper recompense for some work
they have done, such as granting the hunter a large game animal or
producing a bounteous corn harvest. The recompense should take the
form of a sacrificial gift, such as pulque, incense, liquor, soft drinks,
candles, or flowers.

As punishment for transgressions against them, the *nu ñu'un* make
people sick. This aspect of people's relationship to the *nu ñu'un* is
highly significant for Nuyootecos; because almost everyone has suffered from some illness caused by the *nu ñu'un*, it makes human
interactions with them real in a way that they would not otherwise be.
In fact, if you ask people to define *nu ñu'un*, they will often say simply
"it is an illness in the ground."[8]

ñu'un is the *nu ñu'un* of the hearthstones. Rocks, it will be recalled, are considered to be alive. The
burns they endure in the hearth then cause them to suffer tremendously.

8. It is interesting to note that when the *nu ñu'un* retaliate against someone who has offended
them, it is sometimes the case that they do not strike down the person who is directly at fault, but
instead attack a member of the person's household. This makes it difficult to determine the reasons
for an illness, as the actions of any one of a number of people may be responsible for causing a
household member to become sick. But what is perhaps the most important consequence of the
collective accountability of the household before the sacred is that it makes it easy to assert that the

The frequency with which the *nu ñu'un* make people ill also shows that humans are by no means in a naturally harmonious relationship with the sacred. On the contrary, the long lists of offenses against the *nu ñu'un*—which are punished by one's loss of the animating life principle (ánima)—indicate that the human connection to the sacred is most often tentative and discordant. (The word I translate as sacred, *ii*, also connotes something that is dangerous, fragile, and easily disturbed.) This is, in turn, related to the frequency of revelation in Nuyooteco life, which, as we will see, is concerned with reharmonizing individual and collective actions with the underlying order of things.

THE SKY AND RAIN

The Nuyoo region is subject to a long dry season, followed by an intense wet season. The dry season runs from late September through the beginning of May and the wet season from mid-May until mid-September. As in most tropical environments, this alternation between wet and dry has important effects on the region's flora and fauna. After the rains end in September, the luxuriant growth in Nuyoo begins to dry out, and by January the lush, verdant valleys are brown and parched. Wild animals that fed on the harvest grow thin, and it is difficult to find sufficient fodder for domestic animals. All of this is suddenly reversed in late May, when the rains begin again. In the space of a week or two, the valley sides turn green, animals begin to put on weight, and, most importantly for Nuyootecos, the corn they sow begins to sprout. A few days of rain thus cause some dramatic

---

nu ñu'un never act unjustly when they make someone ill. This was made clear to me while I was telling a group of men the biblical story of Job. After explaining that God made Job suffer to test his faith, the men were incredulous. They said that there was no way Job could have suffered for what he did without having done something wrong. When I insisted that he had done nothing wrong, and that otherwise Job would not have had his faith tested, one man suggested that although Job himself may have done nothing wrong, perhaps one of the members of his household did, and God was punishing him for this.

The men's reaction to the story of Job indicates a number of things about Nuyooteco belief. For one, it shows that for Nuyootecos, "deities" like the *nu ñu'un* are much too immediate in people's experience for them to doubt their existence or to need to have their faith in them tested. People took the story of Job not only as a fiction, but one that strained credulity and was therefore not very interesting. It also shows that things such as illnesses are not arbitrary; there is a reason for their occurrence and why they strike down those whom they do. Job did not become ill by chance—the reason illness occurs is because the gods have been slighted. One becomes ill because one has given offense or has failed in some duty. As in many places in the world, sickness is strongly associated with fault and blame.

changes in the environment. Furthermore, the clearing and burning of fields, the sowing of seeds, the agricultural strategies for the coming year, and the harvest itself are all subordinate to the rains. Even if the rains come late in the year, a good crop will be produced if the rain falls in sufficient quantity. People give rain an unrivaled role in the growth of plants and in the creation and sustenance of life in general.

When Nuyootecos talk about Rain (Savi), they speak of it as a potent, volatile substance, almost like an unstable chemical element. Once, while I was on a trip to Zaragoza Nuyoo with several people from Nuyoo Center, a violent thunderstorm forced us to seek shelter in a nearby house. When the storm ended and we resumed our journey, we came across a tree stump that had been hit by lightning and was still smoldering. One of the men pointed out how the falling raindrops seemed to feed the glowing embers, since the tree gave off increasing amounts of smoke. "Rain is like gasoline," he said, "especially where lightning hits." Rain is like gasoline because both are highly charged substances. Yet the potency of Rain is the potency of fertility, rather than combustibility.

The significant role played by Rain in the productive cycle of plants and animals is paralleled by its equally significant role in belief and ritual. Nowhere is this more apparent than on New Year's Eve, when peole gather to await the first cloud of the new year. In this ancient ceremony (Jansen 1982:232–4), people search the sky for the first cloud, standing in groups around the church and municipal buildings or sitting outside their households wrapped in blankets. When someone finally sees the cloud, he or she shouts out, and the fiscales ring the church bells. All take careful note of the direction it is traveling. If the cloud moves south to north, it will be a good year; if it moves north to south, the year will be a bad one. If no cloud appears, people become increasingly anxious. Because the first cloud is a sign of prosperity and vitality, its nonappearance is a sign· of sterility and decline, and people fear there will be many deaths and a poor harvest.

Just as Earth is embodied in everything associated with the land, so too Rain is part of everything having to do with the Sky and moisture. Rain, like Earth, is a fecund substance, a stimulus to growth, and in Mixtec religion fertility is a manifestation of the sacred. Also Rain, like Earth, has several different "faces," or manifestations. There are *ñɨvɨ savi*, or "rain people," who appear as lightning bolts. There are *koo savi*, or "rain serpents," who appear in the midst of violent tempests (figures 6 and 7; see Monaghan 1989). There are *chile savi*, or "rain lizards," which appear in fine mist and dew. But the face of the Rain I want to focus on here is one called the *ñu'un savi*.

The Ñu'un Savi

Nuyootecos use the term *ñu'un savi* in several senses. First, they use it for rain clouds, as when a storm approaches and people say "the Holy Rain comes" *(vaji Ñu'un Savi)*. Similarly, they use it to refer to a damp, high place that often traps passing clouds, or to ponds on the top of a mountain. Finally, and most significantly, they use *ñu'un savi* for what they translate as "the saints of rain," whose Christian names are San Esea and Santa Barbara; however, I will continue to refer to them in the way the Mixtec usually do, as *ñu'un savi*.

Although Nuyootecos give them one or two Christian names, there are many *ñu'un savi* in the world, and each is distinct, just as the *nu ñu'un* in one place is distinct from the *nu ñu'un* in another. We can see the confusion this creates for outsiders in the sixteenth-century Inquisition trial held in Yanhuitlán, in which one witness switched back and forth between singular and plural when discussing Savi, "the demon of water."[9]

According to a man who claims he saw a *ñu'un savi*, it is like a "doll" or "small child," no more than two or three feet tall. It had rust-colored hair and big eyes, "like two plates," so it could see across great distances and understand many things. Many describe the *ñu'un savi* as multicolored. Another man said the legs and feet of *ñu'un savi* are covered with bands of color, as if they were wearing a number of different stockings. One band is yellow, another pink, another red, another green, another white, and another purple. The same is true for their arms and heads. Their bellies, however, are dark, or black *(tuun)*. This coloring may be related to the darkness of rain-bearing clouds *(viko tuun* or *viko savi)* that Nuyootecos contrast to the white, wispy clouds that carry no rain. It may also be related to the darkness *(itun tuun)* of a ripe cornfield, since people consider corn the child of the *ñu'un savi* (see below).[10]

9. "In the village of Molcaxtepec, which is a dependency of Yanhuitlán, there is an Indian named Caxa, who is the pope and guardian of the demons of the kingdom of Yanhuitlán; they call the *demons Caa qui*, that is, the *demon* of water (AGN, Inquisición 37, exp. 5, Contra Don Domingo Cacique, Don Francisco Gobernador y Don Juan de Oaxaca, 1544).

10. Nuyootecos map the processes of plant growth onto celestial phenomena, so that clouds ripen *(jichi,* "turn color") like cornfields and become dark as they "mature."

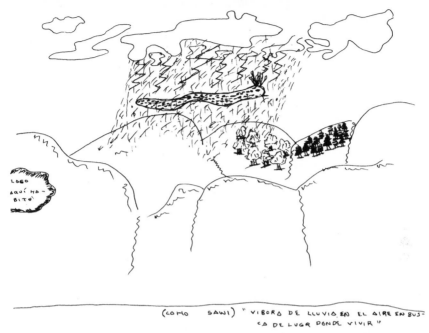

(como   sawi) " vibora de lluvia en el aire en bus-
           ca de lugar donde vivir "

Figure 6. The *koo savi*. In this drawing, a *koo savi*, or Rain serpent, moves
from one home to another. To the left is the lake where it lived, and to the
right is the lake it will create by causing the area to flood. As it flies, the *koo
savi* moves in the center of a rainstorm.

The Rain houses. Like the *nu ñu'un*, the *ñu'un savi* live in "houses," the
ve'i savi, or "Rain houses," which peole treat as shrines (Jansen
1982:189–92). Rain shrines are caves that usually contain pools of
fresh, pure water *(nute noo).* One woman told me that this water
glimmers *(shu'un)* as if it were reflecting candles set alongside the
walls of the cave. All Rain shrines are damp inside, even at the height
of the dry season. People say that the drops of water that fall from the
ceiling of the cave are "raindrops," and that rain clouds pour from the
ve'i savi before a storm. In one Rain shrine near the hamlet of Yucubey,
a resident told me there is a big green drum, like the bass drum the
down musicians play. The *tenuvi* ("Rain people" who function as
shamans, priests, and sacrificers [see chapter 14]) enter this and beat
the drum in the months of April and May. This signals the approach of
the rainy season, and the whole area reverberates with the sound of
their drumming, just as it reverberates with the sounds of thunder

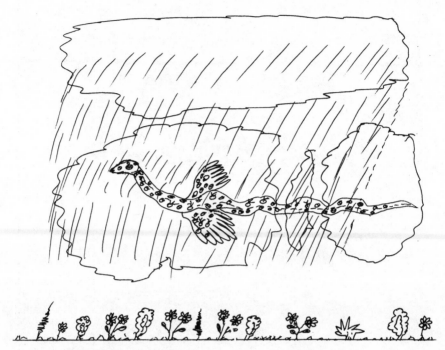

Figure 7. The *koo savi*. Whereas the artist of Figure 6 drew the Rain serpent's plumes growing from its head, this artist depicted the creature with wings. The circles on the Rain serpent's body, some with tassels or shoots coming from them, are the seeds of food plants, such as corn, beans, wheat, and coffee. In figure 6, the artist drew the seeds as small dots.

when lightning strikes and the rain arrives. People also say that in other Rain shrines can hear the *ñu'un savi* "shout" (i.e., thunder) before the clouds come pouring out.

There are several Rain shrines in the Nuyoo region. The best known is atop Yucu Ite, a mountain to the southeast of Nuyoo, also known as the Cerro de la Campana. Another is on Yucu Kasa, to the northeast, in the municipality of Yosondua. A third, as I mentioned, is in Yucubey, near the mountain known as Yucu Koo. The fourth, according to many peole, is atop Yucu Iti, in Yucuhiti. Each mountain also occupies a key directional point and forms a shrine where the tenuvi go to pray for rain.

The location of the Rain shrines in caves atop mountains is significant because many say that mountains contain vast amounts of water. "If the mountains were not full of water," one acquaintance asked in response to my questions, "how else could springs of fresh water flow from them?" The Rain houses are conduits to these storehouses of moisture.

The ñu'un savi and the machete. When Nuyootecos describe *ñu'un savi*, they often mention the *ñu'un savi*'s ax or machete. *Yuchi*, the word for machete, is the ancient Mixtec word for obsidian knife (Alvarado 1962), and Nuyootecos say that obsidian is fossilized lightning. The association of the *nu ñu'un*'s machete with lightning is even clearer in stories where people have gone to trees hit by lightning and found the golden machete of the *ñu'un savi* cleaved to the trunk.

The ax, and especially the machete, are closely associated with males. If a woman or man dreams of a machete, for example, it means that a male child will be born to them. The machete is also the implement men use to clear brush, to cut firewood for the hearth, and to weed fields so that young corn plants may grow (figure 8). "The machete is our nourishment," one man explained, since without a machete "we would not be able to plant; the machete is what allows us to eat."

Given the importance of the machete in agricultural production, all males own at lest one, and rarely does a man leave his house without first slinging a machete over his shoulder. But the machete is more than a simple tool; throughout the region, carrying a machete signals that one is armed and ready to defend oneself. Without it, many say they feel vulnerable—and for good reason. Almost all the serious assaults that occurred in the region while I was there involved machetes. (A second interpretation of the dream of a machete is that the dreamer will be wounded or killed.) As a sign of threat and potential for violence, the machete is a scepter of male power. I once witnessed a fistfight between two men from Yucuhiti where, when it was over, the victor unsheathed his machete and made his rival kiss it as a sign of submission and respect.[11]

It a man's machete is a symbol of his agency, at times functioning as a terribly destructive weapon, then the lightning bolt of the *ñu'un savi* is similarly an expression of its potency. For example, a *ñu'un savi* may sometimes wield its "machete" to punish transgression. If a farmer finds that someone has vandalized his crops (see chapter 6), or if he

---

11. If the machete is positively related to things masculine, then it is negatively related to the feminine. Women are prohibited from stepping over a machete, since this would cause it to break. Males are always a bit uncomfortable when they see a woman wielding a machete, because the sustained contact of females with this symbol of masculinity is felt to be improper and, according to older people, was not permitted in the past.

Figure 8. A man clearing a field with his machete. Many men possess two machetes: a Collins machete for use in the fields, and another finely made blade from Jamiltepec or Ometepec, which, along with its sheath, can cost the equivalent of a month's wages. Men give this second blade a fine edge and often sharpen it while resting in front of their houses. Unlike the Collins machete, this is not used in daily agricultural chores but is something a man carries with him on public occasions, such as a town meeting or on a trip to the Sunday market.

sees that someone's goats entered his fields to eat his corn plants, he can seek revenge by collecting the damaged plants and placing them in the form of a cross, high up in a tree that was once struck by lightning. The *ñu'un savi* can then clearly see the damage caused to their children (see below) and will punish the wrongdoer by "burning" him or his flocks with a lightning bolt.[12]

THE UNION OF EARTH AND SKY

If Nuyootecos, like the ancient Mixtec, partition the sacred into the Sukun, or Sky, and the Ñu'un, or Earth, then it is the coming together

---

12. It is said that some people manipulate the *ñu'un savi* into striking down the innocent, by going to the *ve'i savi* and accusing them of having harmed the children of the Rain. The *ñu'un savi* will be so angry that it will take revenge, irrespective of the truth or falsity of the accusation.

of the two—that sufficient Rain fall on fertile Earth—which provides people with food and the means to survive. The Nuyooteco use of a gendered idiom for distinguishing the two great halves of the cosmos should be placed in this context. When speaking in generalities, it is quite appropriate to refer to Sky as *tatao*, "our father," and each of the principal sacred beings of Sky are in turn associated with symbols and activities that are strongly male in character. The *ñu'un savi* carry the scepter of male potency, the machete. As we will see in chapter 14, the heroic tenuvi—who, like the *ñu'un savi*, are closely connected with lightning and machetes—are the quintessence of maleness. Similarly, when speaking in general terms, Earth can be called *nanao*, "our mother." This is consistent with the notion that the people of Nuyoo emerged from Soko Usha, "womb seven," near Yucunino (see chapter 9), and the idea, to be discussed below, that Earth forms a womb for developing plant seed.

What is most important about the association of each of the great halves of the cosmos with a particular gender are the consistent analogies Nuyootecos draw between the interaction of the sexes to the workings of the sacred. I noted earlier that people identify the onset of the rainy season as a time of renewal and regeneration. They point out that it is when wild animals mate, and it is also the time when the flora in the region dramatically returns to life, as the desiccated valley lands are transformed into green gardens and fertile cornfields.

Just as Nuyootecos view the coming of the rain as a vital event of generation and renewal, they associate rain production with symbols of masculine sexuality. The machete, associated with lightning and the *ñu'un savi*, is a powerful symbol of male potency (see also chapter 9), and the cigars smoked by the tenuvi to bring rain are metaphors for the penis (Monaghan 1989). Given these associations, it is not surprising that people liken rain to semen. As Tata Fausto Modesto Velasco explained, when the rain falls, "it causes the seeds sown there [i.e., in the ground] to grow, just as male liquid causes a baby to grow in its mother." Rain is potent, energizing, and productive, like the semen, or "white blood," of males. Rain, people say, is the father of all plants, and they are its children *(se'ya savi)*.

In the same way that Nuyootecos speak of the generation of plant growth by Rain to be like the male role in procreation, they speak of Earth as providing a womb for developing plant seeds:

Soko kuvi Ñu'un
Earth is womb

Nuvi itun, nuvi yuku,
It ripens the cornfield, it regenerates the forest

Ini Ñu'un va va kue'nu
In Earth it will grow.

We will see in chapter 9 that many Nuyootecos say that for a woman to become pregnant, she needs to have a mass of male blood in her womb, which can be accumulated only if she engages in repeated sexual acts. The blood then thickens and hardens, and a child begins to form. People liken this to when Rain falls in sufficient quantity over an extended period to engender its children, the plants, in the womb of Earth. As one person put it, "Corn without water is like a woman who does not have sexual relations *[kukuachi tee ji ña'a]*, since neither will bear fruit." In this way the interaction of Earth and Sky, which is understood in terms that parallel Nuyooteco understanding of the sexual relations between the human male and female, results in a burst of fertile, vibrant life.

The Daughter of the Earth and Rain

Of all the living things that are produced through the coming together of Earth and Rain, corn is by far the most important for Nuyootecos (figure 9). It is the principal subsistence food, and people speak of it as our "root" and "vein." I suggested earlier that Nuyootecos view corn products as distinctly feminine in nature. Foods such as the tortilla and tamale are metaphors for female genitalia, and processed corn is closely associated with woman's role in the household division of labor. But what is most significant about the corn plant is its identification with a young, desirable, and marriageable woman.

Evidence for this can be found in several places. There are, for example, striking parallels between the marriage negotiations carried on between households and the praying for corn in the house of the Rain. When a man goes to a house of Rain to pray and make sacrifice, he requests that the *ñu'un savi* "feed" him, by providing him with the rain necessary for plants to grow and the corn to sustain himself. He may also ask that the domestic animals he owns abound and that he receive money, but these are secondary requests. His primary concern is with water and corn. We can liken this to the speeches made during marriage negotiations, where it is quite common for the suitor or his spokesman to refer to his potential in-laws' household as "the place from which my tortillas will come, the place from which my water will come." Just as Nuyootecos identify the *ve'i savi* as the source of water

Figure 9. Corn plants. These corn plants are called *niñɨ crusi* because the two ears of corn growing from them form a cross (most plants produce only one ear of corn). The plants are used in a variety of rituals, and farmers will bring *niñɨ crusi* to the church to place them next to the saints.

and corn, a groom identifies his potential father-in-law's house as his source of water and tortillas.

One reason for this identification has to do with the similarities between the relationship the supplicant maintains with the houses of the Rain and Earth on the one hand, and with the household of his affines on the other. He receives water and corn from Rain, which, together with Earth, provides him with his livelihood. Similarly, his affines supply him with the female labor necessary to sustain and reproduce a viable household, which, along with his bride's sexuality, allows him to "eat." Corn and water mediate households, just as women do.

We can also see the association of corn with marriageable women and the association of Rain and Earth with affines in the taboo system. It is a widespread belief that if corn is not properly sown, harvested, stored, and processed, the *ñu'un savi* will remove it from the offender's possession. Treading on corn, leaving a few cobs in the field after harvest, playing with a tortilla, or turning it over and eating it face down, even if done unintentionally, will offend the ñu'un savi (as this is *soonu*, "disrespectful" behavior).[13] Likewise, a woman "who is not properly cared for," that is, one whose husband beats her, or who does not receive enough food, or who is overworked by other members of the household, will leave her husband's household of her own accord, or her kin will arrive to remove her. Both actions impoverish the household. In the case of corn, the household will starve because it will not have enough food. In the case of women, the household will starve because without a woman it will be an incomplete production unit, lacking the necessary female labor to complement its male labor. "Corn is like a woman," people say, because "if you mistreat it, it will return to its household."

The notion that corn should be respected as a male should respect his wife has a sexual, as well as a domestic, dimension. I have heard older men warn younger men, "if you are going to make a woman your mate, you should not just eat one thing." In other words, it is wrong to have sex with a woman without taking her into a household. Nuyootecos also liken illicit relationships—in which men give their paramours gifts of money, corn, and meat—to slighting (soonu) or playing with *(siki)* the tortilla. Older people say that young men who engage in sex with a woman without marrying her are "not really hungry." Like a man who mishandles food, the man who has illicit affairs will find that his cornfield will not produce, or his money will

13. Once, while I was on a trip to Yucunino with several people from Nuyoo Center, we halted for over an hour to pick up corn kernels that lay across the path, which had probably leaked from a hole in a sack someone had been carrying. The people I was with told me they did this so the corn would not be trod on and complain *(ka'a kuachi,* "speak fault") to the ñu'un savi. If it did complain, the ñu'un savi would remove its children from the care of Nuyootecos, and people would be left without anything to eat. The ñu'un savi might remove the corn by causing it to decompose in storage, or by causing it to be used more rapidly than normal, so that the corn crub empties rapidly. It might also wait until the next agricultural year and refuse to supply sufficient rainfall, or it might descend on the cornfields as a windy rainstorm and "collect" all the ears of corn by knocking down the immature plants. In either case the ñu'un savi reasons that if people mistreat corn, then they probably do not really need it, and it would be best to take it somewhere where it is truly appreciated.

Disrespectful behavior toward any of the children of the Rain thus invites retaliation. Cutting down plants for no reason or tearing their leaves off can leave the offender "poor" in the future, as he will not enjoy any harvests. One of the most offensive things one can do is to engage in sexual relations near seeds, stored food, or growing crops or to go to a cornfield after having sexual relations. Given this view of the sensitivity of the children of the rain, it is not surprising that when people go to a Rain house to make sacrifices for bounteous crops, they spend much of the time asking forgiveness for any harm they may have unknowingly caused the Rain's children.

run out, and he will be truly hungry and not able to find food. Just as the tortilla is a "blessing from god," one man explained, so too a woman is a "blessing" from another household.

The final piece of evidence for the association of corn plants with marriageable women has to do with the way Nuyootecos correlate the planting and growth of corn with human gestation and development. This first became clear to me when I attempted to elicit Mixtec names for the stages of plant growth from a group of men who were visiting my house. I had a difficult time communicating what I was after, until finally, after several unsuccessful starts, I read a list of stages of human growth that the same group had enumerated a few weeks earlier. I hardly finished reading when they began to name the stages of corn plant development, starting in sequence from when the corn seed first sprouts to when the plant is ready to be harvested. Upon further questioning, they said that the growth of corn and the maturation of people is indeed a similar process, and one man went on to elaborate, highlighting the significance of the final stages of corn plant growth, when he said the plant bears *(niso)* the ear of corn like a mother bears a child. This is important since the "father" of this "child" is the man who sowed the corn. Thus, in sowing his field, a man begins by dropping the seeds into a hole he makes with a long, sharp, digging stick (figure 10; *yutun tajio*, "stake that we sow with"), the use of which is widely associated in Mesoamerica with the sexual act (Taggart 1983). In Nuyoo, *yutun tajio* can be used as a metaphor for the erect penis, and people told me that they sometimes use the verb *chi'ira*, "they sow," for the act of sexual intercourse.

We can also discern parallels between human sexuality and the planting and growth of corn in the use and symbolism of the machete. Recall that the machete is the principal implement of male labor, and Nuyootecos associate it with virility, dominance, potency, and male sexuality. When a man clears the weeds from around the corn plant, normally twice during the growing season, he provides a dramatic stimulus to growth. In the course of this activity, he grows "cold." The reason he grows cold is that Earth saps his strength. This has nothing to do with the physical exertion required by weeding but involves a general ebbing of life force, or heat, which Nuyootecos call yɨɨ. Yɨɨ is also lost during the sexual act, when a man injects his blood into the womb of his partner and grows cold.

The act of weeding a cornfield also establishes an emotional bond between the farmer and the developing ear of corn. If a man is "sad" and hungry (kukuekani), for example, he will transfer this "sadness"

Figure 10. Sowing corn with a digging stick. The corn men sow in Nuyoo has broad, long leaves, so it is important to leave enough space between the plants to ensure that they will not crowd one another. Most men plant four seeds together, making four holes with their digging sticks in the form of a diamond or rough rectangle, about 15 centimeters along each side, and dropping a seed into each.

to the cob. When it is harvested, people call this cob the *niñi soko li'li*, a scrawny ear with only a few kernels of corn on it, which one woman described as "a corn ear so hungry it hangs its head to one side." The damage caused to the corn by the man's emotional state is similar to the harm caused to a child by its mother when she nurses it after becoming upset. For mother and child, the medium for this transfer is the mother's blood, which is full of yii. For the male farmer and the corn plant, it is the machete or digging stick, implements that, one man explained, cause the farmer to "leave his inheritance" with the corn he sows.

The sexually suggestive role of males in corn production is apparent in agricultural rituals as well. For example, after sowing a field, a man may carry pulque to the plot and pour it onto the Earth, asking that the *nu ñu'un* work so that the crops may grow well. Pulque is associated with the semen, or the "white blood" of males, and this act can be interpreted as an attempt to fertilize the corn in the way a man fertilizes a woman. Also, Mark King has argued that the Mixtec word for *petate* (a straw mat upon which men and women sleep) and the cornfield are morphological reversals of one another (King 1988). These practices and beliefs suggest that just as human fertility requires the union of males and females, and the fecundity of the soil requires the complementarity of the Rain and Earth, so too corn production requires the complementarity of the male farmer and the daughter of Rain and Earth.

What is the significance of the idea that marriage is like the process by which rain falls on the ground and corn grows, where corn is the daughter of the Earth and Rain, and that it becomes a "bride" to the farmer? For one, it reflects a theme I discussed earlier, concerning the Nuyooteco view of marriage as essential to life. Taking a person in marriage, as we saw, allows the household to replace aged members and reproduce itself. The household is, in turn, essential to the survival of its members. By equating marriage with corn production, connubial relations become as necessary to life as consuming basic subsistence foods. And if it were not for the marriage of men with the daughter of the Earth and Rain, human life could not continue.

The parallels Nuyootecos draw between the processes of corn growth and the processes by which a woman is brought into her "true household" in marriage also show the degree to which households need one another to survive. No household can exist in isolation; its continuity depends upon its insertion in a nexus of interhousehold ties. Furthermore, this nexus of ties is not restricted to human households. The *nu ñu'un* live in their houses underground, the *ñu'un savi* are found in the "Rain houses," and, as we will see, the saints reside in the church, the *ve ñu'un*, "house of the sacred." In other words, if it is true that a household needs other households to survive, then it is the totality of ties among all households—not just those of human beings—that is crucial to life.

This last observation suggests that the "social," for Nuyootecos, must be expanded in the same way that our enumeration of households must be expanded. For example, people frequently describe sacrifices at the Rain houses as they do a visit to a human household, and as we will see, the dead return to eat with the living. But to see the full implication this has for Nuyooteco ideas about their lives together, we should first examine the figure of Jesus, since he occupies a strategic place in Nuyooteco thinking about the social, the organic, and the sacred.

CHAPTER 5

JESUS, THE SUN

DURING much of the time I resided in Nuyoo I lived in a house in the town center, which was lent to me by a family I became friendly with in 1983. Next door lived a man named Tañuu Andrés Sarabia López. Tañuu Andrés never had much time for me, unless he was drinking, and then he would come by at odd hours to chat. One morning, about 5:00 A.M., he poked his head in my door as I was making coffee. I invited him to have some with me, and, after I poured him a cup, we sat on a bench outside. As the sky began to brighten, Tañuu Andrés asked if I believed the earth orbits the sun every day. Not wishing to take sides in what was obviously a matter of some importance for him, I tried to duck his question by saying that this is what the teachers say in school. He then told me that he didn't believe it. I asked why, and he took my hand and dipped it in a nearby puddle. The water felt warm in the chill morning air, and Tañuu Andrés asked, "Why would the water feel warm if there wasn't something heating it from below?"

By dipping my hand in the puddle, Tañuu Andrés attempted to prove an ancient Mesoamerican proposition that after the sun sets in the west, it passes under us, heading toward the east, where it rises again the next day. The water in the pool felt warm, Tañuu Andrés reckoned, because the sun had been beneath us.

When Nuyootecos talk about this movement of the sun, they use the term *jiko tiu*, which can describe any revolving or spinning motion. *Jiko tiu* also implies that in revolving or spinning some kind of alternation occurs. Thus, with the proper qualifier, *jiko* can be used for the swinging back and forth of a cradle, or the circling climb of a mountain (Campbell et al. 1986; Pensinger 1974).

Of course, many things alternate with the sun's revolution, not least among them day and night. But what I want to draw attention to is how, from the Nuyooteco point of view, the sun goes on to mediate the division it creates. For example, people say the dead dwell in the *ñuu ánima*, which is under the earth, the place the sun illuminates at

118

night. When the dead come to join their relatives on All Saints' Day, they are able to pass into the world of the living just as the sun dawns—that is, when the sun is between the earth and the sky (see also Klein 1982).

In Christian thinking, Jesus, who dies and comes back to life, is the great mediator, and it is not surprising that Nuyootecos would identify him with the sun (He is, according to one man, the "face" of Sun, just as the *nu ñu'un* are a face of Earth.) But what most concerns me here is how Jesus' creative acts defined a process by which all diverse entities may by mediated, not only the Earth and Sky or the dead and the living. To see this, let us turn to a group of four images of Jesus that play a large role in Nuyooteco ritual life: Santo Niño, Misericordia, Santa Cruz, and Santo Entierro.

THE JESUS SAINTS

There can be little doubt that Spanish priests introduced images such as Santo Niño and Santo Entierro early on, since they portray Jesus at different stages in his life and, in so doing, illustrate the central mysteries of the Catholic faith. The image of Santo Entierro, for example, is an articulated Christ that can be hung on the cross, then taken down, its arms folded and placed in a glass coffin, in a reenactment of the Passion. Yet Nuyootecos I spoke with group these saints together as a set not only because they each represent a stage in the life of Jesus, but also because these saints are, at different times of the year, taken from the altar of their mayordomos and circulated among the households in the community.

Misericordia, Santa Cruz, and Santo Entierro are similar to other mayordomía sains in that they are represented by two images: a large image kept in the church, and a smaller one in the house of the mayordomo. The small images of Misericordia, Santo Entierro, and Santa Cruz are the ones that visit the households, each borne on the back of a man known as the *cargador.* The mayordomo also goes with the saint, along with at least one of the church caretakers. Others may also accompany them, such as the sons of the mayordomo and the cargador.

When Misericordia circulates among the households, the group carrying it sets out at dawn on the first day, usually a Monday in early January, and, after resting on Sundays, completes the rounds in about two weeks. After the party arrives at a household, the cargador enters with the image and sets it on the household altar. One of those who accompany him places a cup of holy water nearby, which the members of the household use to bless themselves. Household members then kneel and pray before the image, burn incense, and perhaps light a candle. A member of the household, usually the eldest person present, prays to the saint for abundant crops, fertile animals, and the health of the children of the household. Then household members offer sacrifices (soko) of squash, coffee, beans, eggs, fowl, fruit, and cash to the saint. The mayordomo and his assistants collect the offerings and pack them away in baskets. People usually offer the mayordomo and his party something to drink and eat. After chatting a while, the men take up their loads and set off for the next household. They visit every Nuyooteco household, no matter how isolated and difficult to reach.

The mayordomos of Santa Cruz and Santo Entierro circulate their saints in March or April, several weeks before Easter. They differ from Misericordia in that instead of setting off singly, they make the rounds together, dividing the households between them. One saint goes to the settlements of Yucunino, Yucubey, and Loma Bonita, in the high, cold zone of the municipality, and the other goes to Zaragoza, Tierra Azul, and Unión y Progreso, located in the temperate to semitropical region. When the parties carrying the two images arrive back at Nuyoo Center, they divide the center's households between them, one visiting one half, the other visiting the other half. Since these saints individually have much less territory to cover than Misericordia, it takes their parties only about a week to visit all the households in the community.

During their rounds, each saint receives a large quantity of agricultural produce in sacrifice. The mayordomo must continuously transport these goods to his house in the center, or else their loads will grow so heavy they will not be able to carry them. When the party returns from their rounds of the households, the mayordomo begins to sell some of the corn, beans, squash and other foodstuffs. Alternatively, he may choose to sell some of this food along the route, to ease the burden.[1]

1. This distribution of foodstuffs within the community has three distinct advantages. First, no profit motive enters into the sale of these items, and they are sold at a price well below that set by the market. The exception to this is the main cash crop, coffee, which is not sold to other Nuyootecos because each household tends to be self-sufficient in what they consume. Rather, coffee is sold to the wholesale buyers who come to Nuyoo to purchase the crop. Second, in the case of Misericordia, the sale of the sacrificial offerings tends to circulate crops from the households in one environmental zone to the households in another. When the saint arrives in the warmer reaches of Nuyoo territory, it brings with it crops from the higher, colder region, which are sought by households searching for

People explicitly link the circulation of the Jesus saints among the households of Nuyoo to the set of myths about Jesus' travels that I introduced in chapter 1. In many Mixtec communities, stories such as these are called *shemblu*, from the Spanish word *ejemplo*, or "example." Storytellers explain that they call them "examples" because they teach moral lessions (see also Taggart 1983:161). Thus, when I would ask why it is so important that we offer food and water to travelers, Nuyootecos would cite the story of the man who refused hospitality to Jesus as the reason. In citing these myths, and in placing a heavy emphasis on the behavior of Jesus and other actors, we can see that morality is not so much discursively given, in abstract codes or precepts, but through exemplary practices. As we will see, these original exemplary practices constitute what we might call "revelation" *(natuvi* in Mixtec), and a long line of exemplary figures, or prophets, have appeared in Nuyoo. But what I want to make clear here is that many Nuyooteco rituals, and in particular the mayordomos' carrying of the Jesus saints from house to house in their annual circuits, are concerned with recreating the interactions of humans with the gods. In the same way Jesus confronted the man in the story with the choice of putting himself in the place of a hungry and thirsty visitor or turning the visitor away, so too the mayordomo's party confront Nuyootecos with a similar choice, giving them the opportunity to emulate the original actors and also experience this sacred event. After all, what they carry is more than a simple representation of the god—as is true of all saints' images, it is the actual god in its concrete, physical form—so the line between ritual and moral action becomes exceedingly difficult to draw.

As I noted at the outside of this chapter, my concern is with how the movement of Jesus/the Sun defines a general process of mediation. In

---

diversity in their diet. People in Tierra Azul or Zaragoza are very happy to ease the burden of the mayordomo by purchasing the upland squash, pulque, and potatoes he brings with him. Finally, the sacrificial items that are not sold along the route are sold in the house the mayordomo's household maintains in the town center. This creates a well-stocked store in the center, where people can purchase needed foodstuffs. Until the 1950s, no permanent store existed in Nuyoo, and the Sunday market was not established until the 1930s. Older, itinerant merchants who worked in the region before the 1960s have many stories about the difficulty they had finding food for sale. Even today the four or five stores in the center are poorly stocked, and they do not sell staples. The sale of the items collected in sacrifice by the mayordomos of Misericordia, Santa Cruz, and Santo Entierro thus creates an effective system of distribution of locally produced goods within the community, goods that would not otherwise have been so readily circulated. When the other 20 mayordomos who also sell goods are added to this total, they come to form a fairly complex distributional network, making a variety of products available to the members of the community.

this context, it is important to point out that when Jesus set off on his travels, he did so not long after the sun's cataclysmic birth (which is also associated with the birth of Jesus). This was a time of creation, when the amoral and asocial world of the tiumi ended and the world of cristianos was brought into being. The interactions Jesus had with the people of the households were part of these creative events. Specifically, Jesus' visits defined society as made up of independent household units and established the manner in which people of different households are to live together, by instituting actions of social mediation. As we will see in chapter 13, Nuyootecos trace the origin of gift exchange to an incident that occurred during Jesus' travels. Here I want to examine the link between Jesus and the institutions of marriage and ritual kinship, by examining the parallels Nuyootecos draw between the ritual circulation of the saint's images from house to house and the persons who travel from house to house via baptismal and marriage rites.

Santo Niño and the Transfer of Persons at Baptism

At first, the criterion by which Nuyootecos group Misericordia, Santa Cruz, and Santo Entierro together—that they annually make their rounds of the households in Nuyoo—does not appear to hold for Santo Niño, the image of the Christ Child. The mayordomo of Santo Niño does not carry the saint on a circuit through the six hamlets, nor does the saint enter each Nuyooteco household on an annual round. However, Santo Niño is central to the *posadas*, a Christmas ritual celebrated throughout Mexico in which people reenact the search of Mary and Joseph for an inn to spend the night. In Nuyoo, this reenactment conforms to a logic where people's participation as members of households is fundamental social action, and where food sharing is the highest form of ethical behavior. Thus, when the religious officials take the images of Mary and Joseph out of the church to go on their search for a place to spend the night, instead of turning the images away, people take them in to their homes and lodge them there through the night.

Each stage of this ritual begins in the early evening of the day after the saints arrive at the house of their hosts. People gather in the patio of the house, and members of the household serve them chocolate, coffee, bread, and perhaps liquor. The musicians are also usually present, to entertain the crowd and play for the saints. Then, after a few hours of prayers, chatting, and listening to the music, it is time for the saints to leave. People carry the saints in procession to the door of another household, where the saints are again lodged for the night. This continues, night after night, until the saints reach the house of the mayordomo of Niño Jesus, on December 23.

The total number of houses that receive the saints is nine, since they go to only one house each night, and the posadas last from December 16th to December 24th. Those who wish the saints to visit make their requests to the mayordomo, who tells them which day is open. By the beginning of the posadas, all the households the saints will visit have been selected. As Christmas approaches (the fiesta of Santo Niño), the number of people who gather each night to accompany the saint grows, and the meals the host households serve become more elaborate.

While the imperative that people show hospitality to Joseph and Mary is one reason Nuyootecos place the Santo Niño image among the other saints that circulate among the households, and the nine households it visits can be seen as iconic of all Nuyooteco households, it is also true that a great number of Nuyootecos have ritual contact with the Santo Niño image as part of the Christmas Eve celebrations.

On December 22, religious officials carry the saints to the house of the fiscal, the church caretaker. On the next evening (i.e., the night preceding the fiesta of Santo Niño), the fiscal serves meals of tortillas and beans to all who arrive for the procession. This celebration is much more elaborate than the one sponsored by those who receive the saint prior to the fiscal, since the fiscal celebrates a fiesta (viko) and sponsorship is part of his household's cargo duties. In contrast, the houses that have lodged the saints prior to December 22 have done so voluntarily, and cargo obligations do not require them to make a large expenditure.

On December 23, the saints are sent on their way again. By the time the saints are ready to leave, the number of people present will have swelled to several hundred, and all prepare to accompany the procession of the saints to the house of the mayordomo of Santo Niño. Their arrival at the house of the mayordomo, late in the evening of the 23rd, or early on the morning of the 24th, marks the beginning of the fiesta of Santo Niño, which lasts from December 24 to December 25. This is one of the largest fiestas celebrated in Nuyoo, and many hundreds of Nuyootecos gather to participate in the rituals.

A man known as the "godfather" of the Santo Niño plays a critical role in the Christmas Eve ceremonies. He is the one who builds and decorates the crib where the Santo Niño image will be placed when it arrives at the house of the mayordomo and who dresses the image in proper clothing. He is also the one who keeps a list of all those who wish to carry the Santo Niño from the church (it is not included with the images in the processions of the first week of the posadas) to the house of the mayordomo. The image is about half a meter in length and weighs only a few kilograms. Each person who wishes to carry the saint makes a donation to the godfather (about 50 pesos in 1984), which he invests in colorful trinkets for the crib. On the night of the procession, each person on the list waits for his or her name to be called. When a person's name is called, he or she approaches the head of the procession, receives the saint, cradles it for a few steps, and then passes it to the next person called. The names on the list easily surpass 100 and include both children and adults. Those in charge organize things so that everyone on the list has a chance to carry the saint before the procession reaches the house of the mayordomo—an event that occurs about midnight—which sometimes requires that the procession make several circuits around the church. When the procession arrives at the house of the mayordomo, the "godfather" places the Santo Niño in the crib, and the mayordomo serves everyone a meal while the prayermakers chant and the musicians play.

To see why the Santo Niño is included among the saints that circulate among Nuyooteco households, I want to return to the earlier discussion of ritual kinship, or compadrazgo. Recall that compadrazgo tries are created when parents decide to "give" their child to another couple. This other couple then brings the child into their household as if it were one of their own. This is the first time the godchild has a relationship with persons outside his or her natal household, and it marks the first of a series of three life-crisis "transfers" in which everyone participates (the other two being marriage and death). Since baptism marks the first of these transfers, the godparents play a leading role in all the others. Godparents participate in the godchild's marriage negotiations, they escort their godchild—if a girl—to the house of her affines on the day of the wedding, and in death they carry their godchild to the cemetery to be buried in, what Nuyootecos say is "our true house" (see chapter 8).

In the Christmas celebration, what is significant about the procession of the Santo Niño is not just that the "godfather" of Santo Niño mediates the transfer from the church (ve ñu'un, or "sacred house") to the mayordomo house (ve'i matomo), as godfathers mediate the transfer of their godchildren from one house to another in marriage, or that the "godfather" decorates the crib and provides the saint with clothing, just as godfathers provide their godchildren with clothing when the child is baptized and married. Rather, what is significant is that each person on the list who contributes to the clothing and crib of the Santo Niño, and who cradles it on its way to the house of the mayordomo, participates in these godparent-like activities. Also, as the person carrying the saint gives it to the next person on the list, they act like parents who "give" their children to another couple in baptism. This ritual, one of the few celebrated in which most Nuyootecos participate (in the others, the Jesus saints are circulated among the various household), exhibits the same set of relationships among individuals, households, and the "child" transferred as in the institution of ritual kinship.

The Jesus Saints and the Transfer of Persons at Marriage

Both Greenberg (1981:112, 118) and Falla (1969) suggest that in rituals similar to the procession of Misericordia, Santa Cruz, and Santo Entierro elsewhere in Mesoamerica, the saint's image is associated with women given in marriage. Falla goes on to argue that the saints enter the house like wives, and then leave like daughters (Falla 1969). It think this is also true in Nuyoo, and I cite two additional pieces of evidence supporting his interpretation. The first is found in the Mixtec codices, manuscripts painted before the Spanish conquest, which are largely genealogical records of the Mixtec ruling elite. One subject that is often dealt with in the codices is the arrangement of dynastic marriages, where the bride is depicted on the back of a male porter on the way from one royal "house" to another. What is interesting about this is that when Nuyootecos carry Misericordia, Santa Cruz, and Santo Entierro from one house to another, they carry them like royal brides in the Mixtec codices—on the back of the cargador, who supports the saint with a tumpline. This suggests that just as carrying the bride from one royal house to another established royal alliances, so too Misericordia and the other saints trace the ties of alliance that marriage generates among Nuyooteco households.

The second piece of evidence that lends support to the association of Misericordia with persons given in marriage has to do with the close connection made between the movements of the Sun (which, as we have seen, has Jesus as its "face") and the movement of marriage parties, which travel to solicit the hands of women from other households. As we saw in chapter 2, marriage parties set off so as to arrive at the household of the potential bride at first light (the time when the sun is at its celestial point of mediation) and in their negotiations are said to speak "the dawning words," which indicate their sincerity.

When Misericordia's party sets off with the saint in January, they leave at dawn and travel only while the sun moves through the sky, stopping to sleep in the house of those they are visiting when the sun begins to set. In other words, the movement of marriage parties and the movement of Misericordia mirror the movement of the sun, and are both understood, like the movement of the sun, to be expressions of moral probity and expressions of the forces which renew life.

THE HEAT OF LIFE

The association of Misericordia, Santo Cruz, Santo Entierro, and Santo Niño with the young women and children transferred from one household to another brings us to my main concern in this chapter: the parallels Nuyootecos draw among baptism, marriage, the exchange of tortillas in the fiesta, the growth of corn in the soil, and the circulation of the Jesus saints among the households of Nuyoo. At the onset I want to make clear that even though I have emphasized the way corn and some of the Jesus saints are identified with marriage partners, and how the transfer of corn to people is likened to the transfer of women from one household to another, I do not mean to suggest that what is involved is a simple projection of marriage practices and sexuality onto the ritual process, corn growth, or exchange. This is because the reverse is also true. To select one example, Nuyootecos compare pregnant women to seeds that have become become wet and sprouted, so that the processes of plant growth are projected onto human sexuality as well, and it would not be possible to say that one is conceptually reduced to the other (Strathern 1980). Rather, what I plan to argue is that the transfer of women in marriage, the giving of children in baptism, the growth of corn in the fields, the pooling of tortillas in the fiesta, and the circulation of the Jesus saints are metaphorically mapped onto one another because they are each currents in a broader process which, for Nuyootecos, sustains and articulates society, nature, and the cosmos. But before discussing this further, I want to introduce one final myth about the life of Jesus.

This myth tells of the flight of Jesus from the evil velu, or "demons," who circulate among the Nuyooteco households in a ritual celebrated in the weeks leading up to Lent (see chapter 6). During his flight, Jesus stops at various households. In one, he finds a farmer sowing a field. Jesus asks the man what he is doing, and the man replies, in a surly manner, "I'm planting rocks, what do you think I am doing?" Jesus then leaves and goes to another house, where he also finds a man sowing. Again he asks what the man is planting, and again he receives a sarcastic response, since the man tells him he is sowing trees. Because of the men's rude replies, Jesus suspects they are of low character and will not help him escape from the velu, so he moves on to a third house. Again, Jesus finds a farmer sowing, but this time the man answers Jesus' question respectfully, telling him that he is planting corn. Jesus spends the night in the man's house, eats with him, and then goes on his way the next morning. As a reward, Jesus causes the man's corn to sprout and ripen overnight, so that when the man looks out on his field he sees that it is full of tall, green corn plants. In contrast, the first man finds nothing but big rocks growing in his cornfield, and the second nothing but tall trees. Later, when the velu arrive at the house of the third man looking for Jesus, he tells them that he has indeed seen Jesus go by, but some time ago, since Jesus passed when the man was sowing his cornfield. "You can see," he says to the velu, "that the corn is now ripe," implying that may months have passed and that the trail is now cold.

Like the man who refused Jesus food and water in the earlier myth, the men who are uncouth and inhospitable return to a primitive state, since the rapid growth of rocks and trees in cornfields is a feature of the era of the tiumi. This is a subject I will pick up again in chapter 11. What I want to highlight here is the way their inhospitable behavior is linked to their production of corn (and, by implication, to the sustenance of their households) since the myth illustrates a connection between moral action and the ability to turn natural processes of growth and reproduction to human use.

Crop fertility, reproduction, and the prosperity of the household are also themes found in the ritual circulation of Misericordia from house to house. Recall that when the saint arrives at a house, the inhabitants treat it with great reverence and "feed" it a large sacrifice. The head of the household then petitions the saint for many children, abundant crops, health, and fertile animals.

In this context, I should point out that Nuyootecos often call Jesus "the man of *yii*." Yii can be glossed as potency, vitality, or fecundity. People consider yii to be that which gives us strength and energy, and most bodily parts can be understood in terms of their role in the provision, distribution, and utilization of yii (Young 1981:46). The source of yii for the body is food, principally the tortilla. When I would tell Tañuu Simón Rojas that my family did not eat tortillas in the United States, he would say to me, "I am a coward if I don't eat tortillas." Without the yii he receives from the tortilla he would be fainthearted, timorous, and unable to work. The tortilla, he said "puts yïï" in people.

The center of yïï for the human body is what Nuyootecos call the ánima, which they associate with the heart and blood. *Ánima* can also be found in the head, hair, nail clippings, and bodily excreta, such as the sweat that clings to clothing (it enters and leaves through the joints and navel). When people lose ánima, and the yïï it contains, their entire organism breaks down. They will not be able to eat, and they will have no energy to work. Even the mind will be affected, since yïï is what determines our ability to think, to understand, and to act in a rational manner.[2]

A tangible sign of the presence or absence of yïï (and ánima) is heat. A warm body is healthful and vigorous, while a lack of body heat, when one becomes "cold," is a sure sign that one's yïï has drained away. Similarly, when people who have lost their ánima have it returned to them through the efforts of a curer, they will feel their head immediately heat up. They are once again "full of yïï."

The most potent source of yïï in the universe is Sun. As we saw in chapter 1, Nuyootecos consider Sun to be the ánima of God, almost an oversoul. The yïï this powerful ánima emits illuminates and heats the world. When I would stand talking in front of my house with Tañuu Andrés Sarabia early in the morning, and the sun's first rays warmed us, he would sometimes say to me "I have now become full of yïï" *(ya nu teeyïïn)*.

Like Sun, Nuyootecos speak of the Earth and Rain as substances that are full of yïï. Earth supplies yïï in the ores and gems that miners find in their excavations. It also supplies yïï in the wild animals that men take in the hunt. Most importantly, it provides yïï through the *nu ñu'un*, who "work" so that plants may grow. "How is it," one man asked, "that we plant only four kernels of corn, and Earth produces several whole cobs?" In each case, the fecundity of Earth is a function of its "yïï." It is interesting that Nuyootecos call the yield on money loaned out at interest the yïï of the money, since it has the same increment-producing quality.

2. Yïï is not evenly distributed among people. Nuyootecos say that differences in strength, leadership ability, and political standing are the result of differences in how much yïï (or, as they sometimes put it, how "hot") individuals are. Men, for example, have more yïï than women, which is demonstrated in their superior strength. Thus some men who cannot lift heavy loads are said to have "the blood of a woman." The cacique, who is the most powerful man in Nuyoo, is felt to have the "hottest" blood of all, and therefore the most yïï. The surfeit of yïï that he and men like him possess gives them an aggressiveness and personal stamina that places them far ahead of others.

Rain is also full of yɨɨ. *Fuerza vi ya kuvi ñu'un savi,* "the *ñu'un savi* is potent," the late Lorenzo Rojas once said to me. Like Earth, Rain is necessary for the incremental growth of plants and for the yield of the harvest on which human livelihood depends. The regenerative power contained in Rain can be seen in the practice of spraying water on people who are ill. The water has the effect of reanimating the sick person, just as spraying water on wilted plants causes them to revive *(nake'eni,* "recover strength," which is used synonymously with *nake'e teeyɨɨ).* As we will see in chapter 9, people also attempt to stimulate the sacred and natural production of yɨɨ through sacrifice.

Beyond its animating presence in organic and cosmological phenomena, yɨɨ is spoken of as something that circulates in social relationships. For example, sponsors of civil-religious hierarchy fiestas and life-crisis commemorations need the aid of other households to amass the goods needed for meals and rituals, and a well-attended event demonstrates that the sponsoring household is a reputable one with a large network of kin, ritual kin, and others it can count on for support. The most important and visible expression of this support are the gifts given to sponsors. Someone who gives a gift to fiesta sponsors communicates trust and affection, and the larger the gift, the more the sponsors are able to distribute. It is therefore significant that Nuyootecos describe the giving of the gift as an act in which partners "lend a word of yɨɨ" to the sponsors and that the gift increment, when partners increase the amount of the gift above what they owe, is called yɨɨ.

Nuyootecos also speak of a variety of interhousehold transactions as circulating yɨɨ. When people "let go" of a child in marriage, they say it is a transfer of yɨɨ to the house of their affines. In this case, the child allows the receiving household to renew itself by replacing senior household members. People also speak of the serving of food to passersby and the giving of a child in baptism as acts that transmit yɨɨ from the members of one house to another.

The notion that gift exchange, hospitality, marriage, and baptism are acts that circulate (and, in a sense, generate) yɨɨ suggests that social relationships are, from a Nuyooteco perspective, not so different from corporeal, organic, and cosmological processes of renewal and connection that they should be considered utterly distinct. After all, in the stories about the time that Jesus walked the earth, those who did not offer him hospitality saw their crops converted to rocks and trees. Likewise, food given in bad faith makes the people who eat it ill, and Nuyootecos understand things such as drought to be related to the breaking of social taboos.

In the last chapter I pointed out that Nuyootecos do not view the world as axiomatically divided into the organic and inorganic, or matter and spirit, but instead see a single life force underlying existence. The idea that social behavior correlates with natural phenomena should be seen in this context, since the assumption that all things are, at base, fundamentally the same implies the existence — even the logical necessity — of homologies and relations of mutual effectiveness between different phenomenal orders. But what I think specifically associates gift exchange, the giving of children in baptism, and the letting go of young women and men in marriage, with the falling of rain on the earth, the growth of corn in the soil, and the rising and setting of the sun in Nuyooteco thought is that each is a channel in a process that creates value (prosperity, renewal, fecundity) through acts of mediation between diverse, and potentially opposed, entities. This process was originally defined by the birth of the Sun, an event that ended the world of the tiumi. It was given concrete social forms in Jesus' travels from one household to another. (As we will see in chaper 13, Nuyootecos trace the origin of gift exchange to an incident that occurred during Jesus' wanderings.) Those wo refuse to participate in these acts of mediation lose control over natural processes of reproduction, as well as their place in society. They may become animals or, as in the myth cited earlier, a child (strikingly reminiscent of the Santo Niño, the icon of the godchild) tells his father that because of his inhospitable behavior he should leave the house and go to live in the bush, to be burned by the Sun, like the presocial tiumi. The tiumi, after all, lived in a primitive, socially undifferentiated, and "cold" world, where there was no agriculture, no households, no marriage, and no Sun.

CHAPTER 6

TACHI, THE WIND

In the preceding chapters I suggested that Nuyootecos imagine themselves as an association of independent households that are bound to one another by mutual necessity. This is clearest in marriage, where households replace aged members, ensuring their continuity. Yet is is also a theme found again and again in Nuyooteco statements about interhousehold relationships. For a household to sponsor a fiesta, or to carry out any number of other activities, it depends upon its ties with other households.

But if the pursuit of particular interests makes households dependent upon one another, their interests can also cause them to be opposed, and this opposition is at least as significant to life in Nuyoo as the solidarity generated by their cooperation. Underneath the elaborate etiquette of politeness characteristic of Mesoamerican people lies, in Nuyoo, an undercurrent of suspicion, fed by gossip, envy, half-truths, and sharp dealings. We can see this in a bit of advice my compadre Herminio López once gave me about how to get on in the community. He pointed down to the ground and said, "outside my household I do not even trust my own shadow." This suspicion, and fear of malice, is fed by acts of petty thievery, senseless vandalism, inexpert attempts at witchcraft, and most seriously, drunken brawls. Nuyootecos frequently label this negative undercurrent as *yatuni*, which they consider equivalent to the Spanish word *envidia*, or "envy." Yatuni—said to be "a burning pain inside oneself"—is likened to the heartburn one feels after eating too much chile. But unlike heartburn, yatuni can last for days, months, and even years. Because yatuni plays such an important role in Nuyooteco thinking about social relations, I want to discuss it in some detail.

YATUNI

Anthropologists have long considered "envy" vital to the institutional order in Mesoamerica. Fear of envy makes it a powerful, if informal, source of social control, and people's attempt to deal with it has consequences for the way they relate to one another across a variety of contexts (Foster 1967, 1972; Wolf 1955). As the advice from my compadre suggests, yatuni is something that is constantly on people's minds, and they will often go to extremes so as not to provoke it in others.

In an interesting treatment of envy, Sabini and Silver (1982:15–33) argue that acts we describe as envious are those that are taken in an attempt to prevent self-diminution. This is a good place to begin discussing Nuyooteco ideas about yatuni. For example, a man who lived near Nuyoo Center built a fine house in 1985 with the help of his sons. Not long after they moved in, he returned from his fields one afternoon to find the banana plants surrounding the house mutilated. After this, he began to leave one of his sons at home during the day, to make sure that it would not be vandalized. He told me that the person who destroyed his bananas was probably someone who did not have a house as well built as his and that the vandal felt yatuni. In other words, he and others who heard about the incident believed the vandal felt diminished by the man's achievements and then sought to protect himself by, in the man's words, "bringing me down." The vandal robbed him of one achievement, a crop of bananas, and might rob him of another, a fine house. Sabini and Silver (1982:15–33) point out that it is not always apparent that actions born of envy are related to self-protection, since the end is obscured by the method, that of harming or demeaning others. However, Nuyootecos are familiar enough with yatuni that even the slightest damage to a house, an animal, or a plant will cause them to search their memories for something they have done to provoke someone to try to "bring them down."

People in Nuyoo speak of yatuni as something that exists between groups of people, as well as between individuals. One day, not long after I had arrived in Nuyoo, I was on my way back from Yucuhiti when a Nuyoo municipal official approached me and said I should no longer visit the other town because "there has always been yatuni between us, and things will never change." At that time their differences centered on the location of a school to be built by the Secretaria de Educación Pública. But they have also competed over the location of the parish seat, the establishment of CONASUPO stores, and even over whose territory the road would pass.

One might gloss the use of the word yatuni to describe the relationship between Nuyoo and Yucuhiti as "ethnic chauvinism," since yatuni, people explain, exists among all the communities of the region and is an abiding dynamic in their relations. It is said that yatuni is why Nuyoo fought land wars with Nopalera from the end of the last century into the 1950s, why young men from Yucuyaa beat up a very drunk Simón López of Zaragoza at a fiesta, and why a group from Nuu Yuvi hacked up Victoriano Sarabia's cow, which had strayed from its pasture onto their land. What is important to note here is that many people may experience feelings of yatuni simultaneously. In the example of the school cited above, this has to do with the extent to which people's collective identities as Nuyootecos or Yucuitenses is bound up with their personal identities. When one town was enhanced over the other by the construction of a school building, the townspeople reacted as a group in the same way they might react individually to a perceived diminution of self—that is, enviously. Nuyootecos thus sometimes speak of yatuni as an element of the collective consciousness that causes people to move in a common direction.

Nuyootecos not only say that contemporary collective action is motivated by yatuni, they also identify it as a historical force. To take one example, older people explain that the campaign of Venustiano Carranza against the Oaxacan Soberanista movement led by Inés Dávila, which resulted in the invasion of the Mixteca by federal troops and the sacking of Tlaxiaco in 1916, was caused by the yatuni Carranza felt for Dávila. Dávila, who was the state governor, and who enjoyed great support in the Mixteca, provoked yatuni in Carranza because of his popularity. In this context, yatuni is a force shaping the events of the past. In giving meaning to historical events and long-term trends, the reality of yatuni becomes ever more powerful, until, as we will see, it assumes a substantial form in the Tachi, or Demon.

Although actions that Nuyootecos characterize as yatuni can be considered strategies to prevent the self from being demeaned, it is nevertheless true that using the word "envy" to translate "yatuni" can obscure both the extent to which people identify it as informing social interaction and the range of contexts in which it can appear. People resort to yatuni as an explanation for the actions of others to a degree that can be described only as chronic, implying a high level of anxiety about precedence and self-consequence that, though usually under control, can be so pervasive that it reduces social intercourse to a series of attacks and counterattacks.

Yatuni differs from our notions of envy in several important ways. One has to do with the close connection Nuyootecos draw between the experience of yatuni and states of health or illness. People describe the feeling of yatuni as "a burning pain in one's heart" or the sensation that "one's heart is aflame." One young man once told me he felt yatuni after fighting with his brother. While in this state he ate dinner, consuming several tortillas with chiles. He then became sick to his stomach and vomited. He attributed his nausea to the physiological imbalance caused by the consumption of hot foods while being "aflame" with yatuni.

The illnesses caused by a surge of yatuni can be serious. People who feel yatuni are kukuekani, "sad, lacking in energy, weak." The late Tañuu Carmen López Feria, for example, said that his bad heart was caused by the severe attack of yatuni he experienced while trying to resolve a land dispute in the 1930s. He became so enraged at the men who caused the problem that when the town police brought them before him (he was serving as a municipal official at the time), he was overwhelmed by yatuni and became dizzy and ill. From that day on he lacked the stamina to walk long distances, which he felt was a symptom of a heart damaged by yatuni.

Yatuni can also cause physical harm to those who are the objects of it. As we saw earlier, Nuyootecos often talk about relationships in terms of physical experiences. Thus, if a man travels to another's household, and the host serves him a meal that later makes him nauseated, he can be sure the man had yatuni for him and that this spoiled the food. In a similar way, someone who desires someone else's children, plants, or animals can, because of yatuni, injure them. As in the rest of the Latin world, Nuyootecos associate envy with the evil eye and say the hateful look envious people have in their eyes (ta'vini ne'yanu) can sicken children and animals and wither plants (Foster 1972:167). People need not act on their envy to harm others; merely feeling it is enough, and envy is strongly associated with illness, sterility, and death.[1]

---

1. People draw an interesting contrast between the state of being *kusɨɨni* ("healthy, content") and kukuekani, which we have seen is associated with yatuni. On one level this contrast is simply one that distinguishes those who enjoy good health from those who are sick. But on another level, this contrast has to do with sociability. This is because one who is kusɨɨni is said to enjoy the good fellowship of others. The times people say they are most kusɨɨni is when they are in a fiesta, which is, as we have seen, a period of intense interaction, where large prestations are made and where key communal symbols are activated. What this suggests is that health, the proximate cause of which is a surfeit of "the heat of life," is associated with those times when people are joyous of one another's presence, i.e., times when they are kusɨɨni. By contrast, the state of being kukuekani is associated with solitude. Thus people say that one who is kukuekani "wanders alone" and "feels abandoned."

In causing harm to those who are the objects of it, as well as those who feel it, yatuni works through the blood and ánima, or heart. The bad heart of Carmen López is one example, another being the idea that nightmares are caused by those who have yatuni for the dreamer. For Nuyootecos, the dream represents the wanderings of the ánima when it separates from the body. I noted earlier that the heart and blood are seats of the ánima, and blood channels yii through the body. Yatuni thus diminishes bodily yii by harming the blood and ánima. This will become important below, when we consider the way demons make people ill.

Finally, yatuni differs from envy in that it is the covering category for a wide range of antisocial acts. An act that is *ta'vini*, "hateful, bitter," such as an irritable reply to a question, is *yatuni*. An act that is *ku'vini*, "cranky," such as passing by someone without uttering a greeting, is yatuni. An act that is kuasunni, "miserly," such as the failure to be generous with one's food, and, by extension, the desire to remain unmarried (see chapter 11), is yatuni. Finally, an act that is *u'vini*, "malicious," such as setting fire to a mountainside, is yatuni. While the focus of *yatuni* may be, like envy, a concern with self-protection, it also embraces almost everything that is negative in social interaction. Those who have it, like the person who passes without offering a greeting, are unsociable, or fail to participate in good faith in the formal arrangements so crucial to communal life. "People with yatuni are like dogs," one man explained: "they do not think or rationalize, they only strike." They are absolutely bad *(niva'a)*, just as the person who is sociable, who demonstrates hospitality, and who shares is "good" *(va'a)*.

The negative and self-defeating nature of yatuni is illustrated by a story Nuyootecos tell of a golden age in the distant past, when rainfall was always abundant, at least two ears of corn sprouted on every cornstalk, and humans grew strong and tall. People owed this prosperity to the efforts of the many tenuvi who lived in Nuyoo. The tenuvi, or "Rain People," are sacrificers who mediate Nuyooteco relationships with Rain (see chapter 15). But people grew envious of the abilities of the tenuvi and denounced them ("like cowards," one man said) to state authorities. Police arrived and imprisoned the tenuvi at a place called Yoshi Ki'vi. The moment the tenuvi left, it stopped

---

We can conclude from this that health and illness are closely associated with the relationships people have with others. Being kukuekani is, like yatuni, something that cuts one off from others; being kusiini means one is connected to others.

raining, and the drought that followed caused the harvest to be lost. Within a short time, animals died of thirst and people began to starve. Nuyootecos sent out a commission to ask the tenuvi to return, but only two came back. These two were able to relieve the drought, but Nuyootecos never again enjoyed the prosperity they did before the tenuvi were arrested.

This story shows that by allowing yatuni to influence them into driving their neighbors out, Nuyootecos destroyed the basis of their own well-being. Yatuni may be part of life, but it is a serious threat. Yatuni is something one should try to repress, and those who allow it to get the better of them are said to be, like the people in the story, "cowards" *(sïïni*—literally, "feminine inside"). In contrast, Nuyootecos admire those who control their impulse to act on the yatuni they feel (as they put it, a "brave" individual) and identify them as good leaders.

In illustrating the consequences of unconstrained yatuni, the story also shows that *yatuni* is opposed to the values that acts of mediation and exchange produce. Thus, if the interaction of Sky and Earth through Rain produce crop fertility, then *yatuni* is associated with drought and famine. It has been broadly recognized that envy is provoked by a violation of reciprocity in Mesoamerican societies (e.g., Dow 1986:84–85; Greenberg 1989:202–3). But what the Nuyoo material goes on to suggest is that *yatuni* is not so much an anomaly, coming into play only when there is a break in normative patterns, but a form of sociation not premised on exchange. This will be important for our examination of *Tachi,* the incarnation of *yatuni.*

THE TACHI

The focus of Nuyooteco thinking about yatuni is the Tachi, which we might translate as "the Demon." However, people sometimes refer to the Tachi as *ya'vi* or *ya u'vi, yaa* being the prefix for sacredness, and *u'vi* a synonym for yatuni. The Tachi, people say, is "sacred envy" (cf. Ingham 1986:105).

Of all the "supernaturals" Nuyootecos distinguish, the Tachi is by far the most immediate to people's experience. Nuyootecos seem to confront the Tachi, unlike the saints or the *ñu'un savi,* on an almost daily basis, passing it on the trails at night, meeting it in their dreams, and suffering from the illness it causes. Many treatments local curers specialize in are designed to ward off the harmful effects of the Tachi, and people wear amulets and take potions to protect themselves from its influence.

The association of the Tachi with yatuni goes back to initial acts of creation. As Nuyootecos tell the story, both Jesus and the Tachi were going to be "grand" *(kuña'nu)*, but the Tachi became envious of Jesus. This caused it to compete with Jesus, by doing the opposite of what Jesus did. Where Jesus — the Sun — grew hot *(itni)*, the Tachi grew cold *(viji)*. Where Jesus was truthful *(nijia)*, the Tachi became deceitful *(shina'vi)*. Where Jesus acted virtuously *(va'a)*, the Tachi acted badly *(nduva'a)*. Where the work of Jesus was good, that of the Tachi was sinful (kuachi) or "envious" (yatuni, or u'vini). As Jesus created people and animals, the Tachi imitated him. However, because the Tachi created things out of envy, its brood ("the children of the Tachi"), turned out to be harmful things like snakes, scorpions, toads, and people unable to talk, walk, or hear. (Nuyootecos say those with some physical deformity have a special sensitivity to the Tachi. Thus the blind are able to "see" the Tachi, and the deaf are able to "hear" it.) The Tachi, then, is matched with Jesus as a creative force, and yatuni is one of the underpinnings of existence.

The Faces of the Tachi

As we saw in chapter 4, Nuyootecos are monists in the sense that they feel the human body, the gods, nature, and society to be animated by the same sacred force. It is true that this generalized force — yïi — has specific manifestations, or properties. Thus far I have discussed Sun, Earth, and Rain. But as Louise Burkhart points out, in this theology distinctions between creator and created, the spiritual and the material, the source and its particular expressions are unimportant (Burkhart 1989). We thus saw that Ñu'un Savi is both an anthropomorphized being (the "saint" of the Rain) and a natural force (the rain cloud). In the same way, people speak of the Tachi as being both a human form and a generalized, natural force. Thus, in addition to "Demon," Tachi is "Wind."

The wind is a particularly destructive phenomenon for Nuyootecos. I saw why in December 1984, when strong, dry winds blew through the Nuyoo canyons, ripping off the roofs of houses, downing fruit trees, shredding the leaves of plants, and knocking over the cornstalks heavy with ripe ears. The damage was considerable. The gusts blew the blossoms off the coffee plants and fruit trees, reducing the following year's harvest by almost two-thirds. Later, in early 1985, the dried brush caught fire and burned out of control for several weeks, destroying acres of coffee, bananas, oranges, and other fruit trees, and even burning one man to death. The Wind is a force that robs life and causes starvation. It is desiccating, and opposed to the growth and fertility brought by Rain. It is for good reasons Nuyootecos say that when the Wind blows, the Tachi is present. In one story the Tachi is associated with the whirlwind. In another, the Tachi has a black donkey as its son, which it sent to kick down corn plants, just as the Wind may knock down the milpa when it whips through the top-heavy plants. The Tachi is opposed to anything that is fecund and life bearing (cf. Ingham 1986:106–10).

Thus far I have spoken of the Tachi as if it were a single entity, but Tachi, like Sun, Earth, and Rain, is a force with a variety of expressions or "faces" distinguished by the places in which they are manifest and the properties associated with them. The main faces of Tachi are the *tachi tuun*, "the black tachi," the *tachi kuka*, "the wealthy tachi," the *tachi si'i*, "the female tachi," and the *tachi niyi*, "the tachi of the cadaver."[2] But before discussing these, I want to mention briefly the "children" of Tachi.

The children of Tachi. As I noted earlier, Nuyootecos say that when Jesus created useful animals, the Tachi responded by creating its "children" *(se'ya* Tachi): snakes, buzzards, toads, scorpions, opossums, black cats, and a kind of lizard *(chile niñi).*[3] The dog and the pig are two

2. Nuyootecos distinguish another kind of Tachi, called *tachi ñu'un,* or "tachi of the earth." When the *tachi ñu'un* come up in conversation, people often refer to those places that make people sick, or areas identified as *sheen* ("extremely fierce," "easily angered"). Such places are sheen because people are made sick around them, even though they gave only a slight offense, or in some cases did nothing at all to deserve punishment. In other words, the tachi ñu'un is a kind of nu ñu'un that consistently acts in a malicious way *(sa'a kini).* It is also called the *nu ñu'un kini,* "polluting nu ñu'un," because it may attempt to frighten someone by either sending a snake across their path or causing them to have horrible dreams *(ñani kini,* or *ñani sheen).* Dreams of dogs, snakes, pigs, and black cats, all of which are animals of the Tachi and *kiti kini ("kini* animals"), are a sign that the dreamer or someone close to him or her will suffer a loss of ánima.

The reason I am hesitant about including tachi ñu'un among the other kinds of Tachi is that some people—primarily those who have been to the Isthmus of Tehuantepec, a region where many have converted to Evangelical Protestantism—have begun to equate the nu ñu'un with the Biblical fallen angels. One man who spent time on the Isthmus considered all the nu ñu'un to be Tachi, or *tentación* ("temptation") and evil, even though he did continue to pray to them for good crops. Older people who have not left the community do not consider the nu ñu'un to be Tachi, although they do say the nu ñu'un do, on occasion, act maliciously. While the classification of the "wrathful" nu ñu'un as a tachi may be an expression of the duality of Mesoamerican religious thought, where the pantheon is often made up of paired opposites, I think the idea of the tachi ñu'un may be due to a "Biblical" interpretation of the local cosmology, where things of the Earth are equated with Satan.

3. Nuyootecos view the buzzard as a particularly loathsome animal. It feeds on rotten meat and has a foul smell. The buzzard, people say, is the form in which dogs see the tachi. The buzzard, also, as one man put it, "exposes lies," since its habit of circling in the skies over carrion shows where thieves butchered stolen animals or, in more dramatic cases, where a murderer left the

other animals sometimes associated with Tachi. Besides calling them the "children of Tachi," Nuyootecos refer to these animals as the "herd" of Tachi *(sana)* and the "angels of Tachi" and classify them as *kiti kini,* "disgusting" or "polluting" animals. Some also say that these "children" are born of the union between a *tachi tuun* and women who have died without bearing children.[4]

The snake is the foremost of the children of Tachi. There are many different kinds of snakes in the region, and each—even the smallest and most harmless—is feared. One reason is that people believe snakes make them ill. For example, snakes may give people the evil eye, just as people who feel yatuni may give others the evil eye. One theory about malaria holds that people are infected with the disease by mosquitoes that have bitten snakes and then bite humans.

Given the harm snakes can cause, people say that when they see one, it is their duty to try to kill it. Once it is dead, its carcass should

---

victim's body. Nuyootecos say several categories of people are like buzzards. I have heard a group of gossiping and envious women referred to as "buzzards." For example, a man and a woman who married someone considerably younger than themselves were called "buzzards." In fact, parents warn their children not to throw stones at buzzards lest they grow up and marry someone older than themselves. This is not a good thing, since the older partner in the marriage saps the *yɨ* of the younger partner during the sexual act, which rapidly ages the younger person.

The lizard, or *chile niñi* ("blood lizard"), is dangerous since it will creep up on an unsuspecting person and, through its glance, suck their blood. This will leave them weak and dizzy. When a chile niñi has sucked someone's blood, its neck becomes bright red and its eyes a deep blue. Like the snake and the buzzard, the chile niñi is found where there is strife and discord. It is always near when a murder occurs or when compadres fight, and even when someone sets fire to a hillside or cuts down corn plants.

The toad also appears in contexts where people "sin." Like the chile niñi, it causes people to become ill by sucking their blood. People say they sometimes discover toads near people who lie sick in bed, where it has crept so as to make the illness more serious. As one man explained, "[just as a person] who has yatuni for us gives more strength to an illness [we suffer]," so too "the toad squeezes *[shini'i]* a person, leaving the victim weak."

4. The children of Tachi are clearly matched with the children of the Rain. The counterpart of the *chile niñi,* "the blood lizard," is the *chile savi,* the "lizard of the Rain"; the counterpart of the toad is the frog; the counterparts of the buzzard are birds like the hawk or eagle; and the snake is matched with the *koo savi.* These different sets of children are also clearly opposites. Where the chile savi is associated with health, order, fertility, and life, the chile niñi is associated with sin, disorder, pollution, and death. This opposition is used as an explanation by Nuyootecos for unusual occurrences. Thus when lightning struck a house in one of the Nuyoo hamlets, people speculated that a toad might have gotten inside and crawled under a bed, since lightning, because of its strong link to Rain, seeks to destroy the children of Tachi.

Another opposition at work in these stories is that between creatures of the Earth and those of the Sky (see note 2). Earth and Sky may complement one another, and their interaction is productive of new life, but, like households, they can also be in conflict with each other.

be placed out of the way; if anyone steps on it, his or her feet may fester. Also, if the snake was killed with a machete, then the blade should be carefully cleaned, either with rubbing alcohol or by urinating on it. Otherwise the blood of the snake will cause the machete to break. The person who killed the snake should also bathe in rubbing alcohol, since it will counteract any of the ills that might befall someone who killed a child of Tachi.

One kind of snake merits special mention, the *koo tuun*, "black snake" or *tilcoate* in Spanish.[5] I bring this up not only because it is the most fearsome of the children of Tachi, but also because people encounter it when they have illicit sexual affairs. Some say the snake coils around its victim, sticks its tongue in the victim's ear, and lashes him with its tail. Alternatively, it may hang the victim upside down from a tree branch. This is significant because it shows that Tachi is a tangible presence in human interaction. Thus, Nuyootecos say that when a *tachi tiu*, or whirlwind, passes through a group of people, they will begin fighting, and the course of the fight will trace the path of the whirlwind. Similarly, people tell the story of a blind man who saw a tachi step into a jar of pulque from which several men were drinking, and the men then began to fight with one another.

What the whirlwind and jar of pulque stories show is that Tachi is at once a natural force, a supernatural being, a corporeal substance, a form of relatedness, and as we will see below, a social type, and Nuyootecos do not feel compelled to draw meaningful distinctions among them. To cite one final example, people in Yucuhiti tell of a man who was on his way to see his paramour when four *koo tuun* slithered out of the grass and attacked his horse. They wrapped themselves around the legs of the animal, which became paralyzed with fear. It was only when the man's sister placed tobacco and chile on the snakes that they released the horse and slithered away. The point here is that it was the man's setting off to consummate an illicit affair that caused the snakes to appear, and Nuyootecos can list many examples where immoral conduct is marked by the simultaneous appearance of the children of the Tachi.

---

5. The *koo yuu* is also an interesting "snake." This is a creature that flies through the air at night, whizzing by people's heads like a bullet. One man told me it is yellow and lives in holes in the ground, fissures in cliffs, and holes in trees. It can be seen as it sticks its head out of its "house" to look at passersby. I suspect that the *koo yuu* is a bat, which Blaffer (1972) said is associated with the "black man" of Zinacantan.

The tachi tuun. The *tachi tuun*, people say, are "the enemy" *(enemigu)*. They are the most sinister face of Tachi, and Nuyootecos call them *nasi* and *yo'vi*, terms that also apply to rich, strong, and violent men.

While *tachi tuun* can be translated as the "black" or "dark" tachi, most people feel they have fair-to-brown skin and are not dark at all. Their blackness has to do with their association with nighttime, the period when they are most active, and the oppositional quality dark has with light, such as the light of Jesus/the Sun. The color black is also associated with yatuni, so that the statement that someone has a black face means they are full of hate and envy.

The *tachi tuun* are also said to have curly hair. Blaffer (1972) suggests that for the Maya, the curly hair of the demon may be the result of its association with the Moors. In the Nuyoo case, two additional reasons for the curly hair of the *tachi tuun* suggest themselves. The first has to do with the coastal region of Oaxaca and Guerrero, which Nuyootecos are familiar with from their trips there to trade for salt. Everyone considers the coastal region a violent place, and a journey there is fraught with danger. In many stories, men encounter a tachi while on their way to the coast, or it arrives in Nuyoo from the direction of the coast. The coast is the home of several towns whose inhabitants are the descendants of African slaves, and the curly—even kinky—hair of the *tachi tuun* may be related to the physical characteristics of coastal populations. A second reason for the curly hair of the *tachi tuun* may have to do with Nuyooteco ideas about gender. The word for kinky, curly hair immediately suggests to Mixtec speakers the pubic region, and, in particular, female genitals. As we will see, certain kinds of women are also a "face" of Tachi.

The tachi kuka. When asked who is most likely to act enviously, Nuyootecos often list three kinds of people: the rich, the poor, and women. Not surprisingly, they also associate these persons with Tachi. A case in point are the *tachi kuka*, "the rich tachi," who use their wealth to entice people, usually poor people, to sell them their souls (cf. Flanet 1977:92–93).

Tachi kuka are known by several different names. One is *tachi yii*, since yii connotes abundance and wealth. They are also known as the *tachi kava* (figure 11), because their houses are in the fissures and holes of cliffs and stone outcroppings, or *kava*. Since each rocky place has its own *tachi kava*, there are thousands of them in the world.

People say that the houses of the *tachi kuka* are like general stores, with shelves piled high with merchandise. Until recently most of the

Figure 11. A man encounters a *tachi* outside its house. As is true of other manifestations of the Nuyooteco sacred, the tachi are associated with particular kinds of places. Here we see the *tachi kava*, whose house is in sterile and rocky cliffs, or *kava*. The circle in the cliff represents the door of the tachi's house, and the arrows suggest the many directions it may go when it emerges.

stores in the region were located in the district capitals of Tlaxiaco and Putla, and all were owned by Mestizos who made their living both by selling to the largely indigenous population of the Mixteca and by acting as middlemen who purchased locally produced cash crops for resale. (These same individuals also control the political life of the district.) We have long been aware of the complex ways ethnic and class phenomena interpenetrate in this kind of situation (e.g., Stavenhagen 1975), and Nuyootecos themselves identify ethnicity as a crucial variable in economic and political control. For example, from the late 1930s through the early 1960s, Spanish and Mestizo merchants paid Nuyootecos low prices for coffee and tried all kinds of tricks to put them into debt (and thereby take possession of the coffee crop). Because most Nuyootecos did not speak Spanish, which prevented them from finding other buyers or sources of credit, they had to deal with these individuals, and those who controlled the trade in coffee actively worked to prevent other buyers and sources of credit from emerging.

It is not difficult to see the parallels between coffee traders and the ideas Nuyootecos have about the *tachi kuka*. Like the *tachi kuka*, these men have not "suffered" for their wealth. As Nuyootecos say, they are people who "do no work, but are very rich." And like the tachi, who take the ánima of the poor and desperate, causing them to die before their time, the merchants make use of their superior position to buy the product of Nuyooteco labor at unjust prices. As Ingham put it for the Tlayacapanese: "The contract with the Devil reifies illicit appropriation of the peasants' labor and reproductivity, the two fundamentals of their security" (Ingham 1986:108; see also Taussig 1980).[6] Nuyootecos, moreover, see this same pernicious force behind a variety of exploiters, so that in addition to Mestizo merchants, the *tachi kuka* are portrayed as hacienda owners, government office workers, and *marijuaneros*, North American or European hippies who ride around in a Volkswagen van trying to carry people off (see chapter 13).

The Tachi and the Household

Nuyootecos often specify that yatuni is not a problem within a household. Because household members hold productive resources in common, the imbalances that cause people to feel yatuni for one another do not occur. Within the household one does not have to defend oneself from attack; one's place is secure, and one can count on other members' support and understanding. Of course, people admit that yatuni exists in some households. However, they also point out that these are invariably households in the process of fissioning. Otherwise, if there are frictions within a household, its members strive to keep them to a minimum and feel that they can survive only by maintaining a united front.

But if *yatuni* should not exist among people of a household, Nuyoo-

6. The agreement one makes with a tachi is a contract or pact *(chiso yu'ura)* in the same way that the covenants with the Earth and Rain are contracts or pacts (see below). However, the agreement one makes with a tachi is a contract that is safe to break. There are many stories about people who are able to fool a tachi, often with the aid of a Catholic priest. They sneak into its house and remove some of the wealth it has stored there, or they may obtain a sacred potion which causes the tachi to sleep through the time set to collect the ánima. This contract can be broken, people say, because the tachi has not worked for its wealth. If one were to break a contract with another Nuyooteco, however, this would be a crime (kuachi), since Nuyootecos "suffer" *(nshino'oma)* for what little they have.

tecos identify it as lurking in the background of relationships between people of different households (for Oaxaca, see Gwaltney 1970:52–53; in Latin America, Wolf and Hansen 1972:80–81). People of different households are suspicious of one another's motives and feel that they must be on guard so as to avoid being cheated or otherwise manipulated. This mistrust makes the relationships between neighbors similar, in some respects, to the long and bitter conflicts between neighboring towns.

The Tachi Si'i

The problematic relationships between households—at once reciprocal and conflictive—are reflected in the connections Nuyootecos make between women and Tachi. As I noted earlier, Nuyootecos say that women, along with the rich and the poor, are the persons most likely to have yatuni for others. Both men and women say that women are "miserly" (kuasunni) and that women do not like to share, loan things, or offer hospitality.

Women, like others who have inordinate amounts of yatuni, are associated with Tachi. For example, people say women are "of the left" (see chapter 1). The left hand is, in turn, "the hand of Tachi," and presenting something with the left communicates hostility and ill will. There is even a "face" of Tachi, called *tachi si'i* ("female tachi"), which people describe as a fair-skinned blond woman. A kind of siren, the *tachi si'i* leads men astray with the lure of sexual favors, often near bodies of water. Several people told me the story of a man from Nuyoo who once saw a *tachi si'i* near a pond by Tierra Azul, and when he went to embrace her, he fell in and drowned. When I heard this story, the narrator turned to the young men present and warned them that they should not become enraptured with any female—even their wives— since they may find that she is Tachi.

Nuyootecos also associate the snake, a child of Tachi, with women. The snake is "a friend" of women, and some men say snakes do not bite women. One man pointed out that in many images of the Virgin Mary, she is depicted as treading on a viper. He reasoned that anyone who is able to maintain such intimate contact with the snake must have a very special relationship with Tachi.[7]

---

7. I noted earlier that Nuyootecos view female sexual organs as filthy (ten'en) and polluting (kini). People also use these terms for Tachi. Also, if woman steps over a male's head or over a lock of his hair, Nuyootecos say she will cause him to become deaf and dumb. The deaf and dumb have a special sensitivity to Tachi, something that makes them sinister in Nuyooteco eyes.

We can also see the connection between women and snakes in Nuyooteco thinking about the machete. Recall that women are prohibited from stepping over machetes, lest they break. Snakes have a similar affect on machetes because they, like a mature woman's sexual organs, are a source of pollution. Moreover, in certain myths an analogy is made between snakes and female genitalia. In one a man falls madly in love with a beautiful woman. After having sex with her, he finds that her vagina is really the gaping mouth of a snake. Soon after, he dies. If males are like machetes, females are like snakes, and they threaten men in the same way the children of Tachi threaten humans in general.

In contrast to female sexual organs, male organs do not carry pollution. In fact, the penis—and things associated with it, such as the machete—can be used as protection from Tachi. As long as he urinates on it afterward, a machete will remain undamaged if a man uses it to kill a snake. (Female urine will not cleanse the machete, but cause it to break.) If a *tachi tiu* (the "whirlwind tachi") approaches, an effective defense is for a man to expose his penis to it as it passes through him. Nuyootecos also tell a story about a man who challenged a tachi to a fight. The tachi agreed, but when the man attacked with his penis, the tachi ran away, and the man was declared the winner. People explain that since the tachi has no penis, it had nothing with which to defend itself. Other examples could be cited, but the point is that while Nuyootecos believe females to have a close relationship with Tachi, males and symbols of masculinity oppose it.

In this context, I want to cite a myth first told to me by a middle-aged woman in Nuyoo Center. I summarize the main elements here:

There was a man who lived alone in a house, with his dog. Every day he would leave for work, and when he returned to the house, he would find tortillas prepared, his clothes washed, and the house cleaned. "How can this be?" he asked himself. "Who is making my tortillas, washing my clothes, and cleaning my house?" He decided that he would pretend to set out to work one day, but instead of going to the fields he would hide himself in the nearby brush. As he peered from his hiding place, he saw his dog stand up and remove its pelt. With its pelt off, the dog became a beautiful woman. This dog-woman proceeded to grind the corn, bake the tortillas, sweep the house and wash the clothes. After a while, the man emerged from his hiding place and had sex with the woman. He then destroyed her pelt, so that she could never again return to being a dog. From then on, the man began to live with the woman in the house (see Taggert 1983:191–99 for versions of this story from the Sierra de Puebla).

Many say that this is the origin myth of the people of Yucuhiti, and that the sons and daughters of this couple spread out and populated the land. Others, however, including the woman who first told me this story, say that this myth recounts the origin of women. In any event, it is clear from this that females, the household, and dogs are closely associated with one another.

In Nuyoo every household has at least one or two dogs, and some have as many as five or six. They serve as watchdogs, sounding the alarm when anyone approaches. Dogs do not usually stray far from their houses. Even when they take them along hunting, people are always careful to leave one or two dogs behind to protect their property.

Nuyooteco also view dogs as dirty and disgusting animals. Dogs are filthy and full of fleas, and people point out that they eat garbage and excrement. People see nothing wrong with striking or kicking dogs, and one of my neighbors once viciously hacked a dog to death after he found it in his kitchen "stealing" food.

Three kinds of people are associated with dogs. The first are those who commit incestuous acts. Nuyootecos call such people "dogs" ("pig" is also an appropriate name) because dogs of the same household, often mother and son, will breed with each other. The second are those who enjoy conflict, who are forever picking fights and challenging others. The reason for this association again lies in the observation of canine behavior. Dogs are highly territorial. Dogs will attack other dogs who happen by the house and will set upon people who draw near. I used to dread returning to Nuyoo Center after dark, since I would be surrounded by packs of yapping dogs, with those from one house replacing those of another as I walked down the street. Like the person who has yatuni, Nuyootecos say that the dog has a burning pain inside it that causes it to strike without warning, and it does not like outsiders coming near its house.

The final type of person Nuyootecos say is like a dog is one who shirks the responsibilities of corporate life. I first discovered this after returning from a trip to a distant Mixtec municipality. I remarked to a group of Nuyootecos that people in the municipality I visited do no communal labor, or tequio. When they heard this, one man said: "No tequio? They must live like dogs there." The others nodded in agreement, since a town where people make no effort to better themselves must be an unpleasant, even anarchic, place.

But what does the association of dogs with the incestuous, the unthinkingly violent, and with those who do no community service have to do with women and yatuni? First, I think what gives the dog its significance as an image of social relatedness for Nuyootecos is that dogs have no allegiance to anything outside the household of their owners, which they jealously guard, so they come to embody the self-interest and self-centeredness people feel is inherent in it. Like a household that refuses to give up its members in marriage (see chapter 8), dogs are incestuous. Like households that own plots of agricultural land and do not allow others to farm them (see chapter 12), dogs drive the people of other households away. Dogs, while they are of the household, form a "society" where interaction is a series of attacks and counterattacks.

Women are like dogs in several ways. First, they are closely associated with the household. Nuyootecos describe women's labor as being "inserted in" the household, and people sometimes say that "the woman *is* the household." Second, women, like dogs, are seen as causing friction within the community. It surprised me how often people blamed women for the breakup of households, for conflicts between households, or even, in one dramatic case, for the secession of an entire hamlet from the municipality of Yucuhiti in the 1930s. Such disputes have many complex causes, the shortage of land being the most important. Yet both men and women inevitably say women's "envious" acts are the root of the problem. Finally, women are like dogs because they are marginalized in most corporate endeavors. As we will see in chapter 8, males in Nuyoo validate their identity as persons worthy of respect and dignity through community service. In the civil-religious hierarchy, they work for the good of the community and defend its interests. Women, on the other hand, do not receive the training men do in civil-religious hierarchy service and do not participate in the forums where men make policy decisions, so that both men and women say females are not motivated to serve in the way men are. If anything, people say women are reluctant to see hard-won household resources expended in ways that do not directly benefit the household. As we saw, both men and women characterize women as kuasunni, "miserly." They say it is up to their husbands to "lead" them in service, motivating them to channel household labor and surpluses into the community.

One might conclude that the ultimate reason for the association between women and dogs is a modified version of the thesis that women are part of "nature" and are therefore asocial, while men are part of "culture" and it is up to them to create society (Taggert 1983:189–91). But the ethnographic facts of the Nuyoo case suggest something else. First, dogs are domesticated animals. They are *kiti*

ve'i, "animals of the household," not *kiti yuku*, "animals of the forest."
Furthermore, out of all the domesticated animals Nuyootecos possess,
dogs are the ones that they most closely associate with humans. They
are the only animals people regularly give individual names to (although not human names), and Nuyootecos spend more time in the
company of dogs than any other animal. Dogs may be animals, but
they are clearly part of "culture."

Nor can one assert that their association with the household makes
women asocial. I noted earlier that senior women play a central role in
the movement of young women from one household to another in
marriage, a process that is essential to building ties between households. Their role is acknowledged in the separate bridewealth payment they receive, and in the marriage ceremony, when the girl's
mother presents her daughter to the boy's mother, a ritual that takes
place in the kitchen, away from the men. Moreover, the relationship
that is most central for the success of the marriage, at least initially, is
that of the mother-in-law and daughter-in-law. It is the mother-in-
law's task to teach the girl to weave and cook and to instruct her in the
ways of the household, so that the girl may someday "cover her place."
Marriage is, in part, a process in which women circulate their daughters among themselves so that the younger women replace them; this
makes women agents in the creation of collective life.

Beyond marriage, there are marked differences between women's
and men's responsibilities for maintaining gift exchange partnerships.
Women produce the tortillas and other foods that circulate in gift
exchange, they are the guardians of the lists of gift credits and debts,
and they are the ones who keep abreast of upcoming fiestas, so they
can return the gifts they owe their partners (cf. Stephen 1991:195–96).
Women will travel to a fiesta and make exchanges without their
husbands, and sometimes men are not even aware their wives are off at
a fiesta making an exchange. Also, widows will continue to participate fully in *saa sa'a* after the death of their husbands. Widowers often
do not, and people view the debts owed by widowers as uncollectable.
As Tañuu Santiago Avendaño once observed to me, women "take the
lead" in gift exchange.

What the ethnographic data suggest is that women's association
with the household does not make them "asocial," but instead gives
them a collectivizing and generalizing capacity that men do not
encompass (Strathern 1988:284–85). After all, if people most frequently experience their relationships with other households through
gift exchange, then we can see that women are the ones who are

responsible for creating the context for this experience. Extending Tañuu Santiago's observations, we can go on to say that women "take the lead" in reproducing Nuyoo as an association of independent households.

How, then, are we to understand the decidedly negative terms with which Nuyootecos speak of female sexuality, and the noxious things with which women are associated, if we can't reduce females and males to a simple nature/culture or asocial/social opposition? It is important to recall that even though men say that women are "polluting," this does not get in the way of the close cooperation of husband and wife in the household or prevent some Nuyooteco men and women from weeding cornfields together. I think this shows that when women are spoken of as "polluting," it is not so much the innate characteristics of males or females that is involved. Keeping in mind women's roles as agents in the creation of community, I think women's danger instead correlates with the social potency their roles give them, coupled with the peculiar status of the household in Nuyooteco thinking about social life.

As we have seen, the household, for Nuyootecos, is both valued and devalued. It is the key to individual survival, yet at the same time it is a threat to social order. The household is a source of envy and bad feelings, and people of different households are often in conflict. This suggests that women's leading role in creating the community as an association of independent households is complemented by their leading role in the conflicts that exist between households. If danger is a sign of potency and consequence (as we will see in chapter 14, Nuyootecos speak of the *cacique*, or headman/broker, in the same they speak of the *tachi tuun*) then when people in Nuyoo associate women with dogs, what they are doing is commenting on the distinct liabilities men and women have as members of domestic units, and the kinds of actions these liabilities entail, rather than some innate female characteristics (Strathern 1988:64–97). Men also have intense domestic interests that motivate them to act in a way that undermines social cohesion, and individual men who do not meet communal obligations can, because of their behavior, be accused of acting like dogs. This will become clear in the next section, where we will see the dual valuation of the household dramatized in the circulation of the velu dancers who depict not only "miserly" women but also rich and selfish men, harmful ánima, dangerous outsiders, and the *jurrios* who pursued Jesus in a ritual that constitutes an order opposite that constituted by the circulation of the Jesus saints.

Figure 12. Dancing *velu*, including a *ñatuun*, with a skirt on. When the velu perform, they often dramatize the problems that exist among household members. In one instance, a ñatuun (grandmother) arrived at the house without her husband, and another of the velu, her "brother-in-law," began to make suggestive comments to her. When her "husband" arrived, he accused his "brother" of being an adulterer, and they began a mock fist fight. People often blame in-marrying women for the breakup of households, and there are at least two cases over the last 10 years where one "brother" (one involving half-brothers, and the other the sons of two brothers) ran off with the wife of another.

THE VELU

Some 8 to 14 dancers make up a velu dance troupe (from the Spanish *abuelo*, or "grandparents"), along with several accompanying musicians. The dancers are divided into two groups: male velu and female velu. Both female and male velu are played by males, for the most part young men. The male velu make up about two-thirds of the dance troupe members and usually wear wooden masks with a beard of goat hair and dried beans for eyes. Although I has not present to see him, one year a man wore a black burlap bag as a shirt, black pants, a black hat, and blackened his face. In Yucuhiti, I saw the velu dress in costumes used in the Dance of the Conquest elsewhere in Mesoamerica, wearing fancy dress and masks with European features.

Figure 13. A velu troupe with its accompanying musicians. Velu troupes typically carry stuffed squirrels, which, in Nuyooteco mythology, are feral children driven by their mother to live out in the wild because they ate so much. In their dances, they may ask people to give them food and money so they can "feed the hungry animal." They may also have the squirrel affixed to a stick with a small hook on its end, to try to snag a bit of food from some unwary merchant in the market. When people give the velu food and money, the dancers pretend that the animal is eating it, which onlookers consider hilarious, in part because feeding a wild animal strikes them as absurd.

Several people told me that the velu also sometimes dress in animal masks—in particular, masks of deer, dogs, monkeys, and pigs. The female velu, or *ñatuun* ("black women"), wear women's *huipiles*, skirts, hats, and kerchiefs to cover their faces. In Nuyoo in 1985, some ñatuun wore rubber masks of fair, blond, blue-eyed women. Usually only the male velu speak, whereas the women remain silent.

The velu make their appearance before Lent and end their dancing on the Tuesday before Ash Wednesday. During this period, they visit the households of the community, dancing and joking in front of each of them. Troupes may also visit neighboring communities, after first asking permission of local officials.

Since the velu dancers receive many presents of liquor while on their rounds, there is always the danger that jokes will get out of hand. Often the authorities send one or two town police officers with them to prevent trouble.

Some municipalities in the region have several velu troupes, each corresponding to a different hamlet. Each troupe has a director who organizes the dances and manages the troupe treasury. As the dancers go around to perform at different houses, people give them money and food. The foodstuffs may be sold, and the proceeds go into the velu fund. In 1984, the velu of the hamlet of San Isidro Paz y Progreso of Yucuhiti had a treasury of 100,000 pesos, which they lent at interest to members of the hamlet. This money was a significant source of local credit, and the hamlet used the profits to pay for public works projects. An older man from Yucuhiti told me that in the past, the 6 to 10 velu troupes of Yucuhiti would give one-third of what they collected to the civil office-holders, to defray the costs of running the municipality.

The Velu as Tachi

The association of the velu with Tachi is unambiguous. Some velu dress as Spanish/Mestizo people, recalling the *tachi kuka*, and some dress as blond, blue-eyed women, recalling the *tachi si'i* (cf. Stanford 1962:189). Their costumes sometimes feature children of Tachi, as well as the dog and pig. People call dogs *jurra* when they misbehave (one woman said that dogs she calls jurra are those that go from house to house stealing food, starting fights, and causing problems), a word that comes from jurrio, or "Jew," which is another name for velu. Female velu are called "black women," a color that suggests the *tachi tuun*, and, as mentioned, one velu dancer even dressed as a *tachi tuun* by darkening his face and wearing a black hat, a black shirt, and black pants. These associations mark the velu as a composite of the negative forces in existence; all the different "faces" of Tachi can be distinguished in their costume.

The sinister qualities of the velu are encoded in the story of their origins, where they first appeared as "kings." Tata Guadalupe Rojas told me the following version in 1986:

> The kings were envious, because Joseph had Mary, and they had asked for her hand first.
> When they went to look for them [in the stable], Joseph and Mary had left and gone to the church on a mule.
> Jesus could already walk, since he was a man of yɨɨ.
> Within two or three days of his birth he was already a full-grown man.
> Eterno had sent him to look over the world and then to report.

The kings asked, "How could he be so powerful? He is newly born,
    and we are much older."
They discussed this among themselves and became very angry.
They said to themselves that they would kill him.
"We are the most important," they said.
"We have been standing up a long time.
"Therefore we will beat him,
"We will grab him,
"We will hang him,
"We will beat him,
"We will go cut a thorny branch," they said.
They chased him all over;
They chased him all over;
Then, within three days of when he was born,
Abraham was present, Saint John was present,
And he came before them.
Because he was already a man.
He was already a man.
He came before them.
And he said, "What blessing will you give me?"
He said, "What blessing will you give me?
"Because I have no name.
"The kings are chasing me;
"They are going to grab me,
"They are going to kill me,
"They are going to hang me,
"They are going to beat me with a thorny branch,
"With a club they are going to beat me.
"They are not going to give me tortilla or water.
"They are going to kill, they say.
"What can I do?
"Are there not people who feel for me?
" 'Where did he go?' This is what they will ask.
" 'Where did he go?' they will say, because they are going to look for
    me, and if the kings manage to kill me, who will remember me?"

A section then follows where Abraham and Saint John baptize Jesus
and give him the name of Jesus. Jesus then names all the things in
creation. Suddenly, the kings arrive:

They [the kings] said, "Who is the man who spoke there?"
They spoke in a loud voice, because they were demons.
Saint John answered softly and slowly, "He is our son."
"What is his name if he is your son?
"What is his name if he is your son?

"If he is your son, if he is your eldest son, what is his name?"

"He is the only son of our family" [Saint John said].

They were stalling, so as not to tell his name to the kings; they said only that he was their son, that he was the eldest, that he was their only son, and they didn't say his name.

The kings were angry, and they grabbed a stone and said, "We will give this to your son to eat, if you do not tell us his name!"

"Do not say this," Saint John and Abraham replied, "because no man eats stone!

"The mason works stone, to construct a house, to put up a house;

"But he works it; we do not say the stone is edible;

"Because tortillas, because water and salt, whatever food, is edible;

"You do not eat [stone] because the mason works it;

"Thus we do not know what you are going to do (with the stone)";

"You will eat [Saint John said] because you are rich, you have experience, you are intelligent and educated;

"You are rich, you have experience, you are intelligent and educated, you who are the kings;

"Because you are standing there with your crowns [feeling proud] but you do nothing!"

They are kings, and on their heads is a metal crown, as [they wear] on Easter Sunday.

"You are rich and intelligent and educated;

"You are rich and intelligent and educated;

"And how are you going to be [when you eat it]?

"You are rich and intelligent and educated;

"You even wear a metal crown on your head;

"You do it! You will eat it!

"Do it, and you will see!" he said to them.

A section follows where Jesus, Abraham, and Saint John convert the rock into bread, tortillas, and other foods, thus showing their superiority over the kings, since the latter were not able to turn stone into food.

And the kings wanted to grab them, to punish them,

And they were not able to do so.

And you think our Lord did not speak?

He spoke, and [he and the kings] battled with words.

They battled with words for a long time.

"You are devils, you are jurrios!" he [Jesus] said.

It is at this time these words were born, and so we pronounce them today.

Because the blessings [Jesus, Abraham, and Saint John] uttered them thus.

And so we now pronounce them, I say;
And thus it does not die out,
It does not disappear.
And so this word,
This story,
Is a story the grandparents told to me.

Besides identifying them as the creatures who pursued Jesus,
Nuyootecos say the velu are the ones who crucified him, so they
sometimes call them "Roman soldiers." Tata Guadalupe refers to
them as kings, because Nuyootecos say the velu ordered a massacre of
children, like King Herod in the Bible. This is the reason the velu
wear masks, one woman explained, "so no one would recognize them
and the villainous purposes that bring them to the house."

Yatuni informs the actions of the velu, just as it does the other
"faces" of Tachi. Recall that Nuyootecos say the *kiti kini*, the animals
the Tachi created out of envy for Jesus, are born of women who did not
bear children. The sexuality of these women was not used in a socially
appropriate way, and they became the mothers of noxious, polluting
creatures. The *ña tuun*, "the black women," represent such women.
Also, in the story of their origin, the velu are rich men, *tee kuka*, who,
in their arrogance, believe they should be able to do anything they
want. When the rich men learn that Jesus is a *tee yii*, "a man of yii,"
and able to do things they cannot, they immediately become envious
of him. As Tata Guadalupe put it, "yatuni caused the kings to begin to
walk."

The velu are also associated with individuals who come from
outside the community. Recall that Nuyootecos view the coastal
region as an especially dangerous place. The people there are violent
and *ni va'a*, "absolutely bad," and some features of the *tachi tuun* and
the velu are reminiscent of coastal populations. One group of velu I
watched announced that they had arrived after a long journey from the
coast:

. . . and there are many good things to eat there;

Your grandmother could not come because she had to stay and take care
    of the goats and sheep and cattle and pigs and horses and mules;

We live very well there, and have plenty to eat, but here you suffer
    hunger.

They went on to say that they were carrying salt, fish, chile, and
coconuts as gifts, coastal products for which people from Nuyoo

sometimes trade. The velu invited the members of one household to come with them to this land of abundance, and asked the members of another to accompany them to work as wage laborers picking cotton (another coastal product). When I heard the velu make this invitation, the head of the household declined, to which the velu replied, "It's just as well, you could never get used to the flies and heat." Although these exchanges have a humorous tone to them, people say that what the velu are doing is trying to entice people away with riches, in the same way that the *tachi kuka* try to entice people to sell their ánima.

THE VELU, THE HOUSEHOLD, AND THE COMMUNITY

When the velu arrive at a household, they come, as one man commented, "to cheat and fool people." They may threaten the people of the house with sickness or, like the kings, say they are there to kill the children inside. Children are frightened of the masked dancers, and their mothers sometimes tell them if they don't behave the velu will take them away.

As befits their sinister motives, the velu often make their visits during the night, coming upon a household unexpectedly. The night, for Nuyootecos, connotes danger; it is the time of Tachi, and it is risky to be about. When the velu arrive at a house, they begin by displaying the polite behavior customary in house visiting, but their blunders, oversights, and misconduct soon make it apparent that these are not people who pay much attention to the social graces. They may greedily demand liquor and money and fail to express their appreciation for the gifts; if they receive only a small amount, however, they then make much of it, comically thanking the people for their generosity. This is part of their custom of "playing" *(siki)*, which earns them the name of *ñivi siki*, "playful people," and their fiesta *viko siki*, "the comical fiesta." Yet siki, in addition to playfulness, connotes disrespect.

Another example of the velu turning etiquette on its head is when they parody the Nuyooteco custom of bringing along presents of food when visiting. Visitors sometimes include in these gifts wild greens and succulent shoots, which they gather on their journey. The ñatuun do a takeoff of this by bringing to the house a basket full of weeds and nettles. One woman told me that the velu once brought seeds with them for her to plant, but these "seeds" were really the eggs of a parasitic worm, which, when it gets into one's feet, causes great discomfort, and in extreme cases can cripple. For their part, people may present the velu with inedible things or throw *nixtamal* water (waste water from corn grinding) onto them.

Beyond showing how the velu farcically imitate Nuyooteco etiquette, these examples also show that the velu are unable to participate in the sharing and the exchange of foodstuffs that are the essential expressions of social reflexivity. Thus people say that tachi cannot eat human food, so that one way to discover if a visitor is a tachi in disguise is to offer him or her something to eat. If the visitor does not take it, or runs away, one can be sure he or she was a demon. Nor can people eat the food of the Tachi. In a widely known story, a man visited a house of a *tachi kuka*, where it offered him so much food that he could not eat it all, so he brought some bread away with him. When he arrived outside, he found the bread, in the light, to be excrement. In other stories the man finds that the coffee given to him is urine, and a bowl of beans is a bowl of goat droppings. This food, like the money of Tachi, is polluted *(kini)*. It is not nutritious; it lacks, as one man told me, "vitamins." The generous hospitality of the *tachi kuka* does not truly purvey well-being, and the fact that the tachi cannot eat human food and that humans find the food of the tachi noxious suggests that Tachi and its minions, the velu, constitute an order that is the polar opposite of an association of households formed through the mediating acts of reciprocity, replacement, and alliance. The nature of this opposed order is perhaps best seen in the association of the velu with certain classes of deceased persons.

The Velu and the Dead

When the velu arrive at a household, they usually address the inhabitants as kin. They call out to people inside, telling them that their "grandfather and grandmother have arrived" or that their "brother and sister have arrived." Alternatively, they may say that they have brought the baptismal brothers and sisters of the household's residents with them and address those inside as "godson" *(se'yan yɨɨ)* and "goddaughter" *(se'yan sɨ'ɨ)*, suggesting that they are related by ritual kinship. The residents of the household in turn refer to the velu as *jii*, "grandfather," and ña'nu, "grandmother." The velu address each other as "brother" if two males are speaking and as "husband" and "wife" if a male velu and a ñatuun speak to one another.

One reason people identify the velu as kin and ritual kin has to do with the way the Viko Velu fiesta complements the Viko Anima, or All Saints'. All Saints' is celebrated from October 31 to November 2, dates that coincide with the beginning of the corn harvest in the region. As in other areas of Mesoamerica, All Saints' is the time when the deceased leave their households in the *ñuu ánima*, "the community of the ánima," and return to visit with the living, an event Nuyootecos look forward to throughout the year.

On the night before the ánima return (children return on October 31, and adults on November 1), each household prepares a large meal for its deceased kin and ritual kin. Along with this meal, the sponsors set out the foods the individual deceased relished most in life, usually on a large table constructed in front of the household altar. The head of the household then goes to each place, inviting the individual ánima to receive the food and asking their pardon for the humble meal. The ánima may also invite other ánima to visit, so that the house fills with the ánima of deceased Nuyootecos.

On the morning of November 1, after the ánima of the children arrive, people go to Mass and visit the cemetery, where they adorn the graves with palm leaves and fruit. In the afternoon, the prayermakers and municipal band members begin to visit the houses in Nuyoo Center, usually in the company of several dozen other men and a host of excited children. When the musicians and prayermakers arrive at a house, they gather around the altar to play and chant. After they finish, household members serve them (and all those who accompany them) the food set out for the deceased ánima. Once they have eaten, they pack up the instruments and set off for the next house.

It is clear that the arrival and feasting of the ánima at All Saints' is modeled on house visiting. This means not only that food sharing and hospitality—essential acts of social reflexivity—are central to the ritual, but also that people maintain an ongoing relationship with the dead in a manner similar to the way they maintain relationships with neighbors and other members of the community.

Feasting during the Viko Ánima is also significant because the celebration occurs during the harvest, after the "months of starvation" pass. As I pointed out earlier, it is during the late summer months through early fall that Nuyootecos have the most difficulty making ends meet, and they call this period "the months of starvation." Yet, as the crowds go from one household to the next, they receive more food than they can possibly consume. Many carry sacks with them to transport what they receive. By the time they return to their homes, their sacks are heavy with tortillas, meat, bread, and sweets—things people may have had to forego during "the months of starvation."

The ánima and the velu. The velu visits to Nuyooteco households closely parallel the visits of the ánima. The velu say they are kin who have come to visit, and, just as when the ánima arrive, the velu are given food to eat and liquor to drink. The velu themselves draw a connection between themselves and the dead by announcing that, for them—as is true for the dead in the *ñuu ánima*—"night is our day, and day is our night." They also sometimes say that the grandmother of the people in the household was unable to come with them, since she could not cross the large river that separates their home from Nuyoo. To reach the *ñuu ánima*, the deceased must cross a river, a river that marks the transition between the world of the living and the world of the dead. The velu's statement that they are ritual kin to the members of the house may also partake of this death imagery, since ritual kin mediate the transfer of persons from their household in Nuyoo to their "true household" in the cemetery, and deceased ritual kin return during the Viko Anima, just as deceased affines and consanguines do.

A feature of the velu that further associates them with the dead is their masks, which for Nuyootecos is the most striking aspect of velu costume. The dream of a mask presages the death of the dreamer or that of a fellow household member. One reason for this association may be that people say the returning ánima on All Saints' are "only head" *(shini)*. Figure 14 contains a drawing by Juan Lopez Nuñez of the returning ánima, whose heads are strikingly similar to the masks of the velu.

As Harris (1982) suggested for the Laymi of Bolivia, the arrival of the ánima in October and the dancing of the velu beginning in January bounds a key period in the local agricultural cycle. The ánima arrive at a time of increasing abundance, when the crops are ripe and there is plenty to eat. Their presence is closely associated with the harvest, because, for one, they created the estates that their descendants depend upon for their livelihood.[8] There is much feasting and happiness when the ánima arrive, and people do not consider them at all threatening.

The velu, on the other hand, appear at the heart of the winter season. This is a cold and sterile period in Nuyoo. The vegetation in the region has withered and died, and people face a time of shortages. Unlike the ánima, the velu arrive at a time of increasing dearth, when the stocks of food from the previous harvest begin to dwindle. People

8. The association of the ánima with the harvest can be attributed, in part, to their being the ones who "suffered" during their lives to produce the estate their descendants enjoy. That this is at least partly the reason for the offerings people leave for the ánima is illustrated in one story told in Nuyoo about a man who squandered the household's wealth, selling its lands and animals. When he died, his son refused to set anything out for him. Because the man didn't leave his son an inheritance, he received nothing on All Saints'.

Figure 14. The return of the dead on All Saints'. This depicts the offerings set out for the dead on the household altar. If a household has many deceased kin and ritual kin returning, and must therefore serve many individual meals, its members will place a table in front of the altar, extending it into the room.

do not welcome the velu, and they may even drive them away. As Harris (1982) noted, this kind of symmetry represents two separate faces of the dead: one benign and helpful, associated with fecundity and prosperity, the other sinister and threatening, associated with death and sterility. It is in this context that we should see the connection between the velu and those who become *tachi niyɨ*, or "tachi of the cadaver."

Tachi niyɨ. It is an ancient Mesoamerican proposition that the final disposition of one's immortal soul depends not on how one lived, but on how one died, since the manner of death determined the god one would serve in the afterlife (Taggart 1983:161; Nutini 1988). For example, after being hit by lightning or drowning, Nuyootecos say the deceased's soul was "taken by the *ñu'un savi*," since the *ñu'un savi* control the rain.

Nuyootecos divide most deaths, however, into ones that are "good" deaths and ones that are "bad" deaths. In a good death, one dies tranquilly, of old age, inside one's house, without much suffering. Bad deaths, on the other hand, are always associated with a tachi and occur, as Nuyootecos put it, "outside the household." In one kind of "bad death," the deceased actually becomes a tachi, a *tachi niyi* or "tachi of the cadaver." Klein (1982) has shown that throughout Mesoamerica the household is an extended metaphor for order and celestial periodicity. By implication, anything marked as "outside the household" connotes disorder, irrationality, and, it might be added, impurity (see also Burkhart 1989). Thus, those who have died "outside the house" (figures 15a and 15b) are also called *tachi yuku* (yuku being the wild, untamed places away from households) and *tachi kini*, since dying outside the house means the deceased has become polluted *(nsa'a kini)*.

The death of someone who becomes a *tachi niyi* can be the result of an accident, such as the man and his daughter who were swept away by a flash flood several years ago, or the result of violence, such as what happened to Julián, a leader of nearby Ocotlán, who was killed by a Nuyooteco sharpshooter during the land wars in the 1930s. Because their kin cannot begin the death rites in a timely fashion—which protects them from the tachi while they make the nine-day journey to the *ñuu ánima*—people who suddenly "die before it is their [appointed] day" do not reach the community of the dead. Instead, they stay rooted to the spot where they expired, remaining among the living but part of the world of the polluted dead. The place where Julián fell is now known as Kava Julián (kava can be a cliff or a rocky outcropping), and people in Zaragoza who live nearby say you can sometimes hear the song Julián was singing when he was shot. The *tachi niyi* are also called *i'na*, "sign, foretoken," since they will reveal their location by gasping, screaming, or making some other strange noise.

Nuyootecos view those who die outside the house as especially dangerous. A *tachi niyi* can filter into the body of someone who passes by and cause its unlucky victim to waste away and die.[9] Alternatively, a *tachi niyi* may try to frighten people, so that their ánima drops out of their bodies, where it lies exposed to danger. This readiness to injure

---

9. If a *tachi niyi* filters into someone, they must be treated immediately, usually with *tatan kini* ("pollution medicine"). *Tatan kini* is designed to make the patient unappetizing to the creature that has the patient's ánima. Curers will therefore have patients drink bitter teas, and even ingest such things as gasoline and mothballs, or rub excrement on their body.

Figures 15a and 15b. Dying "outside the house." This drawing depicts the death of a man in the wilds, with two tachi seizing his soul and bringing it to a cave inside a rocky cliff. The disheveled appearances of the tachi reflect the disordered, "polluted" realm where they exist, "outside the house."

and even kill causes people to refer to the *tachi niyi* as *tachi sheen*, or "wrathful tachi." Some people say that if you die of the illness caused by a *tachi niyi*, you will also become a *tachi niyi*. For good reason, people consider places where many have died "outside the household," such as the battle sites from the days of the Mexican Revolution, as especially dangerous places. It is almost as if the bad death creates a hole that sucks life *(yii)* into it.[10]

The death of someone "outside the household" bears important similarities to the death of those who have sold themselves to a *tachi kuka*. Both die before their time, suffering a sickness that was "not sent by God." Both deaths make the deceased kini, "polluted," and in both cases a tachi eats the deceased. Also, like the person who dies after an accident "outside the household," the person sold to the tachi is unable to make the journey to the *ñuu ánima*. Many stories are told of wakes for those who sold themselves where family members suddenly discover that the shroud is empty, and of caves where the bodies of the dead hang butchered, like so many cuts of meat, waiting to be eaten. Some people say the *tachi kuka* eat these people, defecate, and then re-eat them, evoking the image of an unending, closed cycle of violence and domination. Others say that those who sell themselves become *tachi niyi*, seeking the death and destruction of the living.

What I am suggesting is that the velu, by representing the polluted and polluting dead, specifically evoke the identities of those who have sold themselves to a *tachi kuka* and/or have not "died well." In this, they vividly illustrate what a community is like where individuals isolate themselves from others, place household interests over collective interests, and ally themselves with outside exploiters: it would be populated by the unclean dead, the unsocial rich, and polluting creatures, who turn etiquette on its head, refuse hospitality, commit adultery, poison relations between households, and otherwise make existence corrupt and chaotic. Instead of being bound by transactions that generate prosperity, renewal, and life—reciprocal exchange, the transfer of persons between households, and hospitality—the velu relate individuals and households through transactions that generate sterility, decay, and death—miserliness, hostility, envy, and disrespect.

The collective response to the velu occurs on Shrove Tuesday, when the people of Nuyoo kill the velu. This happens during the comical Viko Velu, which marks the end of their visits to the households.

Although I saw this only in Yucuhiti, Nuyootecos told me that the dif-

10. The word *niyi* may mean *ni yii*, "without the heat of life."

ferent velu troupes gather in Nuyoo Center early on Shrove Tuesday, dancing for the authorities in the municipal building and making the rounds of nearby households. They bring with them the foodstuffs and liquor they have collected and prepare a large feast.[11] They tell those in the nearby households that they will slaughter several large animals to make a delicious soup. However, as they pretend to slaughter the animals, they address each as if it were a principal man of the community, such as a civil authority, a past president, and the cacique. The animals the velu butcher are thus human beings, and the meal they cook is one for cannibals. After they prepare the soup, they pretend to distribute it among those present. They ask people how it tastes, a question that provokes some hilarity but also some repugnance.

The climax of the day comes when people capture the velu and then "burn" them. They chase the velu around the town, and after they subdue them, they hang them on a tree with a rope wrapped under their arms (a form of corporal punishment sometimes used by local authorities). The velu then confess their "sins" (which, I was told, are quite funny). After they confess, they are lowered down, and other members of the troupe place over their backs a reed mat with dried leaves, which they then set on fire. The velu then run "like crazy men," screaming and cursing among the people present. They eventually head for a nearby stream to extinguish the fire and remove their costume, and then they return to join the fun. After all the velu have been caught and burned, the troupe serves a big meal, using the food they collected.

The burning of the velu on Shrove Tuesday can be seen as a response to the kind of order the velu represent. As they make their rounds among the Nuyoo households, the velu dramatize the dangers of yatuni. As people say, "the *velu* go out" (i.e., make the rounds of households) "to remind us." They remind them of what Nuyoo sometimes becomes and the consequences this would have for social life. The velu begin to dance at a time when the days are short and the nights long, a time generally associated with mortality and infertility in Mesoamerica, since the sun is losing its struggle with the forces of evil, darkness, and death.

By burning the dancers in a collective act (just as those who are presocial, like the tiumi, or unsocial, like the household who does not give hospitality to Jesus, are burned), Nuyootecos repudiate the velu.

---

11. In Nuyoo in the 1980s, this part of the ritual was not performed. Portions of it were performed again in the 1990s, after the velu troupe from Nuyoo Center was revived.

The rejection of the velu and what they stand for coincides, moreover, with the gradual lengthening of the day, the coming of the rainy season, and an infusion of "the heat of life" in the universe. However, everyone knows the velu will be back, because they are as much a part of life as yatuni.

JESUS AND THE TACHI

We saw earlier that in both the mythology associated with the Jesus saints and in moving from house to house in ritual, Jesus defines moral actors as members of independent household units and links the relationships that mediate households to broader processes of fertility and renewal. In contrast to this, the sale by individuals of their souls to a tachi and the visits of the velu to the Nuyooteco households produce a different order. The velu lie, steal, cheat, commit adultery, poison their hosts, and consistently violate the rules of etiquette. Their immoral acts subvert the processes of social mediation and are associated not with fertility, prosperity, heat, and renewal, but with sterility, coldness, drought, and famine.

One way to look at the dancing of the velu is as a ritual of reversal, in which their antics constitute a counterpoint to the processions of Santa Cruz, Santo Entierro, Santo Niño, and Misericordia around the Nuyoo households. The velu come at night, whereas the saints come during the day; the velu stay outside, whereas the mayordomo and cargador are invited inside; the saints are offered an impressive sacrifice, whereas the velu are given things of little value or have nixtamal water thrown on them. The list could be extended, but the point is that the velu seem to define the community by demonstrating what it is not and how it could be destroyed.

At the same time the dancing of the velu might be seen as a ritual of reversal, their intimate association with Jesus suggests they represent something else. In the stories of the origin of Tachi, for example, people refer to it as "half" (sava) with Jesus, and they say the two are "brothers," born from the same womb. Also, the rituals involving the Jesus saints and the dancing of the velu share the same mythological charter, since the reason Jesus goes from house to house in the first place is that he is fleeing from the rich "kings." I think this indicates that for Nuyootecos, Jesus and Tachi exist simultaneously and are not just related to each other as social life and its fantastic opposite, or as "ideal" and "real."

The idea that opposed entities like Tachi and Jesus exist in some kind of complementarity is a widespread theme in Mesoamerican religion. Both Tedlock (1982) and Burkhart (1989) have argued that such schemes are structured by something Tedlock called a "dialectical dualism." One thing this means is that "deities" like Jesus and Tachi each contain their own negation. The existence of Jesus immediately implies that which is opposed to what he represents, and the existence of Tachi immediately implies the existence of that which is opposed to everything it represents. As Burkhart (1989:37) put it in her discussion of ancient Mexican religion, "Negative forces were. . . essential, functional components of the cosmos. Disharmony was as necessary as harmony. There was no permanent structure, no mythological hierarchy, no Great Chain of Being, but rather a process or movement."

Based on the Nuyoo material, we can see that this "dualism" extends to ideas about social life as well (Tedlock 1983). Instead of seeing the velu and other tachi as the essence of the antisocial, it is more accurate to view them as representing another side of social life. During Jesus' flight from the velu, for every household that offered him food and a place to stay, there was one that shut him out, and for every household that hid him, there was one that aided the velu. If reciprocity and other forms of social mediation emerged out of people's interactions with Jesus, then the interactions with Tachi and the velu at this time were just as significant for instituting social life, and I think people see the association of Nuyooteco households as also containing within itself its own antithesis: a collection of hostile and envious households.

The problem with calling this "dialectical" is that, while capturing the dynamic interplay of the opposed forms, it implies that the interaction of the two leads to some ultimate synthesis. Instead, the dancing of the velu and the circulation of the Jesus saints dramatize a view of social life where divergence, opposition, and contradiction are simultaneous and not necessarily resolvable, or, as one tañuu I knew was fond of saying, "enemy is friend, and friend is enemy." The notion that the Nuyooteco "community" is a series of forms that are not merged into some higher unity becomes even more evident in the next chapter, which begins by examining an institution, participated in by all Nuyootecos, that is, by its very nature, subversive of household interests: the civil-religious hierarchy.

CHAPTER 7

THE MOUNTAIN OF TIÑU

No account of how Nuyootecos conceive of and organize collective action would be complete without a discussion of service in the civil-religious hierarchy. Unlike other places in Mesoamerica — where rapid population growth, religious change, and the incorporation of local communities into a system of national political parties have combined to make service an infrequent and increasingly empty experience — in Nuyoo everyone serves (even the mildly retarded are given offices), and people spend a great deal of time and money in civil-religious hierarchy activities.

My discussion of Nuyooteco service is divided into four parts. It begins by describing the organization of the Nuyoo civil-religious hierarchy: the number of offices, how they are ranked, and how individuals move through them. I then discuss the way service is marked by gender and examine the notion that men and women have parallel roles in the civil-religious hierarchy. This is followed by a discussion of household and service. Finally, in the last section, I turn from the normative statements Nuyootecos make about service to an analysis of what they actually do when confronted with a cargo. As we will see, people view cargo not only as an opportunity to gain prestige and prove their mettle, but also as a profoundly alienating experience that they do their best to avoid.

THE CIVIL-RELIGIOUS HIERARCHY

There are 54 offices of importance on the "civil" side of the Nuyoo civil-religious hierarchy. The types and duties of these offices are stipulated by Mexican federal law. At the apex of the civil-religious hierarchy is the office of the president, followed by the *síndico*, *alcalde*, treasurer, *comandante*, and comisariado. All serve three-year terms, except the comandante and alcalde, who leave office after only one year.

Each top civil office has several subordinate positions attached to it,

167

called *suplentes*. However, only the first suplentes of the president, síndico, alcalde, and treasurer are "heavy" cargos, in that the officeholder spends a great deal of time and resources in carrying out official duties. Other suplentes, such as the six suplentes of the comandante and the six *vocales* and *comité de vigilancia* of the comisariado, may be required to spend a significant amount of time at their posts, but they are not required to contribute much in the way of cash.

In each of the six hamlets, there is a representative, or agent, whose major duties are to call hamlet members together for meetings, organize tequios, and represent the hamlet before the municipal and state governments. Within each hamlet there is also a head of the local school committee, called *comité* for short, who maintains the school buildings, makes sure children attend classes, and runs errands for the schoolteachers. There are also three comités in the center: two for the primary school and one for the newly created secondary school. Each school committee head has several suplentes. However, those assigned to these posts do little or no work, so people do not consider them formal cargos, and most of the school suplentes serve the community in other capacities as well.

There are also several provisional comités that coordinate efforts on communal undertakings. In the town center is a head of a committee for the town water supply, a head of a committee for road construction, and a head of a committee for electrification. These officeholders, and others like them, are named to oversee specific projects, and once the projects are completed the committee position is abolished. People consider cargos such as the committee head of the water supply light ones, since they require only three or four days of work per year. An individual may hold two or three of them simultaneously, and committee heads of this sort are often not changed for many years, unlike "heavy" cargos, for which, until recently, a one-year tenure was the maximum.

Finally, there are 15 officials charged with caring for the vehicles owned by the Zaragoza, Unión y Progreso, and Tierra Azul hamlets. In the 1980s these hamlets purchased three-quarter-ton trucks for transportation between Nuyoo and Tlaxiaco. The hamlets then named a comité and two to six suplentes to oversee truck maintenance, load and unload freight and passengers, collect fares, and help the driver.

On the religious side of the civil-religious hierarchy, there are 26 cargos (23 mayordomos, 1 fiscal, and 2 suplentes for the fiscal). The principal duties of these offices involve the sponsorship of fiesta and the care and worship of particular saints. The exception to this is the fiscal, or sexton, who does sponsor a fiesta, but has no saint to care for. In times past, each mayordomo *(matomo* in Mixtec) sponsored two fiestas: the *viko luli,* or "small" fiesta, and the main fiesta celebrated on the saint's feast day. The *viko luli* was the time when the mayordomo's helpers *(diputados)* would meet to decide the size of the contributions they would make to the main fiesta and make candles for the worship of the saint (thus people also call the *viko luli* the *naiti,* or "the standing up of the candles"). The *viko luli* were usually held six months before the main fiesta. Now, while all mayordomos celebrate the main fiesta, only four continue to celebrate the *viko luli:* Santiago, Misericordia, Caballería, and Santa Ana.[1]

The mayordomos and fiscales meet every Sunday morning in the church, where they discuss church business and plan for upcoming ritual events. Under the direction of the mayordomo of Rosario, who is the "síndico" of the mayordomos, they perform tequios for the repair of the church building and sow crops on church lands in the municipality. The mayordomos sell these crops at harvest time and use the proceeds to pay for candles and other items they use in rituals.

The number of offices in the Nuyoo civil-religious hierarchy has steadily increased over the years. Some were created in response to needs that arose from within the community, others were created in response to some requirement imposed upon the community by its place in the wider Mexican political system. I mentioned that whenever the federal government builds and staffs a school (there are a total of eight schools scattered throughout the municipality), it requires that the community supply a man to act as liaison between the school staff and the community and to serve as caretaker for the building. Because positions are constantly being added, a relatively high level of participation is maintained, even in the face of population growth. In the mid-1980s, for example, there were roughly 400 households in Nuyoo and 80 cargos, so that members of one-fifth of Nuyooteco households served annually to fill all the posts (for comparison, see Greenberg 1981:155–87). Also we should not restrict our accounting of

---

1. The mayordomo of Santo Niño also sponsors a small celebration in early February, when the image of Santo Niño is moved from where it was placed after the Christmas celebration (on top of the box that holds the monstrance) to its regular niche in the church. Few people are usually on hand for this (in 1984 there were 10 mayordomos, a group of 7 musicians, the mayordomo of Santo Niño, and several prayermakers).

those who serve to officeholders. From the Nuyooteco point of view, tequio, or communal labor, is a type of service *(tiñu)*. I kept track of the days the average man from Nuyoo Center worked tequio in the mid-1980s, and it came to 63 days in 1984, and 56 days in 1985. Even though the majority of men in any year are not officeholders, they still spend as much as 20% of their time in cargo activities.

Cargo Rank

When Nuyootecos rank offices in the civil-religious hierarchy, they do so according to their "difficulty," which they measure in terms of the expenses of office, the amount of time official duties require, and the responsibilities that come with the office. Of the three, the most significant is how much the office is going to cost. The top-ranked cargos can drain a household's accumulated surplus and force it into debt, while the lowest-ranked cargos can cost practically nothing.

The next criterion of importance is the amount of time an official must spend fulfilling duties. In this there is, as with office expenses, a wide variation from one cargo to the next, so that some cargos, like comandante, require an enormous amount of time, while others, such as a committee position, may demand of the officeholder only a few days of service during the year.

The criterion of least significance for evaluating the difficulty of a cargo is the decision-making responsibilities it has associated with it. There are several reasons why these responsibilities should be down so far on the list, but chief among them is that most decisions are made by all the officeholders of a similar rank, and most tasks are performed by groups of cargoholders rather than individuals (see also the discussion of the cacique below and in chapter 14). What this means is that within any given set of officeholders (such as big mayordomos or propietarios), duties are not, in practice, differentiated to a great degree.

The three criteria I listed combine in various ways to produce a cargo's level of difficulty. A position like comandante, for example, which requires much time and shares duties with the top civil authorities, may be more difficult than a small mayordomo cargo, even though the mayordomo cargo requires the officeholder to spend more money than a comandante.

This ranking of cargos by levels of difficulty evokes for Nuyootecos the image of the civil-religious hierarchy as a steep mountain, with various ridges. When one "steps high" *(na ñañu sukun)*, one has reached the ridge of the most difficult cargos, that of síndico, treasurer, and comisariado. People consider the cargo of president to be the most difficult, and it is at the apex of the mountain. On the ridge below the síndico, treasurer, and comisariado are the big mayordomos *(mayordomo ka'nu)*, the fiscal, and the other civil cargos such as agent, alcalde, comandante, and the committee heads of the schools and the trucks. On the lowest ridge are the other mayordomos and the suplentes of the main civil authorities.

In their discussions of cargo ranks, people often make a general distinction between "big" cargos and "little" ones. Big cargos are everything above the lowest ridge of the mountain of tiñu, and little cargos are those on the lowest ridge. This distinction may be based on the way cargos were organized in the past (see below), when the big mayordomos were equal to the big civil cargos, and the agent and committee offices did not exist. The "big" and "little" levels remain significant for individual cargo careers, since once a man has served a "big" cargo, he can never again be given a "little" cargo. Otherwise, movement within each level is lateral, that is, there is no hierarchical progression, say, from mayordomo of Santiago, to treasurer, to síndico, and so on up the "ladder," as is the case in other places in Meso-america. Rather, a man may serve in any combination of cargos on the "big" level, just as he may serve any combination of cargos on the "little" level. A man "steps high" when he makes the transition from the first level to the second. This is not to say that people are unclear about which offices are more difficult than others, or which offices have more authority than others. It only means that the movement of individuals through these offices corresponds in only a rough way with the way in which Nuyootecos rank offices in terms of expenses, time required, and responsibilities.

In 1982, a new federal law required officers in the top posts of municipal governments to serve three-year terms. In places like Nuyoo, where the terms were traditionally one year, the government tried to ease the burden by making monthly cash payments to the municipality, so that the out-of-pocket expenses of officials would be reduced. The arrival of these funds has, however, been the cause of some friction. People say that it is no longer a cargo if officers receive a salary for their work (indeed, the post of secretary has never been considered a cargo, since the secretary receives a wage for his labor) and there is the feeling that the money should be spent on materials for the school or municipal buildings and not be used by the authorities for the expenses of municipal government. But at the same time, most past presidents consider themselves lucky to have served only one year instead of the current three. They observe that although the money from the federal government helps pay some cargo expenses, the time one must spend at one's duties makes the office of president more difficult now than in the past.

Changes such as these have affected the way Nuyootecos rank cargo positions. Older people say that in the past, the religious offices in the hierarchy were just as difficult as the civil offices. Thus the big mayordomos, such as those of Santiago, Rosario, Misericordia, and Santo Niño, were the equals of the síndico, comisariado, and treasurer. However, as the community's articulation with the district, state, and federal government became more complex, and the power of the Church receded, the mayordomo cargos became less difficult than the big civil cargos, and the civil cargos were pushed higher up the mountain of tiñu. Note also that by expanding the term of office to three years, fewer men are able to serve in the offices of president, síndico, comisariado, and treasurer than in the past. This means that recent changes in the cargo system have made the top cargos more selective, as well as more difficult.

CARGO AS A GENDERED ACTIVITY

When I would ask what it means to call a man *nakuinee,* or "brave," people would often say something like "he is someone who can bear hardship" or "he is someone who knows how to suffer without complaining." They would also sometimes say that the "brave man" is one "who knows how to carry out the tasks given him in the general assemblies"—that is, he assumes an office and performs his cargo well. Cargo service for Nuyootecos is a kind of trial by fire, and people say the experience of serving makes a boy into a man and makes men tough and resilient. A man I know once described a situation where another, younger man found that he had been cheated out of his late father's land by some relatives. After going over the story of intrigue and backbiting, he concluded by saying, "When this boy served his first cargo, he began to realize what a man is and was able to sue to recover the land."

Given this perspective on the way males develop strength and character, it is not surprising that people look at those who have held the top cargos in the community as exceptionally intelligent and powerful individuals. The cacique, who people say never failed in a mission entrusted to him by the community, is reputed to be the "bravest" man in Nuyoo (see chapters 14 and 15). For men who aspire to power, cargo is a way of legitimating their standing, both because it shows their willingness to "suffer" for the community and because it affirms their mettle in the face of hardship (Cancian 1965).

One way cargoholders demonstrate their prowess is by vigorously defending community resources. In the past—particularly in the period from the second half of the nineteenth century to early 1950s, when Nuyootecos fought the people of surrounding communities for land—the authorities served as military leaders, organizing raids into disputed territories. Nuyootecos even addressed one war leader who had not served in high offices, the late Simón López, as tañuu, a title usually reserved for past presidents, because of his efforts on behalf of Nuyoo in the battles with Ocotlán and Nopalera. Today Nuyootecos expect their civil authorities to protect and defend the community by initiating legal proceedings against any individual or group that threatens corporate resources.

As I mentioned earlier, it is very important that the community "grow" under a man's term of office. This is, moreover, what Nuyootecos say the whole purpose of cargo service is: to help the community prosper. Thus, when I asked people to name the best presidents over the last 50 years, the ones they listed were those who completed major construction projects or managed to arrange for some government aid to be sent during their tenure. They would also include men who founded new settlements in disputed territories. Individuals such as Santiago Pérez of neighboring Yucuhiti, who founded Teponaxtla and aided in the settlement of Siniuvi on the lands taken from the Hacienda of the Concepción, are even reputed to have been tenuvi, the powerful sacrificers who are able to call the rain and who share a consciousness with animals and lightning bolts.

Nuyootecos often speak of the different levels of success cargoholders achieve in terms of yïï. Those who "step high" have a surfeit of yïï, which is evident in their forceful, well-reasoned speech *(ka'a teeyïï tara,* "they speak potently") and in their hearts, which, as the principal seat of strength and vigor *(teeyïï)* are very large, and make them especially "hot."[2] The potency of big cargoholders manifests itself in a sexual sense as well. People say the cacique is the "hottest" man around and that he carries on many illicit affairs, even though he is in his mid-seventies.[3]

---

2. Their powerful speech is important, since oratorical skills are greatly respected and are the key to success in any leadership position within the community.

3. If cargo is an opportunity for those who serve to show their worth, then Nuyootecos say those who do not serve are "useless" *(ndu tiñu)* and have aged without having amounted to anything of

The big cargoholders are also "hot" in a way that combines their potency with their authoritative control of force. As I pointed out in previous chapters, Nuyootecos, like many other peoples, draw consistent analogies between alimentation and sex. However, they also use *kaji*, "to eat," to connote coercion. Thus, when people say that big cargoholders "eat" a man, what they mean is that they have dominated and punished him. The authorities have the power to publicly chastise, fine, and even exile. When acting as a group, their sentences can be ruthless. In one case I am familiar with, a man had to sell land to pay fines for sexual misconduct; in another the comandantes beat a man for stealing a cow, and in a neighboring town, the authorities hung a man for a similar offense, even though capital punishment is prohibited in Mexico. When people talk about the political authority and sexual potency of big cargoholders, then, they also imply that cargoholders have within themselves a potential for violence that can be merciless and that their rule is not easily questioned. Tiñu, after all, legitimates power. It is legitimate to obey those in office, and it is illegitimate to disobey.

Cargo and the Life Course

When people in Nuyoo speak about cargo, they often do so as a condition of life after marriage, as steps in the progression of an individual to full maturity. As such, the sequence of positions in the civil-religious hierarchy mark stages in the life course and establish a kind of age-grade system for the people of Nuyoo (Moore 1973, 1979).

The key feature of an age-grade system is that it blocks off distinct periods of socialization and training. In the Nuyoo civil-religious hierarchy, each cargo has associated with it certain skills and knowledge that the officeholder should master. For example, in a mayordomo cargo a man will learn about the sequence of public rituals associated with the saint he cares for, while in the síndico cargo, a man will learn how to coordinate groups of laborers and how to set priorities for the expenditure of public resources. As a young man, a cargoholder will be brought face-to-face for the first time with most of the adult males of Nuyoo. He will learn their names, where they live, who their kin are, and details about their personal biographies. While carrying out his duties he may also travel to areas in the municipality he has never before visited and will learn where boundaries are, the names of boundary markers, and the territories disputed with other

---

value *(nijia nusiini, jia'nu ka'a)*. They also say such individuals lack yïɨ.

communities. As he serves in one post after another, his ability to mediate conflicts will improve, as he comes to learn the formal and informal codes for deciding who is right and who is wrong in civil disputes. He will learn how decisions are made and how to avoid making decisions in sticky matters. He will learn how to interact with government officials in Tlaxiaco and Oaxaca, how to draw up "legal" documents, and a host of other skills. People often say that young men should start as suplentes and "go behind" first, so they can study the actions of the older men who "go ahead" *(ichi nuu)*. They describe this process as one where the heart of the officeholder becomes larger, and where he acquires more potency (yɨɨ). Several people have pointed to the sloppy job done by two officials who received important posts at a young age, and attribute this to their inexperience, since they never served as suplentes, or "went behind," before "going ahead."

Besides training men in the duties of office and teaching them norms and community traditions, the sequence of cargos one serves in marks out a career: it enables people to know whether they are ahead of or behind schedule, it provides them with goals they can plan for, and it enlightens them about what they can expect along the way. It is not uncommon to hear men describe their lives, particularly after marriage, as movements between cargo positions. This became clear to me after listening to a man named Joaquín who spent a good portion of his life outside Nuyoo working as a day laborer in Putla, Juxtlahuaca, and other large towns in the Mixteca. When he told me about his life, he punctuated his account in two different ways. While outside the community he marked his experiences as a movement between places: first several years working with his father in Putla, then over to Juxtlahuaca, then back to Putla, then over to Tlaxiaco, and so on. When he reached the point where he moved back to Nuyoo in his late twenties (he is now in his sixties), he began to mark his life as movements between cargo positions. First he was mayordomo of Magdalena, then comité of the school, then mayordomo of Santa Cruz, then mayordomo of Santiago, and finally agent of Zaragoza.

Tata Joaquín's story shows the profound impact cargo has on people's perceptions of themselves. Some men, in speculative moods, even say that "one's whole life is cargo." They point out that although you may move between positions, you are still involved in cargo, since you must repay all the debts you accumulated in office, and you have to perform communal labor at least once a week. The Mixtec word for cargo, tiñu, also suggests this view. While it can be translated as "work," as in *satiñure*, "he is working," it also can be used in the sense of a "role" or "vocation," as it is the rain deities' tiñu to provide rain, and it is the male Nuyooteco's tiñu to work in the fields. It is as if tiñu refers to an existential condition of life, not simply an obligation of community membership. Indeed, as we will see in chapter 11, Nuyootecos liken cargo service to death.

Women and Cargo Service

Thusfar I have spoken of service in the civil-religious hierarchy as if it were an exclusively male activity. Yet cargo service is a complex undertaking with a variety of duties, many of which, it is true, require the work of individual males, but some of which require the work of women, some a husband and wife, and some an entire household.

The vital role played by women in the sponsorship of civil-religious hierarchy fiestas is not at first evident, since men control the ritual activities and dominate the public aspects of the events. Yet Nuyootecos are quick to point out that the women of a household are the ones who prepare the food for the many guests and that this task is central to fiesta sponsorship. A man without a wife was not even eligible for office, because it is impossible for him to fulfill his obligations if there are no women to prepare the quantities of foodstuffs needed to celebrate a fiesta.[4] For civil and religious posts that require fiesta sponsorship, only those who are part of a complete household will be assigned offices.

We can discern the crucial role female household members play in the civil-religious hierarchy fiesta in the remark one man—call him Lucio—made to his brother-in-law, Francisco, during a dispute over how Lucio was treating Francisco's sister. Francisco threatened to take his sister back to his house if Lucio continued to beat her. Lucio's father was serving as a mayordomo at the time, and Lucio said to his brother-in-law, "Fine, if you take your sister, take the chest as well." The chest Lucio referred to was the *mayordomía* chest, where the mayordomo keeps his records, candle wax, and the possessions of the saint. What Lucio was saying, then, was that should his brother-in-law take his wife from him, and the labor she contributes to the household, then he should also assume the office of Lucio's father.

Women clearly feel the burdens of civil-religious hierarchy service

4. Nor was an unmarried man responsible for working tequio. With the recent tendency to marry at a later age, this requirement was changed so that all males 18 years of age and older are eligible, whether they are married or not. Nevertheless, the authorities do not assign offices to unmarried men that have as part of their duties the sponsorship of a fiesta.

to be oppressive. A man I know, whose wife died while he was serving in the hierarchy, was not able "to find a new wife" until he completed his term in office. One woman he proposed to told me, "He is wasting his time, since no woman would marry a man with a cargo." Some women are even accused of provoking fights with their office-holding husbands, so as to return to their father's household and avoid the work demanded by fiesta sponsorship.

Given the important role they play in cargo service, it is perhaps not surprising that one can sometimes hear a woman say something like, "In 1973, when I was mayordomo of San Jose . . . ." This does not mean that she ignores her husband's service, since the "I" can refer to all the members of the individual's household, but it does highlight her role in the successful completion of the cargo and her feeling that she shares in the honor and prestige earned by those who serve. Thus women whose husbands served in all the offices of the civil-religious hierarchy receive the title *ñañuu*, "elder," which corresponds to the male title, tañuu. Also, women who have been through cargo positions will offer advice to those women who come after them on how best to carry out their tasks, much like older men offer advice to younger men who occupy cargos the older men once held.

In a widely cited article, Mathews (1985) pointed out that ethnographers have often ignored the vital role of women in civil-religious hierarchy service (see, however, Reina 1966 and Cancian 1967) and argued, based on a Oaxacan example, that the root of this problem is a bias that sees a domestic/public opposition (connoting less important/prestigious) corresponding to a female/male opposition and a lack of insight "into the way male and female roles interrelate and function within specific socio-cultural contexts" (Mathews 1985:286). Mathews also suggested that the expansion of the Mexican state, and the increasingly complex articulations of local civil-religious hierarchies with state bureaucracies, have tended to marginalize women, since men are the ones who acquire the skills needed to deal with outsiders. Whereas before women and men's roles "paralleled" one another, they have, over time, diverged, so that men's roles now have more autonomy, and hence power, than they had before.

Mathews's points are well taken, but her argument is, in part, a historical one, and she fails to support it with historical data (Stephen 1991:36). It is thus not clear from when these "parallel" roles in the civil-religious hierarchy are supposed to date. In the absence of historical data, the evidence Mathews presented is derived from its presumably older, and more traditional, religious side; it is first linguistic, in that both males and females in religious cargos are referred to as mayordomos, and second observational, based on her finding that male mayordomos organize and coordinate the activities of men, while female mayordomas organize and coordinate the activities of women. Leaving to one side the historical question (see however, note 5), I want to focus on the ethnographic issue of whether we should conclude that men and women's roles in the Nuyoo mayordomías also "parallel" one another.

In any cargo, two kinds of activities are associated with it. One set of activities involves preparations for fiesta sponsorship. In chapter 2, we saw that men's and women's roles do, as Mathews noted, "parallel" and complement one another. A good illustration is in how Nuyootecos judge individual performance in cargo. Women who serve as mayordomas and in other cargos that require the feeding of large groups of people are evaluated based on whether they distribute the right amount of items to those present, whether everyone who is a gift exchange partner receives an adequate countergift, and whether everyone receives a proper measure of food. The performance of male mayordomos is rated on whether there is enough beer, liquor, and soda for guests; whether sufficient corn was accumulated for the meals; and whether enough money was obtained to replace the principal in the mayordomo chest. If a man does not have the money to meet the payments required by his cargo, he will be criticized, yet no mention will be made of his wife, since this was not her responsibility. Likewise, if a proper countergift of tortillas is not made to a gift exchange partner, it is the woman who receives the bulk of the criticism.

The second set of activities associated with religious cargos involve administrative duties. This can be contrasted with fiesta sponsorship in three ways. First, where duties in the fiesta require the management of household resources, administrative cargo duties involve the management of communal resources. Decisions must be made about when to harvest the communal coffee plants (the money is used for ritual expenses incurred by the mayordomo or upkeep of communal property), the disposition of funds in the mayordomo treasury, and what repairs to carry out on mayordomía property, such as musical instruments. Second, whereas fiesta preparations require strategic decisions regarding exchange partnerships with other households, administrative duties require the making of decisions that affect the entire community or hamlet. Mayordomos meet, with other leaders, to decide whether to create new mayordomo positions, whether to bring in outside engineers and masons for church repairs, whether to solicit priests for religious celebrations, and decide when, where, and how long to work tequio on mayordomía properties. Finally, whereas fiesta duties require the household to make decisions about their particular participation in collective activities — often involving the contracting of gift exchange partnerships — the administrative duties of religious cargo require the organization of collective activities. Officeholders decide, for example, how processions will be organized or when Misericordia and the other Jesus saints will set off on their rounds.

In this latter set of religious cargo activities, it would be difficult to assert that women have roles that parallel those played by men. It is men who decide on the expansion of the number of religious cargos, it is men who decide the disposition of mayordomía resources, and it is men, for the most part, who organize the large-scale rituals, such as saint's processions. It is true that some women may have informal input into these decisions, just as it is true that in Nuyoo husbands and wives are both addressed as "elders." But the point is that in administrative aspects of cargo, there is no "separate but equal" gender-based organization as Mathews suggested for the community she studied in the Valley of Oaxaca.[5] Thus, while women gain and lose prestige through their performance in fiesta sponsorship, it is only men who gain and lose prestige through their performance in the administrative aspects of service. For these and other reasons, cargo service is not as important a standard of personal evaluation for individual women as it is for individual men. As people in Nuyoo explain it, "It is the job of a man to lead his wife in cargo."

The Household and Cargo

If it is inaccurate to view cargo as an exclusively male concern, it is also inaccurate to view it as the concern of a single married pair. Recall from our discussion in chapter 1 that household members have a collective identity vis-à-vis other households in the community and form a single productive and consumptive unit. This unity extends to civil-religious hierarchy service as well. Nuyootecos therefore say that it is not so much the individual male, or the husband and wife, but the

5. The Nuyoo material suggests that the parallels Mathews detected in religious cargos might be the result of the loss of mayordomía assets. That is, if the mayordomías in the community she worked in possessed extensive assets, and if, as in Nuyoo, males administered these assets, then the pattern she described reflects not some essential parallelism on the part of men and women in Oaxacan societies, but the disappearance of a set of public activities for which males were responsible.

household that receives the cargo (Cancian 1967:287–88). People even speak of the chest of the mayordomos — a symbol of office — as passing from one household to another, and not as passing from one individual officeholder to another.

When a man is named to a cargo position, household members divide many of the official tasks among themselves. As outlined in chapter 3, it is his wife's job to organize the female labor needed for the processing of large amounts of foodstuffs, especially in those cases where the office requires the sponsorship of a fiesta. She will make up dozens of baskets of tortillas to give to gift exchange partners, so that these tortillas will be returned to her household when needed. However, in a typical extended-family household, she may be joined in this by her daughter and collateral and affinal kinswomen who happen to live with her. These women may also exchange labor in *saa sa'a* with affines and kinswomen in other households and ritual kinswomen, so that in any fiesta as many as a dozen women will be present to help grind corn, cook, and serve food.

Cargoholders can also expect to receive help from brothers and sons living in their household. Sons working as migrant laborers will send cash back to help with fiesta expenses, and there are even cases where cargoholders have sent a son outside the community to work with the single purpose of earning cash for the fiesta. In other instances, sons who have been absent from the community return for the year of their father's cargo to aid him in agricultural chores. In many of the fiestas I attended, sons played important roles in organizing the rituals and keeping track of the goods and money exchanged. Similarly, sons who receive cargos can expect to be aided by their fathers and grand-fathers. Not the least of this aid is the advice of someone who has had experience in cargo service, which is communicated to the cargo-holder within the secure environment of the household.

Of the several adult males who may live in a household, only one is technically eligible to serve at any one time. Nuyootecos will some-times cite this rule when trying to avoid a cargo (see below). In one case I know of, a son successfully argued that his father should not be named mayordomo, since the son held a big civil post and lived with his father in the same household. As people admit, this rule is often not "respected," and members of the same household may serve cargos concurrently. The reason for this, as one president explained, is that there are not enough households with able-bodied men to fill all the cargos if everyone "rests" three or four years between positions. But the same man pointed out that households are not saddled with multiple cargos when one member occupies a big cargo. In those instances where a household has two (or occasionally three) cargos simultaneously, none of the cargos are "big" ones. Although cargo is a heavy burden, the authorities are careful not to overwhelm incumbents. This is important, since all members of a household involve themselves in a cargoholder's service, and if several members serve concurrently, they will not be able to do the job expected of them.

One may therefore say then that just as the household unifies its members with regard to production and consumption, so too it unifies its members in cargo service. In cargo, as in other things, household members act as a unit, and all join in the labor required by the office. There are even cases where one (male) member of a household has served the cargo given to another man in his household. In the example I know best, a father who had just completed a cargo took the place of his son, who was unable to be present in the community over the course of his service because he had joined the military. Here the household not only served the community as a unit, but also demonstrated the substitutability of its personnel. It is for this reason that I refer to civil-religious hierarchy fiesta and life-crisis commemorations as having "sponsors." The plural is meant to include all the members of the household involved in hosting the event.

Before continuing to the next section, I want to reiterate that although Nuyootecos say that males "lead" in cargo service, this does not mean that cargo is an exclusively male domain of activity, just as when Nuyootecos say females "take the lead" in gift exchange, it does not mean that males are excluded from the transactions that create ties among independent households. Instead, a better way to see service and gift exchange is as collectivizing activities that originate in the household but that place different demands on male and female members. And because these demands fall most forcefully on the shoulders of particular household members, they also compel these individuals to confront, more directly, the contradictions they engender. Thus, if women are "inhospitable" and liable to cheat others in gift exchange—to protect household food supplies—then men, who are also interested in protecting domestic interests, often act, in the context of cargo service, "like dogs," and become *tee si'i*, "womanly men."

AVOIDING THE BURDEN OF CARGO

When people in Nuyoo speak about cargo, they all agree that it is something that one should neither profit from nor enjoy. He who has a cargo position, they say, is "filled with cargo" *(tee nchitu tiñu)* and "tied up" *(ni'nira no'o)*. The latter means that the officeholder has so much work to do that he has no time for anything else. People also speak of cargo as a burden one carries. *"Tiñu ve i,"* they say, *"tiñu* is heavy" (figure 16). Accordingly, when a man finishes his service, people say he is "catching his breath" *(nake'e tachi)*, like someone who climbs a mountain with a heavy load and stops to rest a bit before going on. A man may also say *naki'i tachi nuun,* "a cool breeze is refreshing me," and everyone will know that he is resting between positions.

It should perhaps come as no surprise that people approach cargo with great reluctance. On one occasion, I saw a man sit down and cry after the president named him as an office candidate in a general assembly. Although young men who have never held office may welcome the opportunity to prove themselves, others view cargo with dread, and Nuyootecos have developed a number of strategies for giving the appearance of participating fully in cargo service while actually avoiding it.

One thing that made fieldwork difficult in Nuyoo, especially during the first year I lived in the community, is that people do not like to talk about themselves. There is a cultural focus on understatement and humility, and people seldom volunteer information to an outsider. I did not, however, have to try very hard to find out about cargo service. Men were more than willing to speak accurately and at length about the time they served, the public works they finished, and the year they received a new post. After a while it became clear that this unusual behavior, at least for Nuyootecos, was one element in a strategy to avoid cargo service. By proclaiming where he is in his career, and by emphasizing how much he had served and how little he had rested between positions, a man may move his name further down the list of potential candidates or, perhaps, remove it from the list altogether. This is because reputation plays a major role in the selection of officeholders. Those who choose the nominees try to recall who has served recently and who hasn't. They also try to evaluate the financial situation of potential candidates. To the extent that a man can make the most favorable information about himself publicly known (i.e., he has served recently and his efforts caused him to sink into poverty), then those who nominate new officers may place other names before his.

Because the timing and kind of cargo one receives is partly based on assessments of one's financial position (wealthy people are felt to be better able to bear the expenses of heavy cargos, while poor people are

Figure 16. Transferring the saint's chest to the house of the new mayor-domo. Carrying the chest to the house of the new mayordomo is a graphic image of the burden of cargo. These chests are set on a platform next to the household altar of the mayordomo. They contain 20 to 30 pounds of beeswax for candles, *mayordomía* accounts (sometimes going back as far as the eighteenth century), the saint's principal, and other, miscellaneous property, such as hymnals, garments, cult objects, and even tools.

given light ones) it is important to try to obscure the amount of one's assets and income. This is not easy to do. People will take note of how much coffee one has sown, how many animals one owns, and whether one's fields are neatly weeded (something that suggests a surplus in time and/or money). One man I know works some days as a field hand for others, not so much because he needs the cash, but because it is a way of projecting an image of need. Others are careful not to wear new clothes or to leave appliances and other costly items in plain view, since it shows one has money to purchase them. One family has even postponed erecting a new house because, as one of them confided, "as soon as I lay the first brick, I will be given a cargo." They decided to wait until after one of them received a position to begin work on the house, when it won't matter as much.

To put off serving for as long as possible, one should also avoid making a nuisance of oneself. For example, the town police brought a young man into the municipal hall one morning while I was examining documents in the town archive. The night before, he had beaten an older man, who had caught him trying to sneak off with one of his daughters. The president told the young man that they were going to assign him a cargo. The young man protested, arguing that he was only 17 and not eligible to serve. The authorities would not relent, and the president replied that they wanted to teach the young man what it is like to "suffer." Another official explained later that "he will know by the cargo he receives that if he keeps behaving the way he does, he will receive greater punishments." The idea is that by teaching the young man what it means "to suffer," he will respond to the threat of greater punishments and also internalize values such as self-denial, humility, and the importance of doing things for others.

After three years of rest, it is likely that no matter how much a man talks about his record, and how poor he claims to be, he will become a candidate for office. To avoid a cargo at this stage, one can no longer simply rely on manipulating public opinion. One popular strategy is to go to work as a migrant laborer picking tomatoes in Cuautla, Morelos, and stay until the period for naming people to new cargo positions is over. An alternative is what one might call the "out of sight, out of mind" strategy — going into isolated areas of the municipality on week-long hunting expeditions while nominating assemblies are held. So many people did this in 1984 that the municipal president imposed a 500-peso fine on all those who didn't show. People joked that they should now hold assemblies out in the forest, since so many citizens had decided to join the wild animals.

The average Nuyooteco's wish to avoid office also makes the process of nominating candidates and electing officials complex. What is supposed to happen is that during a general assembly in Nuyoo Center, a slate of names is proposed for each vacant office. Those present then vote, and the candidate with the most votes wins. In the past, Nuyootecos held these assemblies on October 31 (during the Viko Anima). It would be dark, and when it came time to name candidates, men would shout from corners, "So-and-so should be president." Others would also nominate candidates, but with hands over their mouths to disguise their voices. People feared, as they do today, that if an official knows they nominated him, they will become targets for revenge once he is in office. At one recent election I attended it took several hours to nominate a slate of three candidates for a minor cargo position. No one wanted to suggest a name, since they feared that the person nominated, or one of his relatives, would retaliate by nominating them. For these minor positions it is often left to the current officeholders to propose names, and the man appointed will focus his anger on them.

Nominations for big cargos, such as president, comisariado, and the many religious cargos, are not made in a general assembly. Rather, a group of men meet separately to select one or two candidates for each position. This nominating group includes the high civil authorities, the cacique, and the mayordomos. In addition, one or two past presidents may be called in for advice. In the meeting, they review the names of the men in the municipality who are eligible, analyze the men's abilities, and match names with the appropriate positions. Past performance in official duties, the personal agendas of the nominators, and the extent to which a man has impressed the nominators with the frequency of his service and his poverty are factors in determining who they nominate. Many of those in the nominating group told me that this can be unpleasant duty, particularly when they feel they have to "defend" a close kinsmen or compadre by coming up with reasons why the man should not be nominated when others want him for an office. This also occurs in the general election, when the president announces the names of the nominees. It is not uncommon to see arguments break out between the authorities and the nominee's allies, as the latter try to get their man removed from the slate. One can also see why many officials are willing to let the cacique make these choices for them, since they can say to the future cargoholder, "I tried to defend you, but the cacique wanted you, and there was nothing I could do about it" (see chapter 14).

When named to a cargo, it is still possible to avoid serving. One way to do this is to plead poverty. In these instances, the authorities will analyze the financial condition of the petitioner and review their decision. They may assign the man to a less-difficult post or even, in some cases, excuse the man from service altogether. The man must, however, make an effort to serve in the office sometime in the future. There are several men in Nuyoo Center who, at some point in their careers, were not able to assume a post when first named, but who did complete it years later. This is important because men who plead poverty or go to other extremes to avoid serving acquire a reputation of "acting like dogs" or being "womanly men" *(tee sɨ'ɨ)*. An extreme example of such behavior is when the officeholder "runs" after receiving the cargo. This happened in the late 1970s, when the man named to be president fled to Tlaxiaco and did not return for over a year. After this, the community began to name the new authorities well ahead of the date they would assume office, to see if they would "run" or not. For most, running is not an option, since the reputation of being a coward is impossible to live down, and the authorities may take one's lands away as punishment.

Once in office, most people serve honorably. There are some, however, who still do what they can to avoid the work. Civil officials, for example, might show up late in the day at the municipal building and use the morning to tend to their crops. Officials might also go to some out-of-the-way place, so that messengers from the center will be unable to find them, or they might go on drinking binges to avoid making difficult decisions. The agent of one hamlet actually stayed drunk for the better part of a year, sobering up only when his term ended. At the same time, it is through cargo service that men define their moral selves, and anyone who is too obvious about shirking his duties will earn a reputation of being a *tee si'i*. Furthermore, the performance of cargoholders is closely monitored. Even the hardest-working official, if suspected of avoiding a responsibility, will be criticized. I recall one day in 1985 when, while passing by a field where a particularly diligent civil official was working, others in my party muttered—and one loud enough for the cargoholder to hear— that "it must be that there is no community business to attend to," since the man has so much time to spend on his crops. The feeling is that cargo, if it is done correctly, should leave the officeholder with no time for anything but his duties.

Finally, cargoholders who are consistent malingerers run the risk of receiving a kind of punishment that seems particularly counter-productive if we view cargo as solely a system for efficient administration: instead of removing an officeholder who has not performed well, the authorities do not excuse him when his term ends, leaving him to serve several additional months. He is thereby forced to endure the duties and expenses of office that much longer. Those who have done particularly bad jobs are held over for an entire term!

Before concluding, I should note that the tremendous effort Nuyootecos usually expend in carrying out their duties, and the criticisms they receive for the slightest omission, makes many of them understandably resentful. The most serious act of violence in the town over the last 15 years occurred when an alcalde accused a young man who had never held a cargo of being "worthless" and "weak." The alcalde had insulted other young men of similar status, but this time he hit a raw nerve. Both parties had been drinking, and after they traded insults, the young man took out his machete and slashed at the alcalde, cutting his forehead and slicing off several of his fingers. People reacted strongly. They banished the young man and publicly rebuked the officials who defended him. But despite widespread sympathy for the wounds the alcalde suffered, most blamed him for the fight, since all were familiar with his tendency to "speak yatuni" about those who had not held office. "It hurts him because he has a cargo and others do not," one woman explained.

Although the fight was a unique occurrence, I found that most cargoholders become progressively bitter during their period of service and develop bad feelings for those who don't hold offices. This is demonstrated by the relish cargoholders privately show at naming their replacements and explains why those named usually accuse the authorities of having yatuni for them.[6]

CONCLUSION

Nuyootecos, like most Native Americans, pay close attention to their dreams, since they believe that dreams are windows to the future and provide insights into the past. Several dreams suggest a cargo is in the offing. In one of them, the dreamer finds himself jumping through flames or trying to extinguish a raging fire. The cracking and popping of the flames, according to one woman, represent the criticism and catcalls made by the large groups of people the official must face when things do not go right. Other "cargo" dreams situate the dreamer in an equally perilous position: in the middle of a large lake, without anything to grab onto, or crossing a swiftly flowing river, with slippery rocks underneath. The idea that dreams such as these—which may cause the dreamer to wake in the middle of the night, sweating and trembling—presage a cargo underscores the tremendous anxiety service provokes in people. This anxiety, I suggest, is rooted in the

6. It is not, however, just those who are "suffering" with cargo who take pleasure in naming their replacements, since those who are not currently serving a cargo may also relish the moments when others receive a position. I have heard people whisper gleefully to one another whenever the expenses of office forced a cargoholder to sell animals and other possessions. Far from showing sympathy for another's predicament, people often find satisfaction in the discomfort cargo causes.

Envy is also an extremely powerful factor in how those who serve together interact. Although officials should work closely with one another, "as if they were brothers," the division of labor is informally arranged, and imbalances frequently arise over the amount of work each officeholder does, so that one officeholder may appear to have an easier job than another. This and other factors cause problems, and by the time a set of officeholders are ready to step down, there is often a great deal of animosity built up among them. In the most serious cases, cargoholders carry on open disputes, with disastrous consequences for municipal government.

juxtaposition of two valued identities in cargo service, which makes
one sustainable only at the expense of the other.

Cargo service, if done property, leaves one's household destitute. In
the past it was not uncommon for a president to have to sell lands to
meet the expenses of office, and other cargoholders may have found
themselves placed in similarly difficult circumstances. In 1986 at least
one officeholder sold land to pay for cargo-related costs, and another
sold four head of cattle. Added to this, the time lost in the performance of cargo duties is substantial. Except for schoolteachers and a
store owner, people in Nuyoo are full-time agriculturalists. When
they assume a cargo this means that they will be unable to sow while in
office or, at best, they will be able to sow only a limited amount. When
they see that they will soon be named to a cargo, many people will sow
a large area, to create a surplus to see them through their year in office
(Dow 1977). But while this surplus may last them the year of their
cargo, once it is gone they are in a difficult position, since they must
wait for a new crop to mature to refill their granaries. Given this
situation, one can see the burden the new three-year term of office
places on the household of the cargoholder. The loss of a laborer for the
better part of three agricultural seasons is a real strain for most
households.

Cargo also forces people to subordinate household-based relationships of alliance to wider corporate interests. For many Nuyootecos,
the most distasteful part of cargo service is the strain it places on their
relationships with friends, relatives, and fellow hamlet members.
Indeed, when asked to name the most difficult cargo, many people
say comandante, because the comandante is the officer who makes
arrests. As comandante, one is frequently put in the distressing
position of having to take friends and relatives into custody. This
predicament can be made even worse if the person arrested asks for a
chance to escape. There is a saying in Nuyoo that "a comandante has
no compadres," since the job does not allow him to show the respect
compadrazgo requires.

In cargo service, then, men are forced to betray their identity as
members of a household by arresting kin, selling household assets,
and not attending to household affairs. Those who give in to their
personal and domestic interests behave "like dogs" and become *tee
sɨ'ɨ*, the male equivalent of envious women. Ethnographers have
reported these kinds of conflicts for many Native Mesoamerican
societies. But the Nuyoo material also suggests that what people
articulate in cargo service—at the expense of the household—is an

image of community distinct from an association of independent households. In the next part of the book, I will explore what this second vision of community is and why cargo service is important to its creation.

PART THREE

THE COMMUNITY AS A GREAT HOUSE

Before the Lords of Apoala . . . conquered this land, there was in it some towns whose residents were called *Tay ñuhu, ña ñuhu, tai nisino tai nisai ñuhu,* . . . and these, they say, had come from the center of the earth, which is called *ñuhu,* and were not descended from the Lords of Apoala, but instead appeared over the earth and took control of it, and these were the true Mixtecs.

For the dead they also have a different term which is: *ñu,* as in *ñu* Andrés, *ñu* Domingo, "the deceased Andrés, Domingo," and this *ñu* comes from *ñuhu,* that is, earth. And so they say *nicuvui ñuhundeyeta,* "the deceased became earth," which is like saying the deceased was entrusted or sent to earth.
—Antonio de Los Reyes, *Arte en Lengua Mixteca,* 1593

CHAPTER 8

BLOOD, MILK, AND SEMEN

NUYOOTECOS often called themselves ta'a. Ta'a contrasts with *to'o*, a generalized term for outsiders. In its broadest sense, ta'a designates objects of the same class, but when used to describe the relationships of humans to one another, it usually suggests a tie of kinship, and Nuyootecos will translate ta'a as "relative."

What I want to show over the next several chapters is that Nuyootecos base the idea that they are ta'a on their sharing of substance with one another. This shared substance is important because it distinguishes Nuyootecos from other people and establishes the boundaries of Nuyoo in terms of the physical makeup of human beings. But more than this, the substance Nuyootecos share relates them as a people to Nuyoo as a place and makes the connection between people and place an especially strong one. I begin by examining the nature of Mixtec kinship.

KINSHIP

Anthropologists have traditionally based their definitions of kinship upon the "natural" facts of sexual intercourse, pregnancy, and parturition. It was assumed that these facts produce a genealogical grid that is the same for all societies. Where societies would differ would be in how they classified elements in this grid. Thus, as Meigs explains, in one society father may be classified with father's brother, while in another society father and father's brother may be lexically distinguished. Similarly, societies may emphasize certain relationships that arise from these natural facts over others. In a matrilineal society, the fact that a child is born of a particular woman is important, while in a patrilineal one it is the fact that the child is born of a particular man (Meigs 1984:118; see also Schnieder 1972, 1984).

In the late 1950s and early 1960s, some began to question the idea that kinship is based on the scientifically defined facts of biological relatedness. After all, our understanding of the genetic basis of

193

reproduction is relatively recent, and our own ideas about kinship, as well as those of other people, existed long before the science of genetics. Instead, it was argued that kinship is a "folk" system of conceptualizing relationships between people. Because this is a cultural phenomenon, nothing requires that it match a genetic model of relatedness.

Early on, it was believed that folk models of kinship would be grounded in cultural ideas about reproduction, so that kinship became whatever processes of heredity, procreation, and gestation people envisaged (Poewe 1981:4–5; Schneider 1968). The substances people understand to be passed between human beings in reproductive acts then came under particular analytic scrutiny. This was because these substances would both relate people as kin and, along with the specific acts involved in their transmission, produce a culturally patterned system of kin relationships. In American kinship, it is the "blood" that mother and father pass to their child in sexual intercourse that serves to relate them to one another and to a host of lineal and collateral relatives. In other societies, the substances transmitted may be bone or skin or many other things. As we will see in the Mixtec case, the crucial substances are semen and milk.

It later became clear that folk models of kinship did not always have to be based upon reproduction. It is true that in many societies, kinship is created through the transmission of substance through sexual intercourse. However, there are societies where shared substance is not the defining feature of kinship (e.g., Witherspoon 1975) and there are societies that define kinship in terms of shared substance but that do not necessarily see it as transmitted through reproductive acts. An example of the latter are the Hua of New Guinea, who Meigs argues make "consanguineous" kin out of people who are not born to the local group, by transmitting substance to them while sharing food. The substance in question is *nu*, which is present both in people and in the food they produce and prepare. If people share food over a long enough period, and continue to live close together so that bodily emissions that also contain nu mingle, then the individuals so associated will become kin through the passing of vital substance to one another (Meigs 1984).

As one can see, the Hua idea of kinship produces a genealogical grid that is quite distinct from one based solely on reproductive acts, because people who are not related to one another by descent can become related to one another through transmissions of nu. What the Hua example shows is that the critical element in kinship may not always be reproduction and, more generally, that there is no single, cross-culturally valid definition of kinship that holds true for all societies (Schneider 1984). If we are to use a notion of kinship to describe social life in a particular society, we must therefore begin by defining just what it is—something that has been conspicuously lacking in discussions of Mesoamerican social organization. As we will see, the acts through which parents create kinship relationships with their children in Nuyoo are both sexual, involving the transmission of substance in intercourse, and nurturing, involving the transmission of substance in feeding.

KINSHIP IN NUYOO

Nuyooteco kinship is like "American" kinship in that it is "shared blood" that connects children to their parents. But unlike American kinship, mother and father contribute blood to their children in fundamentally different ways. A child is first created when the male's semen *(nute kuiji,* "white liquid,") enters a woman's womb (soko). Semen, people say, is blood, which flows from all over a man's body when he becomes "hot" during the sexual act.[1] When semen enters a woman in sufficient quantities, it slowly clots *(nakujio ini)* and begins to grow. The sexual act must be repeated up to 10 times for a woman to receive enough semen to allow her to become pregnant. At this stage, people speak of the woman as a receptacle in which the fetus grows, since she does not contribute in any significant way to the makeup of the child. It is male blood, as semen, that is crucial (cf. Galinier 1987:424). In one Mixtec town where I worked, people were of the opinion that when a child comes out looking very odd, and not at all like its father, it is because the mother had sex with different men while accumulating the necessarily mass of semen in her womb, and these varied sources of male blood produced a child who is equally varied in its characteristics.[2]

Inside the mother's womb, the fetus slowly grows for nine months.

1. I found many differences in Nuyooteco opinions about the physiology of reproduction. Part of this diversity is no doubt due to the combination of an indigenous view of human physiology and reproduction with what people have learned through the birth control lectures provided by the Church and the government-sponsored family planning clinics found throughout the Mixteca. In any event, what I try to do here is simply synthesize the things older people told me about conception, since these ideas shed light on other aspects of belief.

2. The sixteenth-century Mixtec term for children born to an adulterous woman is "mixed-up children," suggesting that they were considered children of more than one semen (Reyes 1976:88; López Austin 1980:337).

The child feeds off its mother's blood, which it receives through the umbilical cord, and "swims" in "female liquid" *(nute si'i)*. After the child is born ("when it falls to the ankles of its mother"), the mother is *ki'mu*, weak, thin, and cold from the loss of blood. Her excessive coldness must be counterbalanced by "hot" things to move her to the median point between hot and cold. Accordingly, the midwife[3] orders the mother to take a sweat bath, to heat up her blood *(nasaa niñi)* and "recook" her veins *(na chi'yo tuchi)*. One midwife told me that the heating of her blood and cooking of her veins converts the blood into a form that is suitable for the child to feed upon outside her womb—that is, breast milk. The child, then, first receives the mother's blood through the umbilical cord and then later as it nurses.

Although males and females contribute substance to their children in different ways—males as they fill a woman's womb with semen, and females as they nurse their child both inside and outside the womb—I found no significant difference in the kinds of things associated with male blood as opposed to female blood. In Santiago Ixtayutla, a coastal Mixtec community, people do not lexically distinguish semen from breast milk; they call both *leche*, and in Nuyoo, both mother and father use the phrase "my blood my milk" *(nu'u niñi shukuin)* to refer to their offspring, even though only one of them contributes blood in the form of milk to the child. Yet the idea that males and females contribute blood in different ways does have consequences for Nuyooteco ideas about kin relationships. Recall that males transmit blood to their children only at the very beginning of the process of reproduction. A woman, on the other hand, transmits blood over a longer period, first as the child matures in her womb and later as it nurses. It sometimes happens that after birth, a child's mother dies or is unable to produce milk to nurse the infant. Another woman then nurses the child. In this case, the child, when he or she grows, will refer to the woman who nursed it as "mother," in addition to the woman who bore it. The reason the nurse is like the birth mother is because she fed her blood to the child, creating a link of shared substance. This is possible because the process of transmission of fluid to the child occurs both inside and outside the womb, allowing more than one woman to participate. While it is also true that a child can have more than one father (if a woman has intercourse with more than one male while she accumulates enough semen to become pregnant), this is usually brought up only in gossip about a woman

---

3. Men as well as women serve as midwives in the region.

who is suspected of having an affair, and these other men are not addressed as "father" by the child.

I cite this example because it highlights an important dimension of Mixtec thinking about kinship: that substance is transmitted through nurturing acts, as well as through sexual intercourse, and that the feeding of one human being by another can create a special bond between them. But before discussing this further, it is necessary to examine just what it is that blood means to Nuyootecos and why its transmission should create such especially close ties between the persons involved.

Blood. Earlier I spoke of yɨɨ, "the heat of life," as the basis of bodily function, the force that gives us strength and vitality. In the human body, yɨɨ flows from the ánima, or "soul," which can be found throughout the body but which exists in its most concentrated form in the heart (which is called ánima).[4] When a person loses his or her *ánima*, due to either a severe emotional overload or the work of a demon, it is as if someone pulled the plug on an appliance. They will not be able to eat and will have no energy to work, since all their yɨɨ is gone. Even the mind will be affected, since the person loses the energy needed to understand and to act rationally. Without ánima, the sufferer will waste away and eventually die.[5]

The presence of ánima is manifest by a warm body, which is healthful and vigorous. To say someone has a cold body means he or she is weak and lethargic, and it is a sign that ánima is gone. When people who lose their ánima have it returned to them by a curer, they know it is back because they feel their head begin to heat up.

Although I have translated ánima as soul, the possession of ánima is not restricted to humans. Everything that is alive—which is almost everything in existence—has ánima, although it is found in greater concentrations in some things than in others. It is most concentrated in the Sun, which as I noted earlier is the most potent source of yɨɨ in the universe and is simply called ánima. Just as the heart is the vital organ that powers our bodies, the sun is the vital center of the universe, and its heat sustains life on earth (see Marcus 1983, 1989;

4. Anima is from the Spanish word for "soul."
5. The heart and blood are also seat of emotions. The salutation, "What does your ánima say?" for example, is answered *kusɨɨnio*, "we are content," or *kukuekainio*, "we are sad," and so on. We can see the close connection of the ánima with the blood in Nuyootecos' observation that a mother who nurses her child after being in an argument runs the risk of making her child sick, by transferring it to the anger she feels. This anger, present in the ánima, finds its way to the child through her blood.

and King 1988, who noted that the ancient Mixtec word for sun translates as "flaming heart").

It is significant that when a curer diagnoses a patient as having lost ánima to a tachi, he or she will sometimes speak of the demon having "grabbed" the patient's "blood," or having "grabbed" the patient's vein. Although concentrated in the heart, ánima is in the blood, and for this reason can be found throughout the body. Thus, people say that someone who has hot blood is strong, vigorous, and aggressive, a sign of a surfeit of yii (often manifested by a luxurious growth of body and facial hair). Someone who has cold blood lacks yii and is weak, infertile, and feeble. Cold blood produces illness and must be warmed up, through sweat baths, the application of rubbing alcohol, and the consumption of "hot" foods.

These statements are significant because they show that blood can serve as a kind of conduit for yii. Although other things may also carry yii beyond the body—hair, nail clippings, sweat, and other bodily excreta—blood is the most effective. Nuyootecos, for example, who often liken yii to electricity, say that people and animals die of electric shocks (while plants and other things remain unaffected) because blood is the best conductor of electricity, even better than high-tension wires. I mention this because if we return to Nuyooteco ideas about reproduction, we can see that as the father of a child fills the mother's womb with his blood, and as the mother nourishes the child with her blood, what they transfer to their children is life in a most potent and concentrated form. It is for this reason that the sexual act leaves men "cold" and breast-feeding a child leaves a woman cold.

Destiny. The passing of blood from parents to offspring is only loosely associated with the inheritance of emotional or physical traits. Some even deny that parents are able to transfer characteristics to their children at all. When I would question people about features shared by children and parents, they would often answer me with examples of children who do not look like either of their parents, or with instances where a hard-working man raised a son who turned out to be lazy. Nuyootecos view character traits, instead, to be determined by one's destiny.

At the moment of birth a child receives his or her *kivi*, "day," or *ta'vi*, "destiny" or "fortune." The kivi or ta'vi of a child includes its physical characteristics (e.g., sex and physique), its personal habits (e.g., neatness), its personality (e.g., gruffness or joviality), and even when and how the child will die. As one man rather pessimistically put it,

Iyo tuni kivɨ nkaku tee kushi
There is one day that the lazy man is born

Iyo tuni kivɨ nkaku saa kui'na
There is one day that the thief is born

Iyo tuni kivɨ nkaku ka'ni niyɨ
There is one day that the assassin is born.

While inside the womb, the child has no destiny. A fetus is neutral, it has no personality, and is unable to think. It is only when the child first appears "in the light" that the "blessing" *(bendición)* of a destiny is bestowed upon it.

I should briefly note here that a view of the person as someone who carries with them, as part of their personal identity, things that we see as either genetically encoded or as just a matter of chance, has important implications for Nuyooteco understandings of death. This is because death is as much a part of one's being as one's height or facial features and is determined by birth, since at birth one receives one's destiny. People even refer to destiny as *orao*, "our hour, our time," since it establishes, in the words of one man, "our limit." Nuyootecos therefore speak of birth and death as symmetrical, as in the adage, "we die on the anniversary of our birth." This will become significant when we consider Nuyooteco ideas about the afterlife in later chapters. Here I simply want to mention the *kitɨ nuvi*, which are also fixed by destiny.

The kitɨ nuvi. People say that at the time a child is born, an animal is also born in the forest. This animal, or occasionally animals, will be the child's *kitɨ nuvi*, literally, its "transforming animal" or coessence. Because the person and animal share the same destiny—a widespread notion in Native Mesoamerica—they also share character traits. For example, someone who is clever will have as a *kitɨ nuvi* a deer, since people reckon that the deer is the animal with the most intelligence. Similarly, someone with a hairy chest may have a puma as a *kitɨ nuvi*. For Nuyootecos, the connection between a person and their *kitɨ nuvi* is so complete that the two share consciousness. Thus, when people dream they are in places or situations that only animals could be in, such as under a rock or in a dark wood, they say they are experiencing the world through the eyes of their *kiti nuvi*. Such dreams take place at night, since this is when wild animals are about.

Nakara and Kinship

When a man or woman says that a child is his or her "milk and blood," neither is—as our discussion of destiny shows—referring to a heritage of traits extending back through the generations. Rather, what they refer to is a set of ties between persons that emerge out of the *way* blood is transmitted between them. As we saw, parents first transmit blood to their child when the father injects semen into the mother's womb during the sexual act, and then when the mother feeds her child her blood. This transmission of life-giving substances does not end when the child stops nursing, however. Nuyootecos say that the food, clothing, and other items that parent's provide their children so that they grow and prosper are related to the blood mothers and fathers transmit to children. Thus they speak of the tortilla as "our blood and our vein"; they say it "puts yïï" in us, and they consider it to be that which gives us the energy to think and act. Even though no one in Nuyoo would confuse a woman's nursing an infant with her weaving a huipil for her 10-year-old daughter, they are part of a single sequence of transactions through which kin create and maintain ties with one another.

In chapter 1, I pointed out that the relationships where parents provide their children with what they need for a prosperous life is called nakara. People gloss it as "they nurture [me], they maintain [me]," and consider such acts as feeding *(nsikaji ma,* "he fed him") and clothing *(nsi kuniji ma,* "he dressed him") to constitute nakara. Recall also from chapter 1 that the household is the foremost expression of nakara. Within the household, all wealth is pooled, and each member looks out for other members' well-being. This suggests that the nurturing acts that create a tie of shared substance between parent and child are related to the acts that create the strong ties among household members, so that kinship and household are intimately connected in Nuyooteco thinking.

In conceptualizing the relationship between nakara, kinship, and the household, it is possible to view nakara as a moral code and to distinguish the Nuyooteco definition of kinship as "shared milk and blood" from both this code and its chief social expression, the household (cf. Gibson 1985). There are, for example, people who live in the same household, and maintain a nakara relationship with one another, but who do not share milk and blood. Yet the issue is not clear cut, since acts of nakara create both domestic relationships (as is marriage) and the link of kinship (as in a mother's feeding her breast milk to her child). This dual instrumentality is significant because, as we will see below and in chapter 10, nakara plays a role in Nuyooteco ideas about relatedness that is analogous to the one played by descent principals in tribal societies: it links the local solidarity of the corporate group with the symbolic solidarity of shared kinship.

Nuyootecos as Kin

I have spent this time discussing Mixtec ideas about kinship because, as I pointed out earlier, Nuyootecos frequently speak of themselves as ta'a, or "kin." Indeed, the terminology of address Nuyootecos use for one another is consistent with this vision people have of themselves as "kin." All members of the community who are older than ego are addressed as "mother" *(nana)*, or "father" *(tata)*. All members of ego's same generation are addressed as "brother" *(ñani,* males speaking), "sister" *(ku'vi,* females speaking), or "cross-sex sibling" *(ku'va).* Finally, those who are younger than ego are addressed as "child" (se'ya). This does not mean that Nuyootecos are unable to distinguish between uterine kin and other community members. When a situation arises where they need to make such a distinction, they use *ta'a yachini,* "ta'a who are close to me" for the former, and simply ta'a for the latter. But as this shows, uterine kin are a subset of ta'a.

The notion that Nuyootecos are kin and are related to one another as are parents and children, or brother and sister, presents a problem, however. If kinship ties between parents and children are defined in terms of shared blood and milk, and if these substances are transmitted through procreative acts, as well as when parents feed their children (both inside and outside the womb), then how can Nuyootecos be kin? People assuredly do not say they are related to elder members of the community because these elders transmitted substance to them in sexual acts, nor do they say they nurse younger members of the community the way parents do with children.

To answer this question, we need to recall that Nuyooteco social symbolism is not only a system of representation, but also a theory of how people create and maintain relationships. In part one of the book, we saw that homologies exist between the way Nuyootecos create and maintain relationships with one another, such as in marriage, and other phenomena, such as corn growth. These homologies exist not because corn growth is reflective of marriage, but because marriage and corn agriculture share a common origin in a process whereby opposed entities are mediated by that which energizes and renews them. More generally, this shows that our examination of Nuyooteco social symbolism should not be restricted to people's relationships with one another, but should also include how they create and maintain relationships with the gods, the dead, and nature. For this reason, I turn in the next section to an event that occurred in the most ancient times, when Nuyootecos emerged from a place called Soko Usha. It is important to begin here because Nuyootecos say the relationships between human parents and children and among fellow Nuyootecos are derived from this original creative act.

NUYOOTECO ORIGINS

Most people in the region are familiar with the tradition that Nuyootecos emerged from Soko Usha in the distant past. Many say the place of emergence was a tunnel, which had its origin in Chalcatongo, a *cacicazgo* seat Nuyoo was subject to during the colonial period. Others say the tunnel came from Huajuapan de León, in the Mixteca Baja. There are even some who say, in what is perhaps a recent accretion to the story, that the people of Nuyoo came through a tunnel that began in Zaachila in the Valley of Oaxaca. While the historical ties encoded in the various places of origin of the tunnel are interesting, they should not concern us here. What is important is the suggestion that Nuyoo's people did not just pass through a tunnel to come to Nuyoo, but were born from Earth.

Soko Usha is near Yucunino, the highest, and traditionally oldest, settlement in Nuyoo. *Soko*, depending on its use, can mean "well," and, more significantly, "womb." *Usha* is "seven," a name given to many sacred places in Mixtec geography. So Soko Usha can be taken to mean "womb seven" (Pohl 1984:177). Many people in Nuyoo and neighboring Yucuhiti think of Soko Usha as a womb. I once heard men from Yucuhiti taunt Nuyootecos by saying, "You people all came from a hole in the ground," to which a Nuyooteco replied, "Well, we all come from a hole" (i.e., mother's vagina). Later, a man in the Nuyoo party went on to relate how Yucuhiti's people were born from a dog.

We can see the womb-like quality of Soko Usha in a drawing made by Juan Lópex Ñunez. In figure 17 he illustrated his ancestors' time underground, giving the distinct impression of a fetal existence.

The people of neighboring Yucuhiti have an origin myth that is distinct from Nuyoo's—that they were born from a dog. Mixtecs, like other people, feel that different human groups are the result of multiple creations (see López Austin 1980:272 for Mesoamerica). In

Figure 17. Nuyooteco ancestors inside the earth.

other words, they do not think a single act brought all people every-where into being. What this means is that, for Nuyootecos, their emergence from Soko Usha makes them unique, just as for other peoples of the region other kinds of origins make them unique. The idea that separate creations produced separate peoples is supported by the somatic differences between members of different commu-nities, since centuries of endogamy have given each group a distinct set of features, which Nuyootecos (and after a while even I) could readily identify. In the Mixteca Alta, people of different towns usually view themselves as distinct varieties of human being.

Body and Earth

The story that Nuyootecos were born from Soko Usha has a signifi-cance that goes beyond the way it distinguishes Nuyootecos socially and somatically from other people in the region. This is because through the process of creation, Nuyootecos became one with Earth and Rain. We can see this in the word for the human body, *ñune'yu*. Ñune'yu, according to Nuyootecos, is composed of two parts, ñu'un (soil) and *ne'yu* (mud; for another example from the Mixteca, see Flanet 1977:103). The "soil" is soil of Earth, and the mud is a mixture of soil and moisture from Rain.

In calling the body, "earth-mud," Nuyootecos are not alluding to some metaphoric relationship between the body and the world. Instead they specifically state that the body is made of the same substance as Earth and Rain. This notion, is, in turn, likened to the idea that Earth and Rain are mother and father to humans. Earth, as we saw, is a "womb" from which Nuyootecos emerged, and when speaking in generalities, it is quite appropriate to refer to Earth as *nanao*, "our mother." This is also consistent with the idea discussed in chapter 4, that Earth forms a womb for developing plant seed. Similarly, the Sky can be referred to as *tatao*, "our father," and each of the "faces" of Rain are strongly male in character. The *ñu'un savi*, as we saw, carry the scepter of male potency, the machete, and the heroic tenuvi (who, as sacrificers, smoke cigars to bring rain) epitomize masculinity (e.g., Monaghan 1987, 1989). But most importantly, Rain, the fertilizing force of the Sky, is likened to semen. Fausto Modesto Velasco once explained, when Rain falls "it causes the plants sown there [i.e., in Earth] to grow just as male liquid causes a baby to grow in its mother."

Earth and Rain also nurture humans in the way parents nurture children in the household. This is related to an agreement made between Nuyooteco ancestors and Earth in the distant past. I have called this "the Covenant with the Earth." Tata Fausto Modesto Velasco told me the following version:

> The story says that there were two men who worked . . . who knows where?
> They went down and cleared the forest and brush, they cut it down.
> And well, if it wasn't the next day they went again to where their piece of work was.
> And it was only forest that regrew.
> The work they did was not there, because the forest regrew.
> And they thought that they would make a plea to [the face of the] Earth, they spoke to the Earth.
> They said, they pleaded, "Give us to eat, give us to drink, clothe us, because from the Earth comes all we need, and thus is our lot."
> And so they asked, they made a covenant *[nchiso yu'ura]*.
> They asked that "that which gives us life come over the world."
> They asked that it give them to drink, it give them to eat, and that [the Earth] should take them in again, because there is no other place they will go [when they die].
> As the Earth gives them to drink, as the Earth gives them to eat, it will gather them in again, we say, and we realize this is true.
> "And now it will produce, and we will obtain what it is we need to eat,

and thus we will live, we live from it," they said.
"And as we live, sickness will arrive, which will enter us, and where
    will we go? To what side will we leave?
"We will go because in the Earth we will lie down again.
"There it will take us in," they said.
The Earth acquiesced.
They were able to do their work.
Because they were not able to enjoy the work they did before.
They went to look for . . . they pleaded with [the Earth] that there
    would be there . . . that there would begin to exist, the work they
    did.
What corn seed! What bean seed! What squash seed they sowed!
"Yaah! It is going to bear fruit!" they said.
But they asked a favor of it.
And thus they were able to work, so the story says.

Fausto concludes with a characteristically Mixtec statement of self-
effacement: "But . . . the people told stories, and I learned their lies,
and I tell them, and this is all I say."

Tata Lorenzo López told me of a related covenant made in the
distant past when Rain did not fall, when plant growth was stunted,
and when people and animals were unable to reproduce. This situation called for a dramatic response, and all those affected gathered to
call for Rain.

All the plants here in the world spoke . . .
The plants that animals eat, the small plants, the fruit trees.
At the time that Earth was placed here;[6]

6. Rain is also associated with Earth. As Tata Lorenzo noted in his account, all moisture comes
from the Earth, not the Sky, "as one might believe." The plants, animals and men, who needed
rain made their supplication to a marsh, and vapor began to rise from the "head" of a rock in the
marsh. This rock is the *nu ñu'un no'yo*, or San Marcos. Water vapor also began to rise out of the ponds
and canyons. From this vapor, clouds began to form and they "became ripe." Soon, Rain fell for the
first time. The source of true moisture, and by implication, Rain, is thus the Earth. Rumblings in
the Earth are signs of Rain, and earthquakes, landslides, cave-ins, and other spectacular tectonic
events all have a direct impact on rainfall, either causing it to stop or making the beginning of a long
wet spell. Even the *ve'i savi*, the houses of the *ñu'un savi*, are caves in the Earth.
    This association of Rain with both Earth and Sky should be understood in terms of Mixtec views
concerning the origin of the world. Information recorded in early Spanish accounts of Mixtec
mythology, and in the Mixtec codices, suggest that in the earliest times there existed no "Earth" or
"Rain" as separate forces, because each was part of a primordial whole. One of the great acts of
creation occurred when Earth and Sky were separated (Mark King, personal communication, 1989).
Water, however, particularly in the form of Rain, remained a primary mediating element between
the major divisions of the sacred. It falls from the Sky as rain but rises from the Earth as vapor. The
cigar smoke of the tenuvi and the bird-like nature of the *koo savi*, which flies up and down with the

They spoke . . . they conferred.
A tree, a plant . . . whatever tree, wherever it stood,
Because there was no rain.
And so they conferred.
The trees, the small animals that are in the world;
They all conferred [including men].
That is the way it was . . . how was this?
And they wished that the plants would reproduce, that they should
    flourish;
And so they spoke with seven marshes and seven gorges;
But, of course, what kind of marsh was it?
There was no water coming from it, since there was only green *tineeca*
    grass growing there.
And some 12 days passed after they spoke there;
Twelve nights and 12 days;
At 10 o'clock in the morning they went there;
And again in the afternoon, when the sun is hidden by the hill there;
And there they spoke with the marsh, they spoke with that marsh;
Water ran there!
And over the marshy land a cloud settled;
Then . . . then at 9 o'clock, at 9 o'clock when it was just dawning;
The rain arrived.
The only thing we say that is in the marsh is Mayor San Marcos, we
    say.
Although it is a rock that is in the marsh, it is potent, vital we say.
Because it is from the [rock] that cloud arose on the hill, we say.
And this cloud carried [rain].
And it passed the drops;
Seven marshes became . . . 14 marshes;
Fourteen gorges, a big river ran there;
It is the marsh that the water comes from, and then returns to in the
    afternoon.
The *ñu'un savi* bestows moisture.
But it only places the cloud.
This [cloud] does not come from the sky, even though we might be-
    lieve otherwise.
Because it is from the Earth that it comes and climbs;
It leaves from the Earth and climbs;
Nor should we think, "where might all this come, might it come from
    afar, and arrive here?" we say [i.e., does it come from the sea?]
It arrives and bestows rain, we say.

---

seasons (and as a snake/bird is both of the Sky and of the Earth), are cosmologically significant
because they link Sky and Earth in the way water does.

[No] Because the stone, even though in the marsh, even though in the
   big gorge, was, and is, sacred.
Because in past times there was no rain.
The people lived only on dry, parched land, we say.
Only the dry earth, only the hard rock;
That was the way it was;
Over the hard earth;
On the hard rock, we say.
It was not able to give the people water to drink;
Dry earth is the way it was.
Over the hard earth;
On the hard rock, we say.
It was not able to give the people water to drink;
Dry earth is the way it was;
Then, suddenly, it [the rock] succeeded.
Water ran there . . . everything flourished.
All that they conferred upon was done;
The plants, the tree, and the drops came . . . and all flourished;
Because there was no rain.
And then . . . well . . .
Even the trees would have dried out.
This is a story that I tell you,
And you will excuse me.
Because it is this story you wish to record.
And you left humbly;
You came and you made conversation.
What little I know . . . where might there be people who will like it?
Because there are different customs where we were born, where we
   live.
And this is all I know . . . what I tell you.
You will please pardon me.[7]

The Codex Vienna, a manuscript painted long before the arrival of
the Spaniards, records a version of these covenants with Earth and
Rain (see Monaghan 1990c). As we will see, the covenants are
fundamental to Nuyooteco thinking about the origins of moral life,
about the different ways males and females relate to corn production,
about the meaning of death, and the nature of sacrifice. Everyone I

---

7. Although it is not explicitly stated in Tata Lorenzo's account, the same kind of agreement that
the Nuyooteco ancestors made with the Earth was made with the Rain. In return for the prosperity
that Rain brings, the Rain may "eat" human bodies, just as the Earth "eats" them in return for the
permission to sow. Thus the people who die during a storm or who have been "burned" by a bolt of
lightning are said to have been "collected" by the Rain to meet the obligation humans incurred
through their agreement with it.

asked in Nuyoo could offer an informed interpretation of the Covenant with Earth, and even children could produce accurate versions of it. This is in contrast to other cosmogonic texts, which are not well known outside of a restricted group of storytellers and shamans. But what I want to highlight here are the analogies that exist between the way Earth and Sky nurture humans and the way human parents care for their children.

When people talk about what happened in the covenants, they often say that the covenants allowed them to "eat Earth," as if they physically consume Earth itself, and "eat Rain," by consuming its children. Nuyootecos describe this relationship as one where Earth and Rain "care for" (nakara) people, in the same way that a mother and father provide their children with all they need to grow and prosper. As one man explained,

Sikajio jen kajio na in tata sa'o
It feeds us, and we eat whatever seeds we make

Ree koo naka kaji va'o
And there will be that which will nourish us well

Sikajio, siko'o, sikunijio
It feeds us, it gives us to drink, it clothes us.

Although I examine Nuyooteco ideas about death in more detail in chapter 10, I want to briefly note here that when someone dies, Nuyootecos say their cadaver does not "rise and go to heaven or anywhere else" but, once it is buried, decays and becomes Earth. What is interesting is that Nuyootecos speak of this process as one where Earth "cares for" (nakara) humans and where the deceased and Earth come to form a single household. People thus call the grave the *ve'i niyi*, "house of the dead," and say of the cemetery as a whole that *ve'i iyo vi*, "our true house is there," and that *ve'io ya'a chi in sombra najia vio ni vi y re sepultura yukua chi yukua kuvi nijia ve'io*, "our house here is only a bit of shade where we rest a while, and the grave there is our true house." The idea is that just as nakara, and the idea of shared substance, implies that those involved make up a household, so too Nuyootecos conceive themselves as forming a single household with Earth, when at death they return to "their true house." As in the relationship of parents to children, we see intertwined here an idea of shared substance, nakara, and household.

I should also note here that the idea that Nuyootecos have come to share substance with Earth and Rain gives them a special attachment to the territory in which they live. This is because their birth occurred in a specific place, Soko Usha, "Womb Seven," at the historical center of their territory (figure 18). This place of birth, which all Nuyootecos can point to, and the substance they share with Earth connect them to this place as well as to one another by ties that are, in a sense, organic, so that there is a complete association between people and locality.

What kind of attitudes toward territory might we find among a people who speak of themselves as linked to a place by the same substance and event? One is a sharp distinction between one's own property and that of others, of the order of the distinction one might make between one's own body and that of others. Indeed, in Oaxaca, the rural political landscape is politically fragmented to an extreme. With less than four percent of the Mexican population, it contains almost twenty-five percent of the nation's municipalities. Many municipalities in the state, and especially in the Mixteca, lack the official qualifications for municipal status, but they have been able to resist merger into larger entities because of the antipathy they have for one another and reluctance on the part of the state government to implement a consolidation policy that will provoke bloodshed.

Intervillage conflict is endemic in Oaxaca (Dennis 1987), and Nuyoo is involved in several long-standing disputes. With Santa María Yucuhiti, whose town center lies a scant five minutes' walk from Nuyoo Center (or, as one eighteenth-century priest put it, "a stone's throw away"), the dispute goes back at least until the early 1600s. The reason the two communities have their town centers so close is it enables them to monitor each other and protect their frontier. This pairing of Nuyoo and Yucuhiti is not unique. Many municipalities in the region have located their hamlets next to hamlets of municipalities that border them, ready to square off across the no-man's-land that separates them. In the Mixteca Alta, many of these settlements date from a period between the mid-1800s to the 1950s, when growing populations, government attempts to introduce new systems of land tenure, and a shortage of good farmland led to bloody struggles between neighboring towns. Leaders established hamlets at defensible positions to protect strategic resources, so that the population of these municipalities tends to be concentrated on their boundaries, with their geographic centers relatively empty, a kind of territorial circling of the wagons.

Outside observers have long marveled at how Oaxacan peoples are ready to fight and die over the tiniest fractions of land, which are often

Figure 18. Nuyooteco ancestors emerging from the earth at Soko Usha. Soko Usha is, like the Aztec Chicomoztoc, or "Seven Caves" (from which came the seven "tribes" of the Chichimeca), a womb-like place. However, Soko Usha does not translate as "Seven Caves," but as "Cave Seven." Because seven is a sacred number, it is often incorporated in Mixtec toponyms without necessarily meaning that the place contains seven caves, springs, trees, and so on.

of no imaginable use. While we will see in part four of the book that the incidence of these disputes rises and falls with population pressure, the strength or weakness of the central government, and a number of economic factors, this extreme sense of territoriality should, at least in the Nuyoo case, be put in the context of a set of ideas about a group of people who not only share the same origin, but who also are intimately linked to the place at which that origin occurred. Nuyootecos, who have fought and died over small parcels of barren, rocky ground, know that their territory is, in many ways, as close to them as a kinswoman, or even as close to them as their own bodies.[8]

8. The idea that the body is of the same substance as Earth can also be seen in the practice of

KIN AND COMMUNITY

The story Nuyootecos tell of their emergence from the womb at Soko Usha and the making of the Covenants with Earth and Rain are significant because they instituted several fundamental social relationships. What these relationships are can perhaps best be seen if we return to Nuyooteco thinking about what the world was like before people came to live in Nuyoo, and before the Covenants with Earth and Rain were made.

According to Nuyootecos, in ancient times a wild forest covered the world. This forest was inhabited by a primitive race of beings called the tiumi, or "people of the wilds" *(nɨvɨ yuku)*. Recall from chapter 1 that when Nuyootecos speak of the tiumi, they usually do so in terms of a set of contrasts with today's people. The tiumi thus lived by hunting animals, which they ate raw because they had no fire. Their dwellings were isolated caves, and they did not form communities (according to some, they were not even able to speak). Nuyootecos also say that "the tiumi did not know what mothers and fathers are" and they "had no families," statements I understand to mean that kinship did not exist for the presocial tiumi.

People today live in communities made up of households because Jesus, or Sun, destroyed the tiumi and, in his travels, defined a set of relationships—in particular, gift exchange, baptism, and marriage— through which households could mediate their differences and create or maintain long-standing ties of alliance. Earth and Rain played a similar role in distinguishing humans from the tiumi. For one, the relationships between humans and Earth and Rain established in the covenants allowed for the practice of agriculture, so people today do not have to hunt like the tiumi. Similarly, the reason humans today are bound by ties of kinship, while the tiumi were not, is that today's people were created by a mother, Earth, and a father, Rain, who transmitted substance to their children in generative acts. Moreover, Earth and Rain continue to nurture their children by providing them with all they need for a prosperous life. To put this another way, recognizing mothers and fathers, and having families, is essential to being human because humanity was created through the transmission of substance in generative and nurturing acts.

The emergence of people from Soko Usha and the making of the

---

painting one's body with mud when ill. One little boy who lived near where I stayed in Nuyoo Center, and who was often sick, seemed to walk around with his forehead covered with mud for months at a time, since Nuyootecos do not wash the mud off until after they are well.

Covenant with Earth were not only key events in the evolution of humankind; they also made Nuyootecos a people. It is because Nuyootecos were born from Soko Usha that they are linked to the place that is Nuyoo, and it is because they were born at Soko Usha that they are distinct from other groups. It follows that if the transmission of substance from one person to another in generative and nurturing acts is essential to being human—it was this set of acts that created civilized life—then the transmission of substance in generative and nurturing acts will also be essential to the community, because it was the same set of acts that produced Nuyootecos as a group. In other words, Nuyootecos are ta'a, or "kin," and speak of one another as "father" and "daughter" or "mother" and "son" because they transmit substance to one another, and care for one another, in a way that is homologous to parents' care and transmission of substance to their children. These relationships, furthermore, are similarly structured because they share a common root: the birth of people from Soko Usha, and the covenants made with Earth and Rain. What I will argue in the next chapter is that Nuyootecos transmit this substance to one another through sacrifice.

CHAPTER 9

SACRIFICE AND KINSHIP

NUYOOTECOS define soko, or "sacrifice," as "presenting something to a god." An act of soko can thus be anything from dropping a coin in the church collection plate to pouring pulque onto the ground for a *nu ñu'un*. It is not appropriate to use soko for an exchange between persons, although in the past it was used for the tribute commoners paid to a lord (Monaghan n.d.).

When Nuyootecos make sacrifice, they do so, as one man explained, "so that things become more abundant." In agricultural contexts, people speak of sacrifice as a stimulus to growth and generative of life, the way we might speak of fertilizer. More generally, when Nuyootecos make their offerings they ask, as another man said, for the things "we need so that we may live." For the people of Nuyoo, sacrifice is a condition of human life.

When making an offering, the sacrificer mutters a supplication in a low voice, slowly, with deference and respect *(ka'a kuachi)*. The sacrificer should also be in a distinct emotional state. As Nuyootecos put it, the sacrificer "thinks sadly and humbly" *(jiani kukuekani)*. This means that the sacrificer comprehends the great and difficult effort that the god must perform and his dependence upon the god for what he requests. The intensity of these feelings may even cause the sacrificer to weep while praying. The supplication is called *ka'a maa kao*, literally, "speaking alone, we alone," which people translate as "succor me."

TYPES OF SACRIFICE

When Nuyootecos make sacrifice, they may have a number of diverse objectives in mind. At times, the sacrifice is expiatory, for a fault committed. It sometimes happens, for example, that people offend a *nu ñu'un* by fouling its house, and it retaliates by seizing the offender's ánima. The items offered then substitute for the ánima which the *nu ñu'un* releases when it feels it has been compensated (figure 19). At

213

Figure 19. A curer offering pulque to a *nu ñu'un* for a patient who has lost his ánima. The curer must speak the name of the *nu ñu'un* who holds the ánima, or else it will not listen and will not release it. Because the curer is often unsure of precisely which *nu ñu'un* should receive the "fine," he addresses all of them. Throughout his prayers, it is important that the curer "think sadly" *(jia ni kukuekani)*, a typically Mesoamerican form of religiosity where one approaches the sacred with great remorse of having causes offense. The patient should also "think sadly" because it is only when the patient acknowledges his or her fault and that he or she is completely dependent on the *nu ñu'un* that the cure can begin.

other times, people make sacrifice as a gift, to receive a gift in return. This occurs in agricultural rituals, where the farmer may make offerings of pulque to the *nu ñu'un*, to stimulate them in its work. Another, more dramatic, example occurred in the late 1940s when Mestizo engineers operated a small lead and silver mine in Nuyoo. One day thre was an accident, and several workers died (all the victims came from outside Nuyoo). Many allege that the engineers them- selves caused the accident to stimulate the production of ore, since the vein had begun to peter out. The engineers, people explain, gave the workers to the *nu ñu'un* by arranging for the entrance to collapse when the men were inside the mine. This "meal" so invigorated the *nu ñu'un* that it began to produce more riches.

Nuyootecos also make sacrifice an act of homage or thanksgiving, where the saints, *nu ñu'un*, or *ñu'un savi* supply something to people, and people make sacrifices to acknowledge the god's generosity. After shooting a deer, for example, a hunger will incense the carcass of the animal and perhaps make an offering of meat to the *nu ñu'un*, by burying a cooked deer thigh at the spot where he shot it. His purpose is to thank the *nu ñu'un* for the animal and to keep it disposed to additional kills in the future. One man put it this way: "We give the *nu ñu'un* something so that it will think well of us *[kuva'ani]*, just as we give something to a relative or a fellow Nuyooteco so they will be content with us, even if it is only half a tortilla. If we did not give these things we would make them feel resentful."

As that indicates, another reason for offering sacrifice can be fear of retaliation for not meeting an obligation. The man's statement also suggests that any particular sacrifice is part of an ongoing relationship between humans and the gods. This is clearly expressed in the text of a prayer uttered by a curer, Tata Felipe Sarabia. In it, Tata Felipe refers several times to past sacrifices he made to the *nu ñu'un* and to sacrifices he will make in the future, highlighting his long and continuous association with the *nu ñu'un*. He uttered this prayer while making offerings to a *nu ñu'un* that had taken a patient's ánima. It is also significant that he did not simply humble himself before the *nu ñu'un*. Instead, he threatened the *nu ñu'un* with chile powder and salt, substances that make the *nu ñu'un* nauseated. He once explained: "You may have to frighten San Marcos [the *nu ñu'un*] into releasing the ánima. It is just like a person, and you have to talk to it like one. You have to lie and beg to get the ánima of a person back. We can hurt San Marcos, and it can hurt us. You have to try to fool it. This is why you need someone who is good at dealing with it." Tata Felipe thus tried to influence the *nu ñu'un* much as he would try to influence a fellow Nuyooteco. He gave gifts, he humbled himself, he pleaded, and at times he threatened. (By his own account, however, he has never actually carried out his threats. He said it would be foolhardy to offend the *nu ñu'un* in this way, but since it does not know how the curer will react, it is frightened just the same.)[1] He approached the *nu*

---

1. The prayer recited by the curer also shows that the reasons people feel obliged to make sacrifice—expiation for fault, a gift for productivity, thanksgiving for something received, and fear of retaliation—are not in any way mutually exclusive. Thus, a farmer making an offering of pulque

ñu'un as beings with whom he could negotiate, with sacrifice being
the channel for these negotiations.

The notion that people negotiate with the gods through sacrifice
brings us to another aim Nuyootecos have when they make sacrifice:
to come into contact with the sacred. We can see this in the practice
where people "bathe" *(sikuchi)* a saint with flowers, by whisking a
bouquet across the saint's image, and then "bathing" themselves, by
whisking the bouquet across their own chest, arms, and face. As
Hubert and Mauss (1968) observed, the act of bathing oneself with
the sacrificial item can be interpreted as an act of purification,
preparing oneself to receive the blessing of the god.

The Sacrificial Objects

Candles, incense, pulque, liquor, flowers, and corn are the things
Nuyootecos most commonly offer in sacrifice. Many of these items are
marked as special substances by the incorporation of the morphological root *ii* (sacred, miraculous, delicate, fragile) into their names (King
1988:134–9). Thus corn is *itun*, candles are *iti*, flowers are *ita*. These
items play a significant role in sacrifice because they represent, in
ritual contexts, key features of both the sacrificer who offers them (or
the person for whom the sacrificer is proxy) and the "god" who
receives them. In this role the sacrificial items serve as tokens of the
relationship between people and the god, which also defines the
process through which the sacrificer's request is fulfilled (Valeri
1985:67).

To illustrate how the sacrificial items become tokens of the relationship between the sacrificer and the gods, let us take corn as an
example. Corn is a good choice because its production, as we will see,
is the condition upon which the first act of sacrifice was predicated.
Perhaps because of this, many other sacrificial items are metaphorically related to it. For example, people often use the *ita nuni*,
"corn flower," in sacrifices during the rainy season, and the *ita saa ñii*,
"tender ear of corn flower," in the sacrifices of the harvest season.
Also, a dream in which a god presents one with white flowers may be
the sign of a good corn harvest. In another example, the tortilla has the
property of "illuminating us," just as the candle does.

Nuyootecos make sacrifices of corn in a variety of contexts. While
sitting to eat in the fields during a meal, a man may break off a piece of

---

for a good corn harvest may also apologize for any faults he has committed and request that he be
shown favor in future harvests.

the tortilla he is eating and throw it to the *nu ñu'un* of the place. People give raw corn to Misericordia when it arrives at their house on its annual rounds, and they prepare *pozole*, a corn gruel, as an offering in the Viko Nuni, "Fiesta of Corn" (see below). Dried corn on the cob may be left in a Rain shrine as an offering to the *ñu'un savi*, and one can often find ears of corn piled around saint's images in the church.

Like other Mesoamerican peoples, Nuyootecos speak of corn as essential to their health and well-being. They sometimes refer to the tortilla as "our flesh and blood" *(kuñuo, niñio;* Furst 1978:199). Without tortillas, we would not, as they say, "be able to live," since the tortilla "is what illuminates us" *(stuuno; kunijio)*. Eating the tortilla enables us to think, to reason, to rationalize. It also gives us the energy to work. People therefore say the tortilla is "our vein" *(tuchio)* or "our root" since, like a vein or root, it is a conduit for yɨɨ. Nuyootecos consume a variety of other foods, such as squash, rice, greens, and beans, because these serve to make a meal of tortillas more delicious, but they never replace the tortilla, since corn is in a class by itself.

Corn is also the measure of productive activity. Today the wage they earn is indexed to the market price of two *cajónes* (about 10 liters) of dried corn. Not long ago, people paid laborers in corn, either as tortillas (10 to 15 for a day's work) or in gourds of dried corn. Women also used the gourds they wore on their heads to measure corn, and each woman knew precisely how much corn her hat would hold and the quantity of tortillas she could make from it. Moreover, many implements used for transporting, measuring, and processing corn are feminine symbols. To take one example, the dream of a *tenate*, a round basket used to carry tortillas and a measure of dried corn, is a sign that a female child will be born to one's household. There is even a design on the Nuyooteco woman's huipil representing the tortilla, the *shita ñɨɨ*, "tortilla of new corn."

Beyond women's labor, corn is associated with female sexuality. The vagina is sometimes called "the folded tortilla," and the saying that one is "going to eat the large tamale *(tikoo)*," a dish made from corn, connotes the sexual act. We also saw that Nuyootecos speak of the corn plant as a young, pretty, and marriageable woman.

Nuyootecos also sometimes call the tortilla *animao*, "our ánima," and in the dreams a curer or patient has following the performance of a cure for the loss of ánima to the *nu ñu'un*, they may see an old man handing them an ear of corn, which means that the ánima has been returned. This association with ánima is similarly apparent in the idea that the tortilla is "our blood" or "our vein," since blood is one of the principal seats of ánima and the channel for yïï. It is as if corn is essential not only to subsistence, but to being human.

Just as corn represents a wide range of human attributes—the sexuality of women, human vitality, the blood, the ánima, people's capacity for labor and rational thought—so too it represents the attributes of a wide range of Nuyooteco gods. Corn has an *ito'o* or "patron" that watches over it, as do all the other species of plants and animals. When I asked a man I was visiting one day about why he didn't cut down a large, unproductive coffee tree on his property and sow a young one in its place, he said he was afraid to because it might be the patron of all the coffee plants, and this would cause all the other coffee he sowed "to leave." As his remarks suggest, the ito'o are usually a superlative member of the species they protect. Thus, San Eustquio, the *nu ñu'un yuku* and ito'o of the deer, is itself a large buck with a cross of white fur on its head.

The ito'o of corn, the *niñi i'ya* (figure 20), is a large ear of corn with a "head" (the tip of the corn ear) that is markedly larger than its base. *Niñi* means "ear of corn," while people translate *i'ya* as "archbishop," "cacica," "king" and "patron." I'ya may be related to *ia*, which in pre-Columbian and early colonial time meant lord or god (Alvarado 1962). Nuyootecos also call the i'ya the "flower of the corn field," both for its shape, which vaguely resembles a flower, and for being the finest, most beautiful expression of the cornfield, in the same way the flower is the finest expression of the plant on which it grows. I should also note that in local mythology, the i'ya is a cleft-headed or two-headed god (ndiosi) who, through negotiations with another god, arranged for humans to enjoy three meals a day. If it were not for these negotiations, people would have gone hungry, since they would have been able to eat only once or twice a day. The i'ya thus plays an important role in making food available to humans.

If a *niñi i'ya* appears in a cornfield, it is a sign there will be an excellent harvest. After the farmer picks it, he should dry it in the sun and then hang it above his household altar, where family members adorn it with flowers and "feed" it incense and candles in sacrifice, "as if it were a saint." It should not be placed in the household corn crib, since it will "eat" the other ears of corn deposited there, causing the crib to empty prematurely.

All corn, not solely the i'ya, is anthropomorphized. People say that corn seeds speak to one another, both in the ground and when they are in storage in the corn crib. People also say that corn has an ánima, and

Figure 20. Corn. The ear to the right is the *niñi i'ya*. Its big head is probably caused by a corn virus, which splits the cob into two or more sections (Richard Ford, personal communication).

therefore sensibilities, just as humans do. Unnecessarily rough treatment of corn can cause it stress and pain. One man told me how, as a child, he was helping clean the house, and he gathered up all the dry corn husks and cobs left on the floor after his grandmother had finished shucking them. Because he did not feel like taking them outside, he burned them in the hearth. When his grandmother came in and saw what he had done she became furious and beat him severely. She asked him, "How would you like to be burned by fire? That is how the corn feels. Don't you think it suffers enough, so that we may eat?" Nuyootecos accordingly treat corn (and all refuse from the corn plant, the tassels, the husks, the stalks) with great respect. When people finish shucking cobs, they take the remains out to their fields and deposit them in a place where they will not be stepped on or otherwise damaged. As the man's grandmother told him, "corn suffers enough." When we consume corn, we consume a living, vibrant, and holy being, and if we cause it to suffer unnecessarily, the protectors of the corn may take it away from us.

The other items Nuyootecos offer in sacrifice have the same general characteristics as corn. On the one hand, they are related metaphorically to a significant aspect of a god. Thus people liken the light and heat of the candle to the light and heat given off by the Sun/Jesus Christ. On the other hand, they may be metonymically related to the god, either as a derivation or manifestation of the sacred, or by becoming a part of the god through its being offered in sacrifice. An example of the former is the maguey, from which pulque is taken, which some Nuyootecos consider the yavi, while others say it is the Virgin of Natividad.[2] An example of the latter are the bouquets of flowers that people use to bathe the saints, so that when the bouquet is set out in a cornfield, the power and sacredness it bears within it after being offered to the saint will protect the plants from winds and animals.

The items Nuyootecos offer in sacrifice are also like corn in that they embody human attributes. Candles are associated with the life span and the destiny of those who offer them.[3] Incense represents

2. Nuyootecos are familiar with the story of the Virgen de Natividad of Chalcatongo, who appeared on the leaf of a maguey (Jansen 1982). The maguey is also associated with the *yavi*. This figure is able to change back and forth between male and female forms and to transform itself into a maguey. The androgynous yavi and its metamorphosis into the maguey is perhaps linked to the idea that pulque is like male semen and female milk—the forms in which blood is transmitted to children (recall also that in at least one Mixtec town, semen and milk are not lexically distinguished). Moreover, the yavi is considered to be the equivalent of the *nosō*, a childlike being who darts through the air in the form of a flaming ball (or, as people in Nuyoo put it, "like a kerosene lamp"). A tone change from nosō to *noso* means breast, and in local mythology, the nosō is often depicted as a child suckling a woman's breast.

3. Candles represent the human person in several ways. For one, the life span is often likened to a candle. The explicit metaphoric link here is that as life is a fragile, delicate thing, so too the candle is a delicate thing, easily knocked over and snuffed out. A candle, in addition, has only a short and preordained time to burn, just as people's lives are short and death is one's destiny.

The flame of the candle is also likened to the mind *(anduni)* or an eye. As the anduni illuminates our thoughts, so the candle's flames illuminate a room. Indeed, as one man put it, when the anduni is extinguished "we are all in darkness." *Na'ma*, "extinguish", and *kuanaa*, "to be in darkness, to become dark", are both metaphors for death.

In addition to being a symbol of the human life span, the candle can also stand for the life and body of specific individuals. For example, it is a bad omen if one lights a candle and the hard wax on the outside of it peels to the sides as it melts down. The sides of the candle are said to be the "sides" of the person who lit it, and the peeling wax is a sign of impending sickness. This same idea can be seen in the use of candles in witchcraft. The name of the victim *(shini,* also "head") is inscribed on the candle, prayed over in the church, and then burned in a mock funeral ceremony (some people hold that seven or nine candles must be used), at All Saints, or in the cemetery. In the latter case the nature of the victim's death will be determined by where the candle is placed in the graveyard. If it is burned in the "unbaptized" part of the cemetery, the victim will die in a violent accident. If it is

much the same thing.[4] The light emitted by the candle is related to the light of the mind. Pulque represents blood, particularly blood in the form of sexual fluids.[5] Flowers are likened to children and the *ánima*.[6] In most cases the analogies are made between the sacrificial items and body parts or human capacities closely related to the ánima—blood, heart, mind, emotions.

---

placed in the "baptized" part, he or she will die of illness.

In a less sinister way, the candle shows the emotional state of the person who offered it. If one is "sad" *(kukuekani)* it will burn low, and if one is content *(kusïïni)* it will burn high. If the person is sick in some way, the candle will simply fall apart and not burn properly.

The idea that a candle offered in sacrifice stands for the life span and body of a specific individual is linked to the notion that candles also embody "the heat of life." All things that radiate warmth and give off light are felt to embody *yïï*, which is, as we have seen, the essence of vital life.

4. Incense, or *sujie ïi*, "sacred resin," is often burned in Nuyooteco offerings. It is considered to be among the finest sacrifices that can be made, and is said to give off *nu'ma vishi* "sweet smoke," which is considered to be especially pleasing to the gods.

In curing rituals the patient often has his or her wrists, heart, inside of elbow joints, and head rubbed ("bathed") with an incense pellet. The pellet is then burned and the curer examines the sparks the pellet throws off, the smoke that rises, and the manner in which the pellet dissolves (this same technique can be used with candles, though incense is the most frequent choice). These things are significant because some of the patient's bodily excretions are rubbed into the pellet when the patient is "bathed" with it. These excretions contain ánima, so that the state of the patient's ánima becomes apparent in the way the pellet burns. As one diviner explained, "the ánima speaks to the incense." When the ánima "speaks" in this way, a part of the patient's destiny and, what is most important if the diviner is interpreting illness, the patient's life force stay with the pellet. By burning the pellet, the curer is thus able to determine the state of the patient's health, or, in divination, to see what will happen to a client in the future, or whether the client will recover lost objects, as well as other things having to do with the client's fate, strength, and mental and emotional state.

5. The drink pulque *(nute kuiji)* is considered to be especially pleasing to the gods. Pulque is produced from the sap of the maguey, in the high, cold country of Yucunino and Yucubey. It can be mildly alcoholic, once it is allowed to ferment. People often make offerings of pulque to the *nu ñu'un*. They may do this in curing ceremonies, in their fields while praying for good crops, or before setting out on the hunt. The offering is made by pouring one or two cupfuls of pulque on the ground, while the *nu ñu'un* is invoked and the purpose of the offering is stated.

Pulque is associated on several levels with blood. Its consumption is said to restore blood, and its whiteness associates it with semen and milk, which, as we saw in the first chapter, are male and female blood. Pulque in fact is sometimes called "milk" and it bears the same name, *nute kuiji*, as semen. The association of pulque with semen is significant in the context of ritual offerings made to stimulate corn production. As we saw in chapter 4, in sowing and tending to his fields, the farmer is felt to transmit "the heat of life" to the corn plant, so that it bears an ear of corn. This same process can be seen in the offering of pulque in the corners and center of the cornfield after the corn has been planted.

6. A wide variety of flowering plants grow in the Nuyoo region, and mayordomos come from as far away as Chila in the Mixteca Baja to gather them for celebrations during Holy Week. Tlaxiaco, the district capital, traditionally demanded a tribute of flowers from Nuyoo and Yucuhiti to celebrate its festivities. People in Nuyoo enjoy cultivating flowers, and many new varieties have

Finally, each sacrificial item is, like corn, a "food" of some sort. This is easy to see with pulque, which some people consume daily. Flowers stand for all fruitful plants, and often carry names of foods.[7] The odor of flowers, the light of candles, and the smoke of incense are all "foods" that gods consume, and the sacrificer feeds to the god during the sacrificial act.

Sacrifice and the Covenants with Earth and Rain

The nineteenth- and early twentieth-century interest in defining sacrifice in universal terms has given way, in our times, to an awareness that sacrifice becomes meaningful only in the context of the particular religious tradition in which it is performed. In Nuyoo, it is impossible to fully understand the efficaciousness of acts of sacrifice, or the characteristics shared by sacrificial objects, outside of the

---

been introduced in the region over the last 50 years.

Just as in the case of pulque and candles, flowers are an integral part of the symbolic vocabulary of Nuyooteco sacrifice. Flowers are grasped with burning candles when praying before a deity, and they are used to adorn saints, both at home and in the church. The ritual symbolism of the flower in Nuyoo is complex, with specific rituals related to the plants that flower during the months they are celebrated.

Women often liken children to flowers, saying that infants bloom forth from their mothers as flowers bloom from a plant and, as the infant grows, that it opens up like the petals of a flower. In dream symbolism, flowers, especially white ones, are signs of an impending childbirth, either to oneself, or to a couple who will be one's future compadres. The relationship between children and flowers can also be seen in depth, as children are buried on a bed of flowers, rather than a bed of palm, as is the case with adults.

While primarily associated with children, flowers may also stand for the ánima. Thus, in the funeral ceremony, the deceased's ánima takes its place in the flowers of the cross that is made on the floor of the house of the person sponsoring the funeral. The crops, people say, represents the body of the deceased.

In addition to their association with children and the ánima, flowers are also linked with edible plants, particularly corn and fruits. People often say that the food they consume is "a flower." In fact, the word for fruit is precisely this, *ita*, "flower." The reason for the connection between food and flowers was explained by an old man from Yucunino, who pointed out that the edible parts of plants begin as the buds of flowers and later develop into the fruits and vegetables people consume.

7. This can be seen in the use of the orchid, *ita viko* ("flower of the cloud"), the *ita nee yuu* ("flower of soup"), and the *ita saa ñɨɨ* ("flower of the tender corn cob") to protect ripe corn fields. Bunches of *ita viko*, *ita nee yuu*, and *ita saa ñɨɨ* are brought as offerings to the church by *mayordomos* and others and left at the feet of the saints' images. Later, the man who wishes to protect his cornfield from the winds and wild animals will collect a few bunches of these flowers, bathe the saints' images with them by whisking them over the statues, and then place the flowers in the four corners of his cornfield. This will prevent the winds from knocking over the top-heavy plants and stop wild animals from entering to feed on the ripe ears of corn. What makes these flowers so powerful is that they have been incorporated into the saint through their being "fed" to it in the act of sacrifice and thus come to contain some of the sacredness and power of the god.

covenant of mutual obligation that exists between humans and Earth and Rain. Recall that in the covenants, Earth and Rain suffer to feed people, and in return people must feed Earth and Rain with their bodies at death. In this way, death became a condition of agricultural production and civilized life. This is important because when Nuyootecos initiate contact with the gods through sacrifice, they base their communication on this primordial agreement (see also Klein 1987: 295–97). In every sacrifice I was able to observe, the sacrificer recited, at some point, the condition of the covenants. For example, one man prayed,

> *Ya'a va nakio nane'yo re sua'*
> Here we lay down our bodies, and thus

> *Nakajire nak'e ii*
> Give us to eat and take us in again.

Another stated:

> I give you these things so that you will give us food to eat, water to drink, so that we may live in the light [niji]; give me to eat because I am not going any other place when I die, but I am going to remain here.

In these examples, the sacrificer explicitly bases his request on the covenants made by his ancestors at the beginning of civilized life and, in his restatement of the human obligation, implies that the god is obligated to grant what he asks. If sacrifice is the channel through which humans initiate contact with the gods, then the covenants make this contact possible.

As I noted, the items the sacrificer offers become significant in light of the covenants. For example, in offering candles to ensure a good corn harvest, what the farmer does is "bathe" himself with one by rubbing it all over his body. "Bathing" imbues the candle with the bather's ánima and destiny (see note 3) and may even be addressed as if it were the person so bathed. The sacrificer then burns the candle in the church before the saints or in a "Rain shrine" for the *ñu'un savi*. As the candle burns, the god to which it is offered "consumes" (the verb kaji is used) it, and the sacrificer reiterates the terms of the covenants—that people be permitted to eat Earth and Rain in return for feeding Earth and Rain with their bodies.

There are occasions when offerings consist of something more than just tokens of people's bodies. In large construction projects, such as in the building of a road where much soil must be moved, a recompense must be made to the *nu ñu'un* (some say the tachi; see chapter 6) whose "houses" the excavations disturbed. Only human bodies will satisfy it for the trouble people have caused. When Nuyootecos constructed the road to Nuyoo Center in 1975, the *nu ñu'un* whose house they disturbed halted progress until they appeased it with sacrifice:

> We had reached the big curve below Yucunino [with the road construction]. Each day we would advance a little, and we would come back the next day, it was like we did not achieve anything. We would work and work, and not advance. Finally, the driver of the earth mover came down from his machine, and prayed *[ka'a kamare]* to the *nu ñu'un*. He promised that if it allowed us to build the road, the *nu ñu'un* could have seven trucks full of people. After this, they allowed the work to proceed, and we finished the road.

This account is obviously patterned after the Covenant with Earth. In that covenant, men were not permitted to sow corn; in the story, men were not allowed to build a road. Like the men who found that tall trees were growing over the land they cleared, Nuyootecos also found that when they returned to the construction site, "their work was no longer there." The solution to their problem was the same as in the covenant. The pain they caused Earth by excavating the roadbed had to be paid for with human bodies, just as the pain the ancestors caused by sowing corn was requited by the promise to "go no other place" but to become Earth, at death.

Besides roads, the construction of bridges, dams, and artificial lakes have all required human sacrifice. People say each bridge on the road from Putla to the coast has people buried in the pylons, and many in Nuyoo believe that in the coastal region municipal authorities take criminals outside the town, kill them, and offer them to Earth (see also Flanet 1977:94). Another example of human sacrifice occurs when someone inscribes someone else's name on a candle and then burns it in sacrifice, or when they offer a piece of someone's clothing to a *nu ñu'un*. The object is to make the victim ill and, if possible, to kill him or her. Here, the politics of sacrifice, as many admit, make it indistinguishable from witchcraft.

We can see from these examples that the Covenants with Earth and Rain instituted, and continue to inform, human relationships with nature and the sacred. It is because they provide a basis for communication with the sacred, and because people affirm them through their deaths, that corn can be grown, roads can be built, houses can be constructed, and the world can be shaped to meet human needs. The covenants are not esoteric myths of origin, but are crucial to human activity in the world.

Sacrifice as alimentary communion. It is significant that Nuyootecos speak of the items they offer in sacrifice as god-food of some sort. Pulque, the sweet smoke of incense, and beautiful flowers are all things that the gods eat. Coupled with this, people describe the act of sacrifice as a meal the sacrificer "feeds" to the gods and refer to the vessels and places of sacrifice as the god's "cups," "plates," or "tables."

But what does it mean that sacrifice, and the human relationship to the gods, is defined in alimenary terms? For one, it shows us the complex relationship Nuyootecos have with Earth and Rain. Recall that the covenant specified that the gods would feed humans by allowing people to practice corn agriculture. This requires that the gods give of themselves to Nuyootecos, or as people put it, they "eat Earth." Corn, after all, is a holy, living being, "the daughter" of Earth and Rain. As I noted earlier, the idea that someone feeds someone else implies a relationship of care, or even love (nakara), and it is through such acts that relationships of identity are created. It is the way parents create a link of shared substance with children, the way godparents bring godchildren into their household, and the way a bride comes to replace her mother-in-law in her "true household." It follows then, that when people consume food, when they "eat Earth," the gods nurture humans in a way that not only shows the concern they have for human existence, like a mother and father, but also in a way that makes every act of eating one of communion. For good reason corn (and other food items) should not be mistreated, since it suffers enough when cooked and eaten by people, and for good reason food should be consumed quietly, with respect, and with full concentration on the meal, since one is coming into contact with the sacred.

In describing sacrifice as a meal offered to the gods, Nuyootecos make clear the price they pay for the divine grants of agriculture. Kaji, "to eat," connotes, depending on the context, dominance as well as identity, incorporation as well as unity, and death as well as transformation. Because the meal the sacrificer feeds to the gods is made up of items that are metaphorically (and, in Prehispanic times, metonymically) related to the human body, sacrifice is also an act in which the sacrificer feeds to the gods his or her body, or those for whom the sacrificer stands as proxy. The price of participation in the promise of the covenants is one where in order "to eat," people must in turn be "eaten," and the act of sacrifice anticipates our ultimate end.

In this context, Nuyootecos say that the *nu ñu'un* and *ñu'un savi* eat three times a day, just as people do. Yet instead of tortillas and beans, the meals of the gods consist of human bodies. Living in Nuyoo, one man explained, one does not immediately recognize this, but there are many people in the world, and several die at every meal of the *nu ñu'un* and *ñu'un savi*. Others likened the gods to a woman who tends chickens. She feeds and cares for them so they will grow fat and multiply. Later she may kill one or two of them so that her family may have meat to eat. She will not, however, kill them all off, since then there will be none left. This is what Earth and Sky do with people. "They care for us and feed us, but later feast on our bodies." The feeding and eating of people by the gods is as basic to Nuyooteco ideas about relationships with the sacred as is original sin in Christian theology.

SOKO AND SELF-SACRIFICE

The Nuyooteco vision of sacrifice — as an act that reaffirms the human commitment to feed the gods with the sacrificer's body — is akin to the kind described for Nepalese Hindus by Grey where, in its ultimate manifestation, the victim is the sacrificer, not an icon of him or her (Grey 1987). As the covenants stipulate, sacrifice goes beyond an identification of sacrificer with victim to actual self-sacrifice. It was an act of self-sacrifice by both parties to the covenants that first brought the relationship between people and the gods into being, and it is self-sacrifice that sustains the covenants, as the gods "suffer" to make their children available for humans, and Nuyootecos "suffer" to reaffirm the pacts made by their ancestors.

In addition to being the first sacrifice, the self-sacrifice recorded in the Covenants with Earth and Rain was the innovation that established civilized life. Prior to this agreement, humans could not practice agriculture and lived in the wilds, like the tiumi. Although not explained in the myths, once the two men were allowed to cut down the forest to plant corn, they were also able to create "cooked" zones for houses and villages. Like Rosseau's social contract, in which society is created by the transfer of each individual's rights to the whole community, Nuyooteco society is similarly based on an initial act of alienation. But unlike the social contract, the Covenants with Earth and Rain are made not only among free individuals, but between humans and the divine, thereby articulating society with the cosmos. Self-sacrifice is thus sociogonic as well as relevant to communication with the sacred, and its efficaciousness derives from precisely the way it repeats the acts that created what the sacrificer hopes to stimulate: agriculture and, by extension, the continuity of social life. This latter point we can be illustrated in the concrete example of the Viko Nuni.

The Viko Nuni

The Viko Nuni is a thanksgiving for the corn harvest made to Earth, to Rain, and to the corn itself. People often celebrate this fiesta when they find an i'ya ear of corn, because when the i'ya appears, "it wants to eat pozole." Pozole *(nujie')* is a dish made of boiled corn with turkey or chicken added, and Nuyootecos sometimes serve it on festive occasions. Since the i'ya ear "wants to eat pozole," this dish is the central sacrifice of the Viko Nuni.

The farmer who sponsors a Viko Nuni piles all the ears of corn he harvests onto a large mat. He may place a cross, or alternatively, a *niñi cruzi* (a cornstalk with two or more ears growing from it, which Nuyootecos say resembles a cross), into the middle of the pile of corn. He then adorns the cross with flowers and places candles around the corners of the mound. The sponsor then circles the pile of corn with an incense burner, thanking both San Marcos (the *nu ñu'un* mentioned in the Covenant) and the *ñu'un savi* for the harvest. He may also pour libations of pulque over the four corners of the mound of corn, and then into its center, continuing to utter his prayers of thanksgiving. Once he finishes with the pulque, he takes the dish of pozole his wife prepares, and sets it on top of the mound of corn. After a day or so, the farmer removes the dish from the corn and places it on a table. He then calls to anyone who wanders close to the house—be they passersby, neighbors from nearby households, or men working in adjacent fields—and invites them to eat a serving. He himself does not eat any, nor does anyone from his household. When Nuyootecos make sacrifice, it is important that they not consume any of the offerings. In part this can be explained by the sacrificial item being a token of the sacrificer's relationship to the gods. Because this relationship is based upon the sacrificer's feeding of himself or herself to the gods, each item offered stands in a metaphoric relationship to the sacrificer's body. If Nuyooteco sacrificers consumed part of the offering, it would be the equivalent of autocannibalism.

It is very important to those who sponsor the ritual that the passerby not be determined beforehand but be someone brought by fate. The passerby, however, is not a wholly indeterminate category of person. Sponsors expect the passerby to be another Nuyooteco, since non-Nuyootecos do not stray far from the two or three main trails that cross the community. The person who receives the offering is thus someone who is randomly selected from among community members.

In "feeding" the gods and then feeding the passerby with the pozole, the sacrificer of the Viko Nuni nourishes the person who receives the offering, making this person stand for both the god to whom the offering has been made and for the collectivity of Nuyootecos. (Farriss 1984:321–24 discusses this in relation to colonial Yucatec fiestas.) But most importantly, he brings himself into the circuit by sacrificing items which stand for his own body. He symbolically feeds himself to the gods—in incense, candles, pulque, pozole, and other items—and then feeds himself to other people, as the passersby consume the offering.

In establishing this circuit, the items the sacrificer feeds to others are those that represent bodily substances. The pozole given to the passersby in the Viko Nuni is made of corn, which in sacrifice represents the human person in several ways, and Nuyootecos speak of it as "our blood and vein." In other sacrifices it may be pulque, which is also associated with blood and with milk. I would further argue that these items are not solely symbolic equivalences of blood and milk, but if we look to the Precolumbian past (see below) function as real substitutes, so that the sponsor can be said to establish a quasi-physical bond between himself and those who consume the sacrificial items. He does this, moreover, in a way that is similar to the way parents give blood to their children.

In the previous chapter, I discussed the way parents and children are linked by blood and how this blood is transmitted through intercourse and through the mother's feeding her child, both inside and outside the womb. This allowed us to see that what is important in Nuyooteco kinship are the acts through which substances are transmitted. The first such act, when Nuyootecos were engendered by Earth and Rain and born from Soko Usha, related them to Earth and Rain as to a mother and a father, and the human body came to be made up of "earth and mud." I am suggesting here that sacrifice allows an analogous relationship to be established between people. The sacrificer does this by feeding himself to passersby through items that represent his blood, so that the passerby comes to "share substance" with him. Although I do not know of another example in the Mesoamerican ethnographic literature where kin-like ties are extended to non-kin through sacrifice, it should not be a hard idea for Mesoamericanists to accept, since we have made the extension of kin-like relationships to non-kin through ritual (compadrazgo), a long-standing focus of theoretical discussion. In any event, that Nuyootecos understand the bonds created between people through sacrifice to be similar to kin-like bonds of shared substance can be seen in another fiesta, the Viko Anima.

As discussed in chapter 6, Nuyootecos celebrate the Viko Anima, or All Saints', from October 31 to November 2, dates that coincide with the beginning of the corn harvest. All Saints' is the time when the deceased leave their households in the *ñuu anima*, "the community of the ánima," and return to visit with the living. On the night before the ánima return (children on October 31 and adults on November 1), the members of each household prepare a large meal for their deceased kin and compadres. Then, on the morning of November 1, after the ánima of the children arrive, people go to Mass and visit the cemetery, adorning the graves with palm leaves and fruit. The priest says Mass in the graveyard, and each household presents him with a list of the names of the household's deceased members. The priest, or a helper, reads the lists aloud after the homily. When the Mass is over, people drift over to the graves they adorned and distribute the fruit to those who stop by to chat. After an hour or so, everyone walks back to the town center, about a half kilometer distant, to begin preparations for the meals to be served to the adult ánima.

When everyone has returned from the cemetery, the prayermakes and municipal band members begin to make the rounds of the houses in Nuyoo Center. Years ago, the band would visit each Nuyooteco household, even though it took more than a week to make the rounds. Now the prayermakers of each hamlet and the members of the band of Zaragoza share this task, so that the musicians and/or prayermakers visit all the houses within a few days of November 1.

The Viko Anima is a time of unity for the individual households that sponsor the celebrations, since its members—both living and dead—are together again. One would therefore expect the Viko Anima to be a time when each household would emphasize its separate identity, celebrating the ties that bind its members. However, in the rituals of All Saints', living non-kin become proxies for deceased kin.

When the musicians and prayermakers arrive at a household on the night of November 1, they are usually in the company of several dozen neighbors and a host of excited children. The rite begins after all gather around the table in front of the household altar. The table is piled with food for the ánima, and the children point to the soda and sweets while the adults eye the liquor and meat. The musicians play dirges, stopping periodically to allow the prayermakers to chant prayers for the deceased. After the prayers end, the musicians signal a transition by switching to lighter music, and the head of the household begins to distribute the food on the table. The adults receive the plates of tortillas, soup, meat, and beer set out for the adult ánima, while the children receive the sweets and breads set out for the ánima of deceased children. Band members are served the largest portions, and when they finish eating, they take up their instruments to play a selection of tunes while the prayermakers chant more prayers. I was told that in the past the tortillas served to the ánima and then fed to the visitors would be ground from red corn instead of the yellow or white corn used today. The whole affair lasts a half hour to forty-five minutes, after which the musicians and prayermakers move off to another household, often bringing with them the members of the household they have just visited, thereby increasing the crowd of people who accompany them.

As in the Viko Nuni, those who prepared the food on the table should not eat it. Away from Nuyoo Center, where people live dispersed across the landscape, the Viko Ánima distribution may go on for more than a week, as household members call in passersby to receive fruit and bread left on the altar. I have even seen the food prepared for All Saints' in these houses spoil, since so few people happened by. This is the only time I ever saw anything left to rot by Nuyootecos, who have a very reverent attitude toward food.

The significance of people not eating the food they offer to their deceased children and other relatives, but instead giving it to the visiting children and adults, is, in the words of one man, that "the guests become like the ánima." If, in the Viko Nuni, the passersby stand for both the god to whom the offering is made and the collectivity of Nuyootecos, then in the Viko Ánima the visitors stand for the sponsor's deceased kin and the collectivity. But most significantly for the discussion of Nuyoo sociality, it is through the offering of items that represent the sacrificer's blood and ánima—highlighted by the red tortillas served in the past—that these non-kin become like kin. Just as parents generate life by transmitting their blood and milk to children, then the sacrificer does the same;[8] and if the blood and milk

8. The vitalization of individuals, the collectivity, and the sacred occurs not just in the Viko Nuni but in all celebrations (viko), such as weddings (viko ta na'a) and civil-religious hierarchy

connect parents with children as kin, then the "blood" the sacrificer feeds fellow Nuyootecos makes them into ta'a.

Writing in the sixteenth century, Bernardino de Sahagún reported that in the celebrations in honor of Xipe Totec and Huitzilopochtli, the Mexica sacrificed their prisoners of war. The capture of an enemy in battle was a mark of bravery in Mexica society, and the captor, or "owner," of the prisoner played a central role in the sacrificial rituals. On the appointed day, the different owners brought their captives to the temple of Huitzilopochtli, where the priests tied each victim, in turn, to a sacrificial stone. Four fully girded Mexica knights then approached to do ritual battle with the captive (sometimes called "the bathed one"), whose only weapon was a wooden sword. After the knights knocked the victim to the ground, his chest was cut open by a waiting priest. The priest extracted the victim's still-beating heart to offer to the sun, and another priest filled a tube with the victim's blood, which he also offered to the sun. The owner of the captive then took the tube and anointed, or "fed," the images of the gods located in the various temples of the Mexica capital. Afterward he returned to

---

fiestas. This, I think, is the appropriate interpretation given to the following statement of Fausto Modesto Velasco, when I asked him about the similarity between the word *viko*, "fiesta," and *vīkō*, "cloud":

> I am going to say a word about what God creates,
> I am going to tell this right now, although it is only three words. . . .
> Let's see. . . .
> There is what we call the viko.
> From the viko comes the tortilla we eat, and he who is *mayordomo* sponsors it, we say.
> And he gives the tortilla we eat, and then there is our *fuerza*, we say [synonymous with *yii*].
> It gives fuerza to us, because what other things does the tortilla give?
> And so there is, there is the vīkō [cloud] in the sky we say.
> And so there is the place, there is the place from which the rain comes.
> This [the cloud] bears rain.
> It is truly male [superior] because God created it.
> The rain comes from this, and it gives fuerza.
> And thus we obtain water so we may drink, we show we are people.
> And so we live by tortilla and water, and thus we will survive.
> And not only [people] we say;
> Because all, even the herds, the plants, whatever edible plant, whatever inedible plant;
> There is not a single thing that grows and lives apart, because all grow of the rain.

Fausto's observations indicate that it is in its provision of fuerza to people that the viko (fiesta) is made like the vīkō (cloud). At the same time the viko energizes the sacred basis of fecundity and renewal—people say "it always rains on a viko," even though it occurs in the middle of the dry season—it energizes the social basis of fecundity and renewal, where, as we will see, people exchange gifts as well as celebrate the transfer of persons from one household to another.

the temple to collect the victim's body and carried it to a house called the *capulco* (where the rituals began with a vigil the night before). The owner then brought the remains home, cut them up, and cooked them in a stew, which he served with corn to his "superiors, friends, and relatives" in an all-night fiesta. Sahagún tells us "the owner of the captive did not eat the meat, because they were believed to be of the same flesh, because from the moment that he captured him he considered him his son, and·the captive considered the owner his father, and for this reason he did not want to eat the meat; he did however eat the flesh of the other captives who died" (Sahagún 1977:146, vol. 1).

Although it occurred in another time and another place, the ancient Aztec use of sacrifice clearly parallels what goes on during the Nuyooteco sacrifices of the Viko Nuni and Viko Ánima. In both, the sacrificial offering represents the flesh and blood of the sacrificer. In both, the sacrificer feeds the offering to the gods and then to associates. We cannot say with certainty that the Mexica viewed sacrifice as an act that created kin-like relations between people, but it is significant that the sacrifices on the Temple of Huitzilpochtli are closely associated with the main corporate unit in Mexica society, the *calpulli*, or "Big House," which sometimes functioned as a corporate, kin-based unit. As we will see in the next chapter, there is also an important link between kinship, corporation, and the idea of the household in Nuyoo.

CHAPTER 10

COMMENSALITY AND COMMUNITY

AMONG specialists in Mesoamerica, the role kinship plays in local social organization has been a matter of some debate. Those who take the perspective that Mesoamerican people are first and foremost a peasantry have usually followed the lead of Eric Wolf, either downplaying the relevance of kinship or ignoring the subject altogether (Nutini 1968, 1976). However, as Eva Hunt observed,

> the increasing evidence from recent anthropological work has shown that wherever the anthropologist deals with peasants who define themselves as Indians (an upon occasion when they see themselves as Mestizos), genealogical linkages, descent groupings, and marriage regulations play a profoundly significant part in the territorial, ritual, economic and other institutional domains of the internal organization of these communities. Although territoriality defines the external boundaries of social units, from the internal point of view the community is defined as having distinct kinship features. (Hunt 1976:98)

Accordingly, some have argued that membership in local corporations is reckoned in terms of descent, as well as by residential criteria. There is, for example, Monzón's early discussion of the calpulli as a "clan" (Monzón 1949), Fox's examination of Quiché expansion in terms of a segmentary lineage model (Fox 1987), and, closer to Nuyoo, Huerta Ríos' analysis of Trique social organization, where he found that partrilineal descent groups play a central role (Huerta Ríos 1981). Some think it is a mistake to view Mesoamerican corporate kin groups as organized according to strictly unilineal principles (e.g., Arzipe 1973; Hunt 1976), yet even in these cases, the link between the categorization of people as "kin" and the corporate groups that they live in is perceived as ancestor focused. It is because people are descended from a common ancestor that they are related to one another, and it is because they are descendants of the same ancestor that they cooperate, act as a unified political force, and hold title to land and other property.

233

Some years ago Ronald Spores, in a review of historical sources on eastern Oaxaca, suggested that the link between kin and corporation in the Mixteca is not so "tribal" and that the term "deme" better captures the Mixtec reality (Spores 1967:11). Murdock originally introduced the term "deme" to refer to certain groups (mostly in the Americas) whose members are bound by ties that go beyond the reciprocal transactions and mutual dependencies that characterize independent peasant households living in proximity to one another. In the deme, the community is made up of consanguines who acknowledge their ties to one another but who do not form a group in which descent is crucial in reckoning these ties (Murdock 1949:62–63). Nevertheless, the idea of shared kinship in a deme can be as intense and as significant as it is for members of a unilineal descent group. As Murdock put it, "Except for family ties, the strongest sense of identification is usually with the community as a whole, which is viewed as a consanguineal unit in relation to other communities in a manner quite comparable to the attitude towards one's own sib in a unilineal society" (Murdock 1949:62–63). Similarly, the Nuyoo material shows that although people define membership in the community in terms of who is and who is not a ta'a, they do not see the blood and milk they transmit to their children as passing on a series of inherited traits; furthermore, although people feel that they are ultimately related to the people who emerged from Soko Usha, this is only in the sense that one generation necessarily begets another. The reckoning of kinship in Nuyoo is by no means ancestor focused, in the classic African or Polynesian sense.

Murdock was vague about what organizes the deme in the absence of descent. He did suggest that a long-standing practice of endogamy is important, since it would otherwise be difficult to sustain the idea that the deme is a kin group distinct from other groups (Murdock 1949:62–63). Indeed, marriage has long been a key element in anthropological definitions of community in Mesoamerica. For the most part, however, the focus has been on community endogamy, and specifically on the way endogamy reinforces community boundaries (e.g., Wolf 1955). The fact that fully 90% of Nuyooteco marriages are with other Nuyootecos highlights the soundness of this interpretation. But marriage also has internal functions. We saw this in chapter 2, which showed how the transfer of persons between households is essential to creating ties of alliance. What I will do here is return to their earlier discussion of marriage, but move from the level of marriage as a transaction between households to the level of marriage

as a community-wide system and explore the role Nuyooteco participation in a system of intermarriage plays in the idea that they are ta'a.

MARRIAGE AND COMMUNITY

When people in Nuyoo speak about the transfer of persons from one
household to another in marriage, they speak of it in terms of destiny.
They say that a woman's leaving her natal household is intrinsic to her
being, since "no woman is born into her true household." This is not
seen as a particularly happy fate, either for the girl or her parents. As
one father put it, a daughter's destiny means that she "doesn't
remember her parents. Once she marries she goes and does not come
back." This is in contrast to her brothers, who "always remember and
care for their parents, because that is where their home is." Another
man likened women in marriage to the poor, ragged, migrant workers
from the nearby Mixtec towns of Monteverde and Atatlahuca, who
come to the region to pick coffee in September. As these people leave
their homes "to find their life," so too must a woman leave her house
and find a place in another.

We saw in chapter 2 that people call the bride's household a "seed
bed" or "nursery." Just as a gardener cares for young plants in a
nursery until they are ready to be transplanted to a permanent site, so
too parents nurture their daughter until she is ready to travel to her
husband's home, "her true household." Nuyootecos view anything
that prevents children from circulating among households in marriage
as a problem. For example, when speaking about those heads of
households who refuse to allow their daughters and sisters to marry,
Nuyootecos will frequently describe them as "stingy" (*shii*) or self-
centered and envious (kuasunni). One such individual, people say,
refuses to allow his sister to marry in order to keep her tending his
household's goats. Several *tee ka'a sha* have approached with marriage
petitions, and she has expressed a willingness to marry (she is now in
her early thirties, a very ripe age by Nuyooteco standards). But each
time a *tee ka'a sha* appears, her brother tells him she would not make a
good wife.

These and other facts fit well with Levi-Strauss's thesis that marriage is a form of the "total" exchange that takes place between
exogamous groups (Levi-Strauss 1969). In Levi-Straussian terms,
Nuyoo is a place where women (and sometimes men) circulate among
the households of the community in a complex exchange, where each
household gives up its daughters in return for its right to receive the
daughters of other households. There are no rules specifying who one

should marry, only who one cannot marry. Negative marriage rules, such as those prohibiting marriage between cousins and ritual kin, situate people in households unrelated to their natal households and create ties of alliance that go beyond those created by consanguineous links. Although the members of the household that "let go" of their daughters and sisters do not enjoy an immediate return, they do know that other households in the community will also "let go" of their children. Thus the man who refused to allow his sister to marry is "self-centered" because his household is depriving other households of a woman, and he is "stingy" because he is making use of his sister's labor for his own benefit, instead of "letting her go" so she may labor in another household (just as the wife he received labors in his).

One factor important in determining the tone of these transactions is that both households benefit from the union of their daughter and son. On the one hand, a son marries so he will acquire the female labor necessary for his survival and life in a viable household. On the other hand, a daughter marries so that she will acquire the male labor that allows her to survive and to have a place in a household. This was a point made by the father of one bride-to-be during a marriage negotiation:

> *Nee naa koto va'a ñivi maa*
> [She marries] in order that people maintain her well
>
> *Nuku ñivi kaji*
> That people feed her
>
> *Nukun ñivi kuniji a kachio*
> That people cloth her, we say.

On the male side, then, marriage may be a "purchase," but the small size of the bridewealth means they do not pay the full price. On the female side, marriage may be a "loan," but one they do not call in. Each household needs other households to sustain and reproduce itself through the transfer of personnel and to make a place for its own children when they must find their "true household." We can see the strong ethos of mutuality that underlies Nuyooteco marriage transactions in the example of the "stingy" man who does not let his sister marry, since the converse is also true: men who refuse to marry (and there are several in Nuyoo) are also "stingy" (kuasunni). They are stingy, people say, because they do not want to support a woman. These men are quite content to live at home with their mothers and sisters, despite having reached marriageable age. Again, taking someone into a household, from the Nuyooteco point of view, is as important as giving up personnel to other households. In terms of the overall system of marriage exchange, informal sanctions on men who refuse to marry are as effective in circulating individuals among the households as are informal sanctions against people who refuse to permit their sisters or daughters to wed.

Nuyootecos, then, are a group of people who circulate their children among themselves, bringing these younger people into their households, where they will grow up to replace elder generations. This activity creates a series of overlapping ties, so that people come to stand in a relationship of both wife giver and wife taker to one another (but without implications of superiority and inferiority or the idea that one side is greatly indebted to the other). It is perhaps for this reason that Nuyootecos often reply to those who ask where they are going, "I am going to visit the household of your sister." Although their response implies they are going to visit people who are related by marriage to the persons who asked the question, it simply means that they are going to visit someone in the community—as if all households were affinally related to one another.

Nuyoo thus appears to conform quite well to the deme model laid out by Murdock, in that centuries of intermarriage has created a sense that people are related to one another as kin and are, in this way, distinct from other groups (see also Spores 1967:11, 1974). However, in the deme model, Murdock saw the long-standing practice of inter-marriage as necessary for building up a sense of *consanguineal* ties among the people in question. In Nuyoo at least, people emphasize that marriage creates overlapping affinal, as well as consanguineal, ties among members of the community. Accordingly, Nuyooteco men may refer to one another as "brother-in-law," and the word ta'a can be used for affines as well as for people related by shared milk and blood.[1] What this suggests is that there is another reason intermar-riage correlates with shared kinship in Nuyoo—and why both are linked to a corporate estate. To see what this is, and why I think we should replace the term "deme" with another term more appropriate to the Mixtec situation, let us return to the discussion of exchange in the fiesta.

---

1. This was also true in the past. Thus in the sixteenth century, *Tnaha dzidzo* was "affine" (Arana Osnaya and Swadesh 1965:84), and "marriage," *Tnaha ndaha* (Arana Osnaya and Swadesh 1965:129), can be translated as "to make a *ta'a* by the joining of hands."

Pooling in the Fiesta

In chapter 3, we saw that the fiesta is a time when Nuyootecos intensely interact with one another as members of households. Through *sa'a* exchanges, they constitute their independence and autonomy, while the symbolism of the gift evokes instances where they provide each other with the resources necessary for their prosperity and continuity. In *saa sa'a*, Nuyootecos articulate an image of the community as made up of discrete households that are dependent upon one another for survival.

Saa sa'a, however, is only one of three distinct, but interconnected, transactions that take place in the fiesta. We can best isolate these if we view them in terms of the sequence of exchanges a typical household sponsoring a fiesta goes through.

The members of the household will begin by attending many dozens of fiestas in the months preceding their own, to make *sa'a* prestations. When it comes time for them to sponsor their fiesta, their partners will arrive to pay these gifts back. In addition, the sponsors will receive gifts from people who do not owe them gifts but who wish to place the sponsors into debt. These people will sponsor a fiesta in the future, and they want the sponsors to attend, bringing with them the gift they owe. These exchanges have the overall effect of keeping everyone involved in the *saa sa'a* complex, so that people are constantly giving and receiving gifts.

The second transaction occurs when the sponsors distribute the goods amassed through *saa sa'a* (and other means) in meals and countergifts to those who participate. As I noted, these distributions can take place over the course of several days. I will return to them in chapter 13, when we examine the relationship between these distributions and changing property relations.

In the final transaction, participants exchange goods among themselves, since each person who brings something to the celebration receives something back, which another participant made (Monaghan 1990c). Just as is true of the reciprocal exchanges of *saa sa'a*, this last has great significance for participants, and I want to make it a focus of discussion here. Perhaps the best place to begin is by discussing the way Nuyootecos reckon who owns tortillas as they pass from hand to hand in the exchanges.

If we start with a couple who wish to initiate a sa'a partnership, we find that early on the morning of the celebration, the senior women of the household (and/or her daughters) will prepare 120 tortillas. Of these, 60 will be for home consumption, and the other 60 will be given to the sponsor of the celebration in gift exchange. The man or his wife will refer to the 60 tortillas prepared for home consumption as *shita maani*, "my own tortillas." The 60 to be deposited with the sponsor they call *shita sa'a*, "sa'a tortillas," or *shita tatu*.

When the man and/or his wife arrive at the celebration, they turn over the goods they have brought to the sponsors. The foodstuffs go to the women of the household, and the liquor, beer, and cash to the men of the household. A man from the household will then note down what the partners brought in the account book. However, the people of the household who sponsor the celebration do not consider the tortillas "their own." Rather, they refer to them as *shita sa'a*, or "sa'a tortillas." After the goods have been counted, a member of the sponsoring household makes a countergift to the couple who brought the tortillas. Both the sponsors and the partners refer to the tortillas of this countergift as *shita sa'a*.

After several weeks, months, or even years, it comes time for the partners to sponsor a celebration. The former sponsors then prepare 60 tortillas in return for those they received from the partners. The former sponsors do not consider these tortillas *shita maani*, "my own tortillas," but *shita sa'a*. When the former sponsors arrive at the celebration, they may say something like "here, take your tortillas back," as they present the basket to their partners. The partner then considers these tortillas to be *shita maani*, "my own tortillas." The tortillas the couple sent out on a journey months or years before are back in their hands once again. As in the first exchange, the old sponsors receive a countergift or 10% to 20% of the initial gift. Also, as in the first exchange, the tortillas in the countergift are considered *shita sa'a*.

Beyond demonstrating the reciprocal nature of *saa sa'a*, the terminology used for the tortillas shows that when they are circulating in gift exchange, they have a special status; they are sa'a tortillas, which have no single owner. The idea that these tortillas have no single owner (no one is able to call them "my own tortillas") makes sense if we imagine the celebration as a giant wheel, where the sponsor is at the hub, and the gift exchange partners are on the spokes. When partners send tortillas down the spokes and into the center, they in effect "pool" their resources to finance the celebration, and Nuyootecos consider the tortillas (and the other goods amassed at the hub) to be collective property. This can be best illustrated by examining how sponsors dispose of the occasional surpluses that remain in their hands once the celebration is over.

In the past, when it became clear that the sponsoring household would have a surplus after a celebration, its members would summon all those who participated back to the house. Household members would lay mats on the floor, and one of the men would divide the surplus into piles, setting goods in front of each participant in proportion to the amount they contributed. Although surpluses are no longer formally redistributed among participants, there is the feeling that any amount that remains over the start-up costs of the sponsors should be returned to those who participated. A large surplus remained after the fiesta of Misericordia in 1985, so the sponsors invited the prayermakers, musicians, and others back for another meal the day after the fiesta ended. In either case, the sponsors do not subtract what they return from what they owe the participants. As one woman explained, the goods were never the property of the sponsors; they belong to everyone who participates.

I highlight the pooling of goods in the celebration because, through this, Nuyootecos create a special kind of relationship that is quite distinct from that created and experienced through *saa sa'a*. As we have seen, when the members of a household make a prestation to the sponsors of a celebration, they signal two things. One is that they support the sponsor's household and can be counted as an ally. The other is that they belong to a unit that, while allied to the sponsor's household, is nonetheless separate from it. Here, *saa sa'a* defines the outer range of commensality. No sa'a exchanges occur among the members of the household, since household members hold everything in common. This marks those who exchange goods as dissimilar by the very fact of their participation in the transaction. *Saa sa'a* thus relates units that are structurally similar to one another (Sahlins 1972).

In contrast to this, the pooling of goods in the celebration creates a more inclusive solidarity. As I pointed out, even though the sponsors control these goods, they belong to all the participants. If *saa sa'a* marks those who exchange as belonging to separate units, with the gift mediating the differences, then pooling makes them into a single unit. As Sahlins noted (1972:188–89), "pooling is the material side of collectivity."

We still might ask, why is the pooling of tortillas in the fiesta significant for Nuyootecos? The term people use for the tortillas they contribute to the pool of goods to be distributed by the sponsor, *shita sa'a*, provides a hint. Nuyootecos define *shita sa'a* as *shita kuaio ta'a*, "tortillas of all of us ta'a." Other things that are *kuaio ta'a* include communal coffee plots, the public buildings in the town center, and the Nuyoo territory. In other words, things that are *kuaio ta'a* are what we might call corporate assets.

Anthropologists and historians have long viewed the control of corporate property, and in particular land, as a defining feature of the Mesoamerican community. I will discuss the composition of Nuyooteco corporate property in chapter 12. What I want to suggest here is that beyond the material manifestations of corporateness, corporateness should also be seen as something people create and experience through their interactions with one another. In other words, it is a value-laden practice as well as a structural characteristic, and it articulates a specific image of "community." But to see what this image is, and how it is articulated through exchange, requires that we examine the pooling of tortillas in the fiesta in more detail.

Before the sponsors of a fiesta distribute the tortillas in the pool of goods they amass, something very interesting occurs that is best seen in an example. After a partner arrives with a prestation, the sponsors serve him or her a plate of beans, along with three to five tortillas. Meanwhile, the women of the sponsoring household count the tortillas and calculate the size of the countergift they should place in the partner's basket. If the partner brought a gift of 60 tortillas, then they will place a countergift of 10 tortillas in the basket. It is very important that the tortillas the partner eats with the meal, and the tortillas the partner receives as a countergift, not come from the tortillas he or she brought in *saa sa'a*. If they were , this would be a great insult, since it would mean that the tortillas were not of any use to the sponsors or that they were deficient in some way. The tortillas the partner receives are rather part of the general pool of tortillas in the sponsors' control. This pool is made up of the tortillas the women of the sponsoring household and their close kinswomen have prepared,[2] plus the tortillas that arrive through *saa sa'a* (as repayments for gifts the sponsor made in the past)[3] and the tortillas that are new gifts to the sponsors, given by those who wish to place the sponsor in debt.[4] Recall that most of these are sa'a tortillas, which differ from everyday tortillas in that they are in circulation among households and are owned by all the households participating in the event. Once they are in the sponsor's possession, no note is taken of who brought which ones, so that the tortillas the

2. In seven mayordomo fiestas for which I was able to calculate the sources of the goods distributed, they amounted to 11.5% of the total.

3. These averaged 36.4% of the total distributed in seven mayordomo fiestas.

4. These averaged 52.1% of the total distributed in seven mayordomo fiestas.

partners receive with their meal, and the tortillas they receive as a
countergift, come from many different households. People in the
celebration, Nuyootecos therefore say, "eat from the same tortilla,"
since the distributions made by the sponsors circulate tortillas among
participants in such a way that everyone is served food that originated
in someone else's kitchen.

In chapters 2 and 4 I discussed the association between tortillas,
such as those circulated in the fiesta, and young women. On the one
hand, men speak of obtaining a wife as enabling them to obtain
tortillas: her household is the place where the groom's "water will
come from, where his tortilla will come from." On the other hand,
Nuyootecos liken women's sexual organs to the tortilla. As I noted
earlier alimentary processes have, for the Mixtec, a sexual connota-
tion. People refer to the sexual act as "eating" (*kajira*), "they eat,"
and the sex organs, particularly female sex organs, as a variety of
nutritious foods, such as "meat," but also as "folded tortilla," and "a
tamale." The corn plant itself is represented as a young, marriageable
woman.

One can also see a relationship between the circulation of items
among households in the fiesta and the circulation of persons between
households in marriage. The exchange of "sisters" between exogamous kin groups in other societies has caused Levi-Strauss to call
women "the supreme gift," since both marriage and the exchange of
items in gift exchange are governed by the same principles of strict
reciprocity, and it should not be surprising that a similar relationship
might exist between marriage and other transactions in Nuyoos as
well. However, marriage in Nuyoo is not like gift exchange, since
there is no direct exchange of persons between households. Instead,
we have a pattern where households make their marriageable women
(and sometimes men) available to others, without demanding a person
back, either immediately or in the future (with the assumption that
other households are doing the same). What marriage is like, then, is
the process through which the pool of tortillas is amassed through the
fiesta by the sponsors, which they go on to distribute among the
people present so that the members of each household "eat from the
same tortilla." In other words, part of the significance of "eating from
the same tortilla" as an image of social relatedness lies in the iconic
relation the pooling and distribution of items in the fiesta has to the
Nuyooteco practice of bringing others' children into their households.

The notion that women form a pool of potential spouses also
suggests that marriageable persons are a resource shared by all,

corporately. After all, the tortillas are *kuaio ta'a*, "a corporate resource," like the municipal buildings and community territory. But although this expands our notion of the range of values considered to make up corporate wealth, it still leaves unanswered the question of what kind of group Nuyootecos imagine themselves to be—and, by implication, why the sharing of tortillas is such an important collectivizing practice. To see the collective image "eating from the same tortilla" articulates, I want to return to another context where people "eat from the same tortilla": the marriage ceremony itself.

Recall that in the marriage ritual, the groom's godparents serve the bride and the groom a tortilla, which the godparents tear in half and then give to the couple to consume. Through this ritual, the bride and groom transform themselves from persons living in separate households into complements, belonging to a single household. By eating from the same tortilla, husband and wife will have true affection for each other, so that "if one is away, the other will feel sad" (kukuekani). Eating together will also diminish conflict between them. As one woman said, "We will be of one heart, one mind" (*in ni nasa'o animao, andunio*), and she went on to add that the couple who eat together will work for the good of the household, instead of their individual interests. Again, the efficacy of the ritual parting and consumption of the tortilla lies not just in its being a sign of the beginning of a nakara relationship between husband and wife. Rather, it is an act that *creates* the relationship; it causes the couple to become one (*in va nsa'a maara*), so that they are "standing up together" (*kuini kuta'a*) and they "accompany one another" (*kuji'i ji; nuu nuu ta'a ji*). The married couple constitute a single legal person, and the only instance in which a woman may attend a town meeting is when she goes as proxy for an absent husband. Nor should we view the sharing of the tortilla as an isolated ritual act, confined to the wedding ceremony. Instead, it is part of a couple's daily life together, and a husband and a wife should share the same food at each meal.

I suggest that something similar to what occurs in the marriage ritual occurs during the exchanges in the fiesta. Specifically, by pooling and then distributing tortillas so that the tortillas of one household are consumed by the members of many different households, the relationship among these households becomes transactionally equivalent to the relationships among people of the same household.[5] As one man explained, "Those who come to the fiesta are

5. Although it is not clear if forms of ceremonial exchange and the items circulated in these

like a single household, with several adult women who prepare the tortillas. No one says, 'Oh, that woman there made these tortillas, while another woman made the tortillas over there.' You take the tortillas as if they were made by a single person." This makes the pool of tortillas like the household granary, in that this pool, like the granary, is a single reserve, and all share equally in the food prepared. Indeed, other people explained that when people do not "distinguish" between the tortillas made by different hands it means they are united. The definitive sign of a breakup of a household, as we saw in chapter 1, is when people do "distinguish" tortillas—that is, when some members begin to prepare and consume their tortillas separate from other members of the household. Furthermore, Nuyootecos consistently identify the fiesta as a time of "unity," when they are most "happy," "content," and "secure"—much as they describe their experience of living in an ideal household.

In their building up of a single store of food, then, participants in the celebration, under the direction of the sponsors, parallel the action of the members of a single household, who cooperate in subsistence activities and share in the fruit of their labors. By not "distinguishing" tortillas, and by giving food to one another in the way that household members do, Nuyooteco actions mirror the kind of care and moral conduct (nakara) one finds among members of the same household. And just as nakara must be continuously demonstrated and experienced for the household to remain intact, so too this replication of commensality in the fiesta is continuous. There are over 80 celebrations held annually in Nuyoo, each lasting two to four days, so that people have ample opportunity to "eat from the same tortilla."

THE COMMUNITY AS A GREAT HOUSE

The last three chapters have examined a set of activities, or forms of sociation, through which Nuyootecos create and experience especially strong connections to one another: In sacrifice, the sacrificer transforms the items offered into blood and milk, which he or she then feeds to others, transmitting to these others substances that link them as kin. In marriage, Nuyooteco children form what might be said to be a common "pool" of persons, who will go to live in other households, so that these other households will be able to renew them-

---

exchanges in the Nahua town of Tlayacapan carry a similar semantic load, John Ingham argues that in this town's mayordomo fiestas a set of "symbolic affinities" are established between the sponsors' household, guests, and ritual kin (Ingham 1986:100–101).

selves. Finally, in the circulation of tortillas in the fiesta, Nuyootecos share a common pool of goods, which, as we saw, evokes not only the Nuyooteco "pool" of marriage partners, but also communal lands and other forms of corporate wealth.

Note that each activity we have discussed parallels the processes through which people create households. It is through the transmission of "the heat of life" in generative and nurturing acts that parents bring children into the household. It is through marriage that they bring new personnel into the household as affines. Finally, it is through commensality that they make godchildren (and others) household members. I am not arguing that sacrifice, intermarriage, and pooling in the fiesta create households; what they do is order relationships among Nuyootecos in "household-like" ways, and the image of community that emerges from this is not one where Nuyootecos live in a household, but where they form something different, a "great house" (with, however, the acts that create ties of shared substance, affinity, and corporate identity informed by nakara, just as they are within the household).

In a recent essay, Levi-Strauss also invited us to see the ambiguous Kwakuitl *numayan*, which some anthropologists have argued is a descent group, as a kind of house. He went on to suggest that the "House" is a type of social organization, and defined it as

> a corporate body holding an estate made up of both material and imma-
> terial wealth, which perpetuates itself through the transmission of its
> name, its goods and its titles down a real or imaginary line, considered
> legitimate as long as this continuity can express itself in the language of
> kinship or affinity, and most often, of both. (Levi-Strauss 1982:174)

Due to his focus on noble houses, Levi-Strauss's interests lie in the transmission of "names, goods and titles," and he did not consider commensal practices in the numayan, which, as we have seen, are crucial both to the household and to the way Nuyootecos create "household-like" relations among community members. Nonetheless, if for us the image of the corporation is the organic unity of the body, then for Nuyootecos it is the unity of the household, and the Nuyooteco corporation, or "great house," is clearly similar to what Levi-Strauss argued for the Kwakuitl numayan, with membership expressed in terms of shared kinship and/or affinity.

The idea that the Nuyoo community is a "great house" may have implications for our understanding Mesoamerican social organization more generally. One finds throughout the region social groups referred to in the native languages by terms such as "Big House" (e.g., the calpulli) and in the Mixteca, John Pohl has pointed out that scribes represented social units in Prehispanic and Postconquest manuscripts as palaces, or stylized houses (John Pohl, personal communication, 1992). Although I see the Nuyooteco "great house" as the summating image of deep purposes and underlying truths about Nuyootecos' lives together rather than a structure generating behavior, the idea that Mesoamerican corporate enterprises could have recruited members based on shared kinship, affinity, and commensality, either singly or in combination, may help to explain why these groups, like the Kwakuitl numayan, have never seemed to fit very easily into the received categories of social structure, such as the descent group—which was, after all, developed to describe societies in other places in the world (Hill and Monaghan 1987; Offner 1983:171).

CHAPTER 11

CARGO AND THE HUMAN CONDITION

DURING a visit to Nuyoo in 1989 I stayed in the house of some compadres in Nuyoo Center. People usually sleep on mats on the floor, often bunched together for warmth and security. One night I found myself next to my compadre's son, who is a restless sleeper. His tossing and turning kept me awake, and I got up to see if I could find another place to lie down. I slipped outside and found my compadre—who was also having trouble sleeping—sitting by the doorstep. He laughed when I told him why I was up and said he wished that his restless son was the only thing disturbing his sleep. He had been named Comisariado de Bienes Comunales and was worried about a dispute with Atatlahuca over boundaries. He had called tequios to repair the boundary markers between Nuyoo and surrounding communities, and he had traveled to the offices of the Agrarian Reform Secretariat in Oaxaca to request official intervention. It would be his responsibility to house and feed the surveyors and other persons the government might send and to pay any other costs associated with their work. This heavy expense, falling so early in his term (he had received the cargo only a few months before) was, he thought, a sign of things to come. He worried that his grandson's education would have to be postponed (which it was) and that he would have to sell his goats (by 1991 his herd of 18 animals was reduced to 4). Having a cargo, he remarked, is "like contracting a disease" (*kue'i*).

In chapter 8, I pointed out that it is the duty of cargo holders to protect, regulate, and distribute corporate assets. It is true that these duties are no longer as significant as they once were, given the loss of the communal cattle herd, the erosion of the value of public funds, and the privatization of lands (see chapter 12). However, they remain important official functions. Cargo holders, like my compadre, take the lead in defending community boundaries; develop public works; decide how to exploit collective resources, such as the forests; decide who has access to unclaimed lands; organize and direct communal labor parties; are in charge of the community-owned vehicles; and even try to find mates for the unmarried. As one official explained it to me, they review a person's situation, and if they see that he or she is in need of a spouse, they call in all those who are eligible partners. In the case of an unwed mother, for example, they will call in all the widowers who live nearby to see if one of them "will take the woman in." In this way they hope to create a viable household.

Cargo holders are also the ones who administer the corporate assets pooled in the fiesta. Recall that nearly every cargo involves the sponsorship of a fiesta, usually at the end of the cargo holder's term in office. During the celebration the cargo holder and other members of his household receive prestations from other households, which they deposit into the pool of goods under their control. They then distribute these items to fiesta participants, in meals and countergifts. As we saw, people liken this pool of goods to the productive assets Nuyootecos hold in common, such as the land, public buildings, and marriageable persons, so that we can say the cargo holder's activities in managing these goods parallels his activities in managing other corporate resources.

Recall also what is significant about the pooling of goods in the fiesta: after the sponsors distribute them, all the participants "eat from the same tortilla." This, in turn, articulates a specific image of what Nuyoo is: a place where people intermarry, where they are kin, where they hold things in common—in short, where they form a "great house." By "eating from the same tortilla," the house becomes not an abstract representation of the group but an ongoing practice, so that Nuyootecos are constantly creating and experiencing themselves as a "great house" in the fiesta. If this did not occur, if people did not "eat from the same tortilla" (with all that this implies) on a regular basis, Nuyoo would be like a household whose members began cooking apart, or like a marriage in which husband and wife do not eat together—on the verge of breaking up. It is through ritual and exchange that Nuyootecos make and remake themselves as a particular kind of community.

Cargo service then, like sacrifice and the pooling of goods in the fiesta, is an activity through which Nuyootecos realize the great house. This is clear in the way they talk about service. For example, Nuyootecos often say that office holders "care for" (nakara) other community members. As one man explained when I asked why he sold a coffee grove to pay for office expenses when he was president in 1972, "The president is the father of the community, and thus when there is a need, the children will come to him." The president, like a father, nurtures the community. Just as it is a father's duty to marry off his children and thereby ensure them a place in a viable household, so too it is the job of the town authorities to look out for their "children" by placing those who lack a mate into a household where they will find care and support. People even phrase their criticism of a bad president in the same terms they would use to criticize a bad father. When one officeholder drank so much that he was unable to attend to visiting state officials in 1983, people denounced him for "abandoning his children" and "leaving them as if they were orphans." And just as roles are reversed when parents grow old, so that the child becomes the provider, so too the "children of the community" should care for a "father of the community" once he grows old. Twice during visits I made to the house of Tañuu Carmen López Feria of Llano Grande, Yucuhiti, younger men stopped by with corn, beans, and other foodstuffs for him. When I asked one of them if he did this because he was a close relative of Tañuu Carmen, the man replied no and explained that he gave the food because Tañuu Carmen served the community and he wanted to be sure that Tañuu Carmen had enough to eat. A man in Nuyoo later commented when I told him about the incident, "We sow so that they may eat because they sowed so that we could eat"—the same response people give when asked why a child cares for his or her parents once the older people are no longer able to work. In other words, just as Carmen had nurtured the people of Yucuhiti through his service to the community, community members now care for him in his old age.

Cargo service, then, is analogous to the act of care and love that creates and sustains the household, and cargo holders have positions within the community that correspond to those of senior household members. When people refer to men who have served as president, they call them tañuu, which translates as "fathers of the ñuu," and their wives as ñañuu, or "mothers of the ñuu." In Nuyoo at least, service and the acts that create ties of kinship share a family resemblance.

THE GREAT HOUSE AND THE HOUSEHOLD

If cargo service is, for Nuyootecos, an activity through which the House is realized, and top cargo holders are analogous to "mothers" and "fathers," then it is also true that the great house is created through the channeling of private household resources into collective activities. In a place like Nuyoo, household surpluses can be captured in two ways: by appropriating what households produce, or by appro-

priating the labor of household members, thereby limiting the amount
they dedicate to household activities (cf. Josephedes 1985). One can
see that cargo is an effective instrument in both respects. It absorbs
surplus production by obliging individual officeholders to spend
personal wealth in carrying out their duties. This can be direct, where
cargo holders spend surpluses already accumulated, or indirect, where
they borrow against future surpluses by assuming gift debt. It absorbs
labor time by obliging office holders to dedicate many days at their
posts in the municipal building or to travel outside Nuyoo on community errands. As people in Nuyoo put it, cargo service leaves them
"thin" and "eats up" their households.

The burden placed on a domestic unit by the loss of labor time in a
society closely geared to an agricultural cycle cannot be overly
stressed. Not being able to work two or three weeks in certain months
means that one may not perform some task that is crucial to the crop's
development and that the harvest may be lost. Many cargo holders do
not even attempt to sow while in office, relying instead on what they
have stored from the year before and purchasing food in the market
with the cash they have managed to accumulate. Others may be able
to call on sons or sons-in-law to work when they are unable. For good
reasons my compadre likened cargo to an illness, since cargo, like an
illness, prevents one from working, and for good reason people expect
that cargo, if it is done well, should leave the cargo holder "thin" and
"eat up" his household. It is in this context that we can understand
Nuyooteco assertions that cargo results in a kind of death.

Cargo and Death

Nuyootecos liken the cargo holder to a man who is deceased and cargo
service to the experience of death. One example of this is the
mountain symbol, which, as noted earlier, people use to represent the
progression through the sequence of civil-religious hierarchy posts,
where the ascent up the mountain corresponds to the individual's
ascent through the different levels of office. The mountain is also
prominent in Nuyooteco images of death, particularly in the notion
that the Nuyooteco dead reside atop Yuku Kasa, a mountain to the
southeast of Nuyoo Center. It is as if the end of the ascent up the
mountain of tiñu implies death, just as the ascent itself is a condition
of life, marking stages in life's course. This connection between life,
death, and the civil-religious hierarchy is even more strongly made in
the aphorism used for the occasion of death, *nte'ne tiñu*, "the tiñu has
ended" (literally, "the tiñu is cut").

People use the term *nte'ne tiñu* in two senses, both of which are relevant here. First, as one man explained, *nte'ne tiñu* means "never again," since the cargo holder, once he completes his term, will never again serve the community in that office. As noted earlier there is generally a one-way movement of people through civil-religious hierarchy posts. The deceased is, then, like a man who has completed cargo, since in death he will never return to life or, as Nuyootecos put it, "he will never pass this way again."

Nte'ne tiñu is also a phrase used in the sense of an obligation that has been met (such as a loan repaid or a ritual duty one has carried out). Death is thus like the completion of a duty or the fulfillment of a responsibility. In Nuyooteco mythology, death becomes a part of human destiny through the Covenants with Earth and Rain, in which people gave up their bodies in return for the right to sow the land (and therefore live as civilized beings). When I asked people to comment on the Covenant with Earth, they would frequently say that "it is about why we have to die," or, more precisely, "it is about why we are buried in the cemetery . . . we go no other place when we die, but to our true house." The tiumi, after all, the primitive beings of precovenant times, lived a long time and did not experience death until the birth of the Sun. According to people today, the giving up of our bodies to Earth and Rain in death is proper because when the farmer digs into Earth with his digging stick, he is stabbing into something that is alive. The soil is flesh, the rocks are bones, and the rivers are veins. Digging into living Earth, or splitting rocks, causes tremendous pain. Furthermore, when we eat corn, we are consuming holy, living beings, since corn is the daughter of Earth and Rain and it suffers when people boil and grind it to make it into tortillas. In return, humans must also suffer death.

Death then fulfills one condition of the covenant, upon which the other condition—crop growth and a civilized life—depends. This makes death an obligation placed upon Nuyootecos by the fact that they are born into society.

In 1607, Fray Gregorio García wrote of the version of the covenants he published that "The Indians say . . . . that this was the first offering made in the world" (García 1981:328, my translation). This is significant because in being the "first offering made in the world," the covenant also became a paradigm for all subsequent sacrificial offerings. This is why whenever Nuyootecos make sacrifice today, they mention the covenants in their prayers, reminding "the faces" of Earth and Rain of the agreement that binds the sacrificer to them and

offering them tokens of their bodies. We saw in chapter 9, for
example, that pulque, which is a very common offering in Mixtec
sacrifices, is equated with the "white blood" (semen) of males, and
that when people offer candles to the gods, they sometimes rub them
all over their bodies before burning them, making the candle a
substitute for their physical organism. The reason for this is that the
covenants made between humans and the sacred required the supreme self-sacrifice. To receive the right to practice agriculture and to
live in the society upon which it is based, people gave up rights to
their bodies; for Nuyootecos even something as personal as one's own
organism is owed as a debt incurred by the fact that we are human and
live in society.

It should perhaps not be surprising that cargo service is broadly
associated with self-sacrifice in Mesoamerican culture (Ingham 1984;
Klein 1987) or that Nuyootecos say "death is the final tiñu" (cargo).
Cargo, like death and self-sacrifice, is something that is a condition of
civilized life. As I noted in chapter 7, after returning from a distant
region in Oaxaca, I mentioned to a group of people that it was no longer
the custom there to work tequio, which, as we saw, Nuyootecos
classify as service. One man commented, "Well, they must live like
dogs there." Dogs, as we saw, are domesticated animals, "of the
household," but are like those who are unable to maintain harmonious
relationships with people of other households. They thus come to be
associated with people who care so much about their own domestic
concerns that they are unable to enter into harmonious relationships
with others. Shouldering a cargo, or working tequio, is to engage in
activity that is minimally necessary for collective life. Just as in the
Covenant with Earth, where people's bodies are "eaten up," in
community service one pays the "debt" incurred (another meaning of
the word tiñu) with household resources, so that Nuyootecos say the
household is "eaten up" and "left thin." The sense of alienation in
cargo can thus be seen as closely tied to the experience of death, and
the purpose of death—to reaffirm the Covenant and renew the
world—is closely tied to the sense of obligation the notion of cargo
evokes.

Note that when Nuyootecos speak of death, sacrifice, and cargo
service, they often do so in alimentary terms. In death, Earth and
Rain "eat" human bodies. In the sacrifices of the Viko Nuni, the
sacrificer "feeds" himself to passersby. In cargo, service "eats up"
the household and leaves its members "thin." In each case the result
is destruction but also a kind of immanent spirituality in which one, as

in the Nahuatl tropes for self-sacrifice recorded by Andrés de Olmos, "falls inward" and is assimilated (Maxwell and Hanson 1992). And this assimilation is expressed in the image of the House. In death, we enter our "true house," and it is through sacrifice and cargo that the "great house" is created. The image of the house thus encompasses a series of processes whereby separate entities are brought into unmediated unity.[1]

The cargo holder, who is at the center of this collectivizing project, assumes a particular status. We can see this in the remarks of a man from the hamlet of Zaragoza who has a particular devotion to the saints in the Nuyoo church and who usually participates in church rituals. When I asked him why he was absent one Sunday when the priest visited to say mass, he told me that he didn't need to go because he knew the mayordomos were there. It is part of the mayordomo's duty to attend mass when it is offered in the church, and one can usually find all 23 of them lined up along the back wall of the room when the priest celebrates. (Earthquake damage had made the interior of the church unsafe, so mass is celebrated in the sacristy.) In any event, the man's point was that the mayordomos become his—and every other Nuyooteco's—representatives before the sacred. "Representative" is also a term many Nuyootecos use to translate "cargo holder," and they frequently address cargo holders as the social units they serve (e.g., tañuu). Through the self-sacrifices of cargo, we can even say the cargo holder comes to embody the corporation, just as the corporation comes to "eat him up" and embody him. If mediation is the social manifestation of the life-renewing properties associated with Jesus/the Sun, then synthesis is the social manifestation of the life-renewing properties associated with Earth and Rain.

At the same time, this synthesis is achieved at the expense of singularity. Specifically, in cargo service, the Nuyooteco vision of themselves as a great house—where the individual becomes the corporation—is reproduced by suppressing the household. Dogs, after all, are one side of the Nuyooteco community as an organization of independent households; what cargo service does is subvert that independence. Even fiesta participation, where all "eat from the

1. Cecilia Klein has shown that in ancient Mesoamerica the house served as an extended metaphor for unity and order, where the celestial world was often depicted as a kind of house, opposed to the disorder of the underworld (Klein 1982). But once again, we see here how the idea of the house for Nuyootecos is not solely a representation of the social order, but also part of a theory of social action.

same tortilla," is, in a sense, the denial of household ties, so that the significance of forming a great house derives from the way it contrasts with, and is created at the expense of, the household. One might even say that in the fiesta, participants begin as inherently domestic individuals—*sa'a* exchanges take place between households—and then, as people "eat from the same tortilla," they are remade in such a way that corporate goals and self-sacrificing action become particularly compelling.

The idea that the great house is created at the expense of the household is something that presents a serious dilemma, however. For most, the answer is to seek some kind of compromise by surreptitiously avoiding service, or by shirking duties. For some, these acts are expressions of independence; for others they inspire great ambivalence and almost pathological responses, such as going on drinking binges and picking fights with others. Yet as long as one stays in Nuyoo, one has no choice but to participate. At every tequio, officials note who participates and who does not. If the tequio is a large one, then they take the names down of those who participate in notebooks for future reference. The town police may be sent to the households of those who are absent to see why they have not answered the blasts of the tequio horn. A man who does not work his days of tequio may be fined or even jailed, as happened to six men who missed several tequios in 1989. If a man consistently misses tequio, officials threaten him with the loss of his lands and exile. The seriousness with which people take this last threat is such that no one, in recent memory, has ever tempted the authorities by continuing to miss work after being warned by the town police.

The inevitability, the lack of choice, and the feelings of alienation associated with cargo are particularly apparent in discussions with Nuyootecos about their reasons for migrating from Nuyoo to urban centers. Most people in Mexico migrate from rural areas for a combination of economic purposes, desire for access to services unavailable in the countryside, and curiosity about the city. Yet every man I spoke with from Nuyoo who was willing to be frank with me about why he migrated told me that the avoidance of cargo service was one of the principal reasons he decided to leave. I first had an inkling of this when one of my linguistic informants, a young man of 18, disappeared one day without saying anything to me. I had been paying him a daily wage slightly above the going rate, and we worked only about two hours a day (which left him plenty of time for other chores), so the need to earn money should not have been a concern for him. I later found out that there was a rumor circulating that the authorities chose him as the head of the new committee for the reconstruction of the municipal hall, so he decided to go to Mexico City while he was still free. He had to keep his trip quiet, because if word reached the authorities that he was leaving, they would have acted before he could depart. There have also been cases where fathers requested cargos for their sons, to prevent the younger men from migrating.

Incidents such as these make cargo into a kind of an "iron cage," an image which occurred to Weber, not coincidentally, while he was analyzing bureaucratic organizations. Nuyootecos, in fact, often speak about civil-religious hierarchy service as something that traps and represses them, and, as we will see, the civil-religious hierarchy cannot be understood apart from the way power is exerted through it. Yet people also feel cargo is something upon which they are dependent, and no one argues that it should be abolished. Like death, cargo is something imposed upon individuals as a consequence of social life. As Simmel noted long ago, "alienation" is not particular to capitalism; or, as Nuyootecos say of someone who has a cargo, *no'o kastigu ñuu nuun*, "he suffers the punishment of community."

PART FOUR

REVELATION AND HISTORY

The nations (of Oaxaca) often fought wars with one another, over trifling matters.

—Antonio de Herrera y Tordesillas, *Historia General,* 1726–1730

When I first arrived (in the area of Nuyoo) I found all the pueblos danced to the tune of a few shysters, or "caciques," who always seemed to occupy a position in the local government.

—Ing. Romeo González, Depto. Agrario, 1934

CHAPTER 12

CORPORATE HOLDINGS
AND LIBERAL REFORMS

OVER the course of this ethnography, I have focused on Nuyooteco statements about their experiences of determining others, and being determined by them, through typical forms of sociation. I have grouped these into two poles: the "community" of independent households, in which people of different domestic units both cooperate with one another to achieve household goals and compete with one another over valued resources, and the "community" of the great house, in which Nuyootecos, as kin, subordinate individual interests to corporate ones. But the larger point is that the Nuyoo ñuu is a conjunction of different images and socialities, which, as people's statements about the dilemmas they experience in civil-religious hierarchy service show, are not merged into a single or cohesive program for collective action.

There are other cases from the ethnography of Mesoamerica that similarly suggest ways of ordering social life not captured by established typologies. Greenberg (1981) for example, wrote of what he called "two principles of organization" in the Chatino town of Santiago Yaitepec. One of these is "based on a grid of reciprocal obligations and ritual redistribution," while the other is "expressly capitalist, premised on unequal exchange and class" (Greenberg 1981:55). In another case, Kay Warren (1978) found that the Maya of San Andrés Semetebaj maintain two different "models of the social order." The first she called "the Law of Christ" or *costumbre* (see also Reina 1966:xii–xix). It represents "diffuse, enduring solidarity" (Warren 1978:57), encouraging people to "unite, love each other, and express mutual understanding" (Warren 1978:43, 67). It is a "guiding principle" for a series of actions, ranging from the way family members, kin, and fellow townspeople behave toward one another to the meaning of the rituals performed in the civil-religious hierarchy. The second model Warren discussed includes the Ladinos, or non-Maya, who live in the town. Here San Andrés becomes a biethnic entity defined in

259

terms of "the Law of the Devil." In contrast to the egalitarian "Law of Christ," the "Law of the Devil" places the Maya in a subordinate position with respect to Ladinos. In its associated mythology, it explains why the Maya lag behind Ladinos in education and wealth and why Ladinos have political power in the community, despite being outnumbered by the Indians.

One conclusion that can be drawn from these examples is that a lack of continuity and coherence in the organization and conception of social life must be viewed in historical terms, in that it is caused by the penetration of capitalism, or some other disruptive change, such as the movement of Ladinos into the community. Although I will show that Nuyootecos today relate to one another in ways that are quite different from what was the case a generation ago, I think we would unnecessarily limit ourselves, and be forced to deny the creativity and fluidity of collective life in Mesoamerica, if we assumed the existence — even to contrast it with its absence — of a single, whole community. There are many examples in the literature of groups that simultaneously maintain distinct "models" of the social order, which they activate according to specific goals or in response to particular events. Gearing (1958) provided a clear example of this in his discussion of the nineteenth-century Cherokee, whom he says assumed different "structural poses" that appeared or disappeared according to the tasks at hand (Gearing 1958:1148). Thus, the Cherokee pursued their hunting activities as an aggregate of individual households. With a murder, however, people interacted in terms of the village clan segments, which cross-cut the households (Gearing 1958). Each of these poses constituted a distinct form of sociation that made the Cherokee village a very different place from one moment to the next in response to specific goals, events, or natural periodicities (for other examples, see Fardon 1985; Gose 1991; Leach 1954; Lipp 1991; Mauss 1979; Salzman 1978; Strathern 1988). Our difficulty in viewing something like this as a regular feature of life in Mesoamerica, instead of some aberration caused by disruptive change, is, no doubt, a legacy of our own image of what an ideal community should be: single, not multiple; homogeneous, not heterogeneous; and all-encompassing, rather than fragmentary (cf. Gose 1991).

In this final part of the book, I will examine Nuyooteco sociality as part of events: not just the recurrent events of birth, baptism, marriage, or death, but also the nonrecurrent events of history. I will not, however, view Nuyoo as a place where history has fragmented an original unity, or where temporary contradictions evolve into an ultimate synthesis—themes that make sense only if we see community as being what is at issue. Instead, I see the "polyphonic" nature of Nuyooteco sociality as being crucial to the way things in Nuyoo change. Because any discussion of change in a place like Nuyo must ground itself in the material conditions of life, I begin in this chapter with agriculture—in particular, how the land on which crops are grown is used and distributed.

COMMUNITY AND CORPORATE PROPERTY

Corporate control over land and other assets has long been recognized as essential to processes of group formation and group continuity in Mesoamerica. However, from the late colonial period to the present, corporate property has been under continuous assault throughout the region by governments whose economic policies encourage individual accumulation, by changes in agricultural technologies that have altered traditional ecological relationships, by outsiders seeking to take control of valuable farmland, and by local people themselves, who see a chance to profit by alienating public resources. This development has the potential to transform rural life (for the Mixteca, see Berry 1981; Carmagnani 1988; Chassen 1986; Pastor 1987), and Nuyoo has been no exception. Over the past 125 years, much of the Nuyoo territory has been placed in private hands, the once-teeming communal herds have disappeared, and the value of the assets held by the mayordomos has sharply eroded. This loss of corporate wealth, has, in turn, had important consequences for the financing of public activities, for interhousehold interactions, and for the way economic assets are distributed among the people of Nuyoo.

Land Use in the Nineteenth Century

I noted in the introduction that the steep and rugged topography of Nuyoo is characterized by a diversity of microclimates, which allow for the exploitation of an unusual variety of plant and animal species. It is clear that throughout history, the ability to produce tropical fruits and vegetables not found in adjacent highland areas provided Nuyootecos with valuable trade items (Monaghan 1994). In the nineteenth century, the most important of these products was the banana, which Nuyootecos would sell in highland Mixteca towns of Chalcatongo and Ocotepec and at the weekly regional market at Tlaxiaco (Apuntes Topográficos 1871:243).[1] Oranges, lemons, limes, mamey, avocados,

1. In 1913, the municipal president of Nuyoo reported that two men from Nuyoo had their

cuajinicuil, zapote, chile, and certain varieties of squash were also local products occasionally traded to highland areas.

Although tropical fruits may have provided Nuyootecos with an important source of trade items and cash during the nineteenth century, the production of corn was the central concern of the Nuyoo farmer. Corn, of course, has been the key component of the Meso-american diet for several thousand years, and we saw in chapter 9 that Nuyootecos view corn as the basis of good nutrition. Nuyootecos eat corn at every one of the three meals they normally consume in a day, usually in the form of large (about 100 grams each) tortillas. People also eat corn on the cob at harvest time, and in the *atole,* tamales, and pozole served during fiestas.

Corn, like the other crops Nuyootecos sow, is sensitive to changes in altitude and climate. In the cold and cloudy upper reaches of Nuyooteco territory, it takes almost a year for a corn crop to mature. In the lower, warmer areas, corn sown in May or June can be harvested only four months after the farmer plants it. Sowing corn in different climatic zones allows people to schedule their agricultural work, so that fields can be sowed, weeded, and harvested sequentially. It also affords some protection against natural calamities, since even though a strong wind or frost might damage a crop at one altitude or stage of growth, it may not affect another sown in a different microclimate (Monaghan 1994; see also Katz 1990).

Nuyootecos produce the bulk of the corn they harvest through swidden techniques, since the steep slopes and rocky terrain make irrigation almost impossible, and the use of ploughs drawn by oxen is limited to a few plots of land. Depending on the altitude, farmers prepare lands for swidden from January to May by clearing the overgrowth on old swidden plots or opening up new plots by cutting down the forest. After the brush and trees have dried sufficiently, the farmer burns them and then sows the plot anywhere from January to May, again depending on the altitude and climate. Nuyootecos sow several different varieties of corn, choosing the seed best adapted to the microclimate of the field where it is to be planted. Most fields require two weedings. This involves hours of standing stooped over in the field, cutting back with a machete the grasses and other plants that threaten to choke off the corn. Beans and squash are also sown in

---

mules stolen on their way through Cuquila after selling fruit in the market of Tlaxiaco "as is our custom every eight days" (ARM, Presidente Municipal de Nuyoo al Jefe Político, September 28, 1913).

the cornfields or in separate plots, after the farmer has finished planting his corn. Like corn, the variety of squash or bean sown depends on climate and altitude. Cornfields must lie fallow for five to seven years before they can be resown.

Swidden agriculture in the Mixteca has important implications for land tenure. Simply put, because people make no great improvements in the land they sow, there is little incentive to establish a private claim to any particular plot. Families may have used fields convenient to their house sites repeatedly, but archival sources and oral history show that until recently individuals did not maintain private title to land. When one decided to sow, one simply went out and used any vacant parcel that looked like it would make a good swidden. The only requirement was that one be a ta'a and fulfill one's communal obligations.

There were, of course, other factors that were crucial to the persistence of this type of land tenure. One is that Nuyoo was not suited for the form of capital-intensive, commercial agriculture practiced in nineteenth and early twentieth century Oaxaca. The most important commercial crop in the Mixteca during this period was sugar cane, which cannot be grown in Nuyoo in any quantity. It was, however, sown on the nearby irrigated lands in the Canada of Yosotichi and around Putla, which were owned, for the most part, by wealthy hacendados of European descent.

There is reason to doubt that Nuyootecos ever achieved self-sufficiency in staple crops, and people often went hungry during the months just before the annual harvest, a period from July to September, known as the *yoo yuu* (Monaghan 1990a; see also Burgoa's comments on the region [Burgoa 1989:359]). During the *yoo yuu* Nuyootecos would descend to Yosotichi and Putla haciendas to work as wage laborers (about a five- or six-hour walk from Nuyoo Center) so that they could obtain enough corn to see themselves through to the harvest (Monaghan 1990a). In the nineteenth century, the Esperón family — who controlled the commercial and political life of the entire Tlaxiaco region — consolidated and expanded these haciendas, forming the giant Hacienda de la Concepción. They became wealthy through the production and sale of aguardiente, a distilled liquor made from sugar cane (Pastor 1987; Monaghan 1990a, 1994).

The only cash crop of any importance that Nuyootecos cultivated during the nineteenth century was the banana, which, as I noted, they sold to the people of nearby highland towns. In several significant ways, banana production is similar to corn production. Bananas, like corn, can be profitably produced by a single household without having to employ outside labor. It is true that bananas must be weeded, and this consumes much of the farmer's time. But with bananas, the weeds do not usually grow very high, because the trees, when planted together, block the sun. According to Simmonds, one man, working full time, should be able to maintain five acres of bananas in good condition (Simmonds 1982:291). What does consume a lot of time in Nuyoo is preventing gophers from eating banana roots and causing the plants to fall over.

Bananas are also like corn in that they exhaust the soil and clean weeding leads to erosion (Simmonds 1982:294–95). This means that plots should be shifted every few years, since production will decline if bananas are continuously grown in the same place. Shifting plots does not significantly lower productivity, since bananas, once sown, will produce a crop within nine months.

The banana, then, may have been a cash crop, but it required only a small investment of capital, and the necessity of shifting it from one plot to another prevented it from becoming the kind of agricultural investment that would have made people want to secure long-term claim to the fields in which it was sown.

Another factor important to Nuyooteco land tenure in the nineteenth century was the community's low population. There were only 226 Nuyootecos in 1826 and 515 in 1869.[2] The low population meant that there would be an abundant supply of land upon which people could make swidden or sow bananas.

The consequences of an abundant supply of land, a low level of agricultural investment, and the dominance of swidden technology for land tenure were spelled out in a letter written by Alcalde Eusebio López of Nuyoo to the subprefect of the Partido of Tlaxiaco in 1856. López was responding to the Liberal government of Benito Juárez's decree that the lands of the community should be privatized:

> The crops that the people of my pueblo plant are swidden sown in the mountains, since there are no level lands that can be used. Because of this situation, the planting that one makes for example in this year cannot be repeated in the same place next year. Only if at least six or seven years have passed and brush has regrown over the plot can one repeat the process of cutting and burning and sow it again. This is the only way lands are sown, since as I said earlier, we lack lands that are called "plough lands" since the places where it is not steep hillsides are rocky and cut by ravines.

2. ARM, Padron de Santiago Nuyoo, April 15, 1826; ARM, Padron General de los Habitantes de Santiago Nuyoo, April 28, 1869.

Therefore I come before you to petition that my community be omitted from the disentailment order.[3]

What López implies in this letter is that with abundant lands for swidden, and the necessity of constantly shifting plots, the person who used any particular plot may never again return to it. For Eusebio Lopez and the alcaldes from other towns in the "swidden belt" between the Mixteca Alta and the Costa, this made any decree ordering land privatization in their villages unworkable.[4]

Cattle, Goats, and Holy Money

Land was not the only productive asset held corporately in the nineteenth century. Nuyootecos also owned a large herd of cattle, mules, sheep, goats, and pigs. According to oral history, the mayordomo of the Virgin of Rosario managed the herd with the help of the other mayordomos and a full-time cowherd, whom the mayordomos hired and paid a wage.[5] All the mayordomos were obliged to work with the herd when many hands were needed, such as in the castration and branding of calves and the repairing of corrals. The Rosario herd, in the late nineteenth century, appears to have been formed through the consolidation of the herds of at least six other mayordomías (called cofradías in the documents), the largest being that of Nuestra Señora de Guadalupe.[6]

Animals from these herds provided Nuyootecos with an inexpensive source of meat, which the mayordomos would butcher during fiestas and distribute in general meals to fiesta participants (see chapter 14). The mayordomos of the Virgin of Rosario also sold

3. ARM, Adjudicaciónes, Eusebio López, Alcalde, al Subprefecto del Partido, October 14, 1856.

4. ARM, Adjudicaciónes, Juan Vicente, Alcalde de Santa María Yucuhiti, al Subprefecto del Partido de Tlaxiaco, October 16, 1856; Manuel Marino, Alcalde de La Municipalidad de Santo Domingo Chicahuaxtla, al Subprefecto de Tlaxiaco, October 16, 1856; Crisanto Castro, Alcalde de San Pedro Yosotato, al Subprefecto del Partido de Tlaxiaco, October 16, 1856; José Basilio Barrios, Alcalde de San Esteban Atatlahuca, al Sr. Subprefecto del Partido de Tlaxiaco, October 18, 1856.

5. Caja de La Virgen de Rosario, estado de cuenta, 1873.

6. In 1803, the following cofradías in Nuyoo possessed a total of 115 head of cattle:

Nuestra Señora de Guadalupe	65
Santiago	24
Jesús Nazareno	11
Santísimo (Sacramento)	5
Las Animas	5
Rosario	5

(APT, Estado que tienen las cofradías de este curato y doctrinas en reales, cera y ganados, 1803).

animals to pay taxes, to buy a chalice, to pay the church tithe, to provide funds for bringing a priest from Tlaxiaco to say Mass during fiestas, to pay for a survey of the town's boundaries, to cover general municipal expenses, and, later, to purchase schoolbooks for the community's children.[7]

Nuyootecos proved to be quite adept at raising cattle, and the size of the Rosario herd stood at 42 animals in 1862. At one point the herd reached 70 head of cattle and 100 head of sheep and goats.[8] Then, beginning in the 1870s, the herd began to dwindle. By 1872 the number of cattle had fallen to 12, and then there were only 8 animals in 1883. The final mention of cattle in the historical record for Rosario was for 1904, and according to older people in the community, the herds managed by the mayordomos completely disappeared during the Revolution of 1910–20, when soldiers overran the community and stole all the animals.[9] Nuyootecos did not reestablish the herds after hostilities ended (see chapter 14).

The cash held by the mayordomos was another corporate asset. Mayordomías, as we saw, are religious fraternities dedicated to the cult of a particular saint. In the nineteenth century they were called cofradías and included four or five deputies (diputados), who served in subordinate positions (see chapter 13). Individual officers served a one-year term and organized the rituals celebrated on the saint's feast day, prepared meals for fiesta participants, joined the members of other cofradías to work on the church or the cattle herd, and managed individual cofradía property. Some mayordomías own plots of coffee today, but in the nineteenth century their most important asset, after cattle, was cash. The mayordomos guarded the money in special chests (yutun), which today also contain wax for candle making, account books, and property that belongs to the saint, such as clothing and jewelry (for the image). Nuyootecos call this money shu'un yutun, "money of the chest" or shu'un ka'nu, "principal." The mayordomo and other cofradía members could use this cash to pay for the

7. The accounts in the chest of the Virgen de Rosario list the following expenditures: in 1823 four head of cattle were sold to buy a chalice; in 1827 three head were sold to pay the diezmo, or church tithe; in 1866 one bull was sold and the proceeds were handed over to municipal officials; in 1873 608 pesos were given to municipal officials; in 1903 several head of cattle were sold, with 12 pesos going for the survey of boundaries with Ocotepec, 3 pesos for schoolbooks and 44 pesos for musical instruments and sheet music. Cattle are also listed as being butchered to celebrate the fiesta of the Virgen de Rosario in 1827 and 1904.

8. Caja de la Virgen de Rosario, estado de cuenta, años 1803, 1843, and 1862.

9. Caja de la Virgen de Rosario, estado de cuenta, años 1872, 1883 and 1904.

celebration of the saint's feast day, but they had to replace it by the end of their term in office and make a payment to the general fund maintained by all the mayordomías. Currently, most mayordomos choose to invest the money in an economic venture, such as making bread or selling liquor, and use the profits to meet the required payments (which, according to some, were as high as 100% of the principal amount at the turn of the century, and today are about 60%). People also loan the money out, at interest, to other community members and then use the interest charged to make the required payments. One consequence of investing in commerce is that the mayordomo houses became, as one old man put it, "like general stores . . . you could go to one and buy meat, go to another and buy salt, and go to a third to buy dry goods." In other words, not only did goods flow into the market economy through corporate organizations, but commodities coming into the community filtered through these organizations.

As I noted above, each mayordomo had to make a payment into what I have called the "general fund" of all the Nuyooteco mayordomías. This fund could at times hold a substantial amount of cash, and officials tapped it periodically in the nineteenth century for municipal expenditures and, beginning in the mid-1870s, to build a new church (see below). The fund still exists today, and Nuyootecos used it in the past decade to help build a new school, to buy and repair instruments for the municipal band, and to defray the costs of the building of a CONASUPO building, a government-subsidized dry goods store. In 1993, the fund contained a little over 20,000 new pesos (about $7,000).

Corporately held property made up the vast bulk of the wealth that existed in Nuyoo during the nineteenth century. If oral history and the complete absence of land titles is any indication, there was no privately held land in Nuyoo, and, most significantly, there was no market in land (though people may have sold crops growing on the land). Church tithe records, which document the numbers of goats, sheep, pigs, mules, turkeys, and cattle held in the Mixteca, mention only one man from Nuyoo, Juan Pérez, as having a privately owned animal (a mule) in the first half of the nineteenth century, although individuals in other Mixtec-speaking communities were listed as holding many animals.[10] Finally, in the few wills that exist from the

10. APT, Libro de Diezmo 1805–06. In 1845, no one is listed as owning cattle or other large animals in Nuyoo, although six men are listed for nearby San Pedro Yosotato (APT, Estado de

period, one can see that the amount of individual property passed from one generation to the next is not very large. People left their children a thatched hut, perhaps some furniture, a few tools, and a peso or two, but never anything exceeding this rather small estate.

THE BREAKUP OF CORPORATE PROPERTY

In the nineteenth century, Liberal Mexican governments passed a series of laws that had the potential to transform land tenure in the region. The most significant of these was the Ley Lerdo of 1856, which required the liquidation of property held by "corporations," such as the Church and indigenous communities, and the transfer of this property into private hands. We do not understand the effects of this policy on indigenous areas of Oaxaca very well, and as we saw in the petition by Eusebio López, many communities in the swidden belt of the Mixteca resisted, often successfully, its implementation.

The division of land into privately held plots did take place in the region, however, and land titles for individual Nuyootecos began to appear in 1890, in response to further disentailment orders issued by the state government.[11] Yet the government was never very effective in legislating change (or at least the changes it intended) in this far-off corner of Mexico. Some plots were privatized, and land was bought and sold, but it appears that most land remained a corporate resource, and the buying and selling of land was a rare occurrence.

Oral history tells us that it was not until the 1930s and 1940s that large portions of Nuyooteco lands fell into private hands—long after the disentailment orders of 1856. What this suggests is that although government edicts may have provided a legal basis for the division of land, and may even have encouraged people to look at land as a private resource, privatization could occur only in the context of other changes that affected the way Nuyootecos used their land. These included the introduction of a new cash crop, a sizable growth in population, and an increase in hostilities with neighboring communities.

---

cuenta de diezmos formada en Tlaxiaco del año de 1845). Again in 1858 and 1859, no individuals are listed from Nuyoo, although the account lists 22 owners of cattle in Itundujia, 10 in Atatlahuca, 17 in Yosonatú, 60 in Chalcatongo, and 6 in Ocotepec (APT, Cuenta general de diezmos de la colectura de la Villa de Tlaxiaco 1858 y 1859).

11. Relevant legislation includes the Circular de 13 de Junio, 1890; Reglamento Para el Reparto y Adjudicación de las Tierras Comunales de 26 de Junio, 1890; and the Circular de 11 de Diciembre, 1890 in *Colección de Leyes, Decretos y Circulares* 1893:13–15, 64, 250–51. The titles took the form of certificates, or *manifestaciónes*, issued by the state government, which specified the owner had registered the land and had begun to pay the property tax on it.

Population Growth, Cash Cropping, and Warfare

As I noted earlier, the only cash crops planted in the region prior to the 1930s were several different varieties of bananas, which Nuyootecos sold in the markets of Tlaxiaco and other highland Mixtec towns where tropical fruits cannot be grown. Bananas will produce fruit only if they are sown at low altitudes, where they will not be injured by occasional low temperatures. Much of Nuyooteco territory is semitropical, and people plant groves of bananas below the town center, and along the sides of the canyons, in lands lying below about 1200 meters.

As a cash crop, bananas do not require an overly large investment of time or money, and Nuyootecos cultivate them with the same techniques they use for corn production. This is not true of coffee, however, a second cash crop Nuyootecos cultivate.

Coffee was first introduced to Yucuhiti in the 1880s (Monaghan 1990a), but it did not become a major crop in the region until the 1940s. Since then it has replaced the banana as the main cash crop for Nuyootecos and has significantly changed the way in which Nuyootecos incorporate commercial agriculture into subsistence activities. Unlike the banana, coffee requires a substantial investment of time and money. Once transplanted, a coffee plant will take up to four years before it begins to bear fruit and several years after that before it produces a mature yield. During this time the plants must be weeded twice annually, a tedious job that must be carried out concurrently with the weeding of corn plants. In this, coffee, unlike the banana, competes directly with corn, the main subsistence crop. Also unlike the banana, coffee requires a sizable investment of labor before it begins to yield any return.

One advantage coffee has over bananas is that it does not exhaust the soil as much as bananas do (Simmonds 1982:294–5), and once coffee trees begin to produce, they will continue to do so for at least 40 years. This makes a plot of land on which coffee is sown very different from a plot of land on which corn or bananas are sown. Because coffee requires a considerable investment, and because it continues to yield a crop year after year for most of the farmer's lifetime, this gives the plot a long-term value that is lacking for plots devoted to bananas or corn.

The high prices people receive for their coffee, particularly since the mid-1960s, has both raised the standard of living in Nuyoo (today few Nuyootecos must leave the community during "the months of starvation," since they are able to sell coffee to buy corn and other food) and transformed Nuyoo from being a net exporter of agricultural labor to a net importer. Whereas in the past, Nuyootecos were the ones to leave to work as migrant farm workers in the nearby lowlands, today they hire Mixtec speakers from highland communities to work for them, so that during the coffee harvest the Sunday market fills with people from other towns looking for work.

The replacement of bananas by coffee in Nuyooteco commercial agriculture took place in the context of important changes in the region that, from the 1860s on, reduced the total supply of land available to individual farmers. One reason for this was an increase in population, which decreased the average amount of arable land available to each farmer. Between 1869 and 1900, municipal records show that the number of Nuyootecos grew over 100%, from 516 to 1,088.[12] Yet the doubling of the number of people in the community did not, in itself, put pressure on Nuyoo's land base. Rather, it was when the population increase was coupled with an escalation in hostilities between Nuyoo and the towns surrounding it that the supply of land was so reduced that a major crisis developed.

With a small population at the beginning of the nineteenth century, Nuyootecos, as was true for the communities surrounding it, did not exploit anything but the most productive and accessible lands in their territory. Lands on the borders of the community were often covered in thick woods, which served as vaguely defined boundaries. The boundary markers between towns were few and irregularly spaced, in contrast to the present, where they are numerous and located within sight of one another. This resulted in a situation where the extent of each town's land was subject to differing interpretations, and people were most likely to interpret boundaries in a way that was most favorable to their own communities (map 4).

The relative peace that existed in the region ended in the 1860s, when Nuyootecos began fighting with the people of Mixtec-speaking communities to the southeast and southwest (Ocotlán and Nopalera, respectively, whose inhabitants Nuyootecos call Luti). Nopalera and Ocotlán were experiencing the same kind of population growth Nuyootecos were, and people from these places began to push onto land claimed by Nuyootecos. People from Ocotlán probably founded Nopalera in the nineteenth century, when some families moved from

12. ARM, Padron General de los habitantes de Santiago Nuyoo, April 28, 1869. The 1890 figure is cited in Cook and Borah (1968:886–8).

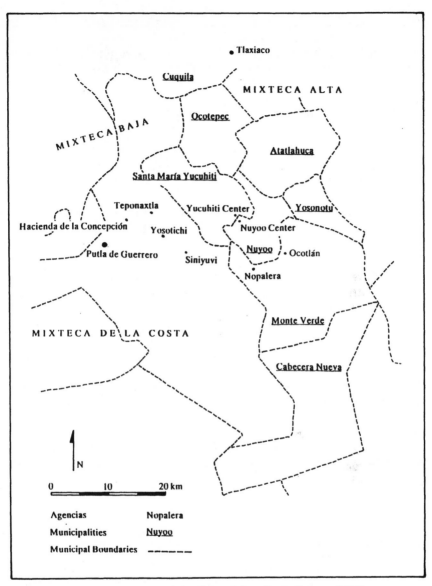

Nuyoo and surrounding municipalities (after Ortíz López 1982).

the east side of the canyon to the west side. The fighting broke out in 1863, when the state government ordered surveys of municipal boundaries throughout the district. The aim of these surveys was to measure the amount of corporate property each community possessed, but it had the effect of bringing the differences that existed between towns over the location of their boundaries to the forefront, and appears to have ignited boundary disputes throughout the region.[13] In the specific case of Nopalera, Ocotlán, and Nuyoo the land they fought over contained the most productive plots for the growing of bananas and, later, coffee. The actual fighting involved armed parties, from 6 to 50 men, heading into the territory of their neighbors, stealing crops and animals, kidnaping women and children, and occasionally massacring the inhabitants of isolated homestead.[14] This raiding continued through the late 1950s, when a local cacique negotiated a peace (see chapter 15) that was then enforced by the state and federal government. It is only in recent years that Nuyootecos have dared to travel to Ocotlán or Nopalera for markets and fiestas.

During the last half of the nineteenth century and the beginning of the twentieth century, Nuyoo also began fighting with the adjacent municipality of Yucuhiti. Although it is true that the colonial Spanish government fixed the boundaries between the two in the eighteenth century, any encroachment by one side on the land of the other—even if it was only a few meters—was enough to cause bloodshed. Such suspicion led to the movement of Yucuhiti's town center in the eighteenth century from the mountains above Nuyoo to the position it

13. For example, in a report by the Jefe Político of Tlaxiaco to the state government on land conflicts in the district, he dates the origin of almost all the disputes to either 1856, 1863, 1890, or 1894, years when the government ordered boundaries surveyed as a prelude to disentailment (AGEO, Conflictos, leg. 83, exp. 19, Noticia de los pueblos que cuestionen en éste distrito sobre límites de tierras, August 8, 1903).

14. In 1907, Nuyootecos complain that the people of Ocotlán set fire to their banana groves and pastures (ARM, Presidente Municipal de Nuyoo al Jefe Político de Tlaxiaco). In 1908 the secretary of Santa Lucía Monteverde complained that Nuyootecos kidnaped a girl of 11 and then stole 67 head of cattle from Ocotlán (ARM, Jefe Político de Putla al Secretario del Estado de Oaxaca, 1908). In 1914, two Nuyooteco children were reported kidnaped by men from Ocotlán (ARM, Presidente Municipal al Jefe Político de Tlaxiaco, 1924). In 1923, raiders from Ocotlán burned three houses in Tierra Azul, kidnaped a young woman, and stole 10 fanegas of corn (ARM, Presidente Municipal de Nuyoo al Jefe Político de Tlaxiaco, 1923). In 1928, people from Ocotlán were accused of kidnaping four young boys from Nuyoo (Archivo del Juzgado de Tlaxiaco, Presidente Municipal de Santago Nuyoo al Juez de Primera Instancia, 1928). Of course, many of these complaints were exaggerated or false (see chapter 14), but they do illustrate the kind of raiding and couterraiding that occurred and the objectives of the raiding parties: the destruction of satellite settlements and the seizure of valuable assets (cattle, corn, women, and children).

occupies today, about 100m from Nuyoo Center. The situation was made even more sensitive by the concentration of Yucuhiti's people along the border with Nuyoo in the late nineteenth century, where they had gone to escape raids organized by the Esperón family into the western half of their territory. As I noted earlier, the wealthy Esperón family were merchants and politicians of Spanish descent (one of them, José Esperón, became state governor in 1874) and owned the sugar haciendas in the nearby Cañada of Yosotichi. In the last half of the nineteenth century, they attempted to expand production by taking control of the forests, pasturelands, and water runs that bordered on the Cañada, which belonged to Yucuhiti's people. The resulting dispute, which turned bloody, caused the people of the area to push back deeper into the mountains, along Nuyoo's border (Monaghan 1990a). With this substantial aggregation of "outsiders" living on Nuyoo's doorstep, Nuyootecos were understandably nervous and quick to repulse any perceived advance.

Nuyoo was thus actively engaged in hostilities with three of the six communities on its borders in the late nineteenth century. In addition, Nuyootecos had a minor dispute with the municipality of Ocotepec, and there were skirmishes with the municipality of Yosonatú. As people recall their grandparents saying, Nuyootecos were constantly in fear of attack and learned to associate outsiders with enemies.

The Appearance of Misericordia

According to oral tradition and documents in the care of the mayordomo of Misericordia, the image of Misericordia miraculously appeared on the steps of the church just before dawn on a December day in 1873.[15] A fiscal, or church caretaker, found it when he went to ring the church bells. In 1876, almost three years after the saint appeared, the first mayordomo of Misericordia was named to sponsor a fiesta on the anniversary of the saint's appearance.[16]

The date and circumstances of Misericordia's appearance are significant. Misericordia appeared on December 8, which is also the feast day of the Virgen de la Concepción, the patron saint of Yucuhiti. Feast days for patron saints are occasions for large gatherings of people, not only from the community celebrating the saint, but also

15. Caja del Señor Misericordia, loose notice, dated 1878.
16. Caja del Señor Misericordia, estado de cuenta, 1876.

Figure 21. Three Nuyootecos, a priest, and Misericordia. The artist represents differences in power and authority by the relative sizes of the different figures—a device sometimes used in sixteenth-century Mixtec manuscripts.

from other communities. The crowds are attracted by the religious rituals, the festive atmosphere, and the market held in the central plaza. The appearance of Misericordia on the feast day of the Virgen de la Concepción would have allowed Nuyootecos to establish a feast that would have competed directly with its rival, Yucuhiti. According to oral history, this is exactly what Nuyootecos attempted to do. Not surprisingly, people in Yucuhiti have always been skeptical about Nuyooteco claims for the miraculous appearance of Misericordia. To this day they discuss it as a plot by Nuyootecos to steal a major regional feast from them, and they say that Nuyooteco leaders went out and bought the saint and then placed it on the steps of the church for the unsuspecting fiscal to see (figure 21). Eventually, in 1878, a Dominican priest from Tlaxiaco, Fray Bernardo López, persuaded Nuyootecos to celebrate the fiesta of Misericordia on First Friday of Lent, although Nuyootecos continue to celebrate its *viko luli* ("small fiesta") on December 8.[17] The tension between the two communities reached a breaking point in 1896, when Nuyoo launched a full-scale attack on Yucuhiti Center, setting fire to the Yucuhiti church and destroying several houses.[18] In their accounts of this incident, Nuyootecos say that Misericordia's miraculous appearance was a sign of divine favor, and it encouraged them to take the offensive against enemy communities.

Although Nuyootecos secured their borders with Yucuhiti, armed conflict with other towns continued for almost a century. A large part of Nuyoo became a kind of no-man's-land, since anyone who worked or lived there could be killed by a hostile raiding party. This was particularly true for the southern part of the municipality, which was in dispute with the people of Nopalera and Ocotlán. I estimate that for almost 80 years, Nuyootecos were unable to farm up to one-half their present territory.[19]

In the last half of the nineteenth century, then, population pressure and warfare with neighboring communities reduced the supply of land available to individual Nuyooteco farmers. This development meant that land was not the unlimited resource it had been in the past. At the same time, the Mexican government ordered the disentailment of property held by corporations. It is true that most Nuyootecos did not register land as a private holding, but the new laws provided a legal basis for claims of private ownership. This became important when coffee replaced the banana as the principal cash crop in the late 1930s and 1940s. Sowing coffee requires a considerable investment, and once sown, it continues to yield a crop for as long as 40 years. People became interested in protecting their rights to the plots they had sown and passing them on to their children. Although Nuyootecos say it was a call by the agrarian reform administration to divide their territory into individual plots in the 1930s that caused them to privatize the

17. Caja del Señor Misericordia, estado de cuenta, 1878.

18. AMY, Presidente Municipal de Yucuhiti al Jefe Político de Tlaxiaco, April 30, 1896.

19. In 1890, Juan Sarabia, the president of Nuyoo, estimated that the people of Nopalera had penetrated 8 to 12 kilometers into Nuyooteco territory from the south. This amounted to 35% to 45% of all Nuyoo territory (AMN, Juan Sarabia, Presidente Municipal de Nuyoo, al Jefe Político, October 12, 1890). In a 1903 report, the Jefe Político of Tlaxiaco estimated that the dispute between Nopalera and Nuyoo alone was over 12 square kilometers of territory. He also valued the land in dispute at 5000 pesos. This made it the second most valuable parcel in dispute in the district, and he reported on no less than 35 disputes between district towns (AGEO, Conflictos, leg. 83, exp. 19. Noticias de los pueblos que cuestionan en este distrito sobre límites de tierras, August 8, 1903). Although Nuyoo's enemies did not control the land in dispute, it was unsafe for farming, and oral history records that anyone working there ran the risk of being slain.

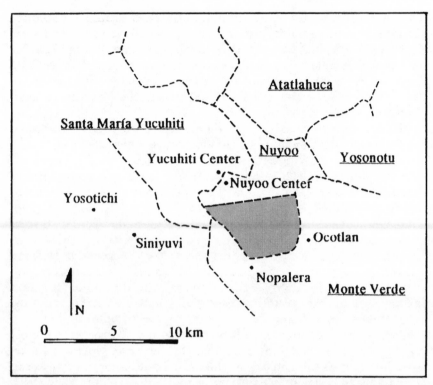

Nuyooteco territory in dispute with Ocotlán and Nopalera. The screened area on the map is the portion of Nuyoo that became unsafe for farming during the war with Luti.

land, people complied at this time because it meant they would have deeds that they could use to protect their claims and to transmit rights to land through inheritance and sale.

It is, of course, one thing to speak about "private" land and another thing to see how this concept works in practice. Following Bloch, "private" in Nuyoo does not mean the kind of "once and for all" rights that we associate with the term (Bloch 1983:92). Rather, in addition to the owner, the community, the owner's hamlet, and a variety of other individuals have rights to any land the owner may hold "privately." The community can take over privately held land if the owner is remiss in communal duties, such as not reporting for tequio, even if the land taxes stipulated by the state are paid. The community or the hamlet may take over any piece of property for public use, without reimbursing the owner. Kin, neighbors, and close acquaintances have the right to use a plot if its owner is not using it. What the person who wishes to use the land needs to do is, simply, ask the owner to lend the plot for a year. The owner does not charge rent, though the borrower may make a small gift of what is produced on the property. I never heard of any Nuyooteco renting land from another Nuyooteco, although people were familiar with this practice from other communities. Renting land, people say, is "selfish" (*kuasunni*).

It is interesting that the idea that land can be alienated in a "once-and-for-all" manner through sale is a notion to which many people do not fully subscribe. Despite an internal land market that has been in existence for at least 60 years, it is common to see Nuyootecos act as though they still have rights to a piece of property after they sell it. For example, it upset one of my neighbors that the man who sold him an orange grove openly continued to pick oranges from it. However, my neighbor felt that he would be accused of being "selfish" if he put a stop to it, so he kept quiet even though he would have liked to drive the man off. It even happens that a seller will decide to take a parcel of land back after selling it, expecting the buyer to return it, even if the sale occurred years before.

If we place this attitude toward land in the context of a society where private landholdings are a relatively recent phenomenon, we can see that privatization has expanded individual rights to use and alienate particular plots, without wholly eliminating either the rights of other individuals or the rights of the corporation to the same plots. Furthermore, even at the time of my fieldwork, no more than one-half of Nuyooteco territory was held "privately." The other half, which Nuyootecos were able to exploit only after the wars with Ocotlán and Nopalera ended, is classified as communal. Some of this land can be said to be "private" in the sense that people have planted coffee on it and intend to leave it to their children. Yet this land cannot be sold, no individual deeds to it exist, and within the communal fraction there is a considerable amount of unoccupied land upon which any Nuyooteco can establish a plot after paying a small tax to the *comisariado de bienes comunales*.[20]

20. Wilk (1984:222–3), in his study of Keckchi farmers in Belize, suggested that once a shortage of good land develops, people begin to recognize continuing usufruct rights to swidden plots. Although the historical information is not specific enough for me to say with certainty that this also happened in Nuyoo, it is a reasonable supposition, since people are clear that plots near house sites tended to be used by the same family over two or more generations, while plots away from house sites were open to whomever wanted to use them.

The Communal Herds, Misericordia, and the Mayordomo Funds

The other corporate assets held by Nuyootecos in the early nineteenth century also came under pressure in the late nineteenth and early twentieth centuries. As I noted, Nuyootecos owned at least 70 head of cattle in 1862, plus numerous pigs, goats, sheep, and mules, despite the passage of a law by the government in 1856 making the holding of communal herds illegal. However, the number of animals began to dwindle in the 1870s as a direct result of Misericordia's miraculous appearance.

Misericordia's appearance coincided with the preliminary phase of the replacement of the old church, described by one observer as *"una iglesia de mala construcción y figura"* (Apuntes Topográficos 1871:243), with a new building. Oral history records that the appearance of the saint motivated people to build the new church on a grand scale. In contrast to the old, thatch-roofed adobe building, the new church was built of brick and mortar under the direction of an architect, skilled masons, and carpenters. This proved to be a very long (they were still working on it in the early 1900s) and expensive undertaking. Not only did Nuyootecos spend many days in tequio on the project, digging sand along the river banks, hauling bricks, and cutting timber, but they also paid salaries to the architect, masons, and carpenters who worked on the project, purchased building materials that they could not manufacture locally, and transported them, usually on their backs, to the site. To raise the needed cash, they liquidated the cattle herd.[21] According to one man, "It was as if they had no choice but to try to build the best church possible." By building the largest and most ornate church in the region, Nuyootecos created a visible sign of their unity, strength, and power.

Although the communal herds no longer exist, the mayordomos still maintain "principal money" in their chests. However, since about 1925, the value these funds has severely eroded. Table 3 shows the average value of the principal held by six mayordomías in days of agricultural labor it could purchase. As one can see, the value of the mayordomo money, measured in terms of the days of agricultural labor

---

21. From 1879 to 1883, the mayordomos and other religious officials contributed 1818 pesos to the construction of the church. They raised this money by selling animals from the cofradía herds and by draining money from the cash account of the mayordomos (Archive of Maestro Eliazar Pérez, Nuyoo Center, Libro que pertenece a este pueblo, por el presidente municipal que consta toda la cantidad del año de 1879 que se paga por los albañiles que va a fabricar al templo del presente pueblo, January 18, 1880).

TABLE 3.
AVERAGE VALUE OF MAYORDOMÍA PRINCIPAL, MEASURED IN DAYS OF
FIELDHAND LABOR IT COULD PURCHASE, 1925–1944

Year	Value
1925	364 Days
1937	176 Days
1944	32 Days
1986	7 Days

it could buy, plummeted by 98% during the 60 years between 1925 and 1986.[22]

Households and Wealth

Corporate assets in land, animals, and cash may have steadily eroded over the last 125 years, but they did not disappear from the community. The lands are still there, animals graze on it, and Nuyootecos raise substantial sums of cash when they need to. What has happened is that these assets are now in the hands of individual households. Today, households are landholding units, they maintain private herds of animals, and the growth of commercial agriculture has placed ever-increasing amounts of cash in the hands of individuals and their households.

As I pointed out in chapter 1, the Nuyooteco household is ideally an extended family, built up around a core of agnatically related men, such as a father and his married sons, or brothers and their wives and children. Farriss (1984:133) has suggested that in the Yucatán, a group of four or five agnatically related men was the favored unit of milpa production during the Colonial period—what she called "the milpa gang." She pointed out that even today in the Yucatán it is customary for a father and sons, or a team of brothers, or sometimes an uncle and nephews, to work adjoining or communal milpa. The advantage is that cooperative work makes the felling and burning of brush easier (Farriss 1984:133). Similarly, in Nuyoo, the extended family household is the unit of agriculture production, and agnatically related men will often make milpas together, burning and clearing large swiddens to plant corn. Nuyootecos often say they find agricultural chores less tedious if they work as a group, instead of individually. Also, a team of men is able to manage different fields of corn sown at different

22. The information in this table is based on the account records in the cajas of the Mayordomías of Misericordia, Rosario, Santo Entierro, Santa Ana, Santiago, and San Sebastián.

elevations better than a lone individual. This is particularly true when the corn ripens and raccoons, deer, and other animals enter the fields to eat the tender ears. The only way to protect one's harvest is to spend the night in the fields. If several different plots are sown far from one another, a milpa gang can guard them all, but a lone individual cannot. Moreover, if several men share the burden, they can spell one another during the night.

I have no direct evidence that large groups of related men cultivated corn in nineteenth-century Nuyoo. However, in the 1924 census—the first to be broken down by residence—75 percent of the households contained more than one married man, and 45% contained three or more married men. Furthermore, only 8.4% of the male population lived in a household without other adult males in it, while 47.7% of the male population lived in households containing four or more adult males.[23] If we assume that the people who lived together also worked together, we can conclude that the household-based "milpa gang" was the primary unit of corn production in Nuyoo.[24]

If we agree that the household was the primary unit of agriculture production in the nineteenth century, it is not surprising that when pressure was put on the community to privatize land, it was divided among the households in the community. Note that this was not, precisely, what the Liberals intended. Because Nuyooteco households often contain several nuclear families, there are cases where as many as eight adult men and women may be considered to "own" a particular plot. Nevertheless, the shift from communal to household ownership of land did have certain long-range consequences, which are related to the contemporary tensions, antagonisms, and frustrations Nuyootecos experience in cargo service.

CORPORATE PROPERTY, THE HOUSEHOLD, AND CARGO

The animals and cash managed by the mayordomos in the nineteenth century were not only held corporately, but were income-producing ventures. Nuyootecos used income from the cattle herds to pay expenses associated with the school, church and municipal government and to buy ritual paraphernalia and provide food for fiestas.

---

23. ARM, Censo de Santiago Nuyoo, 1924.

24. Members of different households could of course have cooperated on agricultural tasks, as they sometimes do today. I suspect that it was quite common for the members of different households to enter into sa'a contracts where they would jointly work to clear, weed, or harvest each other's plots (see below).

Chance and Taylor point out that throughout Mexico, when corporate assets were lost, this did not generally lead to a decline in fiesta activities but to a shift from corporate responsibility for fiesta expenses to individual responsibility (Chance and Taylor 1985:17). Similarly, in Nuyoo, the number of mayordomías did not decrease when corporate assets dwindled, and today we see that it is single households that support the fiesta system. Chapters 13 and 14 will examine the switch from corporate to individual fiesta sponsorship in Nuyoo, since the process was by no means simple, and it involved not only a reordering of the ties Nuyootecos maintain with one another, but also a reordering of the ties they maintain with the sacred. Here I want only to note that what was true for fiesta expenses was also true for other public expenditures—that is, as corporate resources dwindled, the burden of supporting the municipal government and other communal institutions was shifted to individual households.

The first, and most significant, way households assumed the costs of public expenditures was through cargo service. In 1989, for example, when Nuyootecos brought in an engineer to survey lands in dispute with Atatlahuca, most of the costs associated with his visit were borne by the members of the *comisariado de bienes comunales*, who dipped into their household reserves to come up with the money they needed. This stands in contrast to a survey of the town boundaries performed by professional engineers in 1903, which officials paid for by selling off several animals from the communal herd.[25] Nuyootecos also say that the kinds of activities cargo holders have become responsible for have become more diverse and costly. Every year new programs are sponsored by the federal and state governments to develop rural areas, such as road building and school construction, which make new demands of the municipal government and often require that the municipality assume part of the costs of the project. Although difficult to quantify, a large portion of these expenses fall onto the shoulders of cargo holders.

The second way households assumed the costs of financing public activities was through direct taxes levied by the municipal authorities. In 1983, for example, when a water pipe was needed to bring fresh water to Nuyoo Center, the comité for fresh water calculated the cost and divided it by the number of individual households in the center. Officials use this mechanism only for extraordinary expenditures, but

25. Caja de la Virgen de Rosario, Estado de Cuenta, 1903.

the amounts assessed can be heavy. Again, one can see that in the past, officials drew on communal funds to cover similar needs.

Along with the household expenditures required of cargo officials, and the taxing of households for public expenditures, the cost of sponsoring fiestas has increased. For example, in the past, sponsors would serve only a few gallons of aguardiente to guests. Now, besides the aguardiente, they serve many cases of beer, and each case of beer costs the equivalent of five days' labor. Part of the reason for this increase in fiesta costs is that it is through the distribution of wealth by the sponsors of fiestas to other households that sponsors gain prestige. This prestige accrues to all the members of the household, so that households themselves may be ranked by increasing levels of prestige (for a more general statement on this point, see Wolf 1962:215–16). Because celebration sponsors derive prestige through the quality of the food they are able to serve and the amount of liquor they offer guests to drink, when increased amounts of resources become available, it is logical that people will increase the amount and kinds of things they distribute. In 1985, for example, Antonio López Sarabia died, an old tañuu who served in all the major posts of the civil-religious hierarchy and who fought bravely in the land wars with Nopalera and Ocotlán. His survivors distributed 43 cases of beer during his death rites, almost 50,000 pesos worth. At the time, it would have taken a man six months to earn this much cash working as a laborer. The next day the hosts had the 43 empty cases stacked in the patio of the house for all to see, and they were not reluctant to quote the exact number of bottles served or to add that they had slaughtered six goats. In the 1940s, Tañuu Antonio's son-in-law told me, such a distribution would have been unthinkable.

The relationship between the increasing size and quality of fiesta distributions and the influx of wealth from cash cropping and other market activities in Mesoamerica has been widely commented on (Good 1988; Cancian 1965; see also Gregory 1982). My interest, however, is not so much with the implications this has for the fiesta system, but with something else people say about the large distributions the household of Tañuu Antonio López, and others like it, now make.

The Death Rites of Antonio López Sarabia

There are three separate occasions for making distributions during the nine days of the death rituals: when the deceased is buried (usually within 24 hours of death), on the evening before the ninth day after death, and on the morning of the ninth day. On each of these occasions, the heirs of Tañuu Antonio López Sarabia distributed an enormous quantity of food and drink to guests. They slaughtered all their goats and borrowed heavily to pay for the many cases of beer. They invited the municipal band to play, and they bore the costs of nine days of prayers by the prayermakers in a special ritual reserved only for deceased tañuu and ñañuu. At first I thought that this had to do with the prestige of sponsoring a large and well-attended death ritual, since many hundreds of people came to participate and to honor a man who had done so much for the community. Yet when I questioned Tañuu Antonio's family about their expenditures, they said that they made such a large distribution so other members of the community would not become upset or "envious" (yatuni). Others I spoke with agreed that there would have been bad feelings if the sponsors had not made a large distribution. Why would people have felt this way?

Antonio López Sarabia was a dynamic risk taker. Among the other things he accomplished, he was the first to plant large amounts of coffee in Nuyoo. At first people had laughed at him, since they found it hard to believe that anything as foul-tasting as coffee would be a successful cash crop. Of course, they were wrong; by the time of his death, Tañuu Antonio had managed to become one of the largest landowners in the community, and he and his family produced more coffee than anyone else.

The "envy" people in Nuyoo would have felt if Antonio López Sarabia's heirs had not made a large distribution during his death rituals (and if they do not make large distributions in fiestas they sponsor in the future) is directly related to his success as a coffee producer. People say that individuals such as Tañuu Antonio have benefited greatly from their use of Nuyooteco territory. If they hadn't had access to this land, they would not have been able to plant coffee and become so successful. But recall that even though Tañuu Antonio owned the land where he sowed coffee, prior corporate rights to it have not been wholly eliminated. In other words, people clearly remember the land upon which Tañuu Antonio's wealth was based (and which his family continues to profit from) as being communal in the not-too-distant past, and for them, it is covered by corporate claims. That is why people feel it is proper—even obligatory—that the members of Tañuu Antonio's family return some of what they have received. And the way they should do this is through distributions of food and drink in the fiestas they sponsor.

The observations people make about distributions made on occasions such as the death rites of Tañuu Antonio López Sarabia are interesting because they show that it would be a mistake to view envy in essentialist terms, as some kind of character flaw in Mesoamerican people (we might agree that feelings of yatuni are justified even in the case of Tañuu Antonio's wealth). I will return to this in chapter 14, where I relate different "faces" of Tachi to specific historical experiences on the part of Nuyootecos. But what I want to highlight here is how the death rites of Tañuu Antonio show that as Nuyooteco households have come to control corporate resources, the experience of "corporateness" has been created less through the shared ownership and exploitation of productive assets and more through shared consumption. Moreover, this shared consumption is made possible through the extraction of resources through fiesta distributions (and other forms of cargo service), and wealthy households—which benefited most by the shift of corporate assets into private hands—are the ones that are expected to make the largest contributions of resources and time.

The extraction of resources from individual households through cargo service (coupled with a high level of participation in cargo) and the role shared consumption plays in articulating the Nuyooteco image of themselves as a "great house" help us to understand why Nuyootecos express such ambivalent feelings about cargo service. For the individual households involved, there is now more at stake in cargo service than ever before, and the elaborate strategies developed by Nuyootecos to avoid cargo service have to be seen in the context of the increasingly heavy cargo demands placed on individual households over the last hundred years. These demands have amplified the moral and economic tension between the Nuyoo community as a great house and the independent households in which people live. As I pointed out, these burdens have become so onerous that they even cause some to try to avoid the dilemma by migrating to Mexico City.

Grounding the meaning of being corporate in a practice of shared consumption does not efface differences in wealth (Cancian 1965), and this development *has* served to divert attention within the community from the inequities that occurred when land was privatized (see chapter 13). But my goal in this part of the book is to show how, in the context of changing material circumstances, the forms of sociation discussed have been extended, revised, and reconfigured in the last century. The next chapter focuses on the transition from corporate sponsorship of fiestas to individual sponsorship, a process that we will discover is closely related to the appearance of Misericordia in 1873 and the development of the complex gift exchange system I described in chapter 2.

CHAPTER 13

GIFT EXCHANGE
AND PRIVATIZATION

MUCH of the activity in a mayordomo fiesta involves people making presentations to one another. Throughout the celebration, men and women arrive at the mayordomo's house carrying gifts of tortillas, beans, salt, chile, soda, beer, pulque, aguardiente, and cash. The women of the household bustle about the hearth in the kitchen hut, unpacking the gifts and counting out how much each guest has brought. The men dash this way and that, greeting guests and serving food. Groups of people sit around the patio of the sponsor's house, often with large stacks of tortillas in front of them, which were given by the sponsors as countergifts.

Earlier I discussed the economic aspects of these exchanges, where more than 85% of the items distributed in the fiesta first circulate as gifts (see also Monaghan 1990b). I showed that the size and quality of the prestations and counterprestations constitute degrees of social distance, allowing the sponsoring household to take stock of its relationships with other households. The exchanges function this way because the fiesta is a time of crisis for the sponsoring household, and the help provided by kin, ritual kin, affines, and others in financing the event is a defining moment in their relationship.

It had long been a tradition in anthropology to think of gift exchange, such as the Nuyooteco system of *saa sa'a*, as a primitive form of economic activity, lying at the origins of social life, that is in fundamental opposition to commodity exchange, in the face of which it would eventually disappear. However, we are now coming to understand that gifts and commodities are not necessarily opposed to each other and that elaborate gift exchange complexes can exist, and even thrive, within the context of the market (Appadurai 1986; Bloch and Parry 1989, Gregory 1982). It is in this light that I examine the history of the Nuyooteco system of *saa sa'a*. We will see not only that *saa sa'a* remains vigorous, despite increased Nuyooteco involvement with cash cropping and other market activities, but also that the

285

system as it is used to finance fiestas emerged only over the last 125 years and that it was market penetration that precipitated its development.

FIESTAS IN THE NINETEENTH CENTURY

Officials on the religious side of the Nuyooteco civil-religious hierarchy are mentioned in scattered documents produced during the colonial period, but the earliest detailed information on the mayordomías that I have been able to discover data from 1801, in records stored in the chests of the Nuyoo mayordomías. At that time the mayordomías, referred to as cofradías, were structured in conformity with rules set forth in 1731 by Francisco de Santiago y Calderón, Bishop of Oaxaca. In a decree issued for the founding of a cofradía in Tlaxiaco, Nuyoo's district capital, the Bishop stipulated that

1. The cofradía should have a mayordomo and four deputies (diputados), who will each year nominate their successors.
2. At the end of his year of service the mayordomo should present a detailed account of cofradía finances to the priest and other officials. If the mayordomo is unable to give a satisfactory account, of if he has borrowed money from the cofradía and is unable to repay what he owes, then he cannot be re-elected. Re-election can take place only if the mayordomo has no financial interests in the cofradía.
3. The saint's feast day should be celebrated with a mass, vespers, and a procession. The priest should be paid for his services from the cofradía funds. No money should be spent on "superfluous" expenditures, such as dances, chocolate, fireworks, and shows.
4. Each cofradía should have a chest with two keys; one for the mayordomo, and one for the priest. The money of the cofradía should be kept in the chest, with the mayordomo's account book.

Religious officials copied the bishop's decree in at least one cofradía account book for Tlaxiaco dating from 1817 to 1831, suggesting that his rules still provided guidelines for the organization of cofradías in the region at the time that Nuyoo's cofradías first enter the historical record.[1]

It is surprising how similar Nuyoo's current mayordomías are to what Bishop Santiago y Calderón set forth in 1731. For example, each mayordomo arranges to bring a priest to Nuyoo to say mass on the saint's feast day and then makes an offering to the priest for his services. Nuyootecos also maintain the custom of storing mayordomía

---

1. APT, Libro de Cofradía, Hermandad de Nuestro Padre Jesús de Tlaxiaco.

property in a chest, and at the end of his year of service, the mayordomo gives a public account of mayordomo finances. This occurs on the final day of the fiesta, just before the procession of the saint to the house of the incoming mayordomo. An official sets a mat on the floor in front of the saint, and all the mayordomos, musicians, prayermakers, and civil authorities who are present gather around. Also present is the man who is about to receive the cargo. The mayordomo opens the large chest and shows everyone that it contains the cult objects and the 20 or so pounds of wax for making candles that it had when he was given the cargo. The chest also contains a sum of money, called *shu'un yutun*, "money of the chest," or *shu'un ka'nu*, "principal," on which the mayordomo must pay interest over the year of his cargo. He pays the interest on the day he transfers the chest to the new mayordomo, and the other mayordomos check the principal to see if it is complete. The mayordomo must also make a payment for church candles, for incense, for the upkeep of the musician's instruments, and for a "voluntary" increase in the money in the chest. He places these sums on the mat for all to see. The man who collects the different payments (the treasurer of the mayordomos) is in charge of monitoring all mayordomo accounts, and he visits the mayordomo a few days before the public accounting to calculate the amounts owed, so that the mayordomo will know what sums to have on hand. This allows the mayordomo to arrange to borrow the cash if he finds he is short and thereby avoid embarrassment during the public accounting. The treasurer also prepares a written account of the mayordomía finances, which he sets on the mat when the accounts are reviewed. An official then places the account in the chest with the accounts of previous mayordomas, which, in some mayordomías, go back to the early 1800s.

One way that Nuyootecos deviate from the regulations of Bishop Santiago y Calderón is in the number of cofradía personnel. Recall that the bishop stipulated that the cofradías should have five ranked offices. The top position was that of the mayordomo, followed by the first deputy, and then three additional officeholders known only as deputies. However, in Nuyoo today, the only persons responsible for the cargo are the husband and wife who hold the mayordomo postion (and the other members of their household; see chapter 8). What is the reason for this divergence?

Examining the records stored in the mayordomo chests, one can see that in the early 1800s, Nuyooteco cofradías were staffed by a mayordomo and four deputies. Also, one can see that the first deputy often appeared a year or two later as a mayordomo, suggesting that the deputy positions were ranked in the way Highland Maya cofradía positions are ranked, with the first deputy position being the step immediately below the mayordomo position. Moreover, the first deputy was usually a man in his forties or fifties, while the other deputies were usually men in their twenties and thirties. This again supports the idea that the deputy positions were ranked offices in the civil-religious hierarchy, since service in the top offices of the hierarchy traditionally correlates with age.

The mayordomo, first deputy and three additional deputy positions were each probably service positions, and the mayordomo and deputies appear to have been excused from any further work in the civil-religious hierarchy, since their names do not appear on the lists of officials serving during that year. According to oral history, the deputy's duty was to aid the mayordomo in the celebration of the saint's feast day, by helping to adorn the saints, by gathering flowers for the altar, and by arranging for the performance of important rituals.[2] Most importantly, each deputy would provide a fixed quota *(tarea)* of food and money, which the mayordomo would distribute during the celebration of the fiesta. People in the region today say the quota consisted of 360 tortillas, 6 to 12 liters of beans, and a variable quantity of cash, salt, chile, pasta, and liquor. In the past, the money would be used either to buy liquor or, if the mayordomo had enough cash, to buy a steer to be butchered and served to the guests. Yet it appears that the size of the quota could vary, and the mayordomos and deputies would come together well before the fiesta, in the *viko luli*, to determine the amount of goods they would need. One older man, the late Tañuu Fidel Sarabia, once told me that on his first religious cargo in the early 1930s, he had to buy a head of beef to slaughter to serve to his guests, since the saint was an important one. He calculated the amount of money needed to purchase the animal and filled a gourd with corn kernels, one kernel for each centavo. He then invited the deputies over to his house. They all sat around a mat he placed on

2. The *diputado* position can be found in cofradías throughout central Mexico in the Colonial period. For example, in Zacualtipan, the five deputies of the cofradía of Rosario "are charged with arranging the mass, making candles and cleaning the altar of the Virgin" (AGN, Cofradías, vol. 4, exp. 9, Sobre la erección de la Cofradía de Nuestra Señora de Rosario en el pueblo de Zacualtipan, 1757; see also AGN, Cofradías, Los Mayordomos de la Cofradía de Nuestra Señora de Puebla sobre colectación de limosna, Tomo 3, exp. 8, 1798; Cofradía de Nuestra Señora de Rosario de los españoles de Actopam, Tomo 2, exp. 2, 1709; La Cofradía de la Santa Vera Cruz contra Gonzalo de Salazar, Tomo 4, exp. 1, 1557).

the floor, and he went around the room, placing a kernel in front of each man, until the gourd was empty. Then each man looked at the pile in front of him and knew what his quota would be for the fiesta. The number of tortillas was fixed at 60, and the amount of beans was one gourd, a standard measure (see Monaghan 1987).

Comparing the cofradías of the early 1800s with today's mayordomías, we can see that the cofradías differed in that they had many members besides the mayordomo, and all of them pooled their resources to celebrate the fiesta. Although the mayordomo's household may have contributed more than any of the others, it did not contribute significantly more. It is therefore best to think of the mayordomo in the cofradía system of the beginning decades of the nineteenth century as first among equals, especially with regard to the financing of fiestas. The question we need to ask, then, is how and why did this change

Increases in the Number of Deputies

The records kept in the mayordomo chests show that in the 1860s and 1870s, the cofradía system began to undergo some important alterations. This was a period of political upheaval in the Mixteca and in Mexico more generally. Mexico suffered the War of the Reform and then the French Intervention. The unrest severely disrupted the Oaxaca economy, and major skirmishes occurred in the Tlaxiaco region (e.g., Méndez Aquino 1985:197–201; Martínez Gracida 1986:785). In addition, several revolts against the federal government were carried out by Oaxaqueños, some of which began in the Mixteca. Porfirio Díaz made the Mixteca his base of operations against the French, and he stayed in the Putla-Tlaxiaco region in 1866 and 1867, before marching off for the decisive battle of La Carbonera (Berry 1981:200–201). At one time or another during this period, Nuyoo and its neighbors, Yucuhiti and Yosotato, were each looted and burned. In 1871, soldiers also took a significant proportion of Yucuhiti's male population in an embargo, or forced levy, and there are indications that soldiers also tried to destroy Nuyoo Center (Monaghan 1990a). In 1872, government troops occupied the nearby community of Santa Lucía Monteverde, and there was fighting in Atatlahuca, Chalcatongo, and Itundujia (Martínez Gracida 1986:785). This state of unrest, with armed bands criss-crossing the region and looting rural towns, made the accumulation of foodstuffs for a fiesta difficult at best.

The building of the new church in Nuyoo Center began at this time. We saw in the last chapter that this was a major undertaking, since it was the first church in the region to be built of brick, mortar, and plaster. An architect and masons from outside the community supervised the construction, and Nuyootecos performed the heavy labor. The project began in the mid-1870s and was still not completed in 1915.[3] It required such great sacrifice that the building of the church has become a focus of Nuyooteco oral history. For example, people tell of when the masons demanded that their "grandmothers" provide two baskets of sand each morning before work began. This meant two arduous trips down to the dark and chilly banks of the river, where they dug out the sand and then carried it back up on their backs. If they failed to deliver their quota, the masons abused the women and sometimes even entered the houses and beat them.

It was during the 1870s and 1880s that officials sold most of the animals in the communal herds and spent a large portion of the cash held by the mayordomos — all to meet the costs of building materials for the church and wages for the outside workers. What this meant for fiesta financing was a loss of a relatively inexpensive source of meat, the most important food sponsors distribute. It is a tradition in Nuyoo that guests at each celebration receive meat during the fiesta meals. One can imagine that after the sale of the communal herd, meals with meat would have become difficult to prepare. Instead of simply taking an animal from the community herd, or paying for it at a below-market rate, the religious officials would have to undertake the difficult task of raising enough money to purchase a steer in the market. This usually involved a long and risky trip to the coast, since few cattle were available in the communities adjacent to Nuyoo, and those that were available cost considerably more than those sold on the coast.

The 1870s, particularly the last years of the 1870s, were thus difficult times. Food was scarce, the construction of the church consumed increasing inputs of communal labor, and the assets of the mayordomías/cofradías, which were an important source of cash and food for fiesta sponsorship,[4] had all but disappeared. Chance and Taylor (1985) suggest that the loss of corporate assets at the end of the colonial period and the beginning of independence — perhaps the

3. In 1904, a cow was sold by the mayordomo of Rosario to pay for the church door (Caja de la Virgen de Rosario, estado de cuentas, 1904). In 1915, Nuyootecos reported that hostilities had forced them to halt work on the church because they were no longer able to obtain building materials (AMN, Acontecimientos Notables, March 1915).

4. That this was a long-standing practice can be seen in the steady mention of cofradía animals being slaughtered for the fiesta and sold to buy fireworks throughout the nineteenth and early twentieth centuries (e.g., Caja de la Virgen de Rosario, estado de cuentas, 1827, 1904).

most significant development to occur in rural areas during the eighteenth and nineteenth centuries—led to individual sponsorship of cargos. In Nuyoo, as we saw, it was the household that eventually assumed responsibility for fiestas and other cargo expenses. Yet it is also true that in the 1870s Nuyooteco households controlled little private wealth, certainly not enough to sponsor elaborate fiestas. There were few privately owned herd animals in the community, and the income earned from cash cropping would not become significant until coffee began to replace the banana as the main cash crop, in the late 1930s. Although corporate resources were no longer sufficient to meet expenses, shifting the burden to individual sponsors was not, initially, a solution to the problem. How then, did Nuyootecos respond?

Their answer involved distributing the costs of fiesta sponsorship beyond the 5 original members of the cofradía to anywhere from 6 to 10 sponsors, by the simple process of increasing the number of deputies. In other words, instead of having 5 officers in the cofradía, as in the first half of the nineteenth century, by the second half of the nineteenth century, Nuyooteco cofradías had 6 to 10 officers, and instead of preserving the fiesta system by shifting to individual sponsorship, Nuyootecos went the other way and preserved it by making it even more of a collective undertaking.

One can see from chart 1 that this process first began in the 1860s, when the number of deputies began to exceed 4 for the first time.[5] It accelerated in the late 1870s, precisely when Nuyootecos began building the church. In table 4, one can also see the number of deputies level off in the 1890s to between 7 and 8. This corresponds to the period when church construction began to wind down and the Díaz regime normalized the political and economic situation in the countryside. This was also the period when the communal cattle herd began to increase again (although the number of cattle never numbered more than one-fourth of the head that existed before the construction of the church) and when, presumably, more resources were available to aid in fiesta sponsorship.

This situation again changed with the Mexican Revolution. The cattle herd began to disappear in 1912, when roving bands of soldiers

5. The information in chart 1 is drawn from the records in the archive chests of the Nuyoo mayordomías of Misericordia, Rosario, Santa Ana, San Sebastián, Santiago, and Santo Entierro. As far as I could determine, these were the only chests that have survived with their archives intact from the nineteenth century.

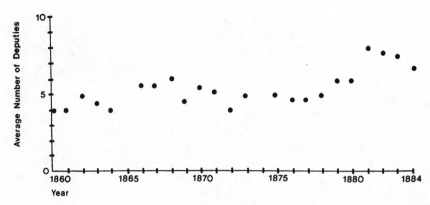

Chart 1. Average number of deputies, 1860–1884.

TABLE 4.
NUMBER OF DEPUTIES IN THE ROSARIO (A), SANTA ANA (B), SANTA
CECILIA (C), AND SANTIAGO (D) COFRADIAS, 1860–1945

	A	B	C	D	Average
1860	4				4.0
1861	4				4.0
1862	5				5.0
1863	5			4	4.5
1864	4				4.0
1865					?
1866	6			5	5.5
1867	6			5	5.5
1868	6				6.0
1869	5			4	4.5
1870			4	7	5.5
1871	5		5	5	5.0
1872	4		4		4.0
1873		6	4		5.0
1874					?
1875	5		6	4	5.0
1876	5		4	5	4.7
1877	6		4	4	4.7
1878	5				5.0
1879	5		5	8	6.0
1880	6		5	7	6.0
1881	8				8.0
1882	8		7	7	7.3
1883	8	7	6		7.0

TABLE 4. *Continued*

	A	B	C	D	*Average*
1884	7	6	5	7	6.3
1885	8		8	7	7.7
1886	8	6	7	9	7.5
1887	6	16	7	6	8.8
1888	8	8	9	7	8.0
1889	15	4	5	7	7.8
1890	8	4	5	4	5.3
1891	7	4	6	5	5.5
1892	9		9	3	7.0
1893					?
1894		11	7		9.0
1895	12	3	6	10	7.8
1896	7	8	9		8.0
1897	14	12		16	14.0
1898	20	15	12	18	16.2
1899	7	11	12		10.0
1900	12	13	23		16.0
1901	16	11	19	14	15.0
1902	19	16	12	5	13.0
1903	24	11	5	11	12.8
1904	11		15	9	11.7
1905		10	18	12	13.3
1906	13	7	20	15	13.8
1907	16	13	17	5	12.8
1908	24	18	23	20	21.3
1909	23		15	18	18.7
1910	26		18	27	23.7
1911	33	16	25	27	25.3
1912	18	11	36	4	17.3
1913	35		26	29	30.0
1914	22	19	26	27	23.5
1915	36	21	44	16	29.3
1916	27	34	25	14	25.0
1917	41		42	32	38.3
1918	38	31	52	29	37.5
1919	41	34	38	46	39.8
1920	34	27	30	40	32.8
1921	38	28	45		37.0
1922	37	38	47	43	41.3
1923	39	44	24	39	36.5
1924	37	23	41	48	37.3
1925	51	34	52		45.7

TABLE 4. *Continued*

	A	B	C	D	Average
1926	51	55	31	33	42.5
1927	51	47	43	38	44.8
1928	61	51	45	73	57.5
1929	19		58	54	43.7
1930				51	51.0
1931	39	33	24	59	38.8
1932	46		46	45	45.7
1933	45		57	47	49.7
1934	51	49	49	53	50.5
1935	37	39	52	67	48.8
1936	51	49	38	51	47.3
1937	65	41	27	54	46.8
1938	26		69	36	43.7
1939	29	32	27	72	40.0
1940	19	27	35	42	30.8
1941	28		74	65	55.7
1942	33		35	53	40.3
1943	17	27	67	62	43.3
1944	35	27	47		36.3
1945		20	15	16	17.0

began to ravage the countryside. According to older people, food was hard to find and it became very difficult for a man and woman to feed their children, much like the situation 40 years earlier. And just as in the 1870s, we see that the number of deputies increased exponentially. This increase in deputies is made more dramatic by the fact that the total population of Nuyoo declined during the war years (see chart 2).

The effect of the Mexican Revolution on the Mixteca was disastrous. Trade dried up, markets were held only infrequently, and agricultural production plummeted. A nadir was reached in 1917, when federal troops sacked Tlaxiaco and the Soberanista forces fled the region. But the unrest continued well beyond the official end of the revolution in 1920, since the earlier loosening of state control allowed hostile communities to attack one another without fear of outside intervention, and private armies continued to operate freely in the region. This continued until the 1930s, when the state was able to exert some control for the first time since the end of Díaz government. If it is true that hard times (particularly when amassing foodstuffs and

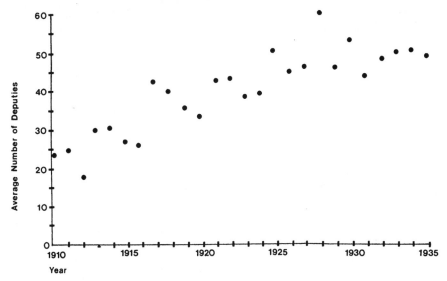

Chart 2. Average number of deputies, 1910–1935.

other goods becomes difficult) precipitate an increase in the number of deputies in Nuyoo cofradías, then this long period of unrest after the revolution, which made travel and trade very difficult and took prime agricultural land out of production, explains the steady growth in the numbers of deputies through the mid-1930s.

We also see an interesting pattern emerge during the late 1930s to mid-1940s (chart 3). This is a period when Mexico experienced a surge in inflation, due in part to the strong demand for raw materials from the Allies during World War II. This is significant because during times of rising wages and prices, the burden placed on cofradía officers is lessened considerably. Recall that one task of the cofradía officials is to "work" the principal money of the cofradía, so that by the end of their year of service, they replace the principal and contribute another 60 percent to 100 percent of the total to community coffers. Traditionally, cofradía members met this payment either by loaning the principal money out at interest or by using it to buy dry goods in the nearby market towns, to resell in Nuyoo at a profit. Animals could also be purchased with the money, and they would yield a profit after the mayordomo butchered them and sold the meat. In any event, it is much easier to replace the principal and meet the interest payments in times of high inflation than it is in times of low inflation. This is

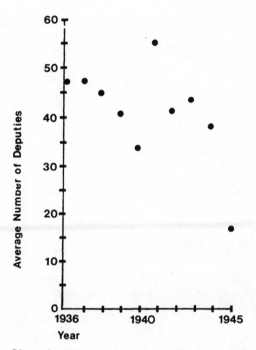

Chart 3. Average number of deputies
1936–1945.

because the real value of the principal money erodes, and it is less
difficult to find an investment that returns 60 percent a year in an
environment where prices are advancing at a rate of 25%, 50%, or even
100% annually, than it is in an environment where prices are increasing at a 2%, 5%, or 7% annual rate. This is significant because it was in
the 1930s to mid-1940s, when inflation heated up and the real value of
the principal money eroded, that the number of deputies leveled off
and even decreased a bit (compare table 3).

In another period of high inflation, from 1890 to 1896, when
Nuyootecos did not increase the amount of principal in the mayordomo chests, the number of deputies also began to level off (see table
4). However, when the principal was increased at a rate exceeding the
rate of inflation, as from 1896 to 1908, the number of deputies again
began to increase, doubling from an average of 7.1 between 1890 and
1896 to an average of 14.2 for 1897 to 1908. Again we can conclude that
as the financial pressures placed on the cofradías decreased, those in
charge did not need to seek the aid of increased numbers of deputies.

Nuyootecos, then, met the burden of increased fiesta costs and the loss of corporate property by spreading the responsibility of fiesta sponsorship among more households. We can see this in Tañuu Fidel Sarabia's account of using corn kernels to calculate the quotas of his deputies. When he did this, in the 1930s, he had 40 or so deputies, each contributing a fixed amount of tortillas and cash, instead of the 4 or 5 deputies a mayordomo would have had two generations before him.

Another important change in the Nuyoo fiesta system made Tañuu Fidel's experience as mayordomo different from that of those who came before him. During the period between 1870 and 1920 (I have not been able to determine exactly when, but indications are it was closer to 1870 than to 1920), the deputy role was uncoupled from the civil-religious hierarchy, so that it was no longer considered a service position. It may have been that the loss of cattle left the deputies with little to do and that amassing tortillas, beans, and a few centavos was not regarded as so difficult that someone could be excused from serving in another office as well. There is also evidence that the amount of food contributed by individual deputies decreased. As I noted, older people in the region define the standard quota as 360 tortillas, and some recall having heard that this amount was the traditional contribution of the deputy to the fiesta. However, none of them ever actually saw deputies contribute 360 tortillas. The most they had seen was 60 tortillas or, on a few occasions, 120. The reason for this reduction in the contribution may have been part of the general process of spreading the burden of fiesta sponsorship to more households.

If I am correct about the reduction in the amount of individual deputy contributions to the cofradía, then this development, along with the removal of the deputy position from the civil-religious hierarchy, would have had an important effect on the relationship of the deputies both to the fiesta and to the mayordomo. Recall that when deputies held service positions, they had many responsibilities. The deputies were in charge of organizing rituals, ensuring that the mayordomo made the proper fiesta distributions, and overseeing the mayordomía accounts. The mayordomo may have been the central administrator of the cofradía, but the deputies were critical to its functioning. When the deputy position was removed from the civil-religious hierarchy, however, the deputies lost their responsibility for the outcome of the cargo. The deputies were no longer held accountable by local government for the results of the fiesta, and they became passive participants, rather than individuals with a personal stake in the fiesta's outcome. The mayordomo household alone began to organize the rituals, make the proper distributions, and ensure that accounts were in order.

In financing the fiesta, a similar process took place. In the old system, each deputy provided about one-fifth of the supplies needed for the fiesta that did not come from communal funds (probably a quota of 360 tortillas). The mayordomo's quota may have been larger than any of the others, but it was not substantially larger.

When deputies no longer held a cargo position their financial responsibility for the fiesta declined. As noted, the size of their individual contributions grew smaller, going perhaps from as many as 360 tortillas to 60 tortillas, or even less. By the time Tañuu Fidel sponsored his fiesta in the 1930s, deputies were individually contributing only 2% to 3% of total fiesta costs instead of the 15% to 20% of the fiesta costs they contributed before.

But what is significant about the uncoupling of the deputy position from the civil-religious hierarchy is that the deputies were no longer obligated to aid the mayordomo. In the first half of the nineteenth century, community elders and the top officers of the civil-religious hierarchy nominated the deputies, just as they nominate the town police and other officials. Yet by the late 1800s or early 1900s, the authorities had stopped appointing deputies. The mayordomo, however, remained an appointed position responsible for the fiesta, and he was then given the additional task of recruiting deputies.

The recruitment of deputies. When the deputy position first ceased being a service position it was probably not difficult for a mayordomo to find four, or even as many as eight, deputies to help in financing the fiesta from among his household's network of kin, ritual kin and neighbors. However, as time went on and ever-more deputies were needed to help, the nature of the task changed. How was the mayordomo to attract several dozen deputies, when these same people had their own civil-religious hierarchy service to perform, and many of them probably also had fiestas to sponsor? Simón Pérez gave me a sense of the difficulties mayordomos faced when he told me of the time he was a mayordomo and asked an older man to be a deputy. The man told him, "You should be looking for people who are like you, who have not yet suffered [that is, young men who had not yet served in the civil-religious hierarchy], not like me, a person who has suffered a lot. Why do you want to put more work on me?" Simón remembered the reply because of the abrupt and embarrassing way the man turned him down.

Finding enough deputies for the fiesta required that sponsors develop several recruitment strategies. One strategy, according to the late Victoriano López, was to use the money in the mayordomo chest. Recall that the cofradía officers had a year to "work" with this money, after which they made an interest payment of 60% to 100%. One way of earning enough to meet the payment was to lend the money at interest. Today, as in the past, when a mayordomo receives a chest there are usually many people who would like to borrow the money. Victoriano said that when the mayordomo would approach someone to be a deputy, he would offer to lend the man some of the money, so that the man would serve.

Another strategy for recruiting deputies was to ply men with liquor or pulque and then ask them for their help, since when they are drunk, people will often agree to things that they might think twice about when sober, and many feel obligated to help once someone has treated them to a drink. The most effective way of recruiting deputies, however, was to enter into an agreement with others who had fiestas to sponsor, such as another mayordomo. Mayordomo A would promise to serve as a deputy and arrive at mayordomo B's fiesta with tortillas, a case of beer, or a bottle of liquor if mayordomo B would return the same goods at A's fiesta held some months later. This is the kind of reciprocal agreement that Nuyootecos call "speaking sa'a."

"Speaking *sa'a*" is an ancient practice in rural Mixtec communities—it is mentioned, for example, in Alvarado's 1593 dictionary of the Mixtec language (Alvarado 1964:14).[6] However, it appears that in these earlier times, what was circulated in sa'a was labor on agricultural tasks. Men in Nuyoo today talk about how the members of one household would enter into agreements with the members of as many as fifteen other households to take turns weeding each other's cornfields. They also note that there was considerable flexibility in how a day of labor could be returned. For example, a man's day of labor could be returned by sending two boys to work, or by the use of a mule for half a day (see Monaghan 1987 for examples). It may be that the

---

6. In his 1580 dictionary of the Mixtec language, Francisco de Alvarado defined *tudzahadi* (equivalent to the Nuyooteco "speaking *sa'a*) as "*ayudarse adinvicem*" ("help in turn," or "help mutually, reciprocally") and "*que en lo que ayudo me ayudan*" (Alvarado 1964:14). He later used the same term to describe the reciprocal exchange of labor in milpa production, a practice found throughout Oaxaca today ("*Ayudar labrar milpa con order que acabando todos juntos una milpa labren otra*" [Alvarado 1962:14]).

same flexibility came into play with regard to fiesta financing when Nuyootecos began to circulate cash and foodstuffs, along with labor, in *saa sa'a*. This might be the reason why Nuyootecos, as we saw, so readily speak of the items circulating in saa sa'a as embodying the labor of exchange partners.

Although, singly or in combination, all these methods for recruiting deputies continue to be employed, the use of gifting to recruit deputies began to predominate. As one man explained the change, "before the mayordomo did not speak sa'a; the mayordomo spoke tarea (quotas)." In part it was because the other methods simply could not be used to secure the cooperation of large numbers of people. After all, there was only so much money in the chest, and plying people with liquor will only work if it is used occasionally and on certain individuals. The use of reciprocal agreements, however, proved particularly effective because one could mobilize others without having to make a formal expenditure. One of the reasons people in the region today say saa sa'a is such a useful practice is that one can secure the cooperation of a large group of people for one's individual projects without having to pay them a wage. In the past, when considerably less cash was in circulation and differences in wealth were even less pronounced, few alternatives to saa sa'a presented themselves. Moreover, a high level of success in contracting partnerships is ensured because it is in the partner's interests to exchange. On average, people sponsor fiestas once every three or four years, since they also celebrate baptisms, weddings, mortuary rites, and for civil officials, patriotic holidays (Monaghan 1990b). By making a reciprocal contract, they are, in effect, able to "bank" labor and resources with another household (Beals 1970). This also assures them they will have precise quantities of specific types of foodstuffs available (since in many reciprocal exchange systems, like must be repaid with like), something that is always a worry because each fiesta requires that a variety of different foods and drinks be served to guests, and the fiesta can be ruined if the sponsors run short of one of the items. Yet the strategy of using reciprocal contracts to finance fiestas had the unforeseen effect of placing the mayordomo in considerable debt, something that led to further changes.

Recall that in the old system, the entire cofradía might produce 1,800 tortillas (5 × 360), with the household of the mayordomo producing only one-fourth to one-fifth of that. The rest would come from the quotas of the four deputies. However, in the new system, to accumulate the same amount of food (if we assume the mayordomo household is able to produce 600 tortillas on its own), the officeholder would have to contract 24 gift exchange partners and would end up owing them 1,200 tortillas (plus cash, liquor, and other items). Here, we can clearly see that the mayordomo not only assumed responsibility for the fiesta, but also was left greatly indebted by it. How Nuyootecos arranged to lighten the burden of the mayordomos so that the position did not leave them destitute marks another major change in fiesta sponsorship.

As older people tell it, it was not uncommon that goods remained after a fiesta ended. The mayordomo would then call the deputies back, and they would gather around a mat the mayordomo laid out in the center of the floor. Then the mayordomo would count the number of surplus tortillas, liters of beans, and sticks of firewood, etcetera, for all to see and divide them among the deputies, reserving a share equal to that of a deputy for himself. This custom continued to 1947, since distributing surpluses to the deputies made eminent sense in a system where participants contribute equal amounts for the financing of the fiesta. As one man put it, not redistributing the surplus was "like stealing."

I first learned about dividing fiesta surpluses among deputies in 1985, from the late Ñañuu María Sarabia, who had invited me to her house to taste some atole she had made. We had been talking about the upcoming fiesta her grandson was to sponsor. The conversation shifted to what fiestas were like when she was young, in the 1940s. She spoke about the distribution of surpluses among the deputies, and I asked her, "If a deputy brought 60 tortillas, and then the deputy received 15 as part of the distribution of fiesta surpluses, did that mean that the mayordomo would owe the deputy only 45 tortillas? Her grandson, who was sitting on the floor next to me, replied—before she could answer—"Of course. Since the mayordomo was returning part of what he had given, then it would be that much less that he would owe." Ñañuu María, however, to her grandson's and my surprise, said that this was wrong. What happened was that the mayordomo continued to owe the deputies what they had given to him, even though he had given them a share of the goods that remained after the fiesta ended. The grandson protested that this did not seem fair. "Indeed it wasn't fair," she said. "That is why people agreed that the mayordomo should be able to keep what is left over after the fiesta, since he supplies the bulk of the things for the celebration."

By the 1940s and 1950s, then, it had become clear to people that it was not right that the deputies, with their responsibilities so diluted,

should receive any surplus from the fiesta. It made sense when each
deputy contributed an amount equal to that contributed by the
mayordomo; it no longer made sense in a system where the deputy
contributed only 2 percent of the fiesta costs and received this back as
gift credits. I mention this because older people date the decline of
the use of the term "deputy" *(latado* in Mixtec) to this event. I first
learned of the existence of deputies after reading the cofradía records
stored in the mayordomo chests, since they never came up in conversation, and only older people could tell me what they were when I began
to ask about them. The deputies, after all, have now become gift
exchange partners, and the transformation from a cofradía system,
with a hierarchy of officers, into a mayordomía, with only one office,
had been completed by the early 1950s.

The most recent change in fiesta financing has been the slow disappearance of the custom of formally contracting gift exchange partnerships. Several things have contributed to this development. First, the
system of *saa sa'a* became ever more complex. This is due in part to
the steady increase in the number of fiestas held during the year. As I
noted, Nuyootecos celebrate fiestas to mark life-crisis events and as
part of their civil-religious hierarchy duties. They finance the life-
crisis fiestas in the same way they finance the civil-religious hierarchy
fiestas—that is, through gift exchange. As the population increased
over the last 30 years, so did the number of fiestas, since there are that
many more baptisms, marriages, and funerals to celebrate. Coinci-
dent with this increase in life-crisis rituals, the number of cof-
radías/mayordomos has also increased over time, from 11 in the early
1800s to 23 by 1920. Furthermore, fiesta sponsorship has become a
duty for many civil cargo holders. The result of this is that the 420
households of the community now sponsor 82 fiestas during an
average year. Because many of the new civil fiestas are celebrated by
several cargo holders conjointly, today, in any three-year period,
roughly 83% of Nuyoo households will sponsor a fiesta.

The fact that most households have to sponsor a fiesta at least once
in every three-year period gives their efforts at financing the events a
characteristic periodicity. About a year or year and a half before a
couple sponsors a fiesta, they begin to prepare for it by depositing, on
average, 36% of the tortillas they plan to distribute with the sponsors
of other fiestas, and an equally large percentage of the beans, cash,
and liquor they will need.[7] These other sponsors must then return the

7. This data comes from several dozen households that sponsored fiestas from 1983 to 1986.

same amount and kinds of goods on the day of the fiesta. Then, when the household celebrates its fiesta, others who have upcoming fiestas, and those bound to the household through ties of kinship, ritual kinship, and propinquity, will arrive to make new prestations. On the average, these people bring with them 52% of the tortillas the sponsors distribute.[8] After the fiesta, members of the sponsoring household will begin to pay off what they owe by returning the gifts in fiestas sponsored by their partners. This means that in terms of participation in gift exchange, the first year after fiesta sponsorship is usually dedicated to returning prestations, since most of those who have made prestations to the couple's household do so with the intention of sponsoring a fiesta before long (although it can take as long as three to five years for partners to sponsor a fiesta so that one may return what one owes). After the first year—once the members of the sponsoring household have reduced their gift debts—they may begin to accumulate gift credits, by attending the fiestas of persons they owe nothing and leaving a prestation. In this way they begin to prepare to sponsor another fiesta. The switch from paying off debts to accumulating credits occurs by the end of the third year, when the members of the sponsoring household begin to make their upcoming fiesta a focus of activity.

The significance of the increase in the number of fiestas celebrated in the community, coupled with the spacing of gift giving and repayment over several years, is that people are constantly in search of gift exchange partners and, consequently, almost everyone in Nuyoo is locked into making exchanges all the time. In terms of the *sa'a* complex as a whole, this has meant that even though the amount of credits versus debts one has accumulated changes (depending on where one stands in the fiesta sponsorship cycle), individual cycles of fiesta sponsorship overlap in such a way that a huge amount of goods is constantly circulating in saa sa'a (Monaghan 1990c).

What happened in Nuyoo over the past century then, is that these contracts became so interconnected and dense—in Nuyoo each exchange is now predicated upon many other exchanges and other fiestas taking place, both in the future and in the past—that saa sa'a functions automatically, coordinating action in a way that has consequences that go beyond the intentions of any of the individual actors. This systemic quality is what distinguishes Nuyooteco strategies for

---

8. The difference between the tortillas sponsors gave out as initial gifts and those they received as initial gifts gives some indication of pace at which the system is expanding.

financing the fiesta from everyday give and take, and what makes it different from anything that existed earlier in Nuyoo. This, in turn, has further shaped the development of the saa sa'a complex, since it is with the increasingly systemic nature of gifting that we see a decrease in the formal contracting of gift exchange partnerships. Although people continue to make formal contracts in which they agree to exchange a specified type and amount of goods, the need for this has been reduced. Because so many people are actively seeking gift exchange partners, and because such large quantities of goods circulate in the system, there is no longer a great concern with having enough of a certain kind of good on hand to distribute.

This however, only explains why the decline in the formal contracting of gift exchange partnerships is a practical possibility. At least as important to this decline are the dispositions of the people participating in the exchanges, particularly the feeling that formally contracting partnerships was somehow "improper" and "embarrassing."

From Deputy to Friend

We saw that one consequence of the uncoupling of the deputy position from the civil-religious hierarchy has been that the mayordomos could no longer rely on the cargo system for deputies but would, on their own, have to find people to aid them. Although mayordomos use a number of strategies to do this, the most common has been the formation of gift exchange partnerships with other sponsors. This has meant that, in contrast to the deputies who were bound to the institution of the cofradía through cargo service, gift exchange partners are now bound to the individual mayordomo through personal ties. The nature of these personal ties are apparent in the way Nuyootecos discuss saa sa'a transactions. As we saw, they speak of a prestation as an "aid" to an esteemed colleague, something that they freely give. The reason for representing gifts as "aid" instead of as a reciprocal transaction—in which people would be very upset if the gift were not returned—has to do with the kinds of persons most likely to give the mayordomo a prestation: affines, ritual kin, neighbors, and members of other households with which the sponsors are on especially friendly terms. Nuyootecos understand a prestation from partner to sponsor to communicate trust, respect, mutuality, and alliance.

The notion that gifts communicate—and constitute—respect, mutuality, and alliance, however, clashed sharply with the mayordomo's having to appeal to people's self-interest for aid in the fiesta, getting them drunk, making loans, and formally contracting a gift exchange partnership. By the late 1950s, with increasing numbers of individuals seeking exchange partners, people became quite sensitive to this conflict and began to drop the custom of "speaking" to partners, which they found to clash with the values transacted in the exchange. To attract the required number of partners, they instead began to rely on their personal reputations as trustworthy individuals who would return prestations and on their ties of alliance and mutuality with other households. One old man put it this way: "Before, we didn't have any friends *[amigu]* come to see us [i.e., participate in the fiesta]. It was just deputies. Now, people are not obligated to come—they come out of goodwill *[kumani]*." This does not mean that the formal contracting of gifts has completely stopped. It continues, but usually it is only older people who do this. Even here, however, it reflects badly on the sponsors if, at their fiesta, there is a preponderance of people who had to be formally invited. As one man explained it, it is like saying, "I can't find anyone who thinks I am a friend or who deems me honorable enough to trust with their goods."

To summarize, the Nuyooteco gift exchange system evolved out of a series of decisions made by Nuyootecos about how to finance fiestas in a situation where corporate assets had been eroded and where households were becoming property-holding units. At first, this involved increasing the number of households responsible for the fiesta, so that the burden of sponsorship might be spread more widely. But the increase in the number of deputies also meant that the position could no longer be considered a cargo. Deputies then had to be recruited through other means; of several different strategies, the most widely used were the extension of reciprocal contracts with affines, ritual kin, and neighbors from the domain of agricultural production to the domain of fiesta sponsorship. (Curiously, sponsors do not always see these reciprocal agreements as part of the fiesta expenses, because, as they say, the goods brought to them by a partner may not have to be returned for some time.) This development, along with the steady accumulation of property by individual households, led to a gradual shifting of the burden of sponsorship to the single mayordomo.

What is of interest here, however, is the way the expansion of the household—in terms of property ownership, fiesta sponsorship, and responsibility for other public undertakings—has altered relationships between households in Nuyoo. The notion that the people who cooperate to finance a fiesta now do so because they are "friends" points to a significant change. In the nineteenth century, the relationships that were important for carrying out one's responsibilities were corporate ones. If one were a member of the great house, then deputies would be obligated to assist in the cargo, and one could use communal property to meet expenses, just as kin living in the same household are obligated to pool resources and support one another. Today, however, these corporate relationships are secondary to the reciprocal alliances contracted and maintained among individual households. If one wants to accumulate the food and liquor needed to sponsor a successful fiesta, it is important that one have a large network of trustworthy gift exchange partners. This network however, is household centered; it has no life apart from the individual household that is its focus, and it serves to define Nuyootecos not as "one body" but as members of independent social units.

The idea that friendship—the building of social networks of alliance and reciprocity—is necessary to mobilize others and achieve social success now extends beyond fiesta sponsorship to a number of other activities. But what seems crucial here is that the development of the gift exchange system in Nuyoo is the outcome of an attempt, by Nuyootecos, to deal with the problems of fiesta finance by extending a form of sociation already in place. This perspective makes plain the importance of understanding community as not only something that change happens to but also a resource—and here I am speaking of community as a loose conjunction of different forms of sociation—that people actively draw upon in order to change. In the next chapter I will examine how this expansion of the household, the privatization of communal assets, and increasing stratification within Nuyoo have been shaped by the Nuyooteco view that social relationships have their origin in the sacred.

CHAPTER 14

A NEW SAINT, A NEW BEGINNING

PATRON saints in the Mixteca, as is true of other areas is rural Latin America, function as prominent symbols of local identity. They are signs of the solidarity of particular groups and of the differences that exist among groups (Gudeman 1976; Ingham 1986). Almost every town in the Mixteca has the name of its patron saint incorporated into its community name, and people speak of patron saints as causing one group to be distinct from other groups. For example, Nuyootecos say that differences in dress, ritual practice, homicide rates, even the temperament of citizens of different towns, exist because each town has a different patron saint.

Given the special devotion people in Latin America usually show patron saints, it surprised me to hear from Nuyootecos that they not only switched patron saints in the past, but are also in the process of doing so again today. People say that Santiago became their patron saint only after their ancestors discovered the image in cave near Yucunino. Prior to this, Santa Ana had been the patron of the community. If, as Nuyootecos say, patron saints are the basis of group identity, then the changing of the saints suggests that the people involved are, in some way, reordering their community and altering their identity. The saint Nuyootecos say is going to replace Santiago is Misericordia.

MISERICORDIA AND THE NEW SOCIAL ORDER

Misericordia miraculously appeared on the steps of the Nuyoo church in 1873. Nuyootecos use the word natuvi, "to make known" or "to uncover," to describe this appearance, indicating that when Misericordia suddenly manifested itself, it was to reveal something of great significance.

Nuyootecos say the world, and its oft-hidden processes, can be understood through dreams, divination, trances, and revelation. As for revelation, Nuyootecos speak of it as a regular feature of their relationship with the sacred. For example, if one goes to the Nuyoo church and asks about the several dozen saints that line the walls, one will see that they are divided into two large categories: those that were "purchased" by community members and those that "appeared." Caballería (Santiago Matamoros) appeared on a stallion brandishing a sword, just as Nuyoo was about to be attacked by enemies intent on destroying the community. Santiago, as I noted, was discovered in a cave near Yucunino, in a place where Nuyootecos would worship the *ñu'un savi*. Others could be listed, since there have been many miraculous appearances in Nuyoo. Even the verb Nuyootecos use for the appearance of Misericordia, natuvi, expresses the constancy of revelation in Nuyooteco life. The prefix *na-* indicates repetition, so natuvi can be thought of as an installment in a continuous process of discovery. Misericordia's appearance was not the first time the sacred made itself known to Nuyootecos, nor, as we will see in the next chapter, would it be the last.

The revelations Nuyootecos experience are not only continuous, but also cumulative. It was the appearance of the sun (natuvi) that destroyed the primitive, asocial, and amoral state of the tiumi and introduced the era of Christian life; it was the tenuvi, the "rain people" who "taught" (natuvi) the people about corn, making agriculture possible; eventually we will experience something called ficio, from the Spanish for "last judgment," when the world as we know it will end. For Nuyootecos, the past is punctuated by a series of miraculous revelations, which have transformed the nature of human life and have given a progressive and meaningful direction to human history.

The process of revelation has a particular expression in Nuyooteco accounts, since the new technologies, social identities, relationships, and moral codes that result are not simply given by the gods. Rather, they are the product of human *interaction* with the gods, where people function as autonomous, though unequal, participants. Thus, it was during Jesus' flight from the evil creatures who pursued him that he stopped at several households. Through his visits with the people of these households, he instituted hospitality and, more significantly, defined society as made up of morally independent domestic units. But this could not have occurred without the active involvement of various humans, who either invited Jesus in to offer him food or who replied abruptly to his questions and turned him away. Morality is not something that the gods, themselves, proclaim (Burkhart 1989:39); its origin lies in primordial human interactions with the gods, which establish the ethical context for subsequent human associations.

As I noted in chapter 12, after Misericordia appeared, Nuyootecos established a new ritual in which a party of men carries an image of the saint around to the households of the community. The men begin their journey on a Monday in early January and complete it about two weeks later. An individual known as the *cargador* carries the saint on his back, with a tumpline. The mayordomo also goes with the cargador, along with at least one fiscal. Others may also accompany them, such as the sons of the mayordomo and the cargador. When the party arrives at a household, the cargador enters with the image and sets it on the household altar. A senior member of the household prays before the saint and makes sacrifices of money and agricultural produce. The mayordomo and his assistants then collect the offerings and transport them to the house of the mayordomo in the center, where they are eventually sold. This ritual probably dates from 1878, when mayordomo records note that civil officials first named a treasurer to keep track of the goods collected by Misericordia.[1]

In chapter 12 I also showed that circulation of Misericordia is based on the stories Nuyootecos tell about the time when demons pursued Jesus. The food and money people offer to Misericordia when the image arrives, and the prayers they make requesting a good harvest, many children, and health for those in the household, re-create this original interaction. Sacrifice plays an important role in this and all human interactions with the sacred, because it is through sacrifice that people communicate with the gods, both reaffirming their adherence to the promises and agreements that occurred in the past and negotiating how these arrangements can be applied to current situations.

Stories like those Nuyootecos tell about Jesus' travels can be found throughout Mesoamerica, and their origin can be traced back to medieval Europe (Laughlin 1977:335). Nuyootecos were therefore probably participants in this folk tradition long before Misericordia appeared. Nonetheless, the ritual circulation of Misericordia only began in the 1870s, suggesting that the ritual does not so much have a latent meaning, but that it establishes a meaning. What we have to ask then is, what was special about the 1870s that made the stories of the circulation of Jesus among peasant households so significant that Nuyootecos would link them to the appearance of the saint? And what did they hope to accomplish when they created the ritual?

---

1. Caja de Misericordia, estado de cuentas, 1878.

Misericordia and the Household

In previous chapters I pointed out that Misericordia came to play a
central role in both the nineteenth-century struggle between the
people of Yucuhiti and Nuyoo over land boundaries and in the
construction of the new church. In the dispute with Yucuhiti, Nuyootecos used Misericordia to try to supplant their rivals as the host of a
regional festival (in that they began to celebrate Misericordia's feast
on the same day as Yucuhiti's patronal fiesta). As for the new church,
the saint's miraculous appearance prompted Nuyootecos to overex-
tend themselves in its construction (it remains today the largest in the
region), which required them to drain the accumulated surpluses of
the mayordomos and sell the communal cattle herd.

We also saw that the late nineteenth century was a time when land
and other forms of corporate wealth began to be transferred to
individual households. As a consequence, households became increasingly responsible for fiesta sponsorship and for providing resources for public enterprises. I do not think it is pure chance that
action in the myths about Jesus' flight from the rich "kings" is set
within a framework of household units. Moreover, the members of the
different households in the myths, as I pointed out, do not act as
members of a corporation but as members of autonomous moral units.
Some provide Jesus with food and water, or misdirect the kings, while
others turn Jesus away and insult him. At the very least, this suggests
that Misericordia's appearance sanctified the leading role households
were beginning to play in local life, at a time when it was assuming
many functions of "the great house."

Misericordia's appearance in 1873 also correlates with a number of
key social innovations in Nuyoo. We saw in the previous chapter that
household-centered relationships began to replace corporate kin-like
relations in the important activity of fiesta financing during the late
nineteenth and early twentieth centuries. If one were a mayordomo in
the first half of the nineteenth century, then deputies would be
obligated to assist in the cargo, and one could use communal property
to meet expenses, just as kin living in the same household are
obligated to pool resources and support one another. By the early part
of this century, these corporate relationships had been replaced by
reciprocal exchanges contracted between individual households, so
that today if one wants to accumulate the food and liquor needed to
sponsor a successful fiesta, one must have a large network of trustworthy gift exchange partners.

Recall that the practice of saa sa'a has a long history in the Mixteca and that in the nineteenth or the early part of the twentieth century Nuyootecos began to circulate goods and cash in saa sa'a along with labor. Nuyootecos say it was during Jesus' visits to the households that this kind of reciprocal gift exchange originated. In one incident Jesus turned a few loaves and fishes into enough food to feed a crowd that had gathered to hear him preach. According to Tata Guadalupe, Jesus said to people, "Have patience with me, for this is a poor gift of food and bread." One often hears this same phrase "have patience with me, for this is a poor gift" uttered by Nuyootecos when making a prestation to a fiesta sponsor. The people who received the food in the story then replied "thank you" *(nkuta'vi)* as those who receive gifts from their exchange partners do today. During each of three or four times I heard Guadalupe tell this story, he stopped to explain to the listeners that those who received the food cannot repeat the words of Jesus ("Have patients with me . . .") since he is a god, so they say *nkuta'vi).* This seems to be a central lesson of the story, and what I understand it to mean is that Jesus, when he distributed the loaves and fishes, set up different identities for people—givers and receivers—and simultaneously established the means for mediating these differences, through the giving of gifts.

The correlation between the origin of a complex system of gift exchange and the mythology associated with Misericordia is not, I think, a coincidence, and suggests that the saint was more than a simple reflection of the changes going on in Nuyoo at the end of the last century. This is particularly evident in the way Nuyootecos replaced the income they lost when the cattle herd and other corporate assets were liquidated.

Since Nuyootecos speak of the appearance of Misericordia as having occurred not at the origin of the world, but as an event their "grandfathers and grandmothers" witnessed, they are all aware that the ritual circulation of the saint among the households is relatively recent. When I would ask people why their "grandfathers and grandmothers" created this ritual, many would say simply that they did it "to collect money." While on its rounds, Misericordia receives cash, coffee, corn, beans, liquor, fruit, squash, and other foods in sacrifice. The mayordomo distributes some of the food in the fiesta of Misericordia, but he sells most of it and, together with the cash he collects, places it in the general fund of the mayordomos. The mayordomos then loan this money out at interest and use it for such things as church supplies, building a new school, aiding in the construction of a CONASUPO building, and defraying municipal government expenses. Other sacrificial rituals channel money into this fund, but the bulk of it comes from Misericordia.

In the nineteenth century, the funds generated by Misericordia gave the saint an active role in resoving the problems caused by the disappearance of corporate sources of income. Some of the money that it collected went into church construction, and some was used to defray the costs of municipal government. Recently, funds accumulated by Misericordia have been invested in a new school and other public buildings. The ritual circulation of the saint may have even served as a paradigm for the system of taxing individual households, which has become an essential mechanism for financing public expenditures.[2]

What I think this indicates is that in the nineteenth century, it was through Misericordia that Nuyootecos innovated. Its ritual and associated mythology allowed Nuyootecos to create new mechanisms for financing collective activities, to develop a moral context for new kinds of relationships between households, and to redefine households as property-holding units. It is true much of the mythology surrounding Misericordia is not original to Nuyoo. Yet if, for Nuyootecos, social relations originate in human interactions with the sacred, the appearance of the saint, and its intimate connection with new social forms, shows that innovations become possible through changes in the way people interact with the gods.

MISERICORDIA AND THE TACHI KUKA

In chapter 6 we saw that the figure of the Tachi embodies a social order where exchange is not a condition of social life: where the members of different households do not marry one another, where the etiquette of house visiting is turned on its head, and where the members of different households treat one another with hostility and suspicion. We also saw that Jesus and Tachi are complementary opposites, or "halves," as Nuyootecos put it. If Jesus is truthful and good, Tachi is deceitful and full of yatuni; if Jesus is associated with the day, Tachi is associated with the night; and if Jesus, as Santo

---

2. Among other things, this suggests that the alienation of resources, at least within Nuyoo, could take place only through sacrificial channels. In other words, sacrifice, as articulated in the Covenant with Earth (where civilized life required Nuyooteco ancestors to give up the rights to their bodies and those of their descendants), is a kind of "natural" model for the nonreciprocal conveyance of property among Nuyootecos: we see it both in cargo service and in the ritual circulation of the saint.

Entierro, Santa Cruz, and Misericordia, circulates among the households, so do the velu, who represent the rich kings who pursued Jesus in myth. Because Jesus and Tachi are two sides of the same phenomenon, where the presence of one immediately implies the presence of the other, then the involvement of Misericordia in the innovations of the nineteenth century implies that Tachi must also be present.

The Tachi Kuka

Of all the different "faces" of Tachi, the one that Nuyootecos most frequently talk about is the *tachi kuka*, or "the wealthy tachi." People bring up the *tachi kuka* in discussions of men who have suddenly become wealthy or whose wealth is so great that it seems impossible that they could have accumulated so much on their own. These individuals, people say, have sold themselves to a *tachi kuka*.

Nuyootecos say the men who sell themselves do so out of either sloth or desperate poverty (I recorded no examples of a woman selling herself to a tachi). Thus people also call the *tachi kuka* the *tachi kushi*, or "tachi of the lazy." The lazy man gets himself into trouble by taking money from a patron to perform a job, and then never does it, or because of his laziness he does not produce the corn needed to feed his family. When the patron demands his money back, or when the family find themselves without anything to eat, the lazy man goes to a tachi for help. The poor man, on the other hand, turns to a tachi as a last resort. In either case, such persons have an inordinate amount of yatuni for others—the lazy man because he wants to have what others have worked for, and the poor man because even though he has made an effort, he has been unable to obtain what his family needs, and therefore also wants what others have worked for.

In exchange for his ánima, the man who sells himself receives storehouses full of dry goods, chests of money, sacks of coffee, hundreds of goats, and dozens of trucks. One man who claimed to have been offered wealth by a tachi said, in response to a question about why he didn't accept, "I have enough to eat, and have little debt, so why should I do such a thing?" While this man rejected the tachi's offer, everyone can list individuals they suspect have made such an agreement, and they privately consider the chance to become rich something that would be hard to turn down.

As I noted, those who sell themselves to a tachi become extremely wealthy, and most of those persons who have amassed considerable wealth, by local standards, are suspected of having done so through this kind of supernatural intervention. What is most interesting about this is that Nuyootecos see these now-wealthy individuals as having cut themselves off from others. This is perhaps best illustrated by the nature of the money given by the *tachi kuka*.

Nuyootecos commonly distinguish two kinds of money: "baptized money" and "unbaptized money." What distinguishes baptized money is that it is "blessed" with holy water by a priest and that it is earned in work or, as they put it, through "suffering" *(shino'o)*. There is, however, a limit on how much "blessed" money can honestly be obtained through "suffering." Like medieval Christians, Nuyootecos condemn those who do not work to create wealth (Bloch and Parry 1989), and anyone who accumulates wealth substantially above this limit can have done so only through illicit means. Moreover, the money they accumulate is money that a tachi or noso (see note 2, chapter 9) stole before it could be blessed. If baptized money is *ii*, "sacred," then unbaptized money is kini, "evil, polluted." In one story told about a man who went to sell himself to a tachi, it filled a chest for him by reaching down and picking up the snakes slithering around on the floor of its cave. As the tachi placed the snakes into the chest, they turned into bank notes. Small snakes turned into 100-peso bills, larger ones into 500-peso bills, and really big snakes became 1000-peso bills. In another story, a tachi gave a man a chest but warned him not to open it until he arrived home. But the man's curiosity got the better of him, and he opened the chest to peek inside. When he did, hundreds of snakes came slithering out and disappeared into the brush, since they had not yet had time to turn into money. Snakes, as "children" of Tachi, are evil and polluted (kini) animals, suggesting that this illicitly obtained money is, in the end, harmful to humans.

The *tachi kuka* are also sometimes called *tachi yii*, just as Jesus is sometimes called "the man of yii." Yii is, in turn, something we might translate as "the heat of life." The incorporation of yii into the names for both Jesus/Sun and Tachi/Wind highlights a very basic perspective one must take when dealing with Nuyooteco religious ideas: that the sacred is composed of different forces, or properties, of life, and issues of fecundity, prosperity, and renewal are always featured in human involvement with the sacred. As we saw in chapter 6, Jesus and Tachi differ in that where Jesus generates vitality through the mediation of potentially opposed entities, the vitality of the Tachi is generated through self-preservation, something that closes in upon itself. Thus, the tachi are often represented as asexual or hermaphroditic (Jansen 1982:496; Monaghan 1987; Ravicz 1965:79), which I interpret as an image of self-containment or self-sufficiency. It is for this reason that those who receive the unbaptized money of a *tachi kuka* live quite well, but it is only their household that derives any benefit from it. For example, many say that if you trade with a certain merchant in San Miguel, you never see a profit. You may buy goods from his warehouse, but if you try to resell them somewhere else, you find you come out with less money than when you started. Some people even go on to say that when the tachi finally takes the man to whom it gave money (usually after seven years), the members of his household find no inheritance, since the money was only for him.

Class Divisions and the Tachi Kuka

Nuyooteco ideas about the role played by Tachi in large accumulations of wealth is significant in the light of economic, political, and social changes at work in the region over the last century. As we saw, these changes have led not only to the emergence of the household as the primary property-holding unit, but also to an increasing differentiation of these households based on their control of land and other forms of wealth. It was often the case in Nuyoo that the first people to register lands as private property were those who had some important knowledge of the world outside the community, such as those who had spent time working in other areas of the country and had come to learn Spanish. Many of these individuals became local leaders (caciques or *"representantes")* and, in registering lands, secured some of the most productive plots for themselves. In fact, a handful of families in the early twentieth century controlled large amounts of land. The division of plots among heirs has since broken up many of these large holdings, but the descendants of several of the men who first registered lands in the late nineteenth and early twentieth centuries continue to be influential in local life (see below).

Coffee has also played a role in giving certain individuals greater access than others to wealth and land. Some individuals have proven themselves adept at growing coffee, and they have been able not only to expand production by using their profits to buy additional lands, but also to control the labor of fellow community members through the paying of wages. As early as 1953, one-half the total coffee production in Nuyoo was in the hands of just 15% of the households.[3] In the 1980s some households produced as much as three tons of coffee

3. AMN, Censo de productores, 1953.

per year, giving them an extremely large income compared with their neighbors.

Although it is true that Nuyoo has never been an egalitarian community, differences in wealth have become increasingly significant for the way people relate to one another. In 1988, for the first time ever, people in Nuyoo Center began to adjust household taxes for public work projects according to a household's ability to pay, by dividing households into three ranks. (About 30% were in the top rank, 60% in the middle rank, and 10%, largely made up of households headed by widows, in the bottom rank.) Moreover, some rich households have attempted to replace received forms of sociation with market relationships. A good example of this is found in fiesta sponsorship.

For a household with sufficient wealth on hand, it makes good sense (in terms of the market economy) not to "lend" goods, interest free, by making prestations to members of other households when preparing to sponsor a fiesta. This is most obvious with cash prestations, since during the times of high inflation in the mid-1980s, money returned after a year's time was worth only half as much as it was when it was given. It is perhaps not surprising, then, that some people began to look at *saa sa'a* participation as a burden instead of an opportunity. This became an issue in the late 1970s, when one of the richest men in the community attempted to sponsor a fiesta without making prestations. When I asked him about his motives some years later, he said that attending others' fiestas and life-crisis commemorations took up a considerable amount of his time, which he thought he could better spend tending his coffee and other crops. Those who regularly work for wages, such as masons, express similar opinions, since wages are paid for each day worked, and a day spent at a celebration translates directly into the loss of a day's salary. In any event, the man decided to use his own money to buy corn, beer, and other supplies and to hire people to process the food for the meals. Without going into any detail about what happened, he did manage to sponsor the fiesta, but public opinion forced him to resume participation in the gift exchange system when it came time to celebrate his next fiesta.

I cite this example because it illustrates how the economic interests of wealthy households are sometimes in direct conflict with the economic interests of less-wealthy households. Almost everyone I spoke to agreed that poorer households are less able to "defend themselves" *(ta'va mara)* — that is, accumulate the goods necessary for the sponsorship of a celebration on their own—so they tend to rely more on gift exchange to finance the celebrations than do wealthier households. This is because poorer households can use *saa sa'a* to convert temporary surpluses into credits of food and money by making gifts to others, surpluses that might otherwise be spent in daily subsistence. The gift exchange system also enables them to stretch out their repayment of debt, since the prestations they receive on the day of their celebration have to be returned only when their partner sponsors a celebration, which may not come for months or even years. The wealthy man who refused to use gift exchange to finance his fiesta thus not only violated local custom, but also, because the participation of many households in the *saa sa'a* system is necessary to keep a steady flow of goods circulating (see Monaghan 1990c), placed himself in opposition to the interests of the vast majority of households.

Although the man's refusal to make any prestations in the sponsorship of his fiesta is a unique case, many feel that members of wealthy households are often reluctant to make exchanges. As one man explained, "The rich are miserly [kuasunni] because they do not go to fiestas; they worry only about themselves, since they have enough to defend themselves." Another man said that the rich "see a little of their wealth going out, and they think, 'there it all goes,' and then do not make more prestations." Later he added that the rich "do not want to aid other people, [since they] think they can do everything on their own."

Many speak of wealthy people's reluctance to enter *saa sa'a* partnerships as a manifestation of something that goes beyond whether or not they participate in gift exchange. A woman once said to me that the problem with the rich is that "they do not feel what it is to be poor" and that "the rich do not know how to eat the food we eat." I understand her to mean that the rich are incapable of putting themselves in the place of others and that they are unwilling to participate in the exchange and cooperation that are so important to Nuyooteco sociation.

The wealthy, then, are seen as having made a pact with a tachi. This pact is the equivalent of an alliance with dangerous outsiders, and the prosperity these community members enjoy both isolates them from others and places them in opposition to the interests of those who have not made such a pact. The offer the tachi present to people is, as many admit, difficult to resist. It is however, universally condemned, and those who sell themselves generate the kind of community the velu dramatize in their dancing. Jesus, after all, when he put names to all the things in creation, called the velu "rich."

The Expansion of the Household and the Tachi Kuka

Joseph Greenberg, in his ethnography on the Chatino community of
Yaitepec on the coast of Oaxaca, tells us that it contains "two conflict-
ing and competing principles of organization: one based on a grid of
reciprocal obligations and ritual redistribution, and the other, expressly capitalist, premised on unequal exchange and class" (Greenberg
1981:55). Indeed, in Nuyoo, changes in the economic and political
environment of the community have exacerbated tensions among
households, since population growth, land privatization, and increasing stratification have combined to increase the space within which
households compete. This conflict is obvious in the case of land, since
households have become the landholding units, and any disagreement
over who has access to which plot of land will be manifested in
conflicts among households. As control over land (particularly land
where coffee is sown) has become the main source of wealth, conflicts
have increased among kin over inheritance, between neighbors over
property boundaries, and between buyers and sellers in land sales.
Such conflicts can also be seen in disputes that cause households to
fission, as brothers argue over dividing their father's lands, and as
children complain about not receiving a proper share of the money
earned from cash crops. And the effects of privatization and stratification do not end with competition over land; instead they ramify, so
that they oppose the interests of different households across a number
of significant contexts, such as fiesta sponsorship.

Although I agree with Greenberg that structural fissures between
households have widened over time, I think it is also important to
reiterate that the salience of the household in Nuyooteco social
organization is itself a recent phenomenon. Beginning in the nineteenth century, population growth, land conflicts with neighboring
communities, cash cropping, and the breakup of corporate assets
resulted in the transference of what was formerly communal wealth to
individual households, making households landholding units that
were also responsible for public expenditures. Consequently, the
relationships among households have become an increasingly important component of social life. Thus we saw that the complex system of
reciprocal gift exchange, which dominates fiesta celebrations in
Nuyoo today, had its origins in the middle to late nineteenth century.
Any increase in interhousehold conflict should be seen as a related
development. It is not that conflict somehow endangers reciprocal
relationships; indeed, reciprocal relationships presuppose conflict. In

structural terms, the two have long been viewed as similar; both are mediating relationships, and both are important in defining opposed social units.[4]

Although I have not seen any documents on the *tachi kuka* comparable to those that discuss Misericordia's appearance, it is clear that the *tachi kuka* have assimilated the identity of persons who were key actors in the transformations of the nineteenth and twentieth centuries. Nuyootecos sometimes represent the *tachi kuka* as nineteenth-century Spanish and Criollo sugar barons of the Putla region, riding horses and wearing fine clothes and wide-brimmed hats (figure 22). People also associate the *tachi kuka* with mestizo merchants (they liken their houses to the warehouse of an infamous coffee middleman from Putla) and with government bureaucrats, such as those from the National Agrarian Commission who, in the 1930s, ordered the division of communal lands.

I am not suggesting that Nuyooteco beliefs about the devil date from the late nineteenth century, nor am I suggesting that the tachi are only an indigenous meditation on the evils of capitalist relations of production (Taussig 1980). The figure of the Tachi instead links actors from many periods—actors who stand out for their excesses and avarice. But what seems to be to be most significant about the Tachi is that just as the appearance of Misericordia in the late nineteenth century allowed Nuyootecos to redefine their relationship with the sacred—and thus create a moral context for action in a setting where households were becoming the property-holding units and inter-household relations had become more complex—so too Nuyootecos redefined their relationship with Tachi as these same households were becoming more stratified relative to one another and as the range of situations in which households compete expanded. If gift exchange originates with human interactions with Jesus—an interaction that Misericordia recreates as it circulates among the households in the community—then the drive to accumulate goods and to preserve what one has gained, and the conflict and isolation that drive engenders, originates with those who sell themselves to the *tachi kuka*. This latter is an act recreated in the visits of the velu and given contemporary relevance by the reappearance of *tachi kuka* in new guises.

---

4. Harris also suggested that the case for treating domestic units as distinct and related through exchange (i.e., that there is a distinction between intra- and interhousehold relations) is valid only with the development of generalized commodity exchange (Harris 1981).

Figure 22. A *tachi kuka*. Here Tachi appears in the embroidered jacket, trousers and broad hat of the Mexican *charro*, or cowboy.

REVELATION AND AGENCY

What I think the appearances of Misericordia and the *tachi kuka* in Nuyoo highlight is not so much that changes in ritual, myth, moral discourse, and exchange are related to changes in the material circumstances of people's lives. Rather, what is at issue is that Nuyoo-tecos responded to changes in their material circumstances in a way that was consistent with a view of social life as something that origi-nates in human interactions with the sacred and, furthermore, that these changes have moral implications expressed in terms of health and illness, prosperity and sterility, and yɨɨ and yatuni. Nuyootecos create and experience community through ritual and myth (which are not easily separated from social interaction and moral discourse), and it is through the telling and retelling of incidents like the appearance of Misericordia and encounters with the *tachi kuka* wearing the faces of *hacendados*, bureaucrats, coffee traders, and mestizo merchants that they reconfigure the practices that organize collective life.

Yet in saying that history and events in Nuyoo are influenced by a narrative logic closely linked to local ideas about how relationships are created and maintained, it must also be said that it is individuals who construct and reconstruct their worlds, not "forces" or "processes" or a disembodied logic; change, especially on the level of a place like Nuyoo, cannot be separated from human purpose. After all, someone had to place Misericordia on the steps of the church, and someone had to link the image of the saint to the myths about the time when Jesus walked the earth.

Differences in wealth and status within Mesoamerican communities have increasingly become a focus for anthropologists and historians working in the region. Research has shown that these differences are not eliminated by "leveling mechanisms" and that they have existed for a long time—although their specific nature may change. This is significant because wealth differences may create divergent, and sometimes incompatible, interests among community members, leading in some cases to "class conflict" (Schryer 1990:27–49), so that we should not confuse community with homogeneity. Economic stratification, far from being the temporary phenomenon an earlier generation assumed, is essential to community organization and continuity in Mesoamerica.

One does not have to live long in Nuyoo to find evidence for wealth differences or to discover occasional points of conflict between rich and poor Nuyootecos (as shown by the discussion of the man who tried to sponsor a fiesta without *saa sa'a*). But something of far greater consequence than the existence of broad, class-like strata for understanding the exercise of power and control in Nuyoo is the position of a single individual, called the cacique. I will briefly examine the development of the cacique position over the last hundred years and discuss how it, like so much else in recent Nuyoo history, is linked to the appearance of Misericordia on the steps of the church in 1873.

The Cacique

In many Mesoamerican civil-religious hierarchies, officials make important decisions concerning the administration of the community only after consultation with a group of individuals who have passed through all the offices in the hierarchy and have become respected elders, or *principales*. In Nuyoo, the number of elders who have this power has always been small, and is now reduced to one man, whom outsiders call the cacique (figure 23). Nuyootecos often address this individual as *tata ji*, "grandfather," and describe him as "the man who commands" *(tee ta'tuni)*, "the powerful one" *(yo'vi)*, and "the dignified elder of the community" *(tee kuña'nu ñuu)*. The cacique sits in on all important meetings of the town officials, and officials give him a prominent place in general assemblies. When Nuyootecos discuss

Figure 23. A cacique addressing the assembled citizens. All the caciques in Nuyoo have been famous orators. Note also how the cacique's authority is marked by his large size and by the way the Nuyootecos who listen to his address are depicted as standing, while he sits.

important matters, his opinion carries tremendous weight, and, like the principales in other places, he is regularly consulted by town officials about public policies.

The origins of the cacique's power can be traced to the late nineteenth century, when there were five or six individuals referred to in both oral history and the documentary record as caciques and/or representantes. It appears that a man could achieve this status in two, not necessarily exclusive, ways. First, he could become a cacique through serving as a successful war leader. Recall that beginning in the second half of the nineteenth century, Nuyoo engaged in an almost ceaseless struggle with Ocotlán and Nopalera, communities lying to the southwest of Nuyoo Center, populated by a people Nuyootecos call the Luti. The men who became war leaders organized raids against the Luti and showed uncommon valor during the fighting. One of them even used to creep into Ocotlán at night to ambush unsuspecting passersby.

The second way a man could achieve cacique status was by learning Spanish, becoming literate, and serving as the communty's representative before the district and state government. The number of people who were able to do this has always been small. According to older Nuyootecos, in the 1940s only four men in the community could read, write, and speak Spanish well enough to hold their own against outsiders, and the 1890 census lists only eight men (and no women) over 30 who were able to read and write.

Literate Nuyootecos would often find themselves employed as town secretaries, a job that required them to answer official correspondence, interpret edicts issued by state and district officials, keep vital statistics, and record the proceedings of official meetings. The secretary also functioned as translator for officials when dealing with Spanish-speaking outsiders. Because there were so few literate individuals in the community, a secretary might serve as many as a dozen years before stepping down. Consequently, the position is not a service position, and its incumbent today draws a salary that is paid by the municipal government. Although the secretary is formally only an employee of civil-religious hierarchy officials, in practice his contacts with the district and national government and his long tenure in office mean that he acquires considerable influence in local decision making; indeed, in many Mixtec communities today he is the real power in the municipality.

The rise of Herminio Velasco. By the early part of this century, the five or six caciques of the late nineteenth century were replaced by a single, powerful cacique, a man named Herminio Velasco. Velasco was born in 1883 and, as a young man, learned how to read and write, even though no one else in his family was literate.[5] When he was only 20 years old, he served as the mayordomo of Misericordia.[6] By 1909 he was town secretary, and he served as president in 1914.

Velasco organized many successful raids into the territory of the Luti. In one carried out in the late 1920s, a band of Nuyootecos outflanked the Luti by crossing into Nopalera from an adjacent community and climbing a mountain in the dead of night. Tañuu Andrés Sarabia, who was a young boy at the time, recalled they held hands during the climb, since it was pitch dark and only one man

---

5. AMN, Censo de Habitantes, 1900.
6. Caja de Señor Misericordia, estado de cuentas, 1903.

knew the way. They fell on Nopalera just before dawn, pouring off a hill, shouting, and firing their guns. The surprise was total, and most of the Luti fled, although Nuyootecos did manage to kill several men who stayed to fight. The raiding party then rounded up all the cattle, horses, mules, sheep, and goats they could find and looted the Nopalera church, taking with them the image of Nopalera's patron saint, San Sebastián (which is now the saint of the San Sebastián mayordomía). When the party returned to Nuyoo, townspeople organized a large feast, and the raiders slaughtered some of the goats they stole, to cook in underground ovens. Herminio Velasco set aside about half the animals to sell in order to pay bribes to district officials, so that when Nopalera raised a complaint, Nuyoo's aggression would be ignored.[7] The rest were also sold, and participants divided the proceeds among themselves. Everyone knew that Velasco pocketed some of the money from the sales, but since he had organized the raids and was the one who dealt with outside officials, this was ignored; eventually, it became a custom to award him a third of the animals. If we are to believe the complaints filed, the raids could net up to 100 head of cattle, mules, goats, and sheep, so Velasco's share of the booty was considerable.

The raiding continued until the 1950s, and through them, Herminio Velasco managed to accumulate a substantial herd of animals. He also began to use the horses and mules to travel to the Pacific coast to trade. One old woman told me she once counted 34 mules in a pack train he sent to the coastal town of Tlacamama to purchase salt and corn. Velasco would stockpile the corn and salt he bought and then sell it during the rainy season, when swollen rivers cut off the trade routes to the coast and the prices of these commodities rose to very high levels in Tlaxiaco and other highland markets. Trade between the highlands and the coast was not something that Velasco initiated, since there are reports of this activity being practiced by Nuyootecos in the nineteenth century,[8] and Nuyootecos probably participated in this trade throughout the colonial period. However, few individuals owned mules, which are necessary if goods are to be transported in any quantity, so that Velasco's use of many dozens of pack animals,

7. For example, in 1908, the Jefe Político of Putla wrote to the Secretario de Estado in Oaxaca, telling him that the people of Ocotlán and Nopalera were complaining that Nuyoo paid a bribe of 300 pesos to the Jefe Político of Tlaxiaco so that he would exculpate Nuyootecos in his official report (ARM, Jefe Político de Putla al Secretario del Estado, 1908).

8. Apuntes Topográficos 1871:243.

and his employment of other Nuyootecos as mule drivers, made his trade unlike anything that had been carried out before. Moreover, in 1826, the community was listed as owning 10 transport mules, suggesting that the trade may have been organized corporately, perhaps as part of the mayordomo cargo.[9]

Besides trading for salt, Velasco raised sheep, goats, and cattle, which he sold in Tlaxiaco and other regional markets. These activities brought him into close contact with the Mestizo commercial elite in Tlaxiaco, and he eventually purchased a house in Tlaxiaco, which he used to store the products he brought and sold. He also loaned money out at interest and maintained extensive plantings of corn and bananas, both of which could be grown and sold at a substantial profit if one had sufficient transportation available—that is, mules and horses—to carry them to highland markets. By the late 1920s, Herminio Velasco was an extremely wealthy man, and if one asks Nuyootecos today about Velasco, one of the first things they mention are the large chests of silver coins Velasco kept in the rafters of his house.

Until a few years before his death in the mid-1950s, when he was supplanted by the current cacique, Herminio Velasco was able to exert a great deal of control over other Nuyootecos. It was he who picked officers to serve in the civil-religious hierarchy, since every year the high cargo officials would come to him with a slate of nominees, and he would make the final selection. Having this power allowed him not only to choose allies (or men he could manipulate) for top posts, but also to terrorize other members of the town, since no one in Nuyoo wants a cargo. Men who crossed Herminio would find themselves appointed to posts before they had their three years of rest. (He even revived a defunct mayordomía in order to fill it with a man who angered him.) Similarly, if one wanted to avoid office, one would try to get on the good side of the cacique so that if one's name came up, he could remove it from consideration.

Herminio Velasco's use of appointments to the civil-religious hierarchy to extend his influence, reward allies, and punish enemies was probably not very different form what went on when there were a half-dozen "representatives" making the decision. As I pointed out in chapter 7, Nuyootecos' attitudes toward cargo cannot be understood apart from the way power is exercised through it, and the vitality and continued relevance of the cargo system in Nuyooteco life is at least partly a function of the way it is used as a mechanism of control. Still,

9. ARM, Registro Civil, Census for Santiago Nuyoo, April 17, 1826.

the concentration of power in the hands of a single cacique was unprecedented, and it allowed Velasco to do things that a group of elders, whose interests may have sometimes conflicted, would not have been able to do. For example, older people say Velasco did not want anyone putting up houses in Nuyoo Center, since this would ruin some of the best pastureland in the community. The town center thus remained largely vacant until his death. He was also in periodic disputes with individual Nuyootecos who lost crops to his animals when they strayed into nearby cornfields. Many Nuyootecos also say he prolonged the war with Ocotlán and Nopalera, because he profited from the raiding and did not want the flow of booty to stop.

What allowed Herminio Velasco to exert such unprecedented control over the lives of Nuyootecos? Simply put, Velasco was able to make many people in the town dependent upon him for their livelihood. There was a core of about a half-dozen men who worked for Herminio Velasco full time, and Velasco employed dozens of Nuyootecos seasonally, when corn was scarce. (I have not run into a single male contemporary of Velasco who had not worked for the man.) He would send some to the coast to purchase salt, and others he would hire to plant, weed, and harvest his cornfields and banana plantings. He would then pay these men in corn. Today, many of those who worked for Velasco speak warmly of his generosity and the large distributions he would make in fiestas, and they say he was the only man you could go to for help when you needed to feed your family.[10] But the pernicious side of this dependence was also apparent to some. As one man explained it,

> The *rico* [Herminio Velasco] would sow enough corn so that they [his household] had extra. They would have enough to feed their families and their workers. The workers would be paid in corn. The wage was four liters of corn a day, but often people were tricked and were paid only three, since the workers had no way to measure. The people who worked for the rico would plant and weed his fields, and since they spent all their time working for him, they did not have time to do their own work [i.e., plant and weed their fields], so when the next year came, they ran out of corn and had to work for the rich man again. (See also Cook 1982:67)

As this man indicates, many Nuyootecos found themselves caught in

---

10. Velasco was famous for providing any Nuyooteco who came by with a meal and for sponsoring celebrations after each successful expedition to the coast, where everyone would be served meat and aguardiente.

a vicious circle in which they became ever more dependent on Herminio Velasco.

By the 1930s, it had become the custom to show Herminio Velasco special deference, with people bowing at the waist and kissing his hand when they greeted him. It is interesting that outsiders say Nuyootecos treated Herminio Velasco "as if he were a saint." Anyone who wanted to speak to him about a private matter would have to bring him a gift, and the mayordomos would always send portions of food to his household on the day of their celebrations.

The only man to challenge Velasco was José López, who, as a young boy, left Nuyoo to join the military. When López returned in 1947, he was literate, had married a mestizo woman, and worked for General Manuel León Navoa, whose company, Minerales de Plomo, S.A., sought to exploit the mineral wealth of the Mixteca. A vein of lead and silver ore runs through the southern part of Nuyooteco territory, and López opened a mine there. While supervising work on the mine, he began to serve in the civil-religious hierarchy, and his wife opened a store in Nuyoo Center. López got Nuyootecos to drain a large pond near the church and used the land to build a covered gallery for the market. He also tried to employ Nuyootecos to work in the mine. As people today recall, López—who strode around like he was still in the military, barking orders and sometimes hitting people—wanted to become a cacique. However, Herminio Velasco began to counsel people not to work for López, and when workers in the mine died in a rock fall, Velasco began to say that the engineers were offering people to the *nu ñu'un*. Then, one night, shots were fired into the López house. Although no one was hurt, López feared for the safety of his family and left Nuyoo. [Also, the mine had begun to peter out, and it was closed a short time afterward.] When I spoke with López in the early 1980s, he told me he was sure that it was the cacique, or one of his henchmen, who fired the shots.

Given the unparalleled amount of wealth Herminio Velasco accumulated and the critical attitude that exists with regard to some of his actions, it is perhaps not surprising that Nuyootecos link the figure of the cacique to the *tachi kuka* and the velu. As we saw, Nuyootecos suspect that anyone who accumulates wealth beyond a certain point has sold themselves to the tachi, and for a man like Herminio Velasco, who had chests full of silver pesos, there is little doubt that he was, as Nuyootecos say, "working with a tachi." Similarly, many terms of address and reference people use for the cacique—such as yo'vi, "the powerful and violent one"; *taji*, or "grandfather"; and *tee kuka*, the "rich man"—they also use for the tachi and velu.[11]

At the same time Nuyootecos voice criticisms of the cacique, they also add—sometimes in the same breath—that the caciques have protected communal lands and have won a variety of concessions for the community from the state and federal government. Many, moreover, point out that the caciques have healed major rifts in the community and that their leadership has enabled Nuyoo to survive in the midst of far larger, but factionalized, rival municipalities. Thus people often speak approvingly of the cacique's ability to "control" others. Households in Nuyoo can be, as we have seen, fractious to an extreme, particularly in a situation of political indeterminacy, and it is difficult for the members of individual households to mobilize widespread support for projects, since outside one's most closely allied kin and ritual kin, the search for allies is likely to be futile. The cacique, on the other hand, can unify Nuyootecos and overcome opposition within the community through persuasion, favors, patronage, and threats. Otherwise Nuyootecos can accomplish things only through consensus, and consensus is often difficult to achieve.

The point, however, is that Nuyooteco solidarity and exclusivity is at least partly the result of this exercise of power and control. This is also evident in the use of alimentary images for the processes of group formation. "Eating" suggests not only a transformative synthesis but also domination, since there are those who "eat" and those who are "eaten." It is perhaps in this light we can understand why, when Nuyootecos speak about the eventual passing of the current cacique (he is now in his seventies), the majority do not express relief at being free from his domination but instead worry that no one will rise to replace him.

Herminio Velasco and the Appearance of Misericordia

Although the idea of a single, powerful cacique at the head of Nuyoo is firmly embedded in Nuyooteco ideas about their lives together, there were, in the nineteenth century, several individuals called caciques. At the time Herminio Velasco began his rise to power many of these men were either dead or, because of their advanced age, no longer played a significant role in public life. At least one of them died at the hands of the people from Ocotlán, and another, who served as

---

11. In some Mixteca de la Costa towns, such as Santiago Ixtayutla, Tachi is referred to as "the cacique."

secretary, mysteriously committed suicide in an isolated area of Nuyoo in 1909, after it was alleged that the people of Ocotlán bribed him to draw up documents justifying Ocotlán's claim to certain lands.[12] The question we should focus on, however, is not whether mortality and age made room for new caciques to emerge, but what it was about the Nuyoo situation at the turn of the century that made it possible for an individual with Herminio Velasco's talents to achieve such unprecedented economic and social control over others and to set himself up as the supreme authority.

The key to cacique status, as we saw, lies in providing successful leadership. In the 1970s for example, the current cacique led a sustained effort to build a road to Nuyoo Center, frustrating the people of Yucuhiti Center, who tried to keep the road within their territory so that Nuyoo would be bypassed. In this sense, the power of the cacique is based upon his taking the lead in issues that have broad communal appeal. A man even corrected me once when I remarked that the cacique brought the road to Nuyoo, saying, "If the cacique did not have the backing of the community, he would not be able to do anything."

Although the key to cacique status lies in his successful pursuit of communal goals, the cacique also tries to manipulate the support he is able to mobilize in a way that furthers his personal interests and adds to his power. Thus, in leading the fight to bring the road to Nuyoo, the current cacique managed to get himself appointed as the labor contractor for the project, a position that allowed him to dole out jobs in the community. I could cite several other examples, but I mention this because the caciques or representantes active in the last decades of the nineteenth century were, early in their careers, central to the organization of the worship of Misericordia. It was men from this group who served as the first mayordomo and the first treasurer of Misericordia. It was also, according to some, a man from this group who, after using a divinatory procedure, determined the feast should be celebrated during Lent, after the priest convinced Nuyootecos not to celebrate it during Yucuhiti's fiesta. The caciques thus seem to be the ones who established the meaning of the saint's appearance for Nuyootecos, and it is clear they took the lead in its promotion as a cult object and in creating the saint's ritual.

---

12. AMN, Informe al Jefe Político sobre la muerte de Manuel Rojas, 1909. Velasco was secretary at the time and the author of the Informe. Given his position, I suspect that he was one of Rojas's accusers.

Why was there such great interest among the caciques in promoting and organizing the worship of Misericordia? Recall that Misericordia appeared at a time of great difficulty for Nuyootecos. In the 1870s, Nuyoo was surrounded by hostile municipalities that were intent on dismembering the community. Not long after the saint's appearance, government troops sacked Nuyoo Center (Monaghan 1990a), and once the Díaz regime solidified its position, Nuyoo came under increasing pressure to comply with government programs of economic change, in particular the privatization of corporate resources. This atmosphere of strife and upheaval mark the early 1870s as one of those times of crisis when the creative responses of individual leaders—so often given in a revelatory idiom and backed by divine sanctions—can be particularly effective for introducing social change (for Meso-america, see Bricker 1981; Gruzinski 1989; Sullivan 1989). The moti-vations of the leaders of such movements, like those of Handsome Lake in Wallace's classic account of the "revitalization" of the Seneca, are often altruistic (Wallace 1970). In Nuyoo's case, it is not to be doubted that the men who organized the cult of Misericordia, and interpreted the meaning of its appearance, acted out of pride in Nuyoo and a wish to mobilize people against outside threats. After all, Nuyootecos used Misericordia to challenge their rival Yucuhiti, and the demonstration of divine interest in the community probably served to assure and inspire people during a difficult period.

At the same time, however, the caciques in Nuyoo had personal and strategic goals that could be achieved through the promotion of Misericordia. As Gosner (1992) has pointed out for the Tzeltal revolt of 1712—which began after the Virgin Mary appeared in the Chiapas countryside—local elites can use popular religious enthusiasm to build a movement that had the effect of solidifying their positions at the apex of the native social hierarchy. Even Handsome Lake was accused of manipulating his revelations for personal gain (Wallace 1970:289–91). For their part, the strategic goals of the Nuyooteco caciques were concretely linked to the issue of privatization. Recall that in 1856, the Ley Lerdo passed by the Juárez government required the transfer of corporate property into private hands. This law did not have an immediate effect in Nuyoo, but there were renewed calls for disentailment by subsequent Liberal regimes, and the first private land titles began to appear in the community in the 1880s. These titles were produced by and for the caciques, some of whom served as town secretaries. (Their descendants carefully guard these titles today, since there are still those who dispute the way they came to control these properties.)

In the nineteenth century, the caciques who claimed private title to land were not so much interested in controlling farmland as in gaining access to pastureland. At that time, the only local product aside from bananas for which there existed significant demand were goats, sheep, and cattle. Also, if one had horses and mules, one could travel to the coast and buy salt to resell in Tlaxiaco or transport fruit, in quantity, to sell in highland markets. The problem Nuyootecos faced, and continue to face today, is that pastureland is limited, so the number of animals one can keep is only limited.[13] Yet when the communal herds, which contained hundreds of head of cattle, goats, and sheep, was sold to build the church after Misericordia appeared, room became available for private herds.

Ownership and investment in cattle by individual Nuyootecos appears to have become increasingly widespread over the 30 years after the communal herd was reduced.[14] It may be that some portion of the communally owned animals was divided among community members in a general *"reparto,"* as occurred with communal resources in other towns in the Mixteca at this time. Privately owned animals were herded together by a paid cowherd, just as the communal animals were. This cowherd also cared for the surviving communal animals, so that pastoral organization did not really change with privatization, just the composition of the herd, which went from being one that contained just a few privately owned animals to one in which most were owned privately.[15]

Although privatization did not initially alter traditional patterns for

13. The shortage of good pastureland was aggravated by the arrival of the *hacienda volantes* from the Mixteca Baja. These were vast herds of goats that were driven from Puebla and other parts of the Mixteca Baja to the Mixteca de la Coasta and back again on an annual migration. The owners would rent pastureland in the towns on their routes, which provided income for local governments but often left the areas denuded, since the herds contained thousands of animals.

14. For example, in 1904 Casimiro López complained to the Jefe Político that the animals belonging to eight different individuals caused damage to his crops when the herd passed by (ARM, Casimiro López al Jefe Político, June 24 and June 30, 1904).

15. Although the number of animals in the communal portion of the herd increased after church construction wound down, they never amounted to more than a fraction of what they were before the project was begun. Part of the reason for this was that the land on which they had pastured the cattle was now grazed by privately held animals, but it was also because work on the church continued until at least 1915 and cattle and other mayordomía property were continuously liquidated to pay for the construction, though at a much slower rate than before (e.g., Caja de la Virgen de Rosario, estado de cuentas, 1904).

the organization of pastoral production, it did create the possibility for differences in the number of animals individual Nuyootecos possessed to emerge. Indeed, by the closing decades of the nineteenth century, we see that some Nuyootecos had many head of cattle while others had none. Both oral history and documentary evidence indicate those who had the most animals were the caciques, or their close relatives. [16]

In this context, I should note that the appearance of Misericordia was used to suppress criticism of the costs of building the church and the liquidation of communal resources, since the saint has a reputation for striking down those who doubt its divinity. Legend has it that the fiscal who found Misericordia on the church steps poked it with his staff, believing, in the early morning light, that the saint was a goat. For this, the saint caused him to become blind. Also, a priest who refused to acknowledge the miraculous nature of the saint, calling it nothing more than "a block of wood," came down with a severe case of dysentery and later died on the way back to Tlaxiaco. More recently, in the 1980s, a man refused to make sacrifice to Misericordia, saying that the mayordomo party carrying the saint was only after liquor. The cargador later complained about this to the municipal authorities, who decided not to punish the man, because, in the words of one of them, "The saint will take care of him." Although Nuyootecos worship Misericordia, they also fear it (the word ii, "sacred," is also used for individuals with prickly personalities), and those in power may have used this fear to mobilize people to support the project. After all, the brutal behavior by the masons building the church could not have been possible if community leaders did not at least tacitly allow it, and the use of the saint, along with the employment of a heavy-handed mestizo, may have been part of a strategy to coerce others into building the church. [17]

16. By 1890, José Gregorio Pérez, who Nuyootecos say was one of the early caciques and who served as town secretary from the 1880s to at least 1900, owned two mules, a horse, several head of cattle, and an unspecified number of sheep and goats (AMN, Recaudación de contribuciones directas, May 24, 1890). Likewise Eluterio López, the brother of Martin López, another cacique, owned at least one yoke of oxen, valued at 55 pesos, which was more than any of the mayordomo saints had in principal money at the time (Escritura de propiedad, May 10, 1894, in private hands). One woman recalled her parents telling her that before the Mexican Revolution (circa 1910) a handful of men owned most of the animals in the herd. Since the cowherd was paid out of mayordomo funds, this meant that the private enterprise of these indivudals was paid for with public funds.

17. The reputations the caciques maintain for brave deeds and violent acts undoubtedly discouraged many from challenging them.

Evidence suggests, then, that the appearance of the saint was used by a group of powerful men to support their position on the liquidation of communal assets, a group—if we are to believe the people of Yucuhiti—who may have been the ones who placed it on the church steps in 1873 in the first place. These men were interested in mobilizing people against outside enemies and in building a monument to their community's faith and power. But they certainly profited from the sales of the communal cattle herd (which had the effect of opening up pasturelands), and the appearance of their names on land titles from the period hints at their support of the Liberal program fostering individual, as opposed to corporate, rights. Although widespread ownership of cattle at the end of the nineteenth century suggests that there may have been broad support for these ideas, those who did not accept the new policies—all of which, it will be recalled, were linked to the church—risked death at the hands of an angry saint.

Through their successes at reducing communal holdings of productive resources, the caciques of the nineteenth century opened the way for Herminio Velasco to establish his own herd on what were communal pastures and to set himself up as the supreme economic power in Nuyoo. Velasco was aided in this by the almost-complete disappearance of cattle and other animals from Nuyoo during the later years of the Mexican Revolution, when marauding bands of soldiers carried off anything they came across. This ensured that there was abundant pasturage when Velasco began to build his own herd. Velasco's intelligence and entrepreneurial skills contributed significantly to his success. But he would not have achieved what he did if it had not been possible to own animals and land privately, and men with careers strikingly similar to that of Velasco appeared in the nearby Mixtec-speaking towns of Yucuhiti and Ocotepec at about the same time.

Although much of this chapter has been concerned with Herminio Velasco's rise to power in Nuyoo, my aim has not been to examine the emergence of modern caciques in rural Oaxaca (which is a history that is yet to be written). Rather, I wanted to explore the role played by Nuyooteco sociality in the creation of new economic and political structures, beginning with the notion that social life is a product of human interaction with the sacred, and then examining the way individual interests and purposes crystallize through revelation. As I noted earlier, nearly every Nuyooteco I know has had a ndiosi (or tachi) communicate directly with him or her. The knowledge that these beings reveal is often of a highly personal nature, such as where to find deer, where a chlid's ánima was lost, or the identity of a thief. What makes Misericordia unique is its use by certain individuals to authorize a particular vision of social life. While they could not have been aware of where their actions would eventually lead, the evidence suggests that they were aware it could be a way of mobilizing others and shifting collective agendas, given Nuyooteco understanding that innovations originate in human interaction with the sacred.

Yet the process through which a revelation takes on significance for the entire community can be much more complex than the bald manipulation that seems to lie at the heart of Misericordia's appearance. As we will see in the next chapter, another revelatory figure has recently become the object of intense interest, and he must be understood in terms of events that are transforming the lives of everyone in Nuyoo today.

CHAPTER 15

THE INDIO DE NUYOO

NUYOOTECOS have migrated in search of work since at least colonial times, when they were part of the steady stream of indigenous people who would descend from the mountains of the Mixteca Alta to labor on the sugar haciendas in Putla and the Cañada of Yosotichi. It is only recently, however, that Nuyootecos have begun to move to Mexico City, to work in restaurants, bakeries, and the informal economy, selling food and other items on street corners. In the 1960s a handful of men established themselves in the city, often after suffering great hardship. By the 1970s, young women also began to migrate. Most of the young adults in the community today have now at least visited Mexico City, and many have spent years working there.

Conventional wisdom holds that people in rural areas of Mexico are "pushed" out of their communities by the drudgery of agricultural work, the low standard of living associated with subsistence agriculture, low wages, overpopulation, and a general lack of social and economic opportunity (see Hirabayashi 1993:77–81). These are factors in Nuyooteco decisions to migrate as well. Yet, as I pointed out earlier, Nuyootecos also migrate to avoid cargo service—a motive not unrelated to the economic factors that press people to move out of the village. It is true that town authorities require cash contributions from migrants to make up for missing tequios and for not serving in offices. At times these contributions can be heavy, consuming a significant portion of the migrant's wages. However, everyone agrees that these contributions are nowhere near as difficult as serving in a cargo. In Nuyoo, at least, burdensome communal obligations are a significant factor in decisions to migrate, and Nuyootecos often cite it as the "last straw" (Hirabayashi's term) in their decision to leave.

Although many migrants leave Nuyoo to avoid "the punishment of community" none of them is proud of this, and they will not admit to the real reason in public. The migrants I interviewed believed that cargo service should continue, since it is performed for the good of

Nuyoo and because it remains, even for them, the way men prove their worth.

In the 1980s, at the time of my initial fieldwork, something very interesting began to occur with regard to urban migrants. Many men and women who left Nuyoo to live in Mexico City in the 1970s began to return. Some say they returned to escape crime and pollution. Others said they returned because they now had children and Mexico City is no place to raise a family. Some lost their jobs, while others said they planned to come back all along, once they saved enough money to build houses, buy animals, and plant coffee. In any event, these return migrants, who are, for the most part, in their thirties, were immediately elected to cargos. In 1991 the sindico, the first suplente to the comisariado, an agent, and three of the mayordomos were men who had recently come from Mexico City back to Nuyoo. I don't want to give the impression that all those who left have come back—the vast majority of those who left continue to live outside Nuyoo territory. However, return migration is clearly a trend, and return migrants make up an ever-increasing proportion of the population in general and officeholders in particular, since they are immediately given cargos upon their arrival, often several in succession.

We have long been aware that migrants from places like Nuyoo transport traditional social patterns to the city, and that the lines of communication between migrants and people back in the village remain strong, so that the town does not lose members as much as it comes to add an urban component (Butterworth 1975; Kearney 1986; Lomnitz 1977). Even though they do not reside in Nuyoo, migrants continue to participate in local life. In addition to making cash contributions to the municipal government, they may also make arrangements with relatives to work for them in the tequios they miss. Migrants with special skills, such as the masons who built the new CONASUPO building in Nuyoo Center in 1985, may return to the community to work when officials request them to do so. Migrants have even begun to vote for municipal officers in "general assemblies" held in Mexico City and send the vote tallies back to Nuyoo.

Despite the ease with which some communal practices have been adjusted to emigration, the long-term residence of a large number of Nuyootecos outside Nuyoo territory, young men's ability increasingly to avoid cargo offices by migration, and the involvement of many residents in life-worlds outside the community cannot be easily encompassed by traditional patterns. What I suggest here is that just as in the nineteenth century, when in response to such things as the introduction of new cash crops, warfare, population growth, and the loss of corporate property, Nuyootecos began to expand the household and redefine relationships among households, today Nuyootecos, in response to migration, are adjusting the civil-religious hierarchy and the standards by which male character is judged, and perhaps most importantly, they are redefining their place within Mexico. The vehicle for these changes is a figure known to history as "the Indio de Nuyoo."

Remigio Sarabia, The Indio de Nuyoo

In his *Cuadro Histórico de la Revolución Mexicana*, Carlos María de Bustamante mentions an incident that occurred in 1812, during Mexico's War of Independence against Spain. The Royalist army in Oaxaca, under the command of José Régules, had Valerio Trujano's rebel forces trapped in the town of Huajuapan de León, in the Mixteca Baja. After several months, provisions in the town ran low, and Trujano looked for someone to take a message out to José María Morelos, the leader of the independence movement after the execution of Father Hidalgo. Morelos was in Chilapa and, according to Bustamante, Trujano chose "an Indian from Nuyoo" to inform him of their situation (Bustamante 1961:408–14).

The "Indio de Nuyoo" had come to Trujano's attention when he crept close enough to the Royalist lines to shoot the commander of Régules' artillery, a Dominican priest by the name of Soto. We do not know how this man came to join Trujano's force. He may have been in the plaza when Trujano rode into Huajuapan, since it was Sunday, the market day, and Trujano ordered his soldiers to detain any Indians who sought to leave, so that he could use them as auxiliaries. He may also have freely joined Trujano's rebel force in the months preceding the siege, since Mixtec speakers fought on both sides of the conflict. In any event, the proven stealth of this "Indio" made him the perfect candidate to slip through the Royalist lines to carry a message to Morelos.

Before he set off, the Indio de Nuyoo covered himself with several sheepskins, so that in the darkness he would look like a stray animal. On his way through the Royalist positions, a sentinel saw him but, mistaking him for a pig, gave him a kick. The Indio de Nuyoo did not cry out, and he managed to hurry away. When he reached a nearby hill, he set off two small firerockets, so that Trujano would know he had crossed through the enemy lines undetected. The Indio de Nuyoo then set off for Chilapa.

Meanwhile, the situation in Huajuapan worsened. Royalist forces had ambushed an earlier relief column, supplies were running low, and Trujano knew they could not hold out much longer. The rebels made a novena to a local saint, and on the last day, just as they were finishing their prayers, the Indio de Nuyoo appeared. He told them he had contacted Morelos and that a large detachment of troops, led by Morelos himself, was on its way. On the next day, July 23, 110 days after the siege began, Morelos arrived, and combined with Trujano's forces from inside the town, they managed not only to break the siege but also to drive the enemy from the field. According to Bustamante, of a Royalist army of well over a thousand men, only twenty-five made it back to Oaxaca City. The rest either died in the battle, surrendered, or threw down their guns and fled. The rebels captured a large number of artillery pieces and small arms, which made them the dominant power in a large area of southern Mexico (Bustamante 1961:408–14).

Most of what we know about the Indio de Nuyoo comes from Bustamante, who visited Huajuapan in 1813 to interview survivors of the siege. Other nineteenth-century historians, such as Carriedo (1842) and Gay (1881), closely follow Bustamante's account, with Gay adding that Indio de Nuyoo crept into the Royalist camp on several occasions to spy on Régules. According to Gay (1950:454–55), he even brought back condiments from Régules' field kitchen, to prove to Trujano that he had been close to the Royalist commander. In the hands of later historians, many of whom have been greatly influenced by the official ideology of the postrevolutionary Mexican state, the story has been considerably embellished and romanticized. One writer, Jesús P. Cota, has the Indio de Nuyoo loyally dying alongside Trujano, later in the war (cited in Mendoza Guerrero 1981:154). Another, Telésforo Mendoza Guerrero, tells us that the Dominican the Indio de Nuyoo shot, Father Soto, was the parish priest of Nuyoo and stole the Indio's sweetheart. By killing the Dominican, Mendoza Guerrero tells us, the Indio de Nuyoo paid the "Spanish adventurers" back for "the offense to his honor, and symbolically, the insults they inflicted on our long-suffering race" (Mendoza Guerrero 1981:141). Professor José T. Cervantes even composed a poem that identified the Indio de Nuyoo as José Antonio Corazón, whose sweetheart, Gila, was stolen by a Spaniard ominously nicknamed "the Black Hand" (cited in Mendoza Guerrero 1981:153).

Nuyootecos also have a version of the Indio de Nuyoo's exploits that is partly based on Bustamante's account but contains additions that come from their own traditions. One thing they note is that the Indio was not the anonymous representative of an entire race but an individual, named Remigio Sarabia. Sarabia is a common surname in Nuyoo, and the parish archive of Tlaxiaco lists a José Remigio Sarabia as having been born in 1798. Many of those who have the surname Sarabia refer to Remigio Sarabia as "father" or "grandfather."

Although oral tradition identifies the Indio de Nuyoo as Remigio Sarabia, Nuyootecos do not appear to have been aware of his significance to Mexican history until the 1930s, when José López—the man who had joined the military as a young boy and attempted to supplant Herminio Velasco as cacique—read about the Indio de Nuyoo in a newspaper account of the siege of Huajuapan de León published in Mexico City. Later, in 1962, the city of Huajuapan de Léon invited Nuyoo to send a delegation to the 150th anniversary celebration of the lifting of the siege. The present cacique, Taji Luis Aguilar, along with a man named Blas Vásquez and another named Zacarias Sarabia Sarabia, who was comisariado at the time, traveled to Huajuapan to participate in the festivities. They learned that city officials had named a street "Indio de Nuyoo" and were on hand to see the unveiling of a monument to the Indio. They also heard officials praise the deeds performed by the Indio de Nuyoo, as in the following speech:

> The Indio de Nuyoo was an outcast and one of the oppressed, a victim of many tyrannies, but he awoke to the peril like an eagle taking off in flight, and with his generous soul that valued humankind more than his own person, saved the fortifications and assured that the vigilance of the besieged would not be in vain, through an effort as meritorious as those who defended the pass at Thermopylae. (Tito Vera Resales, cited in Mendoza Guerrero 1981:168)

For the men in the Nuyoo delegation, their connection with someone spoken of in such heroic terms was a stirring experience. Immediately after the ceremony, they sought out the sculptor who built the monument (a pedestal topped by an image of a man in "Indian" clothing clutching several firerockets and a scroll) to order a duplicate for Nuyoo. The sculptor completed the work in 1965, and Nuyootecos lugged it, piece by piece, from Ocotepec to Nuyoo Center, since there were no roads at the time.

The men who attended the celebration in Huajuapan also worked to promote the recognition of Remigio Sarabia's exploits. Although Blas Vásquez died before I came to Oaxaca, he spent many days looking for information about the Indio de Nuyoo, and Zacarias

Sarabia Sarabia helped secure Remigio Sarabio's baptismal notice for the town (see below). Yet of the three men at the assembly, it was Taji Luis Aguilar who played the largest role in transforming Remigio Sarabia from a historical footnote into a local hero.

Taji Luis Aguilar is now in his mid-seventies, and he has led an eventful life. He was a young boy when his father died. The town schoolteacher, a mestizo who had married a Nuyoo woman, took Luis in as a servant and taught him to read and write. When Taji Luis was 10 or 11, he came to the conclusion that he had no future in Nuyoo (recall that the Mixtec word for orphan translates as "impoverished one") and left for Tlaxiaco. He found a job sweeping government offices, and there he met an official who took a liking to him. The man would sometimes spend his lunchtime with Luis, and he taught the boy how to use a typewriter—a skill comparable to computer programming today.

Luis periodically returned to Nuyoo to visit, and his ability to read, write, and type made him a candidate for town secretary. In 1939 the old cacique, Herminio Velasco, offered him the post, even though Luis was only seventeen. Luis settled in Nuyoo Center, and during this time became a close friend, and later compadre, of the cacique's only surviving son, a man named Epidio. This cemented his ties with the old cacique, and Luis and the cacique became, for a while, close allies. Taji Luis, for example, helped drive José López from Nuyoo, and he may even have been the one that fired the shots into the López house.

Just before Luis returned to Nuyoo from Tlaxiaco, the schoolteacher who had taken him in as a boy died. Luis began to court the man's widow, and they eventually married. Because the schoolteacher left his wife a sizable estate, Luis was soon able to acquire land and plant bananas and coffee.

In the following years, Luis worked his way through the civil-religious hierarchy. He was mayordomo of Santiago in 1942, he served as the first *comisariado de bienes comunales* from 1944 to 1950, and in 1963 Nuyootecos elected him municipal president. Like Herminio Valasco before him, he was also an active participant in the wars Nuyoo fought with Ocotlán and Nopalera. He organized several successful raids, and he once used himself as bait so that Nuyootecos could ambush a band of armed men from Nopalera.

Unlike Herminio Velasco, however, Luis Aguilar wanted to bring the fighting to an end. He and the cacique's son developed friendships with the state deputy from Tlaxiaco, the head of the Department of Indian Affairs in Oaxaca, and several other officials, who advised him on how to settle the dispute. It was while they were "going around to the offices" that the two of them stopped wearing the traditional male costume (rolled-up white cotton pants and a poncho with colorful designs on it) and began to dress in shoes, dress shirt, and long pants, so that, as Taji Luis told me, "they would be taken seriously."

Luis Aguilar convinced people in the community that the war with the Luti would go on forever, unless they secured a presidential resolution that fixed the boundaries between the two communities and allowed government officials to come in to guarantee the peace. Herminio Velasco opposed these efforts, but with the expansion of the Mexican state in the 1940s, Luis was able to use his links with the government to outmaneuver the old cacique. Luis cultivated ties with officials in charge of rural transportation and managed to get himself appointed as the head of various road-building enterprises in the region, which allowed him to employ as many as a hundred fellow Nuyootecos. At the same time, the introduction of coffee made Nuyooteco less dependent on Herminio Velasco for loans, food, and jobs. Luis worked to promote this independence by organizing people into a coffee cooperative, whereby they could sell their crop directly to the government coffee monopoly without having to pass through middlemen such as Velasco, who kept most of the profits. In 1948, in spite of Velasco's opposition, Luis Aguilar obtained Nuyoo's federal title to communal lands, and by the time Velasco died a few years later, people in the community were referring to Luis as *tata ji*, or "grandfather."[1]

In this period, then, the key to power in Nuyoo resided not so much in controlling the economic linkages between the community and the broader economy as in controlling the links between the community and the expanding federal, state, and district bureaucracy. It is interesting to note that Luis Aguilar reversed Herminio Velasco's policy on settlement in the town center, by encouraging people to erect houses and channeling much of the money Nuyoo received for municipal government, schools, and utilities into development projects for the town center, even if it meant losing scarce pastureland. The reason for this is simple. The house of the cacique is next to the office of the comisariado, and he can see the municipal hall from a window. It always amazed me how, whenever the authorities began to transact some piece of business, or an official visitor arrived, Taji Luis

---

1. Epidio, Velasco's son, gradually succumbed to alcoholism and was in no condition to succeed his father. He eventually squandered most of Velasco's wealth, so that his children inherited very little of their grandfather's estate.

would suddenly appear to find out what was going on and, often, to take control. This kind of supervision is possible for him only because administrative activities (and school, ritual, and commercial activities) occur near at hand. Taji Luis has thus been against the establishment of schools, CONASUPO stores, markets, churches, and even cemeteries in the different Nuyoo hamlets. Although he has not always been successful, Nuyoo's hamlets are not nearly as vital or independent as those of surrounding municipalities.

Luis Aguilar was thus able to make himself, by the 1950s, into a classic Latin American broker, controlling the lines of communication between his rural community and the state government. As people say today, "No one knows his way around the offices like Taji Luis." If a Nuyooteco wants something such as a plot of land from the comisariado or a child enrolled in school, they usually go to see Taji Luis and, after paying him a fee, receive his advice and support. This dependence upon Taji Luis Aguilar has given him, not surprisingly, substantial control over the municipal government. A former president told me,

> One day we received an order from the Instituto Nacional Indigenista requiring that the CONASUPO [government-subsidized dry-goods store] be transferred to Yosotato. I did not know what to do, so I went to ask the cacique. The cacique said he knew an office where we could go to complain. I said, "please grandfather, let us go there," but Luis said he could not, because he had a lot of work to do. He had to sow his bean crop for the coming year, and there was no one to help him. Well, I went and called together all the suplentes of the authorities, and the comandantes, and others. A total of 56 men arrived, and we worked to sow Luis' beans. We sowed a huge amount—25 cajónes [125 liters], and Luis had to return to his house twice to get more. After we finished, Luis came to me and said, "How much do I owe you?" I told him that he didn't owe anything; there was, of course, no way anyone could have paid for that much labor. He was asking only to be polite. I said to him, "Could you please help us with the store?" He agreed, and we went to Mexico City, to the head of the Instituto Nacional Indigenista, and the man gave us a letter to the director of the Tlaxiaco office, telling him to leave the store alone. I sent the letter to Tlaxiaco with a messenger, since I knew the director would be angry. He yelled at the young man, but he had to leave the store in Nuyoo.

Taji Luis has often said that the figure of Remigio Sarabia is important because he calls attention to Nuyoo and to Nuyooteco achievements. Although I have no doubt about Luis's civic pride, I think there are additional reasons he takes such an interest in the Indio de Nuyoo—reasons that are related to his position as a broker.

One would not have to stay in the Mixteca long to see that the native people of the region are often treated in a condescending and paternalistic way. In the streets of Tlaxiaco, rural Mixtec speakers are often spoken to as if they were children or were mentally deficient. This has led, in many instances, to attempts by more cosmopolitan Mixtec-speakers to obscure their identity, as we saw in the decision by Taji Luis to stop wearing the traditional male Nuyooteco costume. But Taji Luis—even though he speaks unaccented Spanish, owns houses in Tlaxiaco and Oaxaca City, and has a son who is an employee in the state capital—cannot completely turn his back on his roots, since his power rests on his continuing identification with "Indian" Nuyoo. Government officials favor him because he can deliver a unanimous vote from the community when they call for it, and he can mobilize many dozens of Nuyootecos, in their colorful dress, for political rallies in Tlaxiaco.

I think Remigio Sarabia is important to Taji Luis because the "Indio" makes Luis's Indian identity a more positive one than it would otherwise be. Taji Luis actively organized the celebrations commemorating Remigio Sarabia for many years. He is also the semiofficial narrator of Remigio Sarabia's biography, and I have been with Taji Luis on a half-dozen occasions when he worked the Remigio Sarabia story into his discussions with outside officials. Remigio Sarabia is someone officials are bound to respect, since the ruling political party in Mexico bases its legitimacy upon those who have defended Mexico's sovereignty. In recent decades, each Mexican president has chosen a hero from national history upon which to model his presidency, such as Juárez or Hidalgo. It is not a coincidence that the veneration of the local hero corresponds to the emergence of an official discourse on the nature of political legitimacy in Mexico (see below). The stories of Remigio Sarabia—an "Indio" who nevertheless contributed to Mexico's independence—make men like Luis a part of national events in a way that is more compelling than the passive way most Native Mesoamericans are seen, and he, in effect, copies Mexican officials by modeling his regime on a heroic figure. That the theme of Nuyootecos involvement in Mexican history is of general importance in the Remigio Sarabia phenomenon can be seen in those stories told locally in which he consorts not only with Morelos, but also with patriotic figures who lived prior to 1812, such as Hidalgo, and later than 1812, such as Zapata.

Remigio Sarabia and Migration

Taji Luis Aguilar in not the only person interested in the Indio de Nuyoo and it is doubtful that Remigio Sarabia could have come to play such a significant role in Nuyooteco consciousness—even given *Taji* Luis's potision—if there were not a number of different people whose interests could also be objectified in the Indio de Nuyoo. In fact, despite Luis's efforts, the celebration of Remigio Sarabia was, in the words of one man, "no big deal" for many years. Nuyootecos commemorate Remigio Sarabia's accomlishments on July 23, the anniversary of the lifting of the siege at Huajuapan de León. Before they erected the monument, civil officials would unfurl a large painting of Remigio Sarabia on a cloth screen in Nuyoo Center, and because the town band gathered for the celebration of the patronal feast (which began with the mayordomía fiesta of San Felipe on July 23 and 24), they were available to play *mañanitas* at dawn, and around noon they brought their instruments to the base of the image to play a variety of songs. Typically, no more than two dozen people would gather for this. Sometimes a meal was served in the mayordomo of San Felipe's house for those who came.

This began to change in the late 1970s. The first wave of Nuyoo migrants—men who left in the early to mid-1960s, joined a little later by women from the town—had, by this time, established themselves in Mexico City. They organized a migrant association in Mexico City, which, along with some people from Nuyoo Center, arranged for land to be donated and the monument to be taken out of storage (where it had sat since 1965) and erected, in 1979, on a promontory overlooking the central plaza. From this point on, the celebration on July 23 began to expand. Migrants returned from Mexico City to organize a regular feast on the 23rd, where a general meal would be served at noon, just as in the mayordomías (they also financed it through gift exchange). The office of the comisariado, which had helped to procure the monument and obtain the land upon which to erect it, also began to aid in sponsoring the fiesta, since this office, which was created in the 1940s, was one of the few "big" cargos that did not have a fiesta associated with it. One migrant wrote a short history of Remigio Sarabia, which he had mimeographed and circulated in an assembly of migrants held in Mexico City. During the 1980s more people began to gather for the fiesta, and it became a major part of the celebrations of the patronal feast. By 1991, there were hundreds of people present for the festivities on July 23, and the organizers expanded the program, beyond the speeches and music provided by the band, to include four elaborate skits.

The idea of staging skits as part of a fiesta celebration came from the elementary schoolteachers in the area, who, since at least the 1930s, have made them part of school programs to celebrate national holidays and to mark the last day of classes each year. These programs, in turn, have their origin in education projects designed to promote Mexican patriotism and secular values. The skits organized by the teachers in Nuyoo are usually either comical performances or depictions of an event taken from Mexican history. In 1991, teachers from the community organized one of the skits for the festival of Remigio Sarabia. It examined the suffering of the population of Huajuapan de León during the siege. But three additional skits, not organized by the teachers, dealt with subjects that departed significantly from the themes usually found in school dramas. In one of them, a man and his sick wife visited a local curer. After learning the curer's diagnosis, they went to a government doctor. During the search, the man debated the advantages and disadvantages of traditional and modern medicine. The second depicted the campaign visit of a government official. Mimicking what occurs in political rallies, a representative from each hamlet came before the official and requested something from the government. There is always a humorous tone to the skits, and the men in this one presented absurd requests, such as the installation of a train line to an isolated hamlet so that the inhabitants could get around easier. The official, dressed in a leather jacket and wearing dark glasses, agreed to each request and went on to promise even more outrageous things. Although obviously derived from school performances, the collective authorship of the skits and the consistent use of humor and dancing resonate with genres of Nuyooteco performance such as the velu dances at Lent.

In Victoria Bricker's important work *The Indian Christ, The Indian King*, she demonstrates that ritual dances constitute a Maya aesthetic for the interpretation and understanding of historical events. Using a structuralist framework, she shows how the dances link disparate events to one another (such as the French Intervention and the Mexican Revolution) while dramatizing a theme of ethnic conflict. I would argue that Nuyooteco skits function in a similar way, tying events from long ago with those from the recent past into a narrative that stresses thematic continuities underlying the various events. This brings us to the longest and most elaborate performance of 1991.

This last skit was produced by a dozen men who had spent time

outside Nuyoo working in Mexico City. When they were developing
the skit, they told me they wanted to show "what it was really like"
when people leave Nuyoo to search for work in the city. The performance began with a son speaking to his father, explaining that he
wanted to leave to earn money, to see the city, and "gain experience."
He promised to send money back to his father, but the news made the
father sad and fearful. The father then told the boy that they would
travel together to Mexico City so he could be sure the boy arrived
safely.

The next scene opened with the man and his son in Mexico City,
staring, openmouthed, at the tall buildings. While crossing the busy
streets, they had to run to avoid the cars, which people in the crowd
found very funny. Eventually they found a business advertising for
employees. They knocked at the door, and a guard answered. The
men asked him about the job, and he ushered them into the office of
the owner, who immediately began to interview the boy. The owner
demanded the boy's certificate of graduation from elementary school
and other documents that the boy did not have. It was at this point that
the boy announced "I am a descendant of Remigio Sarabia, 'the Indio
de Nuyoo.'" When the owner heard this, he hired him on the spot,
giving him a broom to start sweeping. The father, seeing that his son
had found a good job, left to return to Nuyoo.

In the skit, the boy worked very hard for a week and, to cut down on
expenses, ate only dried tortillas and water. On payday, the owner
called him in and gave him a check. Looking at the check, the boy
first noticed that the amount was calculated to the second decimal
place. "What," he asked, "am I going to do with two centavos?"
(Less than one cent). The boy also noticed that his pay had been
discounted by a series of charges. He asked the owner about this and
was told that workers must pay for the brooms and other equipment
they use, as well as electricity. "What," the boy then asked, "are
death benefits?" "That is the money you receive when you die," the
boss explained, which caused people in the crowd to laugh.

When the boy left the office, the guard who introduced him to the
owner demanded a tip. The boy protested, but the guard said, "If you
don't hand over some money, you will never work for this firm again."
The boy paid the guard and left the building, only to find two
policemen waiting for him. Knowing it was payday, the police were
shaking down the employees as they left work. When the boy refused
to give them anything, one of them punched him in the stomach and
threatened to beat him unless he paid up. After giving them half of

what he had left, the boy staggered off. Finally, a gang attacked the boy. Although he was able to give them a few good licks, they beat him severely and took what little money he had left. The performance ended when the boy stood up, and made a speech about how much people who go to the city suffer to make a living and how he longed to return to Nuyoo.

One might begin to understand this skit, with its obvious linkage of events in the Remigio Sarabia story to migrant experiences, as reflecting a Mexican discourse on the importance of national heroes in collective self-definitions, as well as Nuyootecos' quest for legitimacy within this broader social and political community. Indeed, I think this has a great deal to do with the efforts of both Taji Luis and the migrants on behalf of the Indio de Nuyoo, and I will return to this subject below and in the concluding chapter. But to understand the full significance Remigio has for Nuyooteco migrants, we must also view him in terms of the special power with which he is imbued, which gives him continuous contact with the sacred. Remigio Sarabia, Nuyootecos say, was one of the "Rain people" (ñivi savi) and thus a tenuvi.

THE TEE NUVI

Tenuvi means, literally, "transforming man."[2] As a verb, *nuvi* is used for anything that is changing from one state of existence to another. The metamorphosis of a tadpole into a frog, for example, is nuvi, as is the healing process, where someone who was once sick is restored to health. But besides describing a transformation, nuvi also implies a continuing connection between apparently diverse things. After all, the tadpole and the frog share an identity, despite the features that distinguish one from the other. When people use the term tenuvi, they use it in precisely this way, indicating a transformative process where someone changes from one state to another, but also an ongoing connection between two states, a connection implied by the transformation itself.

Nuyootecos say all humans maintain a nuvi-like connection between at least two distinct states of being—a human body on the one hand, and an animal body, one's *kiti nuvi*, or "transforming animal," on the other. As I noted in chapter 8, when a human is born, an animal is also born, out in the forest. This creates an intimate bond between the two, since they share the same ta'vi, or destiny. Thus, when one

---

2. Nuyootecos say women can also be *tenuvi* or, more properly, *ñanuvi*, but no one could name any individual ñanuvi, and in myth, the tenuvi are always spoken of as male.

feels hunger, they both feel hunger. When one hurts, they both suffer the pain. The connection extends even to death, so that when one of the two dies, the other also dies. Some people have several *kiti nuvi*, each of a different species. Such persons stand a better chance of a long life than someone who has only one *kiti nuvi*, because the person with several animals only sickens if one of them dies. Many Nuyootecos feel it is best to delay baptism for a few years, since they believe that a child acquired *kiti nuvi* between the time it is born and when the priest pours holy water on its head. By putting off this ceremony, they allow their children to acquire more than one "animal."

The tenuvi are different from other humans in that instead of having a nuvi-like connection with some harmless or insignificant animal, like a deer or rabbit, the tenuvi have a nuvi-like connection with powerful animals, or with lightning bolts (*tajia*) and other Rain-associated phenomena. Also, the tenuvi are able to exercise conscious control over their different coessences, unlike other humans, who often have no precise knowledge of what their "animal" is. The reason for this is that instead of being baptized in the church by a priest, as are most people, those who will be tenuvi are baptized in a special ceremony away from the town center, up in the mountains. The ceremony used to take place in a pond to the northeast of Nuyoo Center, which a landslide obliterated some years ago. When parents brought an infant to be baptized at the pond, they placed the child in a small wooden box, which they set into the swirling waters. If the mist that rose from the pond was red, "like the light of the setting sun," then the infant would soon die. However, if the mist was white, the infant would live a long life as a tenuvi and share consciousness with lightning.

The pond was important because it was there that the patron of the tenuvi lived. Several people, but by no means all, say that the patron was a *koo savi*, a rain serpent that emerged from the water to bless (sikuchi, "to bathe") the child floating in the box by licking it with its tongue. This blessing would imbue the future tenuvi with holy Rain and make him or her one of the Rain people. When the *tee nuvi* celebrated a fiesta they would go to the pool and fetch their patron. It could not stay out of the water long, so they would be quick to return it after they feasted it and the musicians played for it.

Despite differences in the identification of the patron of the tenuvi, all Nuyootecos agree that it is due to their powerful patron that the tenuvi are more intelligent (*anduni va'a nka*) than other humans. The tenuvi are able to diagnose the cause of people's illnesses by merely glancing at them, they can predict the weather, and they know how to cause rain clouds to form. The tenuvi are also heroic figures, and Nuyootecos credit them with defending their community against hostile outsiders. Men such as Santiago Pérez of Yucuhiti, who founded the settlements of Siniuvi and Teponaxtla on the lands of the Esperón family in Yosotichi, are said to have been tenuvi. The tenuvi of opposing communities may duel with one another, in deadly sport. Nuyootecos tell the story of a man from one of the hamlets who suddenly dropped dead one day. Those who rushed to his aid found his body covered with welts. People suspect the man was a tenuvi and died while fighting with other tenuvi. Like the power of the lightning bolt, when the power of the tenuvi is unleashed it has the potential to cause great harm.

Although there are few tenuvi left, people say they continue to play a crucial role in the production of rain. As I noted, Nuyootecos sometimes call them ñɨvɨ savi, "Rain people," and it is their office (tiñu) to work to make the rain fall *(nsikuun savi)*.[3] They do this, one man explained, by "calling" the Rain. They climb four prominent mountain tops *(shini yuku)*, which contain Rain shrines, and smoke seven cigars (figure 24). The cigars smoked by the tenuvi cause clouds to form (clouds are like smoke, people say, because you start with just a bit, and little by little it augments until you have a substantial amount). As the tenuvi smoke one cigar after another, the area circumscribed by the mountains gradually fills with clouds. When the tenuvi become intoxicated by the tobacco, they begin to shout *(kanara)* and call the Rain, just as Nuyootecos shout and call when they become drunk. We hear the booming shouts of the tenuvi as thunder.[4]

The tenuvi, then, are like the other men and women of Nuyoo, but are also set apart. They have "better minds" than others and can do things that normal people cannot do. They are also set apart by their

3. Nuyootecos sometimes call the *tenuvi* "the people of the mountains" *(ñɨvɨ yuku)*, a name that highlights their association with the powerful mountain tops where they make sacrifice, as well as with the sky in general. It also highlights their close association with the sources of prosperity. Nuyootecos say mountains are repositories of water; the caves, or "houses of the Rain," are conduits for the distribution of this water throughout the world. Caves are broadly associated with wealth; in many stories they are described as containing the valuable things in life, such as corn, beans, musical instruments, guns, and even trucks. The tenuvi, as people of the mountain, are mediators of this abundance, able to call it forth for the benefit of Nuyootecos.

4. If their shout comes from the southwest, then the rain will not be long in coming. If it comes from the northeast or southeast, the rain will arrive, but much more slowly.

Figure 24. A tenuvi smoking seven cigars to bring rain. Tobacco grows wild in Nuyoo, and Mixtec people, like other Native American groups, consider it a sacred substance. Nuyootecos use it not only in sacrifice but also to protect themselves from witchcraft and the various *tachi*.

being "Rain people," a human "face" of Rain, and are so closely identified with this sacred force that they can transform themselves into its other manifestations at will. Many say that there is no difference between the *ñu'un savi* and the tenuvi, perhaps because the *ñu'un savi* controls lightning (symbolized by its golden ax), and as we have seen, the tenuvi are lightning. Others, such as the late Lorenzo Rojas, who many people in Nuyoo believe was a tenuvi himself, say that some tenuvi have gone into the *ve'i savi* to live and have become *ñu'un savi*. Certain tenuvi are indeed miraculous figures, and with them, any distinction between the human and the divine is meaningless.[5] But most significantly for our discussion, in being a human "face" of Rain, the tenuvi also serve as bearers of revelation. As I mentioned earlier, it was the tenuvi who first brought (natuvi) men corn to sow, "the daughter of the Rain."

5. In his study of ancient Mixtec ritual and religion Jansen (1982:329–32) noted a similar link between objects of worship, such as sacred bundles, and the ancient kings and queens. He also makes the point that some individuals may carry *ñu'un*, like the man-gods of central Mexico (Jansen 1982:324–25).

Remigio Sarabia as a tenuvi. When people in Nuyoo tell the story of the siege of Huajuapan de León, they say that Remigio Sarabia was able to play the important role he did because he was a tenuvi. They say, for example, that he slipped through the Royalist camp to bring relief for the embattled garrison not because he disguised himself as an animal, but because he *was* an animal (figure 25). Nuyootecos who are familiar with Bustamante's account reason that if Remigio only dressed in sheepskins, as Bustamante wrote, then the Royalist soldiers, one of whom was close enough to kick him, would have easily recognized him as a man. Some go on to say that Remigio Sarabia assumed the form of a variety of animals when he went into the Royalist camp to spy. He even killed a few unsuspecting soldiers, by assuming the form of a chicken and firing a pistol at them, which he hid under his wing. There are also stories in which Remigio Sarabia, who, as a lightning bolt, struck down "100,000 foreigners" who came to invade Mexico.

Some accounts of the Indio de Nuyoo report that he died in later fighting. There is, however, no evidence to support this, and Nuyootecos say that Remigio Sarabia returned to the community after his adventures. (José Remigio Sarabia is recorded as having married in Nuyoo in 1822, and later served as the mayordomo of Santiago.) When he came back to Nuyoo, many say, the community was suffering a terrible drought. Remigio Sarabia was able to save the community because he called the Rain. Some also credit him with "inventing" the rainbow, which he used as a bridge to cross a raging river.

Like the tenuvi, then, Remigio Sarabia was a transformer who had complete and continuous contact with the sacred. (Some people say that the image of Remigio Sarabia on its pedestal is a ndiosi, or "saint," like Misericordia or the ñu'un savi.) this gives the revelations he bears a particular form. Unlike followers of Middle Eastern, monotheistic religions, where prophets are commissioned messengers of God, Nuyootecos never cite a single word he said. Remigio Sarabia is not the mouthpiece for divinely inspired teachings: his revelations are exemplary ones. Like those of the Nuyooteco Jesus—whose interactions with the people of different households created a moral context for the increasingly complex transactions that mediate households—Remigio Sarabia's revelation is embodied in action, which is recorded in the stories of his adventures. Unlike those of Jesus, however, Remigio Sarabia's interactions with Nuyootecos are not the focus of interest—rather, it is his interactions with outsiders.

The central theme in the myths Nuyootecos tell about Remigio Sarabia concern his leaving the community as a young man, to work

Figure 25. Remigio Sarabia creeping through the Royalist lines during the siege at Huajuapan de León. Kitɨ nuvi are always marked in a way that show their human connection. Thus the animal may walk on its hind legs, make human sounds, or, as in this case, have a human-looking face.

for others. Huajuapan de León is distant from Nuyoo, and has long been a center of Spanish settlement. The connection this event has with Nuyootecos' own lives today is no better illustrated than in the skit put on during the celebration in 1991, in which the young migrant declares to the boss that he is a "son" of Remigio Sarabia, who also left the community to work for non-Nuyootecos. Zacarias Sarabia Sarabia, the man who was at the celebration at Huajuapan de León in 1962 with Taji Luis Aguilar, once told me that when he joined the military he was imitating his "grandfather" Remigio, who was also a soldier. Moreover, by leaving the community, Remigio was able to show his worth. Through the trials he faced, he developed into a brave and resourceful young man, which made him a leader after he returned to Nuyoo. When young men and women prepare to go to Mexico City today, they have these same goals in mind. They want to send money back to their relatives (not unlike Remigio, who brought prosperity to the community when he returned, by relieving the drought), but they also want to "gain experience." And the way to show that they have gained experience is to return to the community, assume cargo positions, and vigorously work to improve life in Nuyoo. The men who produced the skit averaged more than eight years' residence in Mexico City, and two of the most recently returned had, along with their wives, begun serving heavy cargos.

The melodramatic scenes in the skit where the young boy is repeatedly abused, robbed, and beaten should be seen in this light. As I noted, people accuse many young migrants of being "cowards" and "running" to Mexico City to avoid serving cargos. For many, this criticism is not off the mark, since it is one of the reasons they migrate. Everyone agrees that the contributions migrants must make in cash to fund community activities are less burdensome than what one loses in time and money in cargo service. In terms of the traditional status hierarchy, then, all migrants are suspect. But by emphasizing how much they suffered—and by drawing a link between their experiences and events in the story of Remigio Sarabia, who returned to serve the community in a way no other could—the men who put on the skit proposed an alternative view of social life that seeks to make their own migration honorable and—because it is formed in terms of an established mandate—traditional.

It may be that other, perhaps competing narratives about Remigio Sarabia will emerge as Nuyootecos find themselves faced with new situations, choices, and opportunities (see below). It may also be that other figures from the Nuyooteco past will be resurrected in order to understand contemporary events. But on a more general level, what we see in their telling the myths and performing the rituals surrounding Remigio Sarabia, is that Nuyootecos are again creating a moral context for newly emerging life careers and patterns of interaction. Instead of marrying, beginning to serve the community in low-ranking cargos, and progressing up "the mountain of tiñu" until, in death, he serves his final cargo, a man may now leave to work away from Nuyoo, where he suffers hardship, gains experience, and then returns to serve, just as Remigio Sarabia did. It is perhaps not too much of a surprise that Nuyootecos named the migrant association they created in Mexico City the "Sociedad de Trabajadores Radicados en México 'Remigio Sarabia.'"

NUYOOTECOS BECOMING MEXICANS

Historically, being Mexican has not been a significant component of Nuyooteco identity. Except for rare individuals such as José López, who fought against the Cristeros in northern Mexico, Nuyootecos have not participated in national movements, and older people are uninformed about what Mexico is, as a political, or even geographical, entity. However, with increasing numbers of young Nuyootecos living away from the region, Mexico has taken on a social, political, and territorial reality that it did not have for older generations. What Remigio Sarabia has allowed these migrants to do is to assert that they are a part of this broader, national community. As I noted earlier, Remigio Sarabia is the same kind of hero that Morelos, Hidalgo, or even Juárez is: a warrior, who fought against foreign invaders to establish or preserve Mexican sovereignty, and who sought no personal reward for his service. As one of these typifications Remigio Sarabia thus connects Nuyootecos both to other Mexicans and to the institutions that closely linked to these heroes—the school system, the government bureaucracy, and the official party.

Although the figure of Remigio Sarabia can be seen as part of an effort to define Nuyoo in terms of national images of the social order, it must be pointed out that Nuyootecos do not speak of Remigio Sarabia as an outsider or as something that outsiders forced upon them. Rather, by winning the battle for independence from Spain, Remigio Sarabia showed that Nuyootecos were essential to the creation of Mexico—just as their birth from Soko Usha made the sharing of blood and milk essential to being Nuyooteco. This is evident in the part of the skit where the owner of the business asks the boy for documents issued by the government affirming and legitimating his status. Since the 1960s, explosive population growth in Mexico City and a relatively low level of job creation has made it more difficult for migrants to find good positions (Hirabayashi 1993:34). Partly because of this excess supply of unskilled and semiskilled labor, the documents verifying the amount of one's schooling have become crucial for job placement, in what Stern called "credentialism" (Stern 1982; see also Hirabayashi 1993). Nuyootecos have always found this to be an irrelevant and somewhat offensive requirement. It is for this reason the boy in the skit replies, in effect, that because he is a "son" of Remigio Sarabia he does not need credentials—he is a good worker and as legitimate a citizen as the owner.

The development of a national identity—in which Nuyootecos see themselves as Mexicans—involved not just Mexico coming into Nuyoo, but also the extension of the boundaries of Nuyoo to embrace all of Mexico. Traditionally, the tenuvi were highly local figures, often depicted as defending the town against outsiders. Remigio Sarabia is like these other tenuvi, but the boundaries he defends are much broader. This can also be seen in different versions Nuyootecos tell of the Remigio Sarabia story, in which those laying siege to Huajuapan de León become not Spaniards, but French and North Americans — all those who have threatened Mexican sovereignty. Another point to note in the Remigio Sarabia story is that in it Nuyootecos become active subjects of history, not the "Indios" to whom history happens. This is clear in the way that Remigio Sarabia, while fighting alongside other Mexicans to create Mexico, does not lose his identity as a Nuyooteco. He remained the Indio de Nuyoo even though he did many things that are not traditionally associated with being "Indian": fighting in the military, speaking Spanish, traveling about the country, and outwitting Spaniards and other educated people. Moreover, his identity as an Indian, rather than being an impediment, was essential to the things he accomplished. After all, if he were not a tenuvi, he would not have been able to get the message to Morelos. In the same way, the migrants do not stop being "Indios" or lose their identity as Nuyootecos once they go to Mexico City. Being Nuyooteco is in fact crucial to their surviving in the city. When one first arrives in Mexico, one goes to other Nuyootecos already living there, who will help in the search for housing and employment. It is through Nuyoo migrant associations that one can get loans and other support, and Nuyootecos spend much of their free time together in the city.

Finally, Remigio Sarabia is a model for the kind of contingent and contextually sensitive identities that Nuyootecos are developing in order to function in the complex and shifting settings outside the village. As a "transformer," Remigio is able to creatively use multiple versions of himself to make his way in the world, just as Nuyootecos who live in Mexico City are able to blend in with the Sunday crowds at the Pino Suárez metro station while on their way to a baptismal celebration, to "eat from the same tortilla" with other ta'a.

SUMMARY
AND CONCLUSION

FOR decades, much of the ethnographic research carried out in Mesoamerica was premised on the idea that indigenous people live in communities with a particular structural form and that there exists a causal link between indigenous identity and this structure. While widespread migration, the growth of refugee populations, and the emergence of new social and ethnic movements have demonstrated the limitations of this view of indigenous ethnicity—people often remain ethnically "Indian" despite the disappearance of a particular type of community organization—it is not only events that have overtaken the model. Alan Sandstrom—whose work is based on research in a Nahuatl-speaking area where people are "traditional" but seem to lack the easily recognized social boundaries that one finds in other places in Mesoamerica—finds that it is an area where people "do not view the village as a coherent community toward which they owe a great deal of loyalty" (Sandstrom 1991:104). His observation suggests that we should question earlier notions of community and identity, and even the idea that we can begin our work by assuming the existence of bounded social groups (Wagner 1974). With this in mind, I suggested that we approach Santiago Nuyoo not by assuming a preexisting structure, but by examining local articulations of how groups form and accomplish goals.

I started with the household and, instead of viewing it as the indivisible building block of social life, I simply asked Nuyootecos to define what a household is. One thing I discovered is that when they speak about the household, they do not usually do so in terms of its "morphology" or how its members are genealogically connected, the way we might (Ravicz 1965:128; Wilk and Netting 1984:2–6). Rather, people define it in terms of generalizable practices, as when they say the people of a household "feed one another" or "clothe one another." These practices are, in turn, related to the ritual acts of feeding and clothing others through which the household is formed and new

356

personnel are brought into it, so that the continuity of households—indeed all groups—is contingent upon a process that organically unfolds from the acts that first create them.

This perspective, however, does not negate the long-standing structural observation that a major concern for people living in places like Nuyoo is how different households relate to one another. From what I observed, and what Nuyootecos told me, the members of different households create and maintain relationships through the transfer of children in baptism and marriage and through the exchange of gifts in fiestas. These transactions must also be viewed in terms of Nuyooteco sociality, since the items that circulate in baptism, marriage, and gift exchange—which end up as food in one's belly and clothes on one's back—are central to the experience of these relationships, so that they come to be more than tokens of something that already exists; in fact, they constitute it in an intensely physical way.

I also found that when Nuyootecos spoke about baptism, marriage, and gift exchange, they would relate these practices to things like rainfall, the origins of corn, the ritual procession of certain saints, or even the journey of the dead to the afterlife. This was significant because it suggested that we have to move beyond the analytic dualisms that come so easily to us, if we are to understand Nuyooteco sociality. Like the sharp line we draw between ritual and moral action, or between affective states and social bonds, the Nuyooteco notion of community would be distorted if we viewed their myths and ritual processions as simply reflective of marriage and baptism. Instead we have to begin with the Nuyooteco proposition that everything is imbued with life, and life has different manifestations, or "faces." These are existential (hot life and cold death, nurturing womb and generative sperm) but may also be gods (Jesus and Tachi, *nu ñu'un* and *ñu'un savi*), natural forces (heat and wind, earth and rain), cosmological divisions (sun and the sea, earth and sky), places (churches and rocky cliffs, lush fields and caves), social categories (visitors and mestizo merchants, females and males), and social processes (mediation and isolation, complementarity and synthesis). The homologies that exist among marriage, the ritual procession of saints, and the growth of corn thus result from their being informed by these broader ideas about life, about how value is created, and about how relationships are maintained. In the specific instance of baptism, marriage, gift exchange, and the processions of the Jesus saints, this involves the vitalization and articulation of diverse entities through the circulation of what Nuyootecos call yɨɨ, a term I translated as "the heat of life."

It is important to realize that the transmission of "the heat of life" from one household to another—in the form of food, items, and persons—does not organize households either corporately, or exclusively, even if it is crucial to social mediation. Decisions about the creation and maintenance of these relationships are made individually, by each household involved, and the values generated, such as the replacement of personnel, are specific to individual households, so that even through these relationships overlap to a high degree, they also extend beyond Nuyoo to include people who are not Nuyootecos.[1] What seems to me to be most significant in defining Nuyootecos as unique and organizing them corporately is the idea that Nuyootecos are "kin" with one another and care for one another in a way that is similar to the way household members care for one another. This vision Nuyootecos have of themselves involves the notion that they share substance with one another, which distinguishes them from all other people and links them to a specific territory. We saw how the acts of sacrifice, cargo service, intermarriage, and fiesta distributions combine to articulate this vision Nuyootecos have of themselves as kin, living in the same household. Like baptism or gift exchange, these acts are related as elements in a broader process through which value is created and relationships are established. But instead of a process of mediation, through which diverse entities are related by the circulation of the things that renew them, this is a process of incorporation, the end of which is not the organization of differences, but their collapse, and the image of synthesis is the house itself, so that the Nuyootecos come to form a "great house."

What the Nuyooteco community is then, is a conjunction of usages out of which arise distinct images of social life. Again, it was important to view these usages not as expressing a prior social reality ("community"), but as constituting and maintaining that reality. Otherwise we might not have realized that sacrifice is a ritual that, like compadrazgo, creates kin-like ties between persons, but seen it merely as expressive of community solidarity, or that fiesta distribu-

1. In 1985, when some households in the hamlet of Ndyonoyuji, Atatlahuca, began to send their children to the secondary school in Nuyoo Center (where they lived with selected Nuyooteco families), Nuyootecos extended the annual circuit of Misericordia to the households of Ndyonoyuji. In other words, if the ritual circulation of Misericordia reaffirms the moral order created by Jesus in the ancient past, where households are bound to one another by reciprocity, alliance, and the circulation of items that bring prosperity and renewal, then the people of Ndyonoyuji, who sent their children to live with Nuyootecos, also participate in this circulation, and it is appropriate that Misericordia visit them.

tions are more than an entailment of social structure (i.e., a leveling mechanism) but are in fact integral to the Nuyooteco making of themselves into a "great house." And, as I pointed out, these usages, or forms of sociation, are not necessarily merged into some kind of overarching unity; nor are they bound into neat periods, where one is switched on and the other switched off, as Gearing and others have suggested. In Nuyoo they often co-occur, and their opposed moralities make life in Nuyoo contradictory and sometimes alienating. At the same time however, it is out of these usages that Nuyootecos maintain visions of themselves that remain distinct from—but not unconnected to—broader social and political formations. When contrasting life in Nuyoo from life in other places, Nuyootecos often say things like "here no one will ever starve"—implying that no matter how desperate one's situation, one can depend on one's ta'a to share food.

In the final part of the book, I examined the way people in Nuyoo attempt to create and maintain relationships with one another in the face of economic, social, and political contingencies that bring possibilities for both change and continuity. Social conventions, rituals, traditions—in short, a culture—do not exist outside of history like some natural species. Rather culture is part of events; it is both constituted by them and constituting of them. Although I discussed such things as population growth, the introduction of new cash crops, and intercommunity warfare, my focus was on a subject that anthropologists and historians have long seen as crucial to group formation in Mesoamerica—the control of property. Beginning with the first half of the nineteenth century, I showed that as corporate lands were privatized, as the communal cattle herd disappeared, and as the value of the cash held in communal accounts eroded, Nuyootecos sought other sources of funds for financing the fiesta system and the municipal government. Since many of what were previously corporate assets ended up in the hands of individual Nuyooteco households, it was logical that the burden of financing collective activities should also be shifted to households, through a system of tithing and through heavier service requirements imposed on household members through the civil-religious hierarchy. This process served to aggravate and extend a central contradiction within Nuyoo, since in civil-religious hierarchy service the "great house" is articulated at the expense of household independence.

I do not mean to suggest by this that Nuyooteco sociality is causally linked to a particular property-holding regime so that, as land privatization proceeds, the notion that Nuyootecos form of "great house" will necessarily disappear. Rather, the erosion of corporate property is something that takes place through Nuyooteco sociality. In other words, established forms of Nuyooteco sociality are crucial to the way things change. This can be seen in several ways. First, Nuyooteco "forms of being with and for one another" are, to paraphrase William Rosberry, part of the life conditions into which individuals are born, so that as circumstances change, they will themselves be part of the way even the most interested actors view these new circumstances. Limits are thus placed on the kinds of activities that can be developed. But while one might view this in Durkheimian terms as constraining, it is also "enabling" (Giddens 1984:169–74; see also Sahlins 1981), something I tried to show by emphasizing that, since at least the early nineteenth century, Nuyoo history can be viewed as involving a reweighting and recombination of different forms of sociality already in place. For example, it does not seem to have occurred to people — in a very forceful way — that a solution to the problem of sponsoring fiestas is to put a halt to feasting altogether.

It is this self-evident relevance — the fact that Nuyooteco sociality is a product of prior activity and thought — that lies behind the security people have in their own destiny. As I noted, Nuyootecos are acutely aware of changes in their lives, but I never heard anyone express the kind of pessimism or fear about the future that one often reads in social scientific reports on rural communities in Mexico. This is not to say that such dire predictions are unwarranted, but it does say something about limits on the imaginations of both sides.

The second way I see Nuyooteco sociality as having an active historical role is that within it there is the potential for creating a new way of life. As we saw, major turns in Nuyooteco history coincide with the arrival of holy figures, resulting in the institution of new technologies, social categories, and moral codes. Unlike prophets in the Judeo-Christian tradition, the revelatory figure is not a divine mouthpiece who pronounces changes to which all must adhere, but instead functions as an exemplar, introducing change through paradigmatic action — something that is consistent with other aspects of Nuyooteco cosmology. This action, moreover, involves interaction with human beings, so that revelation connects events to the sacred and moral order through being, itself, a form of sociation — a way of "being with and for one another" that involves the gods as well as purely human actors. In the case of Misericordia's appearance in 1873, the myths associated with the saint, and its circulation from household to household in an annual ritual, had a number of effects: it located moral action within a framework of independent households, it gave a sacred origin to mediating ties of reciprocity and alliance, it defined these ties as necessary for the survival of individual households, and it perhaps established the pattern for the individual tithing of households that is used for financing collective activities today. Misericordia's appearance was thus crucial to social, political, and economic innovation and signaled an attempt by Nuyootecos to create relationships with one another that were in line with the changing material circumstances of their lives. Activities that were formerly corporate responsibilities were shifted to the household. The use of gift exchange and the expanded role of the household in public activities in turn led to an emphasis on shared consumption in the articulation of the "great house." And it was only after Misericordia appeared that Nuyootecos went ahead with their plans to build an elaborate church. This required that they sell the communal cattle herd and drain the mayordomo treasury. In other words, if not for the appearance of Misericordia, corporate assets would not have been reduced to the extent that they were in the nineteenth century, with the implications this had for household accumulation of wealth. Revelation — the cultural form through which Nuyootecos seek meaning in new circumstances — is thus an abiding resource people draw upon in order to change.

But exchange, sacrifice, and revelation can play such crucial roles in local social dynamics only because individual concerns and purposes crystallize through them. I illustrated this by examining the motivations of those who promoted the cult of Misericordia and the way the saint gave certain men the opportunity to expand their economic and political influence. But I also showed their motivations to be complex, since they used the saint to challenge their rival, Yucuhiti. In Remigio Sarabia, we had a contemporary example of the diversity of interests and motivations that arise and play out against one another in revelatory events, since the figure of Remigio Sarabia objectified the interests of not only a cacique-broker but also young men wishing to alter traditional cargo careers and migrants developing an heroic ethnic identity. The different groups involved in the Remigio Sarabia phenomenon, with their overlapping (and even opposed) concerns, show how the meaning of these revelations is in part a product of negotiation and, at times, contestation.

Again, it is true that these developments are related to economic and political forces that have their origin outside Nuyoo. Also, the power of Misericordia and, later, Remigio Sarabia to authorize change lies in the way they embody legitimating discourses that function on national and even international levels. Misericordia appeared at a time when religious icons played an important part in national political struggles, and some legends about Remigio Sarabia, as we saw, are clearly based on those of Mexican patriotic heroes of the type championed by the official party. Those who promoted Misericordia, and later Remigio Sarabia, were concerned with how they, as individuals, and Nuyoo, as a collectivity, are part of a broader world. Yet at the same time, the power of these figures is highly local, one materializing on the steps of the Nuyoo church, and the other being a Mixtec shaman-sacrificer, with the ability to assume a variety of animal and celestial forms and reveal new knowledge. In inventing a life for themselves that allows them as individuals, and Nuyoo as a collectivity, to exist in newly emerging orders, those organizing and establishing the import of the cults of Misericordia and Remigio Sarabia drew upon local themes and thus preserved their uniqueness, even as they appropriated moral discourses, rituals, and images that have their origins far from Nuyoo.

Saying that Nuyootecos used Misericordia or Remigio Sarabia to "reinvent" themselves should not be taken to mean that these were unique occurrences. On the contrary, there have been many miraculous appearances in Nuyoo, and each seems to have been a time of great creativity. Both the coming of Misericordia and the actions of Remigio Sarabia form part of a long series of revelations which, while not homogeneous in their form or content, are traced by Nuyootecos back to the origins of social life. What seems to be at issue in these revelations is not so much salvation, in the sense of a absolute fulfillment of human needs, but a more limited relief from drought, starvation, infertility, factionalism, or outside threat. Nor do they mark the path to some sort of utopia, but rather, a qualified adjustment of social life to a dynamic sacred. The impetus for this periodic harmonizing comes, in the Nuyootecos' view, from the gods, but it nevertheless occurs with the active participation of human beings.

Finally, it bears repeating that Nuyootecos have never seen themselves as static, and so to say that they periodically reinvent themselves through revelation should not be taken to mean that this involves a process of self-delusion, the simple baptizing of new social patterns as hoary tradition: Nuyootecos freely comment on how institutions have changed over their lifetimes. The proposition that social life has its origins in human interactions with the sacred (where relationships are tied to broader processes of prosperity, renewal, and death) appears to have substantial continuity, yet in revelation tradition is reaffirmed not by ignoring change but by highlighting what is most true about it, thereby unlocking its potentialities. If I understand him correctly, this is that Victor Turner said about Ndembu revelation: that "it asserts the fundamental power and health of society grasped integrally" (Turner 1975:16) And the potentialities of Remigio Sarabia continue to expand, as the first Nuyootecos cross the border into the United States, just as Remigio slipped unnoticed through the Royalist lines at Huajuapan de León. This brings me back to my first day in Nuyoo, and my own association with Remigio Sarabia.

I wasn't in Nuyoo for more than four hours before I was told about Remigio Sarabia. This occurred after the town president arrived at the municipal hall, where the eonomist left me off after the journey from Tlaxiaco. I presented the president with the letters of introduction kindly given me by María de la Luz Topete, the head of the National Anthropology and History Institute's Regional Center in Oaxaca, and Enrique Valencia of the National Indigenous Institute. The president put the letters in his pocket (without bothering to open them) and asked me if I would like to try some aguardiente, a distilled liquor made from sugar cane. I accepted his invitation, feeling good that people were so friendly and remembering the advice I had received from Barbro Dahlgren, a professor at the National Autonomous University of Mexico, to go have a drink in public when I arrived, so that people could see I wasn't an evangelical missionary. Little did I know that the invitation to drink was one Nuyooteco authorities extended to all outsiders, to loosen their tongues and get them to admit what they had really come to Nuyoo to do. Those concerned with cataloging everyday forms of resistance will be interested to know a special fund even exists to pay for the costs of drinks!

To get the aguardiente, the president led me across the sloping, grassy plaza where the Sunday market is held to the patio of the house of Don Carlos, who ladled out shots of the liquor from a large drum. As we drank the aguardiente — which was probably only made a few days before, and had quite a kick to it — I began to speak of my interest in learning the Mixtec language and doing research on Mixtec history. It was then that several men, who had come to the patio to hear what I had to say, told me of Remigio Sarabia. It would be a great help, they explained, if I could find something that showed he really existed, so that they could prove to people in rival communities that Nuyootecos did not make him up for their own self-glorification.

At first I believed that the "historical" basis of the Remigio Sarabia story would be exceedingly difficult to confirm, and originally the whole phenomenon (like so much else I ended up writing about) seemed peripheral to my research. However, people kept asking if I had found anything and telling me how important it was to them. Then one day, as I was in Tlaxiaco waiting for a truck to take me to the dirt road that led to Nuyoo, I spoke with one of Tlaxiaco's parish priests, who mentioned that the church contained a number of baptismal books that appeared to him to be quite old (these are described in Romero Frizzi 1979). I asked to see them and found that some covered the region of Nuyoo and Yucuhiti. Over the next six months, I spent several days reading through the books, since they contained information on migration, birth rates, and other topics. I also hoped that something might be affirming the identity of the Indio de Nuyoo. Then I came to an entry that read, "José Remigio, son of Bernardo Sarabia and María Rojas, baptized on September 2, 1798, one day after having been born."[2] This was proof that a Remigio Sarabia could have been alive during the War of Independence and confirmed what people had told me that day when I was drinking aguardiente.

I returned to Nuyoo, mentioned what I had found to several families in the town center, and then continued with my research. A short time later, the president, Zacarias Sarabia Sarabia, the retired soldier who was at the 1962 celebration in Huajuapan de León, came to my room, along with the head of the local school district and Taji Luis Aguilar. I had never had a visit from people of importance, and it pleased me when they asked how my work was coming. Then they asked if it was true that I had found the documents that proved Remigio Sarabia existed. I told them about the entry in the baptismal book, and the president asked that I accompany them the next day to Tlaxiaco, to show them where it was. I, of course, agreed, and upon our arrival we went straight to the parish archives, where I pulled out the book and showed them the notice. A priest kindly allowed us to take the book to a nearby stationary store so we could photocopy it, and once we finished, Taji Luis turned and said, "Now this should be reported, so that everyone knows that Remigio Sarabia did, and that he was a real hero." The schoolteacher thought of the local radio station, run by the National Indigenous Institute. We went to the station office and spoke to the director, who arranged for an interview in which the four of us reported on the achievements of Remigio

2. APT, Libro de Bautismo de Nuyoo, Yucuhiti y Yosotato, 1772–1803.

Sarabia and the discovery of the baptismal notice. This interview was broadcast on the 173rd anniversary of the lifting of the siege of Huajuapan de León.

After news about our trip to Tlaxiaco began to circulate, and the radio program aired, my position changed dramatically. People in towns like Nuyoo are often suspicious of outsiders. Yet suddenly, everyone, even people I had not met before, knew my name. Town authorities began to solicit my opinion at public gatherings, as if I had proven to them that I was competent at what I do and might have other things of value to contribute. Casual acquaintances also invited me into their houses and introduced me to several older men and women, some of whom were storytellers, who offered to help me with my research. People volunteered to show me their personal land titles and other family documents, and the authorities opened the local archives to me. Not long after this, I began to notice that the story of how I found Remigio Sarabia's birth certificate began to take on heroic aspects, despite my attempts to downplay what had happened. By 1991 my name had been mentioned in many of the oral histories told about the "Indio de Nuyoo."

This, of course, sounds like one those apocryphal "how I was accepted by the natives" stories, and initially it embarrassed me, since the gratitude Nuyootecos expressed was totally out of proportion to the effort I expended on finding the baptismal notice, and they seemed to be playing the part of the humble *inditos* all too well. Lately, however, my association with the Indio de Nuyoo has not bothered me as much. My attitude began to change after I got off the phone one Saturday afternoon with a man from Nuyoo who had made it to Texas and needed some money to pay for a bus ticket north. My wife commented that, since the first young Nuyootecos arrived to work in the United States in 1987, I had become a combination travel agent, lawyer, and banker for people from the town, giving advice, making loans, carrying money back to Nuyoo, tracking down job information, and putting them up whenever they were in our area. I usually get a call every couple of weeks or so, and often it is from people who are doing nothing more than checking in, asking how my family is, and advising us they are here. There are now well over a dozen Nuyooteco men in the United States, and clearly, for this small group of people, I am part of what the United States is. As one of them recently told me, just as I was completing this manuscript, I am the only "gringo" he has had a conversation with, despite being in the United States for almost a year. (He then asked me if I could send him my notes on Remigio Sarabia's biography.) If Remigio Sarabia is a vehicle through which Nuyootecos are defining their relationships with the broader world of which they are a part, then given the role labor migration to the United States is going to play in their future, I guess it is not wholly inappropriate that I be part of the Nuyooteco discovery of their hero, and that he define my relationship with them.

BIBLIOGRAPHY

Acuña, René. 1984. *Relaciones geográficas del siglo XVI: Antequera*. Mexico: Universidad Nacional Autónoma de México.

Aguirre Beltrán, Gonzalo. 1967. *Regiones de refugio: el desarrollo de la comunidad y el proceso dominical en Mestizoamérica*. México: Instituto Nacional Indigenista

Alexander, Ruth M. 1980. *Gramática mixteca de Atatlahuca*. Mexico City: Instituto Lingüístico de Verano.

Alvarado, Francisco de. 1962 (1593). *Vocabulario en lengua Mixteca*. Mexico: Instituto Nacional Indigenista e Instituto Nacional de Antropología e Historia.

Appadurai, Arjun. 1986. "Introduction: Commodities and the Politics of Value." In Arjun Appadurai, ed., *The Social Life of Things*, pp 3–63. Cambridge: Cambridge University Press.

Apuntes Topográficos. 1871. "Apuntes Topográficos del Distrito de Tlaxiaco, del Estado de Oaxaca." *Boletin de la Sociedad Mexicana de Geografía y Estadística* 3:238–54.

Arana Osnaya, Evangelina, and Mauricio Swadesh. 1965. *Los elementos del mixteco antiguo*. Mexico: Instituto Nacional Indigenista e Instituto Nacional de Antropología e Historia.

Arzipe, Lourdes. 1973. *Parentesco y economía en una sociedad nahua: Nican Pehwa Zacatipan*. Mexico: Instituto Nacional Indigenista.

———. 1988. "Anthropology in Latin America: Old Boundaries, New Contexts." In Christopher Mitchell, ed., *Changing Perspectives in Latin American Studies*, pp. 143–61. Stanford: Stanford University Press.

Bakhtin, Mikhail. 1984 (1929). *Problems of Dostoevsky's Poetics*. Edited and translated by Caryl Emerson. Minneapolis: University of Minnesota Press.

Beals, Ralph. 1970. "Gifting, Reciprocity, Savings and Credit in Peasant Oaxaca." *Southwestern Journal of Anthropology* 26:231–41.

Berry, Charles. 1981. *The Reform in Oaxaca, 1856–1876: A Microhistory of the Liberal Revolution*. Lincoln: University of Nebraska Press.

Blaffer, Sarah L. 1972. *The Black-Man of Zinacantan: A Central American Legend*. Austin: University of Texas Press.

Bloch, Maurice. 1980. "Ritual Symbolism and the Nonrepresentation of Society." In Mary Foster and Stanley H. Brandes, eds., *Symbol as Sense*, pp. 93–102. New York: Academic Press.

————. 1983. *Marxism and Anthropology: The History of a Relationship.* Oxford: Oxford University Press.

Bloch, Maurice, and Jonathan Parry. 1989. "Introduction: Money and the Morality of Exchange." In J. Parry and M. Bloch, eds., *Money and the Morality of Exchange*, pp. 1–32. Cambridge: Cambridge University Press.

Blom, Franz, and Oliver La Farge. 1926–27. *Tribes and Temples.* New Orleans: Tulane University, Middle American Research Institute.

Bourdieu, Pierre. 1977. *Outline of a Theory of Practice.* Cambridge: Cambridge University Press.

Bricker, Victoria. 1981. *The Indian Christ, the Indian King: The Historical Substrate of Maya Myth and Ritual.* Austin: University of Texas Press.

Burgoa, Francisco de. 1989 (1674). *Geográfica descripción.* Mexico: Editorial Porrúa.

Burkhart, Louise. 1989. *The Slippery Earth: Nahua-Christian Moral Dialogue in Sixteenth-Century Mexico.* Tucson: University of Arizona Press.

Bustamante, Carlos María de. 1961 (1844). *Cuadro Histórico de la Revolución Mexicana.* Mexico: La Comisión Nacional para la Celebración del Sesquicentenario de la Proclamación de la Independencia Nacional y del Cincuentenario de la Revolución Mexicana.

Butterworth, Douglas. 1975. *Tilantongo: Comunidad mixteca en transicion.* Mexico City: Instituto Nacional Indigenista.

Cámara, Fernando. 1952. "Religious and Political Organization." In Sol Tax, ed., *Heritage and Conquest*, pp. 142–64. Glencoe: The Free Press.

Campbell, Howard. 1990. "Juchitán: The Politics of Cultural Revivalism in an Isthmus Zapotec Community." *The Latin American Anthropology Review* 2:47–55.

Campbell, Sara Stark, Andrea Johnson Peterson, Filiberto Lorenzo Cruz, Catalina López de García, and Daniel Fidencio García Alvarez. 1986. *Diccionario mixteco de San Juan Colorado.* Mexico: Instituto Linguístico de Verano.

Cancian, Frank. 1965. *Economics and Prestige in a Maya Community.* Stanford: Stanford University Press.

————. 1967. "Political and Religious Organizations." In Manning Nash, ed., *Handbook of Middle American Indians*, vol. 6, pp. 283–98. Austin: University of Texas Press.

Carmagnani, Marcello. 1988. *El regreso de los dioses: El proceso de reconstitución de la identidad étnica en Oaxaca.* Mexico: Fondo de Cultura Económica.

Carrasco, Pedro. 1963. "The Civil-Religious Hierarchy in Mesoamerica: Pre-Spanish Background and Colonial Development." *American Anthropologist* 63:483–7.

Carriedo, Juan P. 1949 (1842). *Estudios históricos y estadísticos del estado Oaxaqueña.* México: Biblioteca de Autores y de Asuntos Oaxaqueños.

Chambers, Erve J., and Philip D. Young. 1979. "Mesoamerican Community Studies: The Past Decade." *Annual Review of Anthropology* 8:45–69.

Chamoux, Marie-Noelle. 1987 (1981). *Nahuas de Huachinango: Transformaciones sociales en una comunidad campesina.* Mexico: Instituto Nacional Indigenista.

Chance, John. 1989. *Conquest of the Sierra: Spaniards and Indians in Colonial Oaxaca.* Norman: University of Oklahoma Press.

Chance, John, and William B. Taylor. 1985. "Cofradias and Cargos: An Historical Perspective on the Mesoamerican Civil-Religious Hierarchy." *American Ethnologist* 12:1–26.

Chassen, Francie R. 1986. "Oaxaca: Del porfiriato a la revolución, 1902–1911." Ph.D. diss., Universidad Nacional Autónoma de Mexico.

Cook, Scott. 1982. *The Zapotec Stoneworkers: The Dynamics of Rural Simple Commodity Production in Modern Mexican Capitalism.* Washington: University Press of America.

Cook, Sherburne, and Woodrow Borah. 1968. *The Population of the Mixteca Alta, 1520–1960.* Ibero Americana, no. 50. Berkeley and Los Angeles: University of California Press.

Dahlgren de Jordón, Barbro. 1954. *La Mixteca: su cultura e historia pre-hispánica.* México: Cultura Mexicana.

Daly, John, and Margarita Holland de Daly. 1977. *Mixteco de Santa María Peñoles.* México: Centro de Investigación para la Integración Social.

Dennis, Philip A. 1987. *Inter-Village Conflict in Oaxaca.* New Brunswick: Rutgers University Press.

Diskin, Martin. 1986. "La economía de la comunidad étnica en Oaxaca." In Alicia Barabas and Miguel Bartolomé, eds., *Etnicidad y pluralismo cultural: la dinámica étnica en Oaxaca,* pp. 257–97. Mexico: Instituto Nacional de Antropología e Historia.

Dow, James. 1973a. "On the Muddled Concept of Corporation in Anthropology." *American Anthropologist* 75:904–8.

———. 1973b. "Saints and Survival: The Function of Religion in a Central American Indian Society." Ph.D. diss., Brandeis University, Department of Anthropology.

———. 1975. *Santos y supervivencias: funciones de la religión en una comunidad otomí, México.* México: Instituto Nacional Indigenista.

———. 1977. "Religion in the Organization of a Mexican Peasant Economy." In Rhoda Halperin and James Dow, eds., *Peasant Livelihood,* pp. 215–56. New York: St. Martin's Press.

———. 1986. *The Shaman's Touch: Otomí Indian Symbolic Healing.* Salt Lake City: University of Utah Press.

Durán, Diego. 1964. *The Aztecs; The History of the Indies of New Spain.* Translated by Doris Heyden and Fernando Horcasitas. New York: Orion Press.

———. 1977. *Book of the Gods and Rites of the Ancient Calendar.* Edited and translated by Fernando Horcasitas and Doris Heyden. Norman: University of Oklahoma Press.

Durkheim, Emile. 1960 (1914). "The Dualism of Human Nature and its Social Conditions." In Kurt Wolf, ed., *Essays on Sociology and Philosophy,* pp. 325–40. New York: Harper and Row.

Dyk, Anne, and Betty Stoudt. 1973. *Vocabulario mixteco.* Mexico: Instituto Linguistico de Verano.

Falla, Ricardo. 1969. "Análisis horizontal del sistema de cargos." *América Indígena* 29:923–47.

Fardon, Richard. 1985. "Sociability and Secrecy: Two Problems of Chamba Knowledge." In Richard Fardon, ed., *Power and Knowledge: Anthropological and Sociological Approaches,* pp. 127–50. Edinburgh: Scottish Academic Press.

Farriss, Nancy. 1984. *Maya Society Under Colonial Rule: The Collective Enterprise of Survival*. Princeton: Princeton University Press.

Flanet, Veronique. 1977. *Viviré si Dios quiere, un estudio de la violencia de la Mixteca de la Costa*. México: Instituto Nacional Indigenista.

Fortes, Meyer. 1953. The Structure of Unilineal Descent Groups. *American Anthropologist* 55:17–41.

Foster, George. 1967. *Tzintzuntzan: Mexican Peasants in a Changing World*. New York: Little, Brown and Company.

———. 1972. "The Anatomy of Envy: A Study in Symbolic Behavior." *Current Anthropology* 13:165–86.

Foster, Morris. 1991. *Becoming Commanche: A Social History of an American Indian Community*. Tucson: University of Arizona Press.

Foster, Robert J. 1986. "Exchange and Replacement in Tangan Mortuary Feasts." Paper presented at the 85th meeting of the American Anthropological Association, Philadelphia.

Fox, John W. 1987. *Maya Postclassic State Formation: Segmentary Lineage Migration in Advancing Frontiers*. Cambridge: Cambridge University Press.

Frisby, David. 1990. "George Simmel's Concept of Society." In Michael Karen, Bernard Phillips, and Robert Cohen, eds., *George Simmel and Contemporary Sociology*, pp. 39–55. Dordrecht, The Netherlands: Kluwer Academic Publishers.

Furst, Jill L. 1978. *Codex Vindobonensis Mexicanus I: A Commentary*. Albany: State University of New York, Albany, Institute for Mesoamerican Studies.

Galinier, Jacques. 1987. *Pueblos de la Sierra Madre: Etnografía de la comunidad otomí*. México: Instituto Nacional Indigenista.

García, Gregorio. 1981 (1607). *Origen de los indios del Nuevo Mundo* [Facsimile of the 1729 edition]. Mexico: Fondo de Cultura Económica.

Gay, José Antonio. 1950 (1881). *Historia de Oaxaca*. Mexico: Biblioteca de Autores y de Asuntos Oaxaqueños.

Gearing, Fred. 1958. The Structural Poses of Eighteenth-Century Cherokee Villages. *American Anthropologist* 60:1148–56.

Gibson, Thomas. 1985. The Sharing of Substance versus the Sharing of Activity among the Build. *Man* 20:391–411.

Giddens, Anthony. 1984. *The Constitution of Society: Introduction to the Theory of Structuration*. Berkeley: University of California Press.

Good, Catherine. 1988. *Haciendo la lucha: Arte, y comercio nahuas de Guerrero*. Mexico: Fondo de Cultura Económica.

Gose, Peter. 1986. "Sacrifice and Commodity in the Andes." *Man* 21:296–310.

———. 1991. "House Rethatching in an Andean Annual Cycle: Practice, Meaning and Contradiction." *American Ethnologist* 18:39–66.

Gosner, Kevin. 1992. *Soldiers of the Virgin: The Moral Economy of a Colonial Maya Rebellion*. Tucson: University of Arizona Press.

Gossen, Gary. 1972. "Temporal and Spatial Equivalents in Chamula Ritual Symbolism." In William Lessa and Evon Z. Vogt, eds., *Reader in Comparative Religion*, pp. 135–49. New York: Harper and Row.

————. 1974. *Chamulas in the World of the Sun: Time and Space in a Maya Oral Tradition.* Cambridge: Harvard University Press.

————. 1982. "Review of *The Symbolism of Subordination.*" *Ethnohistory* 29:227–30.

Greenberg, James B. 1981. *Santiago's Sword: Chatino Peasant Religion and Economics.* Berkeley: University of California Press.

————. 1989. *Blood Ties: Life and Violence in Rural Mexico.* Tucson: University of Arizona Press.

Gregory, Chris A. 1980. "Gifts to Men and Gifts to God: Exchange and Capital Accumulation in Contemporary Papua." *Man* 15:626–52.

————. 1981. "A Conceptual Analysis of a Non-Capitalist Gift Economy with Particular Reference to Papua New Guinea." *Cambridge Journal of Economics* 5:119–35.

————. 1982. *Gifts and Commodities.* London: Academic Press.

Grey, John N. 1987. "Bayu Utarnu: Ghost Exorcism and Sacrifice in Nepal." *Ethnology* 26:179–99.

Gruzinski, Serge. 1989. *Man-Gods in the Mexican Highlands.* Translated by Eileen Corrigan. Stanford: Stanford University Press.

Gudeman, Stephen. 1972. "The *Compadrazgo* as a Reflection of the Natural and Spiritual Person." In *Proceedings of the Royal Anthropological Institute of Great Britain and Ireland for 1971*, pp. 45–71. London: Royal Anthropological Institute.

————. 1976. "Saints, Symbols and Ceremonies." *American Ethnologist* 3:709–29.

Gwaltney, John. 1970. *The Thrice Shy: Cultural Accommodation to Blindness and other Disasters in a Mexican Community.* New York: Columbia University Press.

Handy, Jim. 1991. "Anxiety and Dread: State and Community in Modern Guatemala." *Canadian Journal of History* 26:43–65.

Harris, Olivia. 1981. "Households as Natural Units." In Kate Young, Carol Wolkowitz, and Roslyn McCullagh, eds., *Of Marriage and the Market*, pp. 49–68. London: C. S. E. Books.

————. 1982. "The Dead and the Devil among the Bolivian Laymi." In Maurice Bloch and Jonathan Perry, eds., *Death and the Regeneration of Life*, pp. 45–75. Cambridge: Cambridge University Press.

Herrera y Tordesillas, Antonio. 1945 (1726–1730). *Historia general de los hechos de los castellanos en las islas y Tierra-firme.* Buenos Aires: Editorial Guarania.

Hewitt de Alcántara, Cynthia. 1984. *Anthropological Perspectives on Rural Mexico.* London: Routledge and Kegan Paul.

Hill, Robert, and John Monaghan. 1987. *Sacapulas: Continuities in Principles of Highland Maya Social Organization.* Philadelphia: University of Pennsylvania Press.

Hirabayashi, Lane Ryo. 1993. *Cultural Capital: Mountain Zapotec Migrant Associations in Mexico City.* Tucson: University of Arizona Press.

Hubert, Henri, and Marcel Mauss. 1968 (1898). *Sacrifice: Its Nature and Function.* Translated by W. D. Halls. Chicago: University of Chicago Press.

Huerta Ríos, César. 1981. *Organización socio-política de una minoría nacional: Los triquis de Oaxaca.* Mexico: Instituto Nacional Indigenista.

Hunt, Eva. 1976. "Kinship and Territorial Fission in the Cuicatec Highlands." In Hugo G. Nutini, Pedro Carrasco, and James M. Taggart eds., *Essays on Mexican*

Kinship, pp. 97–136. Pittsburgh: University of Pittsburgh Press.

———. 1977. *The Transformation of the Hummingbird: Cultural Roots of a Zinacantecan Mythical Poem*. Ithaca: Cornell University Press.

Hunt, Eva, and June Nash. 1967. "Local and Territorial Units." In Manning Nash, ed., *Handbook of Middle American Indians*, 6:253–82. Austin: University of Texas Press.

Ingham, John M. 1984. "Human Sacrifice at Tenochtitlan." *Comparative Studies in Society and History* 26:379–400.

———. 1986. *Mary, Michael and Lucifer: Folk Catholicism in Central Mexico*. Austin: University of Texas Press.

Jansen, Maarten E. R. G. N. 1982. *Huisi Tacu. Estudio Interpretativo de un Libro Mixteco Antiguo: Codex Vindobonensis Mexicanus I*. Amsterdam: Centrum voor Studie en Documentatie van Latijns Amerika.

Josephides, Lisette. 1985. *The Production of Inequality*. London: Tavistock

Katz, Esther. 1990. Prácticas agrícolas en la Mixteca Alta. In Teresa Rojas Rabiela, ed., *Agricultura indígena: Pasado y presente*, pp. 239–70. México: Ediciones de la Casa Chata.

Kearney, Michael. 1972. *The Winds of Ixtepeji: World View and Society in a Zapotec Town*. New York: Holt, Rinehart and Winston.

———. 1986. "From the Invisible Hand to the Visible Feet: Anthropological Studies of Migration and Development." *Annual Review of Anthropology* 15:331–61.

King, Mark B. 1982. "Historical Metaphor and the Communication of Legitimacy in the Mixteca, 500 B.C.–A.D. 1500." M.A. thesis, Vanderbilt University.

———. 1988. "Mixtec Political Ideology: Historical Metaphors and the Poetics of Political Symbolism." Ph.D. diss., University of Michigan, Department of Anthropology.

Klein, Cecelia. 1982. "Woven Heaven, Tangled Earth: A Weaver's Paradigm of the Mesoamerican Cosmos." In Anthony F. Aveni and Gary Urton, eds., *Ethnoastronomy and Archaeoastronomy in the American Tropics*, pp. 1–35. Annals of the New York Academy of Sciences, no. 38.

———. 1987. The Ideology of Autosacrifice at the Templo Mayor. In Elizabeth H. Boone, ed., *The Aztec Templo Mayor*, pp. 293–370. Washington, D.C.: Dumbarton Oaks, Trustees for Harvard University.

Kroeber, Alfred. 1948. *Anthropology*. New York: Harcourt-Brace.

Kuiper, Alberta, and William R. Merrifield. 1975. "Duixi Mixtec Verbs of Motion and Arrival." *International Journal of American Linguistics* 41:32–45.

Laughlin, Robert M. 1977. *Of Cabbages and Kings: Tales from Zinacantan*. Washington: Smithsonian Institution Press.

Leach, Edmund. 1954. *Political Systems of Highland Burma: A Study of Kachin Social Organization*. London: G. Bell and Sons, Ltd.

Leslie, Charles. 1960. *Now We Are Civilized: A Study of the World View of the Zapotec Indians of Mitla, Oaxaca*. Detroit: Wayne State University Press.

Levi-Strauss, Claude. 1969 (1949). *The Elementary Structures of Kinship*. Boston: Beacon Press.

———. 1982 (1975). *The Way of the Masks*. Translated by Sylvia Modelski. Seattle: University of Washington Press.

Lewis, Oscar. 1970 (1951). *Life in a Mexican Village: Tepoztlán Restudied*. Urbana: University of Illinois Press.

Lipp, Frank. 1991. *The Mixe of Oaxaca: Religion, Ritual and Healing*. Austin: University of Texas Press.

Lomnitz, Larissa. 1977. *Networks and Marginality: Life in a Mexican Shantytown*. Translated by Cinna Lomnitz. New York: Academic Press.

López Austin, Alfredo. 1980. *Cuerpo humano e ideología: Las concepciones de los antiguos nahuas*. Universidad Autónoma de México.

López López, Benito Moisés. 1984. *Estudio de la comunidad municipal de Santiago Nuyoo, Oaxaca*. Trabajo Recepcional, Universidad Veracruzana, Facultad de Medicina.

Mak, Cornelia. 1959. "Mixtec Medical Beliefs and Practices." *América Indígena* 19:125–50.

———. 1977. "Picturesque Mixtec Talk." *Tlalocan* 7:105–14.

Marcus, Joyce. 1983. "Zapotec Religion." In Kent V. Flannery and Joyce Marcus, eds., *The Cloud People: Divergent Evolution of the Zapotec and Mixtec Civilizations*, pp. 345–51. New York: Academic Press.

———. 1989. "Zapotec Chiefdoms and the Nature of Formative Religions." In R. Sharer and D. Grove, eds., *Regional Perspectives on the Olmec*, pp. 148–97. Cambridge: Cambridge University Press.

Martínez Gracida , Manuel. 1986 (1883). *Colección de cuadros sinópticos de los pueblos, haciendas y ranchos del estado libre y soberano de Oaxaca*. Oaxaca: Dirección de Desarollo de Sistemas de la Secretería de Programación y Presupuesto.

Mathews, Holly F. 1985. "'We Are Mayordomo': A Reinterpretation of Woman's Roles in the Mexican Cargo System." *American Ethnologist* 12:285–301.

Mauss, Marcel. 1967 (1950). *The Gift*. Translated by Ian Cunnison. New York: W. W. Norton and Company.

———. 1979 (1904). *The Seasonal Variations of the Eskimo*. London: Routledge and Kegan Paul.

Maxwell, Judith, and Craig Hanson. 1992. *Of the Manners of Speaking that the Old Ones Had: The Metaphors of Andrés de Olmos in the TULAL Manuscript*. Salt Lake City: University of Utah Press.

Meigs, Anna. 1984. *Food, Sex and Pollution: A New Guinea Religion*. New Brunswick, N.J.: Rutgers University Press.

Méndez Aquino, Alejandro. 1985. *Historia de Tlaxiaco*. Mexico: Compañía Editorial y Distribuidora, S.A.

Mendoza Guerrero, Telésforo. 1981. *Monografía del distrito de Huajuapan, Oaxaca*. Huajuapan: published by the author.

Mintz, Sidney, and Eric R. Wolf. 1950. "An Analysis of Ritual Co-Parenthood (Compadrazgo)." *Southwestern Journal of Anthropology* 6:341–68.

Monaghan, John. 1987. "'We Are People Who Eat Tortillas: Household and Community in the Mixteca." Ph.D. diss., University of Pennsylvania, Department of Anthropology.

———. 1989. "The Feathered Serpent in Oaxaca." *Expedition* 31(1):12–18.

———. 1990a. "La desamortización de la propiedad comunal en la Mixteca: resistencia popular y raíces de la conciencia nacional." In María de los Angeles Romero Frizzi, ed., *Lecturas históricas del estado de Oaxaca. El Sigo XIX*, pp. 343–85. Oaxaca: Instituto Nacional de Antropología e Historia.

———. 1990b. "Reciprocity, Redistribution and the Structure of the Mesoamerican Fiesta." *American Ethnologist*, 17:148–64.

———. 1990c. "Sacrifice, Death, and the Origins of Agriculture in the Codex Vienna." *American Antiquity* 55:559–69.

———. 1994. "Irrigation and Ecological Complementarity in Mixtec Cacicazgos." In Joyce Marcus and Judith Zeitlin, eds., *Caciques and Their People*, pp. 143–61. University of Michigan Anthropological Papers, no. 89. Ann Arbor: Museum of Anthropology, University of Michigan.

———. n.d.. "Sacrifice and Power in Mesoameria."

Monzón Estrada, Arturo. 1949. *El calpulli en la organización social de los Tenochca*. Mexico: Instituto de Historia.

Moore, Alexander. 1973. *Life Cycles in Atchalan*. New York: Teachers College Press.

———. 1979. "Initiation Rites in a Mesoamerican Cargo System: Men and Boys, Judas and the Bull." *Journal of Latin American Lore* 5:55–81.

Murdock, George. 1949. *Social Structure*. New York: Macmillan.

Nutini, Hugo G. 1968. *San Bernardino Contla: Marriage and Family Structure in a Tlaxcalan Municipio*. Pittsburgh: University of Pittsburgh Press.

———. 1976. Introduction: The Nature and Treatment of Kinship in Mesoamerica. In Hugo G. Nutini, Pedro Carrasco, and James Taggart, eds., *Essays on Mexican Kinship*, pp. 3–27. Pittsburgh: University of Pittsburgh Press.

———. 1988. Pre-Hispanic Components of the Syncretic Cult of the Dead in Mesoamerica. *Ethnology* 27:57–78.

Nutini, Hugo G., and Betty Bell. 1980. *Ritual Kinship: The Structure and Historical Development of the Compadrazgo System in Rural Tlaxcala*. Princeton: Princeton University Press.

Nutini, Hugo G., Pedro Carrasco, and James Taggart, eds. 1976. *Essays on Mexican Kinship*. Pittsburgh: University of Pittsburgh Press.

Oettinger, Marion. 1980. *Una comunidad tlapaneca: sus linderos sociales y territoriales*. Mexico: Instituto Nacional Indigenista.

Offner, Jerome. 1983. *Law and Politics in Aztec Texcoco*. Cambridge: Cambridge University Press.

Ortíz López, Pedro. 1982. *Análysis morfosintáctico del constituyente nominal del mixteco de Santa María Yucuhiti, Oaxaca*. Mexico: Instituto Nacional Indigenista.

Ortner, Sherry. 1974. "Is Female to Male as Nature is to Culture?" In Michelle Zimbalist Rosaldo and Louise Lamphere, eds., *Woman, Culture and Society*, pp. 67–87. Stanford: Stanford University Press.

———. 1978. *Sherpas Through Their Rituals*. Cambridge: Cambridge University Press.

———. 1984. "Theory in Anthropology since the 1960s." *Comparative Studies in Society and History* 26:126–66.

Parry, Jonathan. 1986. "*The Gift*, the Indian Gift, and the 'Indian Gift.'" *Man* 21:453–73.

Pastor, Rodolfo. 1987. *Campesinos y reformas: La Mixteca, 1770–1856*. México: El Colegio de México.

Pensinger, Brenda. 1974. *Diccionario mixteco, mixteco del este de Jamiltepec, pueblo de Chayuco*. Mexico: Instituto Linguístico de Verano.

Poewe, Karla. 1981. *Matrilineal Ideology: Male and Female Dynamics in Luapula, Zambia*. London: Academic Press.

Pohl, John. 1984. The Earth Lords: Politics and Symbolism of the Mixtec Codices. Ph.D. diss., University of California at Los Angeles, Department of Anthropology.

Ravicz, Robert. 1965. *Organización social de los mixtecos*. México: Instituto Nacional Indigenista.

———. 1967. "Compadrinazgo." In Manning Nash, ed., *Handbook of Middle American Indians*, 6:238–52. Austin: University of Texas Press.

Redfield, Robert. 1941. *The Folk Culture of Yucatán*. Chicago: University of Chicago Press.

———. 1960 (1955). *The Little Community and Peasant Society and Culture*. Chicago: University of Chicago Press.

Reina, Ruben. 1966. *The Law of the Saints: A Pokoman Pueblo and its Community Culture*. Indianapolis: Bobbs-Merrill.

Remmereswaal, Jamie. n.d. "Nusabi: Informe del Reconocimiento Etnografico del ex-distrito de Tlaxiaco en la Mixteca Alta." Manuscript on file at the Centro Coordinator del Instituto Nacional Indigenista, Tlaxiaco, Oaxaca.

Reyes, Antonio de los. 1976 (1593). *Arte en lengua Mixteca*. Vanderbilt University Publications in Anthropology, no. 14. Nashville, Tenn.

Romero Frizzi, María de los Angeles. 1979. *Información sobre el acervo documental de archivos en La Mixteca, Oaxaca*. Estudios de Antropología e Historia, no. 18 Oaxaca: Centro Regional de Oaxaca, Instituto Nacional de Antropología e Historia.

———. 1985. Economía y vida de los españoles en la Mixteca Alta, 1519–1720. Ph.D. diss., Universidad Iberoamericana.

Romney, A. Kimball. 1967. "Kinship and Family." In Manning Nash, ed., *Handbook of Middle American Indians*, 6:207–37. Austin: University of Texas Press.

Roseberry, William. 1989a. Anthropology, History and Models of Production. In William Roseberry, ed., *Anthropologies and Histories: Essays in Culture, History and Economics*, pp. 145–74. New Brunswick: Rutgers University Press.

———. 1989b. "Marxism and Culture." In William Roseberry, ed., *Anthropologies and Histories: Essays in Culture, History and Economics*, pp. 30–54. New Brunswick: Rutgers University Press.

Sabini, John, and Maury Silver. 1982. *The Moralities of Everyday Life*. New York: Oxford University Press.

Sahagún, Bernardino de. 1977 (1956). *Historia general de las cosas de Nueva Espana*. Mexico: Editorial Porrua.

Sahlins, Marshall. 1972. *Stone Age Economics*. Chicago: University of Chicago Press.

————. 1981. *Historical Metaphors and Mythical Realities: Structure in the Early History of the Sandwich Island Kingdom.* Ann Arbor: University of Michigan Press.

Salzman, P. C. 1978. "Identity and Change in Middle Eastern Tribal Societies." *Man* 13:618–61.

Sandstrom, Alan. 1991. *Corn Is Our Blood: Culture and Ethnic Identity in a Contemporary Aztec Indian Village.* Norman: University of Oklahoma Press.

Schneider, David. 1968. *American Kinship: A Cultural Account.* Englewood Cliffs, N.J.: Prentice-Hall.

————. 1972. "What is Kinship All About?" In Priscilla Reining, ed., *Kinship Studies in the Morgan Centennial Year,* pp. 32–63. Washington: Anthropological Society of Washington.

————. 1984. *A Critique of the Study of Kinship.* Ann Arbor: University of Michigan Press.

Schryer, Franz J. 1990. *Ethnicity and Class Conflict in Rural Mexico.* Princeton: Princeton University Press.

Schwartz, Norman B. 1983. "The Second Heritage of Conquest: Some Observations." In Carl Kendall, John Hawkins, and Laurel Bossen, eds., *Heritage of Conquest Thirty Years Later,* pp. 339–62. Albuquerque: University of New Mexico Press.

Selby, Henery A. 1974. *Zapotec Deviance: The Convergence of Folk and Modern Sociology.* Austin: University of Texas Press.

Sheridan, Thomas E. 1988. *Where the Dove Calls: The Political Ecology of a Peasant Corporate Community in Northwestern Mexico.* Tucson: University of Arizona Press.

Simmel, George. 1964 (1917). "The Field of Sociology." In Kurt Wolf, trans. and ed., *The Sociology of George Simmel,* pp. 3–25. New York: The Free Press.

————. 1971 (1908). "The Problem of Sociology." In Donald N. Levine, ed., *George Simmel on Individuality and Social Forms,* pp. 23–35. Chicago: University of Chicago Press.

————. 1990 (1909). *The Philosophy of Money.* Edited by David Frisby. Translated by Tom Bottomore and David Frisby. London: Routledge and Kegan Paul.

Simmonds, Norman W. 1982. *Bananas.* Longman: New York.

Smith, Carol. 1990. "Introduction: Social Relations in Guatemala over Time and Space." In Carol Smith, ed., *Guatemalan Indians and the State: 1540–1988,* pp. 1–30. Austin: University of Texas Press.

Smith, Mary Elizabeth. 1973. *Picture Writing from Ancient Southern Mexico.* Norman: University of Oklahoma Press.

Sperber, Dan. 1975. *Rethinking Symbolism.* Translated by A. L. Morton. Cambridge: Cambridge University Press.

Spores, Ronald. 1967. *The Mixtec Kings and Their People.* Norman: University of Oklahoma Press.

————. 1974. Marital Alliance in the Political Integration of Mixtec Kingdoms. *American Anthropologist,* 76:297–311.

————. 1984. *The Mixtecs in Ancient and Colonial Times.* Norman: University of Oklahoma Press.

Stanford, Thomas. 1962. "Datos sobre la música y danzas de Jamiltepec, Oaxaca." *Anales del Instituto Nacional de Antropología e Historia* 15:187–200.

Stavenhagen, Rodolfo. 1975. *Social Classes in Agrarian Societies.* Translated by Judy Hellman. Garden City, N.Y.: Anchor Press/Doubleday.

Stephen, Lynn. 1991. *Zapotec Women.* Austin: University of Texas Press.

Stern, Claudio. 1982. "Industrialisation and Migration in Mexico." In Peter Peek and Guy Standing, eds., *State Policies and Migration: Studies in Latin America and the Caribbean*, pp. 173–205. London: Croom Helm.

Stern, Steven J. 1983. "The Struggle for Solidarity: Class, Culture, and Community in Highland Indian America." *Radical History Review* 27:21–45.

Strathern, Andrew J. 1971. *The Rope of Moka.* Cambridge: Cambridge University Press.

Strathern, Marilyn. 1980. "No Nature, No Culture: The Hagen Case." In Carol MacCormack and Marilyn Strathern, eds., *Nature, Culture, and Gender.* Cambridge: Cambridge University Press.

———. 1988. *The Gender of the Gift.* Berkeley: University of California Press.

Sullivan, Paul. 1989. *Unfinished Conversations: Mayas and Foreigners between Two Wars.* New York: Alfred A. Knopf.

Taggart, James M. 1975. *Estructura de los grupos domésticos de una comunidad nahuat de Puebla.* Mexico City: Instituto Nacional Indigenista.

———. 1983. *Nahuat Myth and Social Structure.* Austin: University of Texas Press.

Taussig, Michael T. 1980. *The Devil and Commodity Fetishism in South America.* Chapel Hill: University of North Carolina Press.

Tax, Sol. 1937. "The Municipios of the Midwestern Highlands of Guatemala." *American Anthropologist* 39:423–44.

———. 1953. *Penny Capitalism: A Guatemalan Indian Economy.* Washington: Smithsonian Institute of Social Anthropology.

Taylor, William B. 1979. *Drinking, Homicide and Rebellion in Colonial Mexican Villages.* Stanford: Stanford University Press.

Tedlock, Barbara. 1982. *Time and the Highland Maya.* Albuquerque: University of New Mexico Press.

———. 1983. "A Phenomenological Approach to Religious Change in Highland Guatemala." In Carl Kendal, John Hawkins, and Laurel Bossen, eds., *Heritage of Conquest Thirty Years Later*, pp. 235–46. Albuquerque: University of New Mexico Press.

Townsend, Richard. 1979. *"State and Cosmos in the Art of Tenochtitlan.* Dumbarton Oaks Studies in Pre-Columbian Art and Archaeology, No. 20. Washington: Dumbarton Oaks.

Valeri, Valerio. 1985. *Kingship and Sacrifice.* University of Chicago Press: Chicago.

Wagley, Charles, and Marvin Harris. 1955. "A Typology of Latin American Subcultures." *American Anthropologist* 57:426–51.

Wagner, Roy. 1974. "Are there Social Groups in the New Guinea Highlands?" In Murray Leaf, ed., *Frontiers in Anthropology* pp. 95–122. New York: D. Van Nostrand.

———. 1975. *The Invention of Culture.* Englewood Cliffs: Prentice-Hall.

Wallace, Anthony F. C. 1970. *The Death and Rebirth of the Seneca.* New York: Alfred A. Knopf.

Warren, Kay B. 1978. *The Symbolism of Subordination: Indian Identity in a Guatemalan Town.* Austin: University of Texas Press.

Watanabe, John. 1990. "Enduring Yet Ineffable Community in the Western Periphery of Guatemala." In Carol Smith, ed., *Guatemalan Indians and the State: 1540–1988*, pp. 183–204. Austin: University of Texas Press.

———. 1992. *Maya Saints and Souls in a Changing World.* Austin: University of Texas Press.

Weber, Max. 1962 (1922). *The Sociology of Religion.* Translated by Ephraim Fischoff. Boston: Beacon Press.

Weiner, Annette. 1978. "The Reproductive Model in Trobriand Society." *Mankind* 11:175–86.

———. 1980. "Reproduction: A Replacement for Reciprocity." *American Anthropologist* 7:71–85.

Weiner, James F. 1988. *The Heart of the Pearl Shell: The Mythological Dimension of Foi Sociality.* Berkeley: University of California Press.

Wilk, Richard. 1984. "Households in Process: Agricultural Change and Domestic Transformation among the Kekchi Maya of Belize." In Robert Mc C. Netting, Richard Wilk, and Eric Arnould, eds., *Households: Comparative and Historical Studies of the Domestic Group*, pp. 217–44. Berkeley: University of California Press.

Wilk, Richard, and Robert Mc C. Netting. 1984. "Households: Changing Forms and Functions." In Robert Mc C. Netting et al., eds., *Households: Comparative and Historical Studies of the Domestic Group*, pp. 1–28. Berkeley: University of California Press.

Williams, Raymond. 1976. *Keywords: A Vocabulary of Culture and Society.* New York: Oxford University Press

Witherspoon, Gary. 1975. *Navajo Kinship and Marriage.* Chicago: University of Chicago Press.

Wolf, Eric R. 1955. "Types of Latin American Peasantry: A Preliminary Discussion." *American Anthropologist* 57:452–71.

———. 1957. "Closed Corporate Peasant Communities in Mesoamerica and Java." *Southwestern Journal of Anthropology* 13:1–18.

———. 1962 (1959). *Sons of the Shaking Earth.* Chicago: University of Chicago Press.

———. 1986. "The Vicissitudes of the Closed Corporate Peasant Community." *American Ethnologist* 13:325–29.

Wolf, Eric R., and Edward C. Hansen. 1972. *The Human Condition in Latin America.* New York: Oxford University Press.

Young, James Clay. 1981. *Medical Choice in a Mexican Village.* Rutgers University Press: New Brunswick, New Jersey.

INDEX

Affinity, 17, 39–41, 57, 59, 62, 73–77, 148; and Earth and Rain, 112–15; and gift exchange, 91–93; and image of the corporation, 237, 242–46; and ritual kinship, 69–70

Agriculture 23–26, 38–39, 78, 104–5, 159–60, 262, 263, 326–27; and Covenants with Earth and Rain, 216–27, 251–52; and Earth, 98; and land tenure, 263–65; milpa gang, 279–80; and nu ñu'un, 101, 112, 117; swidden, 262–65, 268, 279; and verticality, 262

Aguardiente, 263, 363

Aguilar, Luis, 339–44, 347, 352, 364

Aguirre Beltrán, Gonzalo, 6, 8

All Saints'. *See* Viko Anima

Alvarado, Francisco de, 109, 218, 299

Anima, 45–46, 98, 102, 128, 134–35, 156, 157, 197–98, 215, 217–18, 221, 223, 229–31, 313. *See also* Sun

Apoala, Santiago, 51, 97, 191

Appadurai, Arjun, 285

Arana Osnaya, Evangelina, 237

Arzipe, Lourdes, 10, 233

Atatlahuca, San Esteban, 235, 247, 265, 289, 358

Banana, 26, 30, 261, 263–64, 269–70, 272, 291, 325, 340

Beals, Ralph, 83, 300

Berry, Charles, 261, 289

Birth, 58, 109; and agriculture, 111, 115–17

Blaffer, Sarah L., 140, 141

Bloch, Maurice, 13, 276, 285, 314

Blom, Franz, 3

Blood, 98, 112, 116–17, 128, 134–35, 195–98, 218, 228. *See also* Kinship; Semen; Yɨɨ

Body, 203–4

Bonfil Batalla, Guillermo, 10

Borah, Woodrow, 270

Bourdieu, Pierre, 13

Bricker, Victoria, 330, 345

Bridewealth, 66–67, 74
Burgoa, Francisco de, 263
Burkhart, Louise, 23, 32, 46, 137, 166, 308
Bustamante, Carlos María de, 337, 338, 351
Butterworth, Douglas, 336
Buzzards, 138

Caballería, 308
Cacique, 31, 170, 172, 173, 185, 272, 315, 321–34, 339–43; and building of church,
    332; and civil-religious hierarchy, 325–27, 342; and coffee, 341; government
    contracts and, 329, 341; hamlets, municipal government and, 341–42; and Mis-
    ericordia, 301, 329–34; and private herds, 324–26, 332, 333; and Tachi, 327–28;
    terms for, 321, 327–28; as war leader, 322–24
Calpulli, 232, 233
Cámara, Fernando, 6, 8
Campbell, Sara Stark, 118
Cancian, Frank, 172, 177, 180, 282
Candles, 216, 220–23, 227, 228
Carmagnani, Marcello, 261
Carranza, Venustiano, 133
Carriedo, Juan P., 338
Cash crops, 30, 261–64, 269, 270, 272, 273, 283–84, 291, 318, 325
Cattle, 265–67, 278–79, 281, 290–94, 324–25, 331, 333
Cemetery, 208, 220, 251
Cervantes, José T., 338
Chalcatongo, 202, 261, 289
Chambers, Erve J., 10
Chamoux, Marie-Noelle, 9
Chance, John, 10, 281, 290–91
Chassen, Francie R., 261
Chicahuaxtla, Santo Domingo, 265
Chicomoztoc, 210
Chilapa, 337
Christmas, 122–25. *See also* Posadas; Santo Niño
Church: in Nuyoo Center, 289–91, 310, 331; property, 169
Civil-religious hierarchy, 31, 167–89, 247–55; as an age-grade system, 174–76;
    cacique and, 325, 327, 341–42; changes in, 169–70, 302; election of new officers,
    184–85; eligibility, 176, 180–82; and feasting, 302, 344; and federal government,
    169–72; and hamlets, 168; and households, 87, 166, 188–89, 359; images of, 170–
    71, 173, 247, 250; leadership in, 321–22; and the life course, 174–76; and marriage,
    248; offices in, 167–70; rank in, 170–72; salaries in, 171–72; and school, 168, 169;
    terms of office, 171–72; and training, 174–76; women in, 176–79. *See also* Service
Clan, 233
Class, 259, 315, 318, 321

Clothing, 36–39; given by ritual kin, 69–72, 123–25; in marriage, 69–70, 236; and nakara, 36–39, 41, 200–201, 208, 356

Coffee, 19, 26, 30, 142–43, 183, 235, 266, 269–70, 272, 283–84, 291, 313, 315–16, 336, 340, 341

Cofradías, 266, 286–306

Communal herds, 265–67, 278–79, 290–94, 331, 333. *See also* Mayordomos

Community, 3–16; closed corporate community model, 6–9; and communication, 11–16; in epochal analysis, 10; in folk-urban continuum, 3–6; and gift exchange, 86–87; as a great house, 244–46; in Mesoamerican ethnology, 3–14, 260–61, 321, 356; as model of social reality, 11–14; and moral codes, 11, 12, 259–60; ñuu as, 11, 27; Nuyooteco definition of, 13–14, 258–60; power and control in, 328; and ritual, 11; and service, 9, 13; as structure, 14; as theory of social action, 13–16. *See also* Sociality

Compadrazgo, 37, 52–54, 358; and death, 158–59; as giving a child to another household, 54, 124–25; and nakara, 54, 72. *See also* Clothing; Ritual kinship

Conasupo 26, 27, 132, 267, 312, 336, 342

Cook, Scott, 326

Cook, Sherburne, 270

Corn, 357; and affines, 93; and ánima, 230–31; and blood, 217–18; and farmer, 115–17; and children, 93; and Covenants with Earth and Rain; 224–25; handling of, 113–15; and human gestation and growth, 115–18, 221; and marriage, 112–17; metaphors for, 112–217; niñɨ cruzi, 227; niñɨ i'ya, 218–19, 227; patron of, 218; processing of, 55; and the Rain, as daughter of, 67, 109–110, 112–17, 225, 251, 350; and ritual kin, 93; and sacrifice, 216–22; and saints, 222; types of, 115–16, 262; wages paid in, 217; and women, 67, 93, 217, 242; and yɨɨ, 127, 200, 217. *See also* Pozole; Tortilla; Viko Nuni

Corporal punishment, 89, 164, 174

Corporate assets, 240–41, 261, 265–68, 278–79, 311, 330–31, 359–61; cargo holders as administrators of, 178–79, 247–48, 265–68

Corporateness as a practice, 240–55. *See also* Great house; Pooling

Corporation, 232–34, 241. *See also* Great house; Pooling; Civil-religious hierarchy; Service

Cosmogony, 43, 226–27

Covenants with Earth and Rain, 15, 204–8, 211–12, 251–52, 312

Culturas populares, 10

Cuquila, Santa María, 221

Dahlgren de Jordón, Barbro, 363

Dance, 150–52, 165

Dávila, Inés, 133

Death, 160–63; and Earth, 191, 208; rituals, 221, 282–83; and sacrifice, 250–53; and service, 250–55

Deme, 234–35, 237

Demon. *See* Tachi

Deputies, 169, 266, 286–306; duties of, 288–89, 297–98; increase in numbers of, 291–98, 305; recruitment of, 298–300, 305. *See also* Civil-religious hierarchy; Cofradías; Mayordomos; Service

Dennis, Philip A., 26, 209

Descent, 7, 233–35

Destiny, 198–200, 347–48; and the Sun, 199. *See also* Kiti nuvi

Díaz, Porfirio, 289, 291, 294, 330

Disentailment, 264–65, 268, 275, 278, 330–31, 333; and intercommunity conflict, 272

Diskin, Martin, 84

Divorce, 57, 61–62, 67, 176–77

Dogs, 145–49; as child of Tachi, 138; and envy, 135; and households, 145–49, 253; men and, 149, 181, 185, 188, 252; and social relatedness, 145–49; Tachi as parent, 138; and velu, 151, 152; and women, 145–48; and Yucuhiti, origin of, 202–3

Dow, James, 8, 9, 136, 188

Dreams, 36, 99, 109, 135, 136, 187–88; and kiti nuvi, 199–200, 217–18

Dualism, 165–66

Durán, Diego, 17, 48

Durkheim, Emile, 360

Earth, 97–104, 118–19, 191, 211–12, 251–52, 357; and agriculture, 98, 101, 251–52; and body, 203–4, 207, 210, 228–29, 251; as cosmos, 100; and death, 191, 208, 251; face of, 98–99; and hunting, 101; and nakara, 208–9, 211–12; and Rain, 97, 110–11; and sacrifice, 101–3, 222–27, 251–52; shrines of, 97; and soul loss, 103–4; transgressions against, 98, 103, 251–52; as womb, 111–12, 202–4. *See also* Nu ñu'un

Elders, 321–23, 325–26, 328. *See also* Cacique; Ñañuu; Principales; Tañuu

Envy, 131–36, 165, 187; and households, 143–49, 166; and illness, 133–35; and privatization, 283–85; as self-protection, 132–33, 135; and social control, 131–32; as sociation not premised on exchange, 136; Tachi as, 136–37, 312; velu as, 155. *See also* Tachi; Velu

Esperón, José, 273

Ethnic groups, 58–59, 91–92, 202–3, 259–60

Ethnicity, 11–13, 22–23, 26, 141–43, 338, 341, 343, 355, 356

Ethnophysiology, 112, 115–17; body, 203–4. *See also* Birth; Blood; Heart; Kinship; Procreation; Semen

Evil Eye, 134

Falla, Ricardo, 125

Fardon, Richard, 14, 260

Farriss, Nancy, 8, 228, 279

Fiestas, 79–80, 230, 244, 285, 359–60; attendance, 86, 90–93; civil-religious hierarchy and, 79–80, 248–49, 314; as crisis, 89–90, 285; distributions in, 238–40, 282–84, 358–59; financing of, 288–89, 297–98, 299–301, 316–18; gift exchange in, 80, 82–85, 89–90, 285–86, 299–301, 316–18; and great house, 243–46, 253–54; number celebrated, 79–80, 302; pooling in, 238–45, 248–49, 253–54; start-up costs, 83, 240; and stratification, 316–18; surpluses in, 240, 301–2

Fiesta sponsorship, 181; gender and, 56–57; households and, 180, 254, 302–3; spouses and, 176, 248. *See also* Fiestas

Fiscal, 123, 168–69. *See also* Mayordomos

Flanet, Veronique, 65, 141, 203, 224

Flowers, 216, 220–22, 227, 228

Food sharing, 36–39, 41, 47–49. *See also* Fiestas; Gift exchange; Nakara

Ford, Richard, 219

Fortes, Meyer, 7

Foster, George, 88, 90, 132, 134

Foster, Morris, 13

Foster, Robert J., 75

Fox, John W., 233

French Intervention, 289, 345, 355

Friendship, 304–6

Frisby, David, 16

Furst, Jill L., 217

Galinier, Jacques, 195

García, Gregorio, 95, 251

Gay, José Antonio, 338

Gearing, Fred, 260, 359

Gender, 42; and corn, 67, 93, 112–17, 242; and cosmology, 101, 110–12; and fate, 235; and fiesta sponsorship, 56–57; and gift exchange, 148–50; and the household, 56, 147–50; and labor, 55, 57–60; and left/right symbolism, 58–59; and machete, 109–10; origin of women, 145–46; and pollution, 59–60, 148–49; and service, 147, 172–74; and Tachi, 144–49, 313

Gibson, Thomas, 200

Giddens, Anthony, 14, 360

Gift exchange, 14, 15, 178, 179, 285, 357, 358; and alliance, 88–93; and alternating disequilibrium, 88–90; cheating in, 81; and commodity exchange, 285–86; as communication, 84, 89–90, 240, 304–5; competition in, 90; and conflict, 318–19; and core exchange partners, 238–40; countergift, 83–85, 178, 239, 285; and debt, 88–90, 301–2; among different towns, 86–87; and expansion of the household, 318–19; in fiestas, 80–81, 238–40, 344; in financing fiestas, 82–83, 89–90, 285–86, 299–306, 310–12, 316–18; and the household, 87, 91–92; images of, 81–82, 89, 238–42; increments in, 89; inflation and, 316; items exchanged, 80–81; and Jesus, 122, 311; and labor, 84–87, 180, 280, 299–300; men and, 148–49; origins of, 122, 311; partners' relationships, 89–90, 304; and pooling, 238–40, 241–42; reciprocity in, 81, 239; and record keeping, 81–83, 92, 148, 239; and self-interest, 86; and sociation, 300; and stratification, 316–19; and surpluses, 85, 90; systemic nature of, 302–4; women and, 148–49, 180; and yïi, 129. *See also* Saa sa'a

Goats and sheep, 265–67, 278–79, 290, 294, 324–25, 331, 333

González, Romeo, 257
Good, Catherine, 16, 282
Gose, Peter, 260
Gosner, Kevin, 330
Gossen, Gary, 12, 58
Grave, 208, 251
Great house, 15; and corporateness, 244–46, 284
Greenberg, James, 8, 125, 136, 169, 259, 318
Gregory, Chris, 282, 285
Grey, John N., 226
Gruzinski, Serge, 330
Gudeman, Stephen, 52, 307
Gwaltney, John, 74

Hacienda, 143, 263, 273, 335
Hacienda da la Concepción, 173, 263
Hacienda Volante, 331
Hamlets, 26–32, 78–79, 152, 341–42; and gift exchange, 90–91
Handy, Jim, 16
Hansen, Edward C., 144
Hanson, Craig, 253
Harris, Marvin, 6
Harris, Olivia, 159, 160, 319
Heart, 45–46, 98, 102, 128, 134–35, 156–60
Hewitt de Alcántara, 7, 10
Herrera y Tordesillas, Antonio, 257
Hidalgo y Costilla, Miguel, 337, 343, 354
Hill, Robert, 246
Hirabayashi, Lane Ryo, 335, 354
Hospitality, 42–50, 164; charter for, 42–56; and envy, 144; and the fiesta, 48; Jesus and, 42–50, 121–23; and nakara, 48; reflexivity and, 49, 119–23; and Tachi, 157, 163; in Viko Anima, 158
Households, 32–50, 356–57; and agriculture, 40–41, 278–79; composition, 36, 39–42; corporate nature of, 35–36, 53–54, 103, 181; death outside of, 160–63; definition of, 41–42, 356–57; as dwellings, 32–34; and envy, 143–49; expansion of, 305–6, 310, 318–19; and fiesta sponsorship, 290–91, 302–4, 310; fissioning of, 39–41, 87, 91–92, 244, 318; and gift exchange, 87, 91–92; and the great house, 249–55, 359; and hospitality, 47–50, 119–23; Jesus, 42–50, 309–12; kitchens in, 34, 37, 56–57, 242; labor division in, 55–61; and marriage, 55–61, 235–37; and men, 149; as a moral unit, 50, 75–77; and nakara, 34–42, 356–57; opposed to wild places, 32–33, 45, 49–50, 161; and property, 36, 40–41, 244, 280, 281, 310, 359–60; and ritual kinship, 53–54; and service, 87, 179–81, 188–89, 249–55, 280–84, 305–6; stratification of, 315–19; and Tachi, 318–19; and velu, 156–57; and Viko Anima, 229–31; and women, 56, 147–49

Huajuapan de León, 202, 337–39, 344, 345, 351, 352, 363–65
Hubert, Henri, 216
Huerta Ríos, César, 233
Huitzilopochtli, 231, 232
Hunt, Eva, 58, 233
Hunting, 101, 215

Incense, 215, 221, 222, 227, 228
Indio de Nuyoo, 337, 338, 340, 342–44, 346–47, 351–55, 361–66
Inflation, 295–97
Ingham, John M., 136, 137, 143, 243, 252, 307
Inheritance, 28, 159
Intercommunity conflict, 26–32, 132–33, 147, 174–75, 208–10, 247–48, 270–75, 322–
    24, 340–42, 361; and agriculture, 275–77; and caciques, 322–24, 326, 340–41; and
    competing feasts, 273–75, 310; and settlement patterns, 209, 273, 275, 277
Ixtayutla, Santiago, 196, 328
I'ya, 218

Jansen, Maarten E. R. G. N., 32, 46, 99, 100, 101, 105, 107, 220, 314, 350
Jesus, 42, 119–30, 149; and creation, 43, 46, 308; and gift exchange, 310–12; and heat,
    46–47; as a moral force, 46–47; and Sun, 44–47, 118–19; and Tachi, 136–37, 152–55,
    165–66, 312–13; and tiumi, 49–50; and velu, 152–55; visits to households, 42–50,
    119–22, 126–27, 149, 308–12, 351, 357; and yɨɨ, 127–30, 314. See also Misericordia;
    Santo Entierro; Santo Niño; Sun
Josephedes, Lisette, 250
Juárez, Benito, 264, 343, 354
Juxtlahuaca, 17, 175

Katz, Esther, 262
Kearney, Michael, 48, 336
Kindred, 91–92
King, Mark B., 45, 51, 117, 198, 205, 216
Kinship, 9, 28, 185, 193–95, 232–37, 358; blood in Nuyooteco, 194–98, 200–201, 221,
    228, 230, 234, 252; milk in Nuyooteco, 196–98, 200–201, 220, 221, 228, 230, 234;
    nomenclature, 201; in Nuyoo, 193–212, 228–32; and tiumi, 211; relationships, 36–
    41; through the transmission of substance, 195–98, 200–201, 227, 230–31. See also
    Nakara
Kitɨ Nuvi, 199–200, 217–18, 347–48, 351
Klein, Cecelia, 119, 161, 223, 252, 253
Koo Savi, 105–8, 205, 248
Kroeber, Alfred, 6
Kuiper, Alberta, 81–82

Labor, 84–87, 143, 314. See also Service; Tequio; Wage labor

La Farge, Oliver, 3
Landa, Diego de, 95
Land tenure, 8, 261, 263–65, 275–77, 283, 310, 315–16, 318, 330–31, 359–60
Laughlin, Robert M., 309
Leach, Edmund, 260
León Navoa, Manuel, 327
Leslie, Charles, 81
Levi-Strauss, Claude, 235–36, 242, 245
Lewis, Oscar, 6
Liberal reform. *See* Disentailment
Lightning, 105, 109–10, 139, 173, 207, 348–51. *See also* Ñu'un savi; Rain; Sky
Lipp, Frank, 260
Loma Bonita, 26, 27, 30, 31, 120
Lomnitz, Larissa, 336
López, José, 327, 339, 340, 353
López, Simón, 173
López Austin, Alfredo, 58, 195, 202
López Fería, Carmen, 134, 135, 249
López Nuñez, Juan, 202
López Sarabia, Antonio, 282–84
Luti. *See* Nopalera, San Sebastían; Ocotlán

Machete, 59–60, 109–11, 115–16, 145; as protection against Tachi, 145. *See also* Ñu'un savi
Maguey, 220
Marcus, Joyce, 99, 198
Markets, 28, 261, 294, 324
Martínez Gracida, Manuel, 289
Marriage, 39–41, 234–37, 257; age at time of, 61, 62; bridewealth, 66–67, 74; church ceremony, 68; civil ceremony, 67–68; clothing and, 69–70, 236; and corn, 112–15; 241–46; and corporate resources, 242–43; in deme, 234–35; divorce, 57, 61–62, 67, 176–77; eating from the same tortilla and, 70–72, 243; endogamy, 234–35; exchanges in, 63–67, 70, 73–77; and household division of labor, 55–60; images of, 51–52, 56, 62, 63, 66, 67, 73, 93, 235, 236; and Jesus, 122, 125–26; as moral duty, 64–65; and nakara, 65, 69–72, 243; negotiations about, 63–65; as replacement, 67, 73–77, 117; and saint's processions, 125–26; and service, 176–77; strategies behind, 60–61, 63–64, 236; as a system of exchange, 234–37; types of, 61–62; uxorilocality, 76; viko ta na'a, 67–77; virilocality, 235; and yɨɨ, 67–129. *See also* Tee ka'a sha
Masks, 150–51, 155, 156, 159, 160
Mathews, Holly, 177, 179
Mauss, Marcel, 88, 216, 260
Maxwell, Judith, 253
Mayordomos, 80, 168–72, 174, 185, 221, 222, 327, 344; accounts, 266, 286–87, 302; and building of church, 278–79, 289–90, 361; of Caballería, 169; cash held by, 266–

67, 278–79, 295–96, 361; chests of, 176, 183, 266–67, 286–87, 302; and cofradías, 255, 286–306; and commerce, 266–67, 280–81, 295–96; duties of, 168–69, 178–79; eligibility for, 176, 180–81; general fund of, 266–67, 295–96, 361; and gift exchange, 86, 87, 324–25; herd animals of, 265–67, 278–79, 281, 290–94, 325, 361; and interest payments, 267, 295–96, 299; of Magdalena, 175; of Misericordia, 119–20, 169, 172, 273, 309, 311–12, 329; property of, 178–79, 265–67, 278–81, 325; as proxies, 253; rank of, 170–72; and recruitment of deputies, 298–300; of San Felipe, 344; of Santa Ana, 169; of Santa Cruz, 119–20, 175; of Santiago, 169, 172, 175, 265, 340; of Santo Entierro, 119–20; of Santo Niño, 122–25, 169, 172; tequios of, 169; of Virgin de Rosario, 169, 172, 265–66; women as, 176–79. *See also* Civil-religious hierarchy; Service

Meigs, Anna, 193, 194
Méndez Aquino, Alejandro, 289
Mendoza Guerrero, Telésforo, 338, 339
Merrifield, William R., 81–82
Mestizos, 22–23, 26, 340
Mexican Revolution, 266, 291–95, 333, 345
Mexico City, 335, 336, 342, 344, 345, 352–55
Midwives, 196
Migration, 16, 155–56, 263, 270, 284, 335–37, 344, 354–55, 361; agricultural laborers, 184, 270; to Mexico City, 254–55, 335, 336, 344, 346–47, 352–55; migrant association, 336, 344, 353, 355; Remigio Sarabia and, 344, 352–55, 361; return migration, 336; revelation and, 336–37; and service, 180, 184, 254–55, 335, 336; to United States, 365–66
Mining, 214–15, 327
Mintz, Sidney, 52–53
Misericordia, 15–16, 119, 240, 309, 333–34, 358, 361, 362; appearance of, 273–75, 278, 284, 307–12, 320, 321, 330, 332, 360–61; and building of church, 278, 310–12, 332, 361; and caciques, 329–34; and expansion of the household, 311–12, 361; feast of, 274–75; and fiesta sponsorship, 310–17, 361; and gift exchange, 310–12, 361; and intercommunity conflict, 273–75, 310; and marriage, 125–26; and municipal finances, 311–12, 361; and privatization, 332–34, 361; procession of, 119–22, 125–27, 165, 179, 309, 313, 358; sacrifice to, 309, 311–12, 332; and tachi kuka, 312–13; viko luli of, 274–75
Mixteca, 19–26
Modesto Velasco, Fausto, 204, 205
Monteverde, Santa Lucía, 30, 31, 235, 289
Monzón Estrada, Arturo, 233
Moon, 49
Moore, Alexander, 174
Morelos, José María, 337, 338, 343, 354, 355
Municipality, 27–28; administration of, 167–68; finances of, 152, 280–82, 311–12, 316
Murdock, George, 234, 237

Myth, 42–43; as moral lesson, 121

Nakara, 36–39; and affines, 39–41, 65; clothing and, 36–39, 200, 208, 356; feeding and, 36–39, 41, 200–201, 208, 356; and Earth and Rain, 208–9, 211–12; the household and, 34–42, 200–201, 225, 243–44, 356–58; in marriage, 69–72; as a moral code 200–201; relationships of identity through, 54, 69–72, 225, 242–44, 356–57; and ritual kin, 54, 69–72, 225; service as, 248–49
Ñañuu, 177, 248–49. *See also* Civil-religious hierarchy; Service
Nationalism, 353–55; patriotic heroes in definitions of, 343, 347, 354, 362
Ndiosi, 100, 351
Netting, Robert McC., 42, 356
Nopalera, San Sebastían, 28, 31, 133, 173, 270–72, 275–77, 282, 322–24, 326, 340–41
Northamerican invasion, 355
Noso, 220, 314
Nutini, Hugo G., 160, 233
Nu ñu'un, 23, 34, 97, 98–114, 160, 327, 357; and agriculture, 101, 128; and corn, 113–14; as face of Earth, 99–100; and gender, 101; houses of, 100, 102, 204; and hunting, 101, 103; images of, 99–100; and mine, 327; as ndiosi, 100; and Rain, 205; sacrifice to, 101, 102, 103, 213–15, 217, 221, 223–24, 226, 227; San Barrancón, 100; San Cristóbal, 100; San Marcos, 100, 205, 206, 227; and soul loss, 103–4, 215; transgression against, 103, 113–14. *See also* Earth
Ñuuánima, 118–19, 157, 159, 161, 229
Ñu'un savi, 97, 105–11, 137, 204–6, 347, 349, 350, 357; and ax, 109–10; houses of, 107–9; images of, 106; and machete, 109–10, 204; and rainfall, 97, 107–9; and sacrifice, 215, 226; as saint of the Rain, 106; and Santiago, 308; and Tenuvi, 349–50; and yɨɨ, 129. *See also* Rain; Rain shrines; Sky
Nuyoo Center, 20, 27–29, 31, 78–79, 85, 105, 120, 132, 145, 146, 163, 170, 185, 209, 224, 229, 247, 250, 273, 281, 316, 322, 326, 329, 330, 336, 339, 341, 344, 348, 363

Oaxaca City, 343
Ocotepec, Santo Tomás, 85–86, 261, 273, 333, 339
Ocotlán, 28, 31, 161, 173, 270–72, 275–77, 282, 322–24, 326, 328, 329, 340–41
Oettinger, Marion, 11
Offner, Jerome, 246
Olmos, Andrés de, 253
Ortner, Sherry, 13, 48

Pack animals, 324–25
Pantheism, 98–99, 130, 137, 197–98, 314
Parry, Johnathan, 88, 285, 314
Pastor, Rodolfo, 261, 263
Patron saints, 307
Peasants, 6–8
Pensinger, Brenda, 118

Pérez, Santiago, 173
Pérez Simón, 298
Poewe, Karla, 194
Pohl, John, 101, 202, 246
Pollution, 59, 103, 149, 155, 162; and agriculture, 59–60; medicine for, 161; and sexual intercourse, 59; and Tachi, 144, 149, 155, 157, 314
Pooling, 238–45, 248–49, 253–54; and corporateness, 240–46
Posadas, 122–25. *See also* Compadrazgo; Fiestas; Mayordomos; Ritual kinship
Pozole, 217, 227–28. *See also* Corn; Sacrifice; Viko Nuni
Pregnancy, 126
Principales, 321–23, 325–26
Procreation, 112, 195–98
Privatization, 268, 272, 275–77, 279, 283–84, 310, 315–16, 318, 330–32, 359–60
Pulque, 116, 214, 220, 221, 227, 228, 252
Purification, 216, 220, 223
Putla, 142, 175, 263, 289, 319, 335

Rain, 97, 99, 104–17, 135–36, 205, 211–12, 348, 349, 357; and agriculture, 104–5, 251; and body, 201, 203–4, 251; children of, 109–11, 350; and Earth, 97, 110–11; faces of, 105–6; fiesta and, 230; first cloud of new year, 105; images of, 105; mountains and, 108–9, 349; and nakara, 208–9, 211–12; sacrifice to, 222–27, 251–52, 349; and semen, 204; and Tachi, 139; and yïï, 128, 129, 201. *See also* Ñu'un savi; Rain shrines; Sky
Rain lizard, 105–6
Rain serpent, 105–8
Rain shrines, 112–13, 223, 249, 350
Ravicz, Robert, 41, 52, 314, 356
Redfield, Robert, 4–7, 10
Régules, José, 337, 338
Reina, Ruben, 173, 259
Religion, 26, 32–33, 165–66, 226; Catholic, 26; Protestant, 26, 138
Religiosity, 213–14
Revelation, 104, 307–8, 312, 319, 333–34, 350–52, 360–63; and agency, 320–21; and exemplars, 360–61; and expansion of the household, 310–19; and history, 308, 320–21, 353; and migration, 336–37, 361; and morality, 121, 308; and privatization, 318–19; and Remigio Sarabia, 351–53, 361, 362; and stratification, 318–19; and tenuvi, 350–53, 362. *See also* Misericordia; Remigio Sarabia
Reyes, Antonio de los, 19, 51, 191, 195
Ritual, 121
Ritual kinship, 52, 185, 188, 229, 247; clothing exchange in, 69–72, 123–25; and gift exchange, 91–93; in marriage, 68–70; nomenclature, 54; occasions for, 53, 72; and Santo Niño, 122–25, 130; and tiumi, 52; and velu, 157–59. *See also* Compadrazgo
Rojas, Guadalupe, 41–42, 45, 49, 152, 155, 311
Rojas, Lorenzo, 129

Romero Frizzi, María de los Angeles, 364
Romney, A. Kimball, 36
Roseberry, William, 8, 360
Rousseau, Jean Jacques, 226

Saa sa'a, 80–83; and exchange of labor, 380, 299–300. *See also* Gift exchange
Sabini, John, 132
Sacred, 104, 105
Sacrifice, 101, 102, 129, 213–32, 358; as alimentary communion, 223–32; and ánima, 221, 223; and body, 221, 223, 225–32, 251–55; and communication, 215–16; as a condition of human life, 213, 224–25, 251–55; and Covenants with Earth and Rain, 222–27, 251–53; and food, 222; after hunting, 215; to Misericordia, 120–21, 127, 311–12; nu ñu'un and, 213–15; objectives of, 213–16; offerings, 216–22, 227–28, 349–50; purification and, 216; and religiosity, 213, 214; to Santa Cruz and Santo Entierro, 120–21; and self-sacrifice, 226–32, 251–55; and service, 251–55; and tenuvi, 349–50
Sahagún, Bernardino de, 46, 231–32
Sahlins, Marshall, 84, 240, 360
Santa Cruz, 119; and marriage, 125–26, 179; procession of, 119–20, 122, 125–26, 165, 313
Santiago, 307, 308
Santiago Nuyoo, 19–22; demography, 31, 264, 270, 280, 323; environment, 19–22, 104–5, 221; hamlets, 26–32, 78–79, 341–42; and intercommunity conflict, 28–32, 247–48, 270–75, 310, 322–24, 326, 340–41, 361; origins of, 202–3, 209–10; territory of, 29–30
Santo Entierro, 119; and marriage, 125–26, 179; procession of, 119–20, 122, 125–26, 165, 313
Santo Niño, 47, 119, 122–25; godfather of, 123–25; and compadrazgo, 122–25, 130; procession of, 122–25, 165, 313
Sarabia, Ñañuu María, 301
Sarabia, Remigio, 337, 338, 340, 342–44, 346–47, 351–55, 361–66
Sarabia, Tañuu Andrés, 323–24
Sarabia, Tañuu Fidel, 288–89, 298
Sarabia López, Andrés, 118–19
Sarabia Sarabia, Zacarias, 339–40, 352–64
Salt trade, 141, 155–56, 324–25
Salzman, P. C., 260
Sandstrom, Alan, 356
San Sebastián, 324
Santa Ana, 307
Santiago y Calderón, Francisco de, 289
Satire, 345, 346
Schneider, David, 11, 193, 194, 195
School, 345

Schryer, Franz J., 6, 8, 9, 11, 321
Schwartz, Norman B., 10
Semen, 111, 112; and pulque, 116–17. *See also* Blood; Kinship
Service, 15, 146; alienation and, 254–55; attitudes towards, 182–89; costs of, 247–48,
    283–85; and death, 176, 250–55; as debt, 252; dreams of, 187–88; as a gendered
    activity, 172–79; great house and, 359; household and, 179–81, 284–85, 359;
    images of, 170–71, 173, 175, 181–82, 247–50; and migration, 180, 184, 284, 335–36,
    353; as nakara, 248–49; and ñañuu, 177, 248–49; and power, 174, 183–84, 254,
    325–26; purpose of, 173; and social control, 183–84, 254, 325–26; strategies to
    avoid, 182–87, 254, 284, tañuu and, 173, 248–49; tequio as, 170; as vocation, 175–
    76; and women, 147; and yïi, 173, 175. *See also* Civil-religious hierarchy; Deputies;
    Mayordomos
Sheridan, Thomas E., 8, 9
Silver, Maury, 132
Simmel, George, 13, 14, 16, 255
Simmonds, Norman W., 264, 269
Sin, 47–48, 103
Siniyuvi, San Pedro, 173, 349
Skepticism, 103–4
Skits, 345–47
Sky, 97, 104, 118–19, 204, 205, 357. *See also* Rain
Smith, Carol, 16
Smith, Mary Elizabeth, 33
Snakes, 138–40, 144–45, 314. *See also* Tachi
Sociality, 14–15, 122, 201–2, 226, 230–31, 248–49, 259, 354–55, 356–62; and agency, 14,
    16; alienation and, 252–55; and alimentation, 174, 225–26, 241–46, 250, 252–53, 328,
    355; and change, 15–16, 306, 312, 320, 359–63; corporateness as, 241, 252–54; and
    Covenants with Earth and Rain, 226–27; eating from the same tortilla, 241–44; and
    history, 260–61; and household association, 15, 50, 157, 165–66; mediation, 118–30,
    253; and national identity, 354–55; Nuyooteco images of, 15, 51, 131, 145–50, 248–49;
    revelation as a form of, 333–34, 362–63; synthesis, 253; Tachi and, 314–15, 318–19;
    and value, 130. *See also* Envy; Kinship; Gift exchange; Great house; Nakara;
    Revelation; Ritual; Sacrifice; Service; Storytelling
Soco Usha, 27, 111, 202, 209–12, 228, 234, 354
Soul, 45–46, 98, 102, 156. *See also* Anima; Blood; Destiny; Heart; Kiti nuvi; Soul loss;
    Sun; Yïi
Soul loss, 102–4, 161
Sperber, Dan, 13
Spirit/matter distinction, 98–99, 130. *See also* Pantheism
Spokesmen. *See* Tee ka'a sha
Spores, Ronald, 99, 234, 237
Stanford, Thomas, 152
Stavenhagen, Rodolfo, 12, 142
Stephen, Lynn, 148, 177

Stern, Claudio, 354
Steward, Julian, 7, 8
Storytelling, 42–43; as sociation, 42–43, 121
Strathern, Andrew J., 88–90
Strathern, Marilyn, 13, 126, 148, 149, 260
Stratification, 259, 315, 318, 321; and conflict, 318–19, 321; and fiesta sponsorship, 316–18; and gift exchange, 316–18
Sullivan, Paul, 330
Sun, 32, 99, 357; and ánima, 45–46, 118, 197–98; Corpus Christi, 46; and cosmology, 118–19, and Jesus, 43–47, 119–20; light and heat of, 46–47, 128, 197–98; and mediation, 118–19, 130; as a moral force, 46–47, 64–65; and Tachi, 136–37; and tiumi, 49–50, 308; Viko Nkanii, 46; and yɨɨ, 128
Swadesh, Mauricio, 237
Sweatbath, 100, 196

Ta'a, 85–87, 193, 233–35, 237, 355, 359. See also Kinship
Tachi, 32, 43, 45, 52, 58, 99, 136–66, 223, 284, 312–13, 333, 357; cacique and, 327; children of, 137–40, 155, 314; as envy, 133, 136–37, 312; faces of, 137, 313; and food, 58, 157; houses in cliffs, 141–42; and Jesus, 136–37, 141, 152–55, 165–66, 312–15; in left/right symbolism, 58, 144; and men, 149–50, 313; money of, 314–15; and pollution, 138; poor and, 313–15; and priest, 143; and rich, 141–43, 313–15, 317, 318–20; and social order not premised on exchange, 157, 314–15; and Sun, 136–37, 141; tachi kuka, 138, 139, 141–43, 157, 163, 313–15, 318–20; tachi niyɨ, 38, 160–63; tachi ñu'un, 138; tachi sheen, 163; tachi sɨ'ɨ, 138, 144–45, 152; tachi tiu, 145; tachi tuun, 138, 139, 141–43; tachi yuku, 163; and velu, 150, 152, 314–15; and women, 139, 141, 144–50, 313; as Wind, 99, 137–38, 140, 145, 222, 314. See also Velu
Taggart, James M., 115, 121, 145, 160
Tañuu, 173, 248–49, 253. See also Civil-religious hierarchy; Elders; Principales; Service
Taussig, Michael T., 143, 319
Taylor, William B., 281, 290–91
Tax, Sol, 4, 12, 34–35
Tedlock, Barbara, 166
Tee ka'a sha, 51–52, 63–65, 67–69, 173, 235
Tenuvi, 111, 135–36, 173, 204, 308, 347–53, 355; ñanuvi, 347. See also Rain
Teponaxtla, San Juan, 173, 349
Tequio, 27, 42, 246, 252, 254, 276, 278; for cacique, 342; days worked in Nuyoo Center, 170; eligibility for, 176; in hamlets, 27; and migrants, 335, 336; as service, 170; and síndico, 27
Tierra Azul, 26, 28–31, 42, 120, 144, 168
Tiñu, 175–76. See also Civil-religious hierarchy; Service
Tiumi, 32–33, 41, 49–50, 52, 65, 122, 127, 130, 164, 211–12, 226, 251, 308
Tlacamama, 324
Tlaxiaco, 22, 133, 142, 175, 185, 221, 261, 265, 266, 269, 274, 286, 289, 324, 325, 332, 339, 340, 343, 363, 364, 365

Tobacco, 140, 204, 349, 350
Topete, María de la Luz, 363
Tortilla, 55; in gift exchange, 80–81; in marriage, 69–72; mediating households, 113
Town secretary, 323, 329, 340
Townsend, Richard, 99
Trujano, Valerio, 337, 338
Turner, Victor, 363

Unión y Progreso, 26, 30, 31, 120, 168

Valencia, Enrique, 363
Valeri, Valerio, 216
Vásquez, Blas, 339–40
Velasco, Herminio, 323–28, 333–34, 339–41
Velu, 32, 43, 45, 126–27, 149–66, 317; cannibalism, 163–64; and carnival, 151, 163; costume, 150–51; and dance of the conquest, 150; as dance troupe, 150–52; and the dead, 157–63; and dogs, 151, 152; and food, 156–57; as Jews, 152, 154, as kin, 157–59; as kings, 152–53; ñatuun and, 150–52, 154, 156; performances of, 156–57, 164; as ritual kin, 157–59; ritual of reversal, 165–66; as Tachi, 150–51, 154, 156; viko sikɨ, 156. *See also* Tachi
Viko Anima, 119, 157–60, 184, 220, 229–32
Viko Luli, 80, 169, 288. *See also* Fiestas; Mayordomos
Viko Nkanii, 46
Viko Nuni, 217, 227–28, 230, 232. *See also* Corn; Sacrifice
Viko Sikɨ, 156. *See also* Tachi; Velu

Wage labor, 155–56, 263, 270, 313, 316, 325–26
Wagley, Charles, 6, 13
Wagner, Roy, 13, 356
Wallace, Anthony F. C., 330
War of Independence, 337–38, 343, 345, 351, 354, 355, 363–65
War of the Reform, 289
Warren, Kay B., 11–12, 259–60
Watanabe, John, 8, 11, 12–14, 16
Weber, Max, 255
Weiner, Annette, 75
Weiner, James F., 13, 15
Wilk, Richard, 36, 39, 42, 87, 277, 356
Williams, Raymond, 13–14
Witchcraft, 131, 220, 224
Witherspoon, Gary, 194
Wolf, Eric R., 6–9, 52–53, 132, 144, 233, 234, 282

Xipe Totec, 231

Yavi, 220

Yïi, 115, 127–30, 141, 155, 197–98, 220, 221, 230, 357–58; and blood, electricity, 198; and gift exchange, 80, 88–91; and heat, 197–98; and kinship, 197–98; and Rain, 129, 230; and service, 172, 175; in speech, 173; and Tachi, 163, 314–15; in tortilla, 200. *See also* Blood; Heart; Sun

Yosondua, Santiago, 108

Yosonotú, Santa Catarina, 273

Yosotato, San Pedro, 22, 27, 78, 265, 267, 289

Yosotichi, Cañada of, 22, 263, 273, 335, 348

Young, James Clay, 127

Young, Philip D., 10

Yucubey, 26–28, 30, 31, 91, 107, 120, 221

Yucuhiti, Santa María, 19, 22, 108, 109, 132–33, 146, 147, 150, 152, 163, 173, 202, 209, 265, 269, 272–75, 289, 310, 329, 330, 332, 333, 349, 361, 364

Yucunino, 22, 26–31, 111, 120, 202, 221, 224, 307, 308

Yuku Kasa, 250

Zaachila, 202

Zapata, Emiliano, 343

Zaragoza, 27–31, 78–79, 85, 105, 120, 132, 145, 146, 163, 170, 175, 229, 253